RESEARCH IN ACCOUNTING IN EMERGING ECONOMIES

RESEARCH IN ACCOUNTING IN EMERGING ECONOMIES

Series Editors: Mathew Tsamenyi and Shahzad Uddin

Recent Volumes:

RESEARCH IN ACCOUNTING IN EMERGING ECONOMIES
VOLUME 10

HF
5616.5
R47
2010
web

RESEARCH IN ACCOUNTING IN EMERGING ECONOMIES

EDITED BY

MATHEW TSAMENYI

Birmingham Business School,
Birmingham University, UK

SHAHZAD UDDIN

Essex Business School,
University of Essex, UK

Emerald

United Kingdom – North America – Japan
India – Malaysia – China

s/o

Feb. 14, 2011

c 458 s

BN

Emerald Group Publishing Limited
Howard House, Wagon Lane, Bingley BD16 1WA, UK

First edition 2010

Copyright © 2010 Emerald Group Publishing Limited

Reprints and permission service
Contact: booksandseries@emeraldinsight.com

No part of this book may be reproduced, stored in a retrieval system, transmitted in any form or by any means electronic, mechanical, photocopying, recording or otherwise without either the prior written permission of the publisher or a licence permitting restricted copying issued in the UK by The Copyright Licensing Agency and in the USA by The Copyright Clearance Center. No responsibility is accepted for the accuracy of information contained in the text, illustrations or advertisements. The opinions expressed in these chapters are not necessarily those of the Editor or the publisher.

British Library Cataloguing in Publication Data
A catalogue record for this book is available from the British Library

ISBN: 978-0-85724-451-2
ISSN: 1479-3563 (Series)

Emerald Group Publishing Limited, Howard House, Environmental Management System has been certified by ISOQAR to ISO 14001:2004 standards

Awarded in recognition of Emerald's production department's adherence to quality systems and processes when preparing scholarly journals for print

INVESTOR IN PEOPLE

CONTENTS

LIST OF CONTRIBUTORS

Pawan Adhikari	Bodø Graduate School of Business, Bodø, Norway
Rafiuddin Ahmed	James Cook University, Townsville, Queensland, Australia
Mohobbot Ali	University of Dhaka, Dhaka, Bangladesh
Chedli Baccouche	Institute of Accountancy and Business Administration (ISCAE), Manouba, Tunisia
Ataur Rahman Belal	Aston University, Birmingham, UK
L. Nelson Guedes de Carvalho	University of São Paulo, São Paulo, Brazil
Stuart Cooper	Aston University, Birmingham, UK
Khaled Dahawy	The American University in Cairo, Cairo, Egypt
Prasanta Dey	Aston University, Birmingham, UK
Stephan A. Fafatas	Washington and Lee University, Lexington, VA, USA
Abdel Karim Halabi	University of the Witwatersrand, Johannesburg, South Africa
Harun Harun	Tadulako University, Palu, Indonesia; The University of Waikato, Hamilton, New Zealand
Md. Rezaul Kabir	Aston University, Birmingham, UK
Md. Habib-Uz-Zaman Khan	East West University, Dhaka, Bangladesh; Macquarie University, Sydney, Australia
Niaz Ahmed Khan	University of Dhaka, Dhaka, Bangladesh

Souhir Khemir	Institute of Accountancy and Business Administration (ISCAE), Manouba, Tunisia
Ahmed Kholeif	Edge Hill University, Ormskirk, Lancashire, UK
Gerlando Augusto Sampaio Franco de Lima	University of São Paulo, São Paulo, Brazil
Iran Siqueira Lima	University of São Paulo, São Paulo, Brazil
Vinícius Simmer de Lima	University of São Paulo, São Paulo, Brazil
Frode Mellemvik	Bodø Graduate School of Business, Bodø, Norway
Esinath Ndiweni	Cardiff School of Management, University of Wales Institute, Cardiff, UK
Taiabur Rahman	University of Dhaka, Dhaka, Bangladesh
Peter Robinson	The University of Western Australia, Perth, Australia
Khaled Samaha	The American University in Cairo, Cairo, Egypt
Kevin Jialin Sun	University of Hawaii at Manoa, Honolulu, Hawaii, USA

LIST OF REVIEWERS

Mohammad Faisal Ahammad
Nottingham Trent University, UK

Kamran Ahmed
Latrobe University, Australia

Frank Birkin
University of Sheffield, UK

John Brierley
University of Sheffield, UK

Manuel Castelo Branco
University of Porto, Portugal

Jui-Chin Chang
*School of Business, Howard
University, USA*

Susela Devi
University of Malay, Malaysia

Charles Elad
University of Westminster, UK

Simon Gao
Napier University, UK

Mostafa Hassan
Sharjah University, UAE

Ron Hodges
University of Sheffield, UK

Zahirul Hoque
Latrobe University, Australia

Wendy James
Zayed University, UAE

Rowan Jones
University of Birmingham, UK

Wares Karim
*Saint Mary's College of California,
USA*

Ahmed Kholeif
Edge Hill University, UK

Kevin Lam
*School of Accountancy, Chinese
University of Hong Kong, Hong Kong*

Neil Marriott
*Winchester Business School,
University of Winchester, UK*

Keith Maunders
University of Hull, UK

Kamil Omotseo
*De Montfort University, Leicester,
UK*

Asheq Rahman
Massey University, New Zealand

Lucia Limam Rodrigues
University of Minho, UK

Rudra Sensarma
University of Hertfordshire, UK

Michael Sherer
University of Essex, UK

Ven Tauringana
*University of Bournemouth,
UK*

Andy Wayne
*Idilmat Capacity Development
Solutions, Accra, Ghana*

Idlan Zakaria
University of Essex, UK

CALL FOR PAPERS

SPECIAL ISSUE ON "ACCOUNTING IN THE ASIA-PACIFIC REGION"

Increasingly, it is noted that accounting infrastructure in less developed and emerging economies is undergoing tremendous change given the diffusion of international standards, increased globalization, and quests for economic growth and financial stability.

For example, it is envisaged that the International Financial Reporting Standards (IFRSs) and the International Standards on Auditing (ISAs) issued by the International Accounting Standards Board (IASB) and the International Federation of Accountants (IFAC) will become the global language for financial reporting and auditing in the world. Currently more than 100 countries around the world require or permit IFRS reporting for companies. Many emerging economies, including those in the Asia-Pacific region have followed suit in announcing their convergence deadlines. For example, China and India announced the intention to converge in 2011. This move is seen by many as a welcome move, as emerging economies cannot be seen to be left behind in the race to adopt high-quality global financial reporting standards.

Furthermore, international standards also comprise the International Standards on Ethics (ISEs) and International Education Standards (IESs) as well as International Public Sector Accounting Standards (IPSAS) issued by IFAC.

From the capital market regulator's perspective, this move brings definite advantage to emerging economies' businesses that are operating in an increasingly global environment and enable these capital markets to reap the benefits of reporting consistent, high-quality transparent accounting information under the IFRS and ISA regime. It is envisaged that such transformation will entail structural, legislative, regulatory changes, as well as changes in both private and public sector accounting environments.

However, studies examining the implications of such convergence to IFRSs, and other related accounting issues for emerging economies in general and the Asia-Pacific region in specific have not been forthcoming.

The aim of this special issue of *Research in Accounting in Emerging Economies* is to promote informed debate to establish a more realistic understanding of accounting practices in the Asia-Pacific Region. While the papers in this special issue will be from the Asia-Pacific Region, policy implications and associated reviews will be of interest to other emerging economies as well as developed countries generally.

We invite historical, theoretical, empirical, practical, and review papers, whether quantitative or qualitative, from scholars across disciplines on the following issues affecting accounting practices in the Asia-Pacific region. Issues of importance include, but are not limited to, the following accounting issues in the Asia-Pacific Region:

- Historical development of accounting, including the development of the profession
- IFRS and financial reporting
- Developments within ASEAN, Asian Oceanian Standard Setters Group, and other regional groupings
- The impact of structural adjustment programs and international financial agencies
- The impact of culture, ethnicity, and history on accounting practices
- Education, training, and the role of professional accounting bodies
- Management accounting practices
- Corporate governance
- Environmental accounting
- Accounting in family-owned businesses
- Accounting in small- and medium-size enterprises (SMEs).

The deadline for submission is 28 February 2011. Accepted papers will be published in 2011/2012. Please prepare your manuscript according to *Research in Accounting in Emerging Economies* guidelines. For details, visit http://info.emeraldinsight.com/products/books/series.htm?PHPSESSID = gv6b3l19piv9558ph9flrlgd50&id = 1479-3563

All enquiries and electronic submissions of papers should be sent to one of the guest editors:

Associate Professor Dr. S. Susela Devi, University of Malaya, Malaysia
E-mail: susela@um.edu.my

Professor Keith Hooper, Auckland University of Technology, New Zealand
E-mail: khooper@aut.ac.nz

ABOUT THE VOLUME

Accounting research in emerging economies has been growing significantly over the past two decades due to the increasing recognition of the roles that accounting systems play in these environments. Globalization of capital markets, competition, the emergence of international accounting standards and structural adjustment programs have all brought accounting issues in emerging economies to the fore. Research papers in the current volume have highlighted the implications of the aforementioned issues. The papers have examined various issues including the adoption of International Financial Reporting Standards (IFRS) and International Public Sector Accounting Standards (IPSASs), management accounting change in the context of public sector reforms, corporate reporting disclosures, and auditing.

The papers published in this volume have provided us the opportunities to further engage with wide-ranging empirical and theoretical issues that will have policy implications and also generate future academic debates. Overall, the volume advances debate on the role of accounting reforms in areas such as accounting standards, disclosures, and corporate govern-ance in both the public and private sectors in emerging economies. We believe the audience will find the papers interesting and insightful in terms of theoretical development, practices, policy implications, and future research directions.

A TRAIL OF UNINTENDED CONSEQUENCES: MANAGEMENT ACCOUNTING INFORMATION IN A VOLATILE ENVIRONMENT

Esinath Ndiweni

ABSTRACT

Purpose – *This article highlights the unintended consequences that resulted from the (abuse/use) use of management accounting information in a large automobile corporation in Zimbabwe.*

Methodology – *The article uses a case study and draws on Giddens' structuration theory to help us understand how management accounting practices are produced and reproduced through interactions in organizations.*

Findings – *It reveals how the use of management accounting information can lead to the domination of other employees in organizations and result in unintended consequences such as redundancies.*

Originality – *The article lays emphasis on the unintended consequences resulting from actions of different players in the motor industry and their impact on workers and wider society. It also brings to the fore the dialectic of control which allows subordinates to mobilize resources and act otherwise. It concludes that management accounting practices are*

Research in Accounting in Emerging Economies, Volume 10, 1–27
Copyright © 2010 by Emerald Group Publishing Limited
All rights of reproduction in any form reserved
ISSN: 1479-3563/doi:10.1108/S1479-3563(2010)0000010006

"situated practices" which reflect the dominant discourses and can be harnessed to liberate or enslave other players in organizations. The article suggests that adopting structuration theory helps us analyze the role(s) of accounting information and illuminate possible unintended consequences associated with accounting-based decisions.

Practical implications – *Accountants should guard against misuse of accounting information, to justify political decisions made by managers.*

Research limitations – *The political and economic volatility of the environment obscured the interactions between engineers and accountants because the central focus shifted to survival beyond the crisis.*

Keywords: Structuration theory; dialectic of control; unintended consequences.

1. INTRODUCTION

The practice of management accounting (MA) continues to be a contested territory between engineers and accountants, and more so recently when its boundaries have blurred encroaching into strategy and marketing (Simmonds, 1981; Bromwich, 1990; Roslender, 1995; Lord, 1996; Coad, 1996; Roslender & Hart, 2002). Scholars have adopted a plethora of approaches drawn from various theories in an attempt to understand the role of accounting and accountants in organizations (Scapens, 1990; Miller & O'Leary, 1993; Ezzamel, 1994; Hoque & Hopper, 1994; Buhr, 2002; Conrad, 2005; Gurd, 2008). However, the MA literature in emerging economies remains essentially dominated by the technical perspective, thus positivistic, with the exception of a few recent studies (Uddin & Hopper, 2001; Alawattage & Wickramasinghe, 2008; Hassan, 2008).

The main aim of this article is to understand the role of MA and how it interfaced with other disciplines such as engineering, quality assurance, and marketing. Of particular interest was its role during the implementation of a quality management system at Zimford, a car assembly plant in Zimbabwe. One thesis in the literature suggests that MA techniques should change to suit new production technologies, leading to accountants being closely involved with the costing of quality initiatives (Anderson & Sedatole, 1998).

The article contributes to the sparse literature that adopts a sociological approach to understanding the role of accounting in emerging economies of Africa. It utilizes insights from Giddens' structuration theory (ST) to help us understand the role of MA information in a car assembly plant in Zimbabwe. ST was chosen because of its ability to link structures and agents; thus, allowing for analyses of action at both macro and micro levels. Insights from ST revealed how MA intertwined with the sociopolitical context, resulting in a trail of *unintended consequences*, which are revealed later in this article.

The next section of the article presents key themes from the literature on MA practices in developed and least developed countries (LDCs). The third section considers the core concepts from Giddens ST while the fourth explains how the empirical study was conducted. Section five presents the analysis and interpretation of the data while section six presents the discussion and conclusion.

2. LITERATURE REVIEW

Several writers in the 1980s alleged that there was a crisis in MA (Johnson & Kaplan, 1987; Howell & Soucy, 1987; Hayes & Jaikumar, 1988; Primrose, 1991). Their contention was that the manufacturing environment had changed with the adoption of new technologies such as flexible manufacturing systems, computer-aided design, and total quality management (TQM) to name a few, rendering traditional MA techniques inadequate. Bromwich (1990) and Bhimani (1996) rejected the crisis thesis in reference to the United Kingdom and European experiences. However, writers called for changes in the role of MA to encompass new fields such as measuring and costing quality initiatives (Roth & Morse, 1983; Morse & Roth, 1987; Albright & Roth, 1992; Anderson & Sedatole, 1998 in the United States; and Tayles & Woods, 1998; Ghobadian, Gallear, Woo, & Liu, 1998 in the United Kingdom). In the 1980s and 1990s there were further calls to expand the scope of MA to encompass strategic decisions (Simmonds, 1981; Bromwich, 1990; Kaplan & Norton, 1996; Smith, 1997). Subsequent literature showed disillusionment with the prospects of strategic MA (see Lord, 1996; Coad, 1996; Guilding, Cravens, & Tayles, 2000).

On the other hand, some critical accounting writers focused on the role accounting plays in power relations in organizations (Miller & O'leary, 1993,

1994; Ezzamel, 1994; Ezzamel & Willmott, 1998). However, these writers downplay the power of subordinates – an aspect adequately addressed by Giddens' *dialectic of control*. Several writers have applied insights of ST to accounting studies (Roberts & Scapens, 1985; Willmott, 1987; Capps, Hopper, Mouritsen, Cooper, & Lowe, 1989; Macintosh & Scapens, 1990; Whittington, 1992; Macintosh, 1995, 1996; Dirsmith, Heian, & Covaleski, 1997). Early studies focused on the analysis of the power of MA systems (MASs) through the three dimensions of social structures, namely *signification*, *legitimation*, and *domination*. Latter studies focused on the role of MA and processes of change in developed countries (Conrad, 1999, 2005; Gurd, 2008).

A comprehensive review of the literature on MASs in LDCs (see Hopper, Tsamenyi, & Uddin, 2009) was revealing. They noted that research was prevalent on MAS in state-owned enterprises (SOE) but very little was known about its role in nongovernmental organizations (NGOs) and small and medium enterprises (SMEs). These organizations play a key role in development and alleviating poverty in LDCs. They urged researchers to stray into these areas and identify MASs that are compatible with the development agenda. Their paper conceded that it did not find MASs that were unique to LDCs. Further, they warned that MASs were susceptible to abuse by political elites and were embroiled in the socio, political, and economic context. Commenting on the definition of MASs, they cautioned about the dangers of a narrow technical definition of MASs and how it may lead to unanticipated consequences (Hopper et al., 2009). This article pulls some threads from some of the latter concerns/themes and sheds light on how they were played out at Zimford. Further there is a limited understanding of MA in volatile environments except for (Kattan, Pike, & Tayles, 2007) contribution about organic MAS in Palestine. However, at Zimford the MASs themselves did not change, but what changed was the use of MA information to justify decisions that had profound impact on the vulnerable factory floor workers.

The unique contribution of this article is the volatile context within which it is set, followed by its emphasis on the *dialectic of control* exercised by different professions and the *unintended consequences* resulting from accounting-based decisions. This type of analysis is less prevalent in emerging economies where the technical perspective plays a dominant part in explaining the role of accounting and accountants, thus downplaying the issues of power and *unintended consequences* of accounting-related decisions.

3. THEORETICAL FRAMEWORK

There has been a proliferation of diverse perspectives on accounting that have illuminated our understanding of the accounting phenomenon and its possible roles in organizations (Burchell, Clubb, Hopwood, Hughes, & Nahapiet, 1980). In their seminal paper they directly challenged the idea that accounting is a passive reflector of economic reality, and argued that it was both a product and a producer of sociopolitical processes (Alvesson & Willmott, 1996). This article follows this latter thinking. ST is most suited for the phenomenon under investigation because it overcomes the problem that pervades social theory, depicted by the notion that social reality is a product of either structures or human agency. Instead, it replaces this *dualism* with a *duality of structure*, whereby both structure and human agency are dynamically interlinked. It is concerned with understanding the relationship between the activities of knowledgeable human actors and the structuring of social systems (Giddens, 1976, 1984). In this article the knowledgeable human actors are engineers, accountants, and other players at Zimford, while social systems comprise social practices such as MA which are reproduced through their interactions. On the other hand, structures comprise rules and resources that are drawn upon during interactions. The article utilizes selected concepts from Giddens' ST to analyze the institutional context and the interactions of managers in the motor industry. These include (a) *agency*; (b) *unintended consequences*; (c) the *duality of structure*; (d) *dimensions of social structure – signification, legitimation, and domination*; and (e) *the dialectic of control*.

3.1. Agency and Unintended Consequences

Giddens defines action or agency *as the stream of actual or contemplated casual interventions of corporeal beings in the ongoing process of events-in-the-world* (Giddens, 1976, p. 81). Thus, in this article agents are the key players in the motor industry such as policy makers in government ministries, engineers, quality assurance managers, and accountants.

Thus it can be argued that agents are self-aware and monitor their own actions and those of others. Closely linked with the agent's action is the concept of *unintended consequences* that result from these actions. On the other hand, *unacknowledged conditions* also arise as a result of unintended consequences in the process setting conditions for future action. These concepts are critical in the analysis of the outcomes of the actions of accountants and politicians in this study. For example, when policy makers set tariffs for imported cars, they rationalize their actions and also monitor the impact of the policy on the industry and the overall economy. Actions such as these may lead to both intended and *unintended consequences*. The intended outcome with tariffs is to protect local manufacturers while the *unintended consequences* may be fewer imported cars, overpriced locally manufactured cars which are out of reach for many locals. The unacknowledged conditions of action could be imports of cheap used cars from any quarter of the world resulting in further *unintended consequences* in the form of shortage of spare parts, skills to service such cars, and a waste of scarce foreign currency.

On the other hand, engineers and accountants set the prices for the cars assembled to enable Zimford to make profit. However, interference by politicians through ministerial directives resulted in special lower prices of vehicles for government ministers; reduction of profits for the company; cash flow problems; and profiteering by individual government ministers on reselling the same. The key insight is that agents rationalize their actions and have motivations, but may not fully control the outcomes. In a volatile sociopolitical environment actions of agents distorted the role of MA as accounting information was drawn upon to justify different actions and motivations. An elaborate discussion is given later in the article. The next concept to be considered *is the duality of structure*.

3.2. The Duality of Structure and Structural Dimensions

By the *duality of structure*, Giddens means that social structures are both constituted by human agency, and yet at the same time are the very medium of that constitution. They can be conceived to be both the medium and the outcome of social action, both a resource for production and a reproduction of practice, both enabling and constraining. Any type of social production necessarily entails the (often unintentional) reproduction of the structures used in that action (as the most unintended consequence of that action). The "duality of structure" connects structures with action and allows us to consider both the institutional realm and the action sphere in our analysis.

Structure is seen as interacting through modalities of interpretative schemes, resources, and norms, respectively, with human actions of communication of meanings, power, and sanctions. Because of the recursive nature of interactions, structure can be understood both from an institutional and an action viewpoint. From an institutional point of view, the *signification* dimension represents the interpretative schemes, which participants use to interpret past results and future actions. In this article senior managers used accounting information as their interpretive scheme while operations managers drew from quality assurance systems for their understanding of the organization. The interpretative schemes are the modes of typification incorporated within actors' stocks of knowledge, applied reflexively in sustaining communication. They comprise the procedures, which mediate between the (virtual) structure and the (situated) interaction (Giddens, 1984, p. 28).

On the other hand, the *domination* structure comprises allocative and authoritative resources that agents draw upon in the exercise of power. The former arises from command over objects, goods, and other material phenomenon, while the latter arises from the capabilities to organize and coordinate the activities of social actors. Both types of resources facilitate the transformative capacity of human action, while at the same time providing the medium for domination (Macintosh & Scapens, 1990). Different professional groups in organizations tended to draw from different resources and effectively shifted power relations at certain points in time. For example, at the peak of the economic crisis in Zimbabwe, allocative power of resources became more important giving ascendancy to accountants ahead of engineers. Among their critical skills was an ability to source scarce foreign currency to import knock down kits from Japan to continue production. Accountants also rationed money across competing priorities such as staff salaries and production. Other professional groups mobilized political resources to justify their employment in the organization, resulting in greater cooperation among different actors. This insight from ST was helpful in understanding the behaviour of different groups at Zimford.

The *legitimation* dimension involves the moral constitution of interaction and is mediated through norms and moral codes, which sanction particular behaviours. This structure institutionalizes the reciprocal rights and obligations of the social actors, thus defining accountability patterns. Accounting information comprising budgets and break-even points was enlisted to justify decisions that often led to *unintended consequences* such as redundancies and plant shut downs. The final core concept to be considered is the *dialectic of control*.

3.3. The Dialectic of Control

Giddens introduces the concept of *dialectic of control* which refers to the "transformative capacity of human action" (Giddens, 1984). This is about the ability of individuals or groups to resist what is being imposed on them. It intrinsically involves the application of "means" to achieve outcomes, brought about through the direct intervention of an actor in the course of events, while power represents the capacity of the agent to mobilize resources to constitute the means. Noteworthy is the fact that power always involves "relations of autonomy and dependence" where no party is either autonomous or entirely dependent. Thus, stresses the ability of subordinate groups to use existent structural rules and resources as tools in their resistance to domination. ST stresses that the resources upon which the exercise of power depends are asymmetrically distributed *structured properties of social systems*, but their use involves a complex *dialectic of control*. At Zimford ISO 9000 and the engineering curriculum were the structuring properties that privileged engineers during the implementation of a quality management system. This article demonstrates the presence of the dialectic of control at all levels of interaction, whether macro or micro. For instance, agents were influenced by what happened at the structural societal level, but they could also influence the constitution of the social system. Similarly, policies put in place by the Ministry of Industry and Commerce could be resisted by agents in the motor industry resulting in their revision. In short, no party to the interaction had complete autonomy over its activities, but in contrary depended on the other for its success. On the other hand, at micro level, that is, organizational level, subordinates had power to frustrate the work of their superiors and different professional groups had different power resources that they could tap when necessary. Examples of the operation of this concept at Zimford are revealed in the analysis section of this article.

4. RESEARCH METHODS

The article utilized a case study of an automobile plant located in Zimbabwe, a less developed country that provides the broader context that influenced the interactions. The plant was jointly owned by the state and a Japanese multinational corporation herein called Zimford. The research site was chosen for two reasons: (1) Assembling/manufacturing vehicles is associated with sophisticated technology. (2) It also provides a fertile ground for the interaction between accountants and engineers, marketing, and other key actors in organizations.

Yin (1993) suggests that case study method is appropriate when the topic is broad, covers contextual conditions, and relies on multiple sources of evidence. The rationale for the adoption of case study approach resonates in the recent literature where researchers in accounting were encouraged to get involved with the messy data in organizations (Kaplan, 1984; Scapens, 1990; Otley & Berry, 1994). Otley and Berry (1994, p. 46) posit that management control cannot be fully understood in isolation; therefore, a more contextual approach is required. Furthermore, case studies have a potential to reveal rich insights about the phenomenon under investigation (Berry et al., 1985; Tomkins & Colville, 1984; Laughlin, 1988), thus providing a prima facie case for the use of case-based research methods. Extending case study–based research to developing countries, particularly in Africa, is likely to add new insights to our understanding of the role of accounting and other controls in organizations, in that part of the world.

The fieldwork was carried out during the months of August to October 1999 when Zimbabwe was experiencing severe social, political, and economic problems which affected interactions at the research sites. The author reported at Zimford as if she was one of the employees. This unfettered access afforded her an opportunity to adopt an ethnographic approach. In addition, the study used multiple data sources from the motor industry, Zimford, and external organizations. These comprised semi-structured interviews, a review of documents, direct and participant observation, newspaper clippings, archival material to printed sources generated at the local and national level. A total of 16 interviews were held, 4 of which were with external participants in the motor industry. The external interviewees were selected due to their influence in drafting policies that affected the motor industry. The first to be interviewed was the permanent secretary in the Ministry of Industry and Commerce. Her ministry was working on a policy document to regulate the motor industry in the light of competition from South Africa. The president of the Motor Industry Association whose role was to liaise between the industry and policy makers while lobbying for changes in favour of the vehicle manufacturers was also interviewed. His views about the future of the industry helped the author understand the context within which Zimford operated. Included in the list of interviewees was the director of Tariff Commission who set tariffs to discourage cheap imports and protect local producers and the principal of the Motor Industry College. The college developed the curriculum that was used to train key workers in the industry. Of importance to this study were the MA and quality assurance syllabi. These were relevant in helping us understand the contest between engineers and accountants in the factory.

Interviewees at Zimford included the general manager, production engineer, quality assurance manager, management accountant, financial director, marketing and sales, and human resource managers. The selected interviewees had worked for Zimford for more than five years. Five years was a significant cut-off period because Zimford started implementing a quality management system three years ago, so these managers had insights about the situation before and after the introduction of the system. The interviews averaged between thirty and forty-five minutes and up to one hour in instances where there were interruptions. The secretary of the Workers' Committee was also formally interviewed, while other employees were interviewed informally. Their experiences on changes in social practices since the introduction of quality initiatives were sought. It was also critical to understand the perceptions of the interviewees about the impact of MA on their work. One-off official interviews were scheduled in the Boardroom at Zimford while informal repeat interviews were in the respective offices of the managers. The author relied very much on partial ethnography (Van Maanen, 1995) and critical reflections on the data in order to make sense of the empirical material (Alvesson & Willmott, 1996; Alvesson & Skoldberg, 2000). In the remaining sections, ST is used as a *sensitizing device* to help us understand the role(s) of MA at Zimford.

5. EMPIRICAL FINDINGS AND ANALYSIS

5.1. Background Information about Zimford

Zimford was registered in 1961. Barely, four years later, in 1965 it closed temporarily due to sanctions imposed on Rhodesia for rebelling against Britain following the unilateral declaration of independence (UDI). It reopened its doors in 1967 under the control of Industrial Development Corporation (IDC), a state-owned *parastatal*. IDC was incorporated in 1963 with a mission to identify and invest in areas of strategic importance to the nation. After UDI in 1965, its focus shifted to facilitate sanctions busting. After independence in 1980, the focus shifted again to reflect nationalistic sentiments. For nearly 10 years (1980–1989) the members of the board of directors (BOD) were political appointees. Zimford then only carried out contractual assembly. The franchise holders delivered their kits to Zimford for assembly contract and were charged fees. Because of the nature of that arrangement, there was no need to hold stocks; thus cash flows were favourable since there were no high set up costs, for example, credit control and credit rating were not important.

Zimford's activities were perceived to serve national interests and this legitimated what went on in the organization, until 1988 when a financial scandal involving government ministers erupted. The government, using its authoritative resources, had given a directive to the company to supply vehicles to ministers. Accountants and engineers agreed prices that would not undermine the company. However, the scheme was abused by ministers who bought several vehicles and sold them in the open market at a profit. The directive from the government had been implemented because nationalistic interest was dominant and thus shaped the signification structure of the organization. However, the scandal resulted in *unintended consequences* that led to resignations from government and suicide by one of the disgraced ministers. Most of the offenders were condoned, undermining the judiciary, in turn, discrediting the government.

To redeem its reputation the government introduced major reforms, which led to Zimford entering into a joint venture with a Japanese multinational corporation in 1989. The interference by the state declined with the introduction of this external partner and the advent of trade liberalization of the 1990s. However, the government retained its rights to appoint members of the BOD. In spite of being a minority shareholder, the Japanese multinational corporation had two resident technical advisers on the BOD. The technical advisers were experts in engineering and marketing. The BOD of Zimford comprised three engineers, two finance persons, and a marketing specialist. The chairperson was a professional accountant, while the chief executive officer (CEO) was an engineer. One of the key insights of ST is to abolish the *dualisms* such as *macro* versus *micro* and focus on the duality between them; hence, the analysis interrogates both simultaneously because what happens at societal level has a bearing on activities in the organization. Likewise, in this article there will be no abstract separation of the two.

Power relations between professions at Zimford were depicted through numbers and positions. Overall, there were 11 engineers in managerial positions and about 4 accountants, while the remainder were marketing, human resources (HR), and information technology. The engineers were concentrated in the production and quality assurance units, not a surprising feature considering the nature of manufacturing. Accountants had no direct link with factory workshops or quality assurance units in spite of the calls in the literature for them to get involved with quality costing (Tayles & Woods, 1998). The post for management accountant was lower in the hierarchy, and thus yielded less power. The next section analyzes the role of engineers and their perceptions of accounting at Zimford.

5.2. Analysis Using ST

5.2.1. Role of Engineers and Their Perceptions of Accounting

The main aim of this study was to understand the role of MA and how it interfaced with other disciplines such as engineering, quality assurance, and marketing. Of importance, was the role of MA in costing quality initiatives. The responses to interview questions were analyzed in the light of the literature review which emphasized changes in manufacturing technologies and explored potential contributions of MA to costing quality initiatives. (1) Is the management accountant involved in the measurement of the costs of quality projects? (2) Does the MAS capture the costs and benefits of implementing quality management systems? There were suggestions in the literature that accountants had the expertise to help companies measure the costs of quality initiatives (Anderson & Sedatole, 1998). The views of engineers are considered first followed by marketing and human resources; and finally, accountants' views about their role.

At Zimford the role of MA and how it interfaced with other professions can be understood in the context of the dominant discourses reflected in structural dimensions of *signification, domination,* and *legitimation.* The three are intricately linked and cannot be separated except for the purposes of analysis. Prior to 1986, Zimford's existence served national interests and little attention was paid to the number of vehicles produced. Engineers were the dominant professional group whose ingenuity resulted in about 17 different models being produced, albeit in insufficient quantities. Performance was perceived in terms of 900 cars per month and bonuses were also linked to outputs.

Most of the vehicles were sold to government ministers and civil servants. All this increased the visibility of engineers in the signification structures at Zimford, and reinforced the existing interpretative scheme that was based on the number of vehicles and models produced. Drawing on this success engineers proposed to expand the plant.

> We applied investment appraisal techniques such as payback and convinced senior management about the need to undertake the investment. Management approved the investment of Z$24 million dollars in a new plant. However, due to the dramatic changes that occurred in the political and economic landscape of Zimbabwe, it was on hold (Production Manager).

In addition, the engineers who had received three months training in Japan introduced several changes in the work organization and arrangements at the factory.

> With help from Japanese advisers, the factory layout has been reorganised, leading to improvement in material handling saving the company of Z$10 million dollars (Production Engineer).

As part of improvements, the engineers developed a quality assurance manual and in 1996 started implementing a quality assurance system throughout the factory. This initiative was timely because of the importance of ISO 9000 certification. It got its legitimacy from global trends that defined competitiveness in terms of ISO 9000 compliance. This development became a major interpretative scheme supplanting the focus on production targets. This had company-wide acceptance throughout the factory floor to marketing and sales. Despite the calls in the literature for management accountants to get involved in measuring quality costs, at Zimford, engineers were self-reliant in terms of their training. In other words, the institutions such as training colleges reinforced engineering dominance through their broad curriculum that taught costing, MA, and marketing. However, the curriculum in Zimbabwe did not include quality assurance modules.

Engineers estimated cost savings after reorganizing work arrangements. For example, after adopting *kaizen,* losses due to poor work were reduced from Z$1,100 million to about Z$300,000. Engineers boasted about their ability to compile costs and savings on quality systems without involving accountants. However, accountants acknowledged the savings made but argued that quantification was fraught with errors, instead focused on revenue generated from month to month. Here there was evidence of generation of MA information by engineers without reliance on professional accountants.

There were several other accounting activities at Zimford that were performed by engineers such as reviewing standard costs. For example, the work-study officer (engineer) determined the labour costs and the quantity of direct materials consumed in the process of production per model. The assembly fees varied per model depending on the quantity and quality of material used and the labour costs in each operation. The cost of materials was based on standards that were calculated quarterly. Due to rapid changes in the economic environment the previous quarter's actual costs were adjusted by a contingency factor to arrive at the standard costs for the next quarter.

In conclusion, in their interactions with accountants, engineers did not see any added value in what accountants did. The financial director was consulted to approve fully costed engineering projects. His major consideration was not on the accuracy of the calculations but on whether the firm had the resources to implement the projects. However, this view changed when the political and economic crisis worsened forcing different professions to cooperate. The accounting language slowly became an important interpretative scheme when the whole organization focused on survival and procuring sources of finance to secure their future. Here dependence between professions flourished and the politicians were seen as the main enemy, for having destroyed the economy.

5.2.2. Perceptions of the Role of Accounting by Marketing

On the other hand, marketing revealed closer relationships with both production and accounting (Roslender & Hart, 2002). When working with production the concern was to maintain quality while reducing cost of production. There was also evidence of customer profiling so as to increase sales. Their main customers were dealers.

> At the moment (1999) we have 43 dealers. As part of streamlining our activities and increase efficiency there are plans to rationalise dealership and organise sub-dealers. Our target is to reduce our dealers to 20. Within our group, Autospares (Pvt) Ltd a company that manufactures motor vehicle spares is responsible for compiling customer profiles. It places more emphasis on assessment of facilities such as showrooms and workshops. The character of our dealer network leaves a lot to be desired. We are helping dealers with personal visits and offering service (Marketing Manager).

As part of streamlining activities they were attempts at grading dealers.

> We are in the process of grading our dealers into A to D grades. For example, dealer Grade A – one who buys 1000 cars a month, B, one who buys 30 or 50 and so on. The criterion for rating includes an assessment of investment in premises (owned or rented), the number of branches owned, number of employees and the total asset base. We analyse facilities rather than viability. This way we intend to eliminate briefcase businessmen in the past we have had to withdraw cars from some dealers who could not sell them quickly (Marketing Manager).

One drawback of selling through dealers was that the company did not control the mark up added by each dealer. Depending on their economic circumstances some dealers added a high mark-up. This practice might explain the disparities in prices for the same model across the country. The marketing manager acknowledged his involvement with accounting on a reactive basis, assisting with credit control and debt collections. Beyond purely financial accounting activities geared to reduce bad debts, there was little analysis of competitors and market share. Marketing and Sales were also active in compiling customer complaints, however the opportunity costs associated with complaints were neither explicit in MA nor the cost of quality reports. However, both Marketing and TQM audited output and compiled customer complaints.

It has been noted that involuntary costs arise whenever customers choose alternative suppliers because of actual or perceived quality deficiencies (Garvin, 1987). Attaching monetary values to such costs might not be easy; however, nonfinancial performance indicators might suffice (Smith, 1997). Overall, the interactions between marketing and accountants did not reflect conflict nor competition but mutual trust. There is potential to develop the links between MA and marketing curricula. However, observations show that sometimes, academics stifle interdisciplinary cooperation by drawing up disparate standalone curricula for their subjects, yet in the field professional groups work together amicably (Galpin, Hilpirt, & Evans, 2007).

5.2.3. Perceptions of the Role of Accounting by Human Resources

The HR manager stressed that they relied on accounting for processing payroll information. However, this was an understatement considering the consultations between accountants and personnel on cutting down costs through short-working weeks and staff retrenchments. For example, in November 1998, 120 contract employees were laid off followed by a further 48 in January 1999 and a temporary shutdown.

Accounting information was used to justify the actions taken while downplaying the *unintended consequences* associated with social strife. The workers who lost jobs had worked at the factory plant all their lives. Alternatively, the impact of retrenching other managers would have been less due to the marketability of their skills. Accounting was used for legitimating senior management decisions. On the other hand, HR continued to provide staff benefits such as subsidized meals, staff loans, assistance with funeral costs, and procurement of private household goods through the Purchases Office of the company.

> We offer subsidised meals where workers contribute Z$50 per month. We also have a Clinic for our staff. Staff can purchase goods through the company purchases department and we recover the money in instalments from their salaries (Personnel Manager).

Zimford being a quasi-government owned corporation upheld the tradition of providing staff welfare. The Japanese partner did not stop this practice because Japan also has paternalistic tendencies. This culture was morally acceptable and not questioned as the economic situation deteriorated. The rhetoric about minimizing costs was construed in terms of the factory floor, rather than cutting down welfare-related costs. For example, the price of a single meal in a commercial restaurant was higher than the monthly contribution made by staff. Finally, the accountants were asked about how they perceived their role at Zimford.

5.2.4. Accountants' Perspectives about Their Role at Zimford

The role of MA had not changed at Zimford in spite of the introduction of a quality management system three years ago. The management accountant described their conventional role as:

> To empower people to conceive the impact of what they are doing financially; to give the right financial data to other departments to ensure cost control; to enable people to help us achieve cost control, unless we give them the right data they cannot help us; and to help other departments appreciate what accounting is all about. Others think we cause problems, particularly if they have overspent their budgets (General Accounting Manager).

This description flies in the face of everyday reality where employees lose their jobs because of how accounting information is used. Centrally, to Zimford's policy is the devolution of budgeting to individual departments that is intended to empower managers. The impact of this policy is clear in engineering departments but less so in others.

> At the end of every year managers of each department are asked to produce their capital budgets. We approve proposals if there is finance. We judge projects based on their strength, i.e. justification and cash flow projections (General Accounting Manager).

Once more decision making is based on accounting rationale and not the other qualitative softer matters which affect the generality of the workers and their families.

When pressed to disclose whether the new factory arrangements and the introduction of a quality management system had changed the role of management accountants, he said:

> We try to dovetail the accounting system to capture the changes that are happening production wise. To me it is supposed to be part of that system. We regard QA as a cost centre. We look at it as one of the overheads. We give QA department data pertaining to quality such as training costs. The onus is on the quality personnel to raise queries with accounting about the items we have allocated to them (General Manager Accounting).

It is clear from the above answer that MA is not integrated with the quality costing or management system.

> We recognise that quality costs go beyond labour for the cost centre. In addition to costs that pertain to quality, we also have one off quality costs such as Research & Development expenditure (R&D). This is not part of the cost centre but is capitalised or

> written off at once. The integration is manifest only through cost centres. We cannot go and pick up a quality cost, except R&D. We have not seriously thought of all those costs pertaining to quality (General Manager Accounting).

However, the review of the cost reports showed that accountants made blanket provisions for *inplant damages, warranties*, and *modifications* during assembly. Even, in instances where actual cost of reworks could be ascertained there were no attempts to do so. Management in general, was reluctant to divulge information on average reworks per month. The warranty section prepared reports on reworks and services and depending on the causes of failure passed some claims to the franchise owner, while the company settled others. The passing of the risk to the franchisor is one of the advantages of foreign direct investment (FDI). In other words, the external alliance partner would pick up costs associated with adherence to assembly manuals. Because of this practice, the warranty report was neither integrated into the MAS nor the publicly available quality management reporting system.

The depiction of the role of MA reflects the dominance of the technical perspective, which the author suggests limits our understanding of the role(s) of accounting. A lack of reflection by the general accounting manager prevented him from seeing the multifaceted roles of accounting. He denied involvement of accounting in strategic decisions, yet senior management depended on it to justify such decisions. According to the accounting manager, Zimford had not considered introducing ABC or any other techniques associated with new manufacturing technologies. However, the key performance indicator was profit margin. This was a shift from the former interpretative scheme which focused on number of vehicles produced. The economic crisis that engulfed Zimbabwe led to a radical change in the signification structures privileging accounting-based information, such as turnover, profit margins, and break-even points. However, what emerged from the study was how MA information was (ab) used to justify many decisions at the plant. Paradoxically, while subscribing to the supremacy of the technical perspective on the ground MA was implicated in the social construction of reality in a volatile environment. There was nothing authentic about the numbers that affected people's lives in profound ways.

5.3. Unintended Consequences

The ascendancy of MA information led to a series of *unintended consequences* that are highlighted in this article. Other *unintended consequences* resulting from the political and economic crisis included a cut in salaries, redundancies, short-working week, and a resort to hiring part-time temporary staff. Workers were reduced from 700 to 554 by 1999. Accounting information was enlisted to help management arrive at some of the above decisions. Other social pressures such as retaining the workforce under difficult conditions led to higher prices charged for vehicles in order to absorb all costs incurred at Zimford. The cost accounting model used was informed by the volatile economic situation and rampant inflation. The deterioration in the company's fortune was seen to be politically motivated, although it played itself out through MASs. The level of desperation characterized the problems faced by industries operating in Zimbabwe. Most of these harsh conditions were directly linked with the economic consequences of the actions of the various agents of the state.

Some factors that contributed to high prices for vehicles were social costs related to staff benefits. Under African culture, the company takes care of its workers by extending facilities such as subsidized meals, staff loans, and facilities to procure household items through the company's buying office. Staff debts are recovered gradually from their salaries. This practice ignored the present value of money particularly during inflationary times. Staff medical expenses had also increased because of opportunistic infections associated with HIV. There were hidden costs to the company in terms of lost man-hours due to high absenteeism, aggravated by nepotism because under Zimbabwean culture when there is death in the family all relatives do not report for work. A good recruitment policy of asking employees to recommend relatives now resulted in opportunistic losses. How did the accounting system take into account such losses?

In short, the sociocultural context got intertwined with the MA practices to an extent that they assumed a new identity formed by the institutions that practiced them. If this mutation were not possible, both MA and TQM systems would not have had a place in a volatile political and economic environment like the one that prevailed in Zimbabwe during the time of research. The overriding explanation is that both MA and TQM systems were not really imported from outside into the organizations, but they were truly redefined and reconstructed by the crucial actors within the motor industry to suit their own needs (adapted from Hancke & Casper, 2000, p. 174). This observation confirmed the suggestion made by Burns and Scapens (2000) that management practices are *path-dependent* on existing routines and institutions.

By drawing on MASs and the wider social discourse of profit making, senior managers helped to institutionalize MA practices. As long as the profit motive was not under threat, MA practices that served the company well in the past were reproduced. They became routinized and were implemented mechanically, resulting in the institutionalization of the MAS. When viewed from this angle, accounting assumed a dominant role and became part of the structures of accountability. This allowed the MAS to become a dominant interpretative scheme through which staff preferred to understand the performance of the company. How much was the turnover for this month and how much of it was in foreign currency? This had become the language that was understood by everyone at Zimford.

The MAS in place legitimated decisions made by engineers such as expanding the plant, in spite of it being underutilized. On one hand they were nationalistic sentiments, which were balanced with the interests of the multinational investor. The MAS that eventually prevailed at a particular point in time was determined by the dominant structure at that time. For instance, engineers might downplay the cost of quality and expect the accountant to price the car according to industry norms rather than reflect their inefficiency.

On the other hand, the nationalistic sentiments of the indigenous employees who did not own companies would rather have the management accountant absorb all costs as overhead and attach them to the product. An international investor who required a fair return on his/her investment would rather have a MAS that traced all costs to the product and sold it at a profit. The scenario in Zimbabwean manufacturing firms showed the dilemma that management accountants face in volatile environments.

5.4. Dialectic of Control

Giddens' *dialectic of control* stresses that all social relations involve both autonomy and dependence. Overall, the interviewees at Zimford recognized that it was an engineering dominated company and let engineers do their jobs without interference. The factory floor was the preserve of the engineers and the general workers. Management accountants did not go into the factory to observe and measure the costs of quality. However, HR manager felt that there was need to involve them in the training of staff on quality management. Accounting played a support role to engineering and focused more on the preparation of financial statements and procuring finance for the operations of the company. Notwithstanding the desire to cooperate, ST reminds us that the exercise of power is never unidirectional.

For example, gang workers at Zimford often discovered solutions to problems at the plant but withheld information from management. There could have been many reasons for that type of behaviour, may be to retain their jobs. When subordinates feel victimized they develop subtle forms of resistance (Alawattage & Wickramasinghe, 2009). In such instances knowledge was used as a competitive weapon in managing the *dialectics of control*. In the past workers at Zimford were rewarded for making suggestions on how to improve work processes. ST reminds us that human beings are never docile agents; they have this transformative capacity to change their circumstances or act otherwise.

Another incident of lack of cooperation related to the protection of the identity of fellow workers who made costly mistakes. The workers refused to divulge the names of the offenders and preferred that managers traced errors to gangs/teams and not to individuals. For them, there was power in numbers; the company could not dismiss all of them at once. This was another example of the power of subordinates that ST emphasizes is inherent in all interactions. However, workers could caution each other behind management's back as part of peer surveillance but would withhold some important information from management.

General factory floor workers felt sidelined by management and used any avenue to vent their frustrations. When an opportunity arose they would talk to the media about their plight.

> These days management does not communicate about targets. It appears there is a communication break down between management and us. The Workers Committee was dissolved last year. We have been unable to hold elections. Things are not transparent for us here and we do not know what fate is awaiting us and we are the only ones sidelined (Disgruntled worker).

Some retrenched workers enlisted the services of war veterans who posed as trade unionists to harass company management and demand equitable redundancy packages for laid off workers. Many companies lost millions of dollars due to extortion. The statements by workers to the press claiming maltreatment tended to attract informal ways of settling disputes.

The *dialectic of control* played out at different levels of interactions at times between politicians and executives in the motor industry. The executives exploited the media to vent their problems to the embarrassment of the government. For example, one executive said:

> Both the foreign currency and the fuel shortage are impacting severely on our operations, as is the case with all industrial operations. We are arranging to have supplementary supplies from those of our associates and subsidiaries with access to

foreign currency accounts. Apart from having a negative impact on the company's sales the severe foreign currency shortages are seriously compromising the company's credit reputation with its foreign suppliers, with whom we have had a long-standing open account relationship. Management has discussed this issue with government officials at all levels including the Ministry of Industry and Trade, the Ministry of Finance and Economic Development and the Reserve Bank of Zimbabwe to no avail (The Daily News, November 15, 2000).

On the other hand, the government also accused management of complacency, lack of creativity, and unsound decisions by the plant's management. The concept of *dialectic of control* underscores the fact that various professionals recognized their dependency on each other. For example, senior management recognized its dependence for profit on middle managers and gave them leeway to pursue their own agenda based on professional expertise. When the situation demanded, for example, the need to increase sales or profit, senior managers would use whatever resources at their disposal to influence their subordinates. The same applies to subordinates, they were not totally powerless but had resources that they mobilized to counter senior management domination. This logic prevailed between accountants and engineers as they negotiated their work processes. In other words, this concept partly explains the cooperation between professionals in organizations, particularly during a crisis.

6. DISCUSSION AND CONCLUSION

Prior to the severe political and economic crisis in Zimbabwe, production and quality assurance systems were the determinants of organizational culture at Zimford. Thus, the interpretative schemes adopted then to cement meanings centered on the number of vehicles and models produced. The focus was on engineers and improvements on the factory floor as a result of the quality assurance system that was being implemented, however, there was a shift in the *signification, domination, and legitimation* structures as the crisis intensified giving ascendancy to accounting information. The study took place at the climax of the crisis, when the focus by everybody had shifted to accounting information. The actual activities carried out by accountants had not changed significantly, except that there were changes in inflation, foreign currency, interest rates, and Zimford needed timely information to navigate the stormy waters.

Macintosh and Scapens (1990) suggest that MASs represent modalities of structuration in the three dimensions of *signification, legitimation,* and *domination*. In the *signification dimension*, MASs are the interpretative schemes, which senior managers use to interpret past results, take actions, and make plans. For example, the HR manager gave turnover figures for the past five years over the phone without reference to any records because he had internalized them in his understanding of company performance. The language of accounting was traded in meetings and all senior managers identified with it. The chairperson of the BOD of Zimford explained in an interview, *"we are operating at a level at which we break even – we intend to reduce our break-even point from 300 to 200 cars per month."* Once again, reiterating the importance of the accounting numbers in interactions in these companies in the motor industry.

In the *domination dimension*, MASs are a facility that management at all levels can use to coordinate and control participants. For example, holding managers accountable for the budgets and requiring an explanation for variances was still a common occurrence at Zimford where, budgets were reviewed every three months. The control of resources reflected power relations, and during tough economic conditions accounting structures became dominant, because there were scarce resources to be allocated and controlled. Therefore, by signifying what counts MA provided a discourse for the domination structure through which some participants were held accountable to others, while at the same time provided legitimacy for the social processes which were involved.

In the *legitimation dimension*, MASs communicated a set of values and ideals about what was approved or disapproved; they justified the rights of some participants to hold others accountable and used certain rewards and sanctions. When budgets were tight senior management used anything including accounting information to justify cutting down staff and reducing expenditure. For example, the break-even point became crucial in making decisions about plant closure, temporary shut downs, etc. However, which members of staff were laid off was generally a political decision, for example, at Zimford the general workers at the factory were laid off. For a manufacturing company, such as Zimford these were key workers compared to office staff who could find work elsewhere. If *unintended consequences* were taken into account perhaps different decisions could have been taken. For instance, laying off managerial staff could have impacted fewer families.

The three dimensions of structure are intertwined (Macintosh & Scapens, 1990). Senior managers reported to the BOD who in turn reported to shareholders using financial statements. This type of reporting fulfilled both stewardship and agency functions. However, it should be noted that these *signification, domination, and legitimation* structures were not *fixed*; they shifted as the agents reproduced them. The results of interactions formed the basis for future actions, though at an abstract level and for analytical purposes only we seem to hold them static. The developments at Zimford showed how the *dialectic of control worked,* and the fluidity within which interactions took place. On one hand, middle managers drew on the production and TQM systems and viewed those as their main accountability structures, while senior managers depended on the accounting systems.

At Zimford, there were so many other external factors that influenced interactions of the key players. Because this was a quasi-owned government organization, Ministers of Industry and Commerce meddled in its affairs. The actions of politicians contributed a fair share to the problems experienced at Zimford. When Zimbabwe severed relations with the IMF in the 1990s over the implementation of the structural adjustment programs, it suffered from shortages of foreign currency. An assembly plant such as Zimford depended on imported kits from Japan; this action directly reduced the annual production volumes and the associated break-even point. The shortage of foreign currency reserves put paid the investment in plant expansion and construction of a paint shop. The unacknowledged conditions set the scene for future actions.

> Plans for a new paint shop are on hold until sales pick up sufficiently to justify the high cost of Z$600 million (CEO).

The developments at Zimford impacted negatively on the government as well because it was a major shareholder. The political rhetoric that led to forceful invasions of farms owned by whites, harassment of NGOs also bore unintended consequences. NGOs retaliated by cancelling orders of vehicles from Zimford in protest at the behaviour of government. Turnover declined as private companies placed orders with Zimford's competitors. A lack of respect for private property rights led to a flight of investment capital. Zimford was operating at 40% of capacity during the time of the study.

> There is very little investment in the country. Existing companies are not expanding and are not spending money on buying vehicles. There is generally a lack of confidence in the prospects of the country due to macro-economic problems. If anything goes up, people are not going to buy. Only those companies which require a transport fleet/wish to replace the existing fleet continue to purchase vehicles (Marketing Manager).

The main aim of the article was to apply social theory to help us understand the role of MA at Zimford. The article concludes that how MA interfaces with other disciplines depends on the sociopolitical context that prevails in a particular organization. The imperatives that are often dictated by positivistic research downplay the importance of context. The insights from this study can help us appreciate why the proposed potential of strategic MA has not come to fruition. The main focus of the analysis was on the series of *unintended consequences* that many accountants in positions of power readily ignore. There is nothing wrong with MA techniques; however the motives of the actors can be harmful to other players in organizations.

The main conclusion of this article is that the social context determined the potential roles of different professionals in organizations and was implicated in the reproduction of MASs that prevailed. The concept of interdependence between players was demonstrated by the notion of *dialectic of control*. The impact of accounting based decisions on workers; other professionals and society in general were captured by the concept of *unintended consequences.*

The other macro economic problems had also changed the tone of interactions at Zimford. All the planning tools, whether accounting based or not had been made redundant because of the upheavals in the economic landscape, for example, using the pay back period to appraise investment was overtaken by events. This article has shown that MA cannot be viewed as solely a neutral technical planning and control exercise but a phenomenon involving power and legitimacy. It is a "situated practice" a result of interactions of different players as they reproduce their reality. This viewpoint was discernible during unsettled periods in organizations such as those affected by the economic crisis in Zimbabwe. The political and economic crisis in Zimbabwe led to unity among the contending professional groups, creating a new culture of cooperation. How this culture of cooperation will be sustained beyond the crisis period remains to be seen. By raising these problems the article shows how the social, political, and economic context affects MA. At the same time the article shows that accounting information was enlisted as and when convenient to legitimate decisions taken by management, however leaving a trail of *unintended consequences.*

ACKNOWLEDGMENT

I acknowledge constructive comments from two anonymous reviewers on an earlier draft of this article.

REFERENCES

Alawattage, C., & Wickramasinghe, D. (2008). Changing regimes of governance in a less developed country, corporate governance in less developed countries. *Research in Accounting in Emerging Economies, 8*, 273–310.

Alawattage, C., & Wickramasinghe, D. (2009). Weapons of the weak: Subaltern's emancipatory accounting in Ceylon Tea. Paper presented at the RAAE Workshop, Birmingham University, January 9, 2009.

Albright, T. L., & Roth, H. P. (1992). The measurement of quality costs: An alternative paradigm. *Accounting Horizons, 6*(2), 15–27.

Alvesson, M., & Skoldberg, K. (2000). *Reflexive methodology*. London: Sage.

Alvesson, M., & Willmott, H. (1996). *Making sense of management: A critical introduction*. London: Sage Publications.

Anderson, S. W., & Sedatole, K. (1998). Designing quality into products: The use of accounting data in new product development. *Accounting Horizons, 12*(3), 213–233.

Berry, A. J., Capps, T., Cooper, D., Ferguson, P., Hopper, T., & Lowe, E. A. (1985). Management control in an area of the NCB: Rationales of accounting practice in a public enterprise. *Accounting, Organisations and Society, 10*(1), 3–28.

Bhimani, A. (1996). *Management accounting: European perspectives*. Oxford, UK: Oxford University Press.

Bromwich, M. (1990). The case for strategic management accounting: The role of accounting information for strategy in competitive markets. *Accounting, Organisations and Society, 15*(1/2), 27–46.

Buhr, N. (2002). A structuration view on the initiation of environmental reports. *Critical Perspectives on Accounting, 13*(1), 17–38.

Burchell, S., Clubb, C., Hopwood, A. G., Hughes, J., & Nahapiet. (1980). The roles of accounting in organisations and society. *Accounting, Organisations and Society, 5*(1), 5–27.

Burns, J., & Scapens, R. W. (2000). Conceptualising management accounting change: An institutional framework. *Management Accounting Research, 11*(1), 3–25.

Capps, T., Hopper, T., Mouritsen, J., Cooper, D., & Lowe, T. (1989). Accounting in the production and reproduction of culture. In: W. F. Chua, T. Lowe & T. Puxty (Eds), *Critical perspectives in management control*. Basingstoke: Macmillan Press Ltd.

Coad, A. (1996). Smart work and hard work: Explicating a learning orientation in strategic management accounting. *Management Accounting Research, 7*(4), 387–408.

Conrad, L. (1999). *Control issues in the regulation of privatised industries: A case study of the gas industry*. Unpublished Ph.D. thesis, University of Essex, UK.

Conrad, L. (2005). A structuration analysis of accounting systems and systems of accountability in the privatised gas industry. *Critical Perspectives on Accounting, 16*, 1–26.

Dirsmith, M. W., Heian, J. B., & Covaleski, M. A. (1997). Structure and agency in an institutionalised setting: The application and social transformation control in the Big Six. *Accounting, Organisation and Society, 22*(1), 1–27.

Ezzamel, M. (1994). From problem solving to problematization: Relevance revisited. *Critical Perspectives on Accounting, 5*(3), 269–280.

Ezzamel, M., & Willmott, H. (1998). Accounting, power and resistance in the plant with a problem. Paper presented at Osaka Conference, Osaka, Japan.

Galpin, T., Hilpirt, R., & Evans, B. (2007). The connected enterprise: Beyond division of labour. *Journal of Business Strategy, 28*(2), 38–47.

Garvin, D. (1987). Competing on the eight dimensions of quality. *Harvard Business Review* (November/December), 101–109.

Ghobadian, A., Gallear, D., Woo, H., & Liu, J. (1998). *Total quality management: Impact, introduction and integration strategies.* London: CIMA.

Giddens, A. (1976). *The new rules of sociological method.* London: Hutchinson/New York.

Giddens, A. (1984). *The constitution of society.* Berkeley, CA: University of California.

Guilding, C., Cravens, K. S., & Tayles, M. (2000). An international comparison of strategic management accounting practices. *Management Accounting Research, 11*(1), 113–135.

Gurd, B. (2008). Structuration and middle-range theory: A case study of accounting during organisational change from different theoretical perspectives. *Critical Perspectives on Accounting, 19*(4), 523–543.

Hancke, B., & Casper, S. (2000). Reproducing diversity, ISO 9000 and work organisation in the French and German car industry. In: S. Quack, G. Morgan & R. Whitley (Eds), *National capitalisms; global competition and economic performance – Advances in organisation studies.* Amsterdam: Johnson Benjamin Publishing Co.

Hassan, M. K. (2008). The corporate governance inertia: The role of management accounting and costing systems in a transitional public health organisation. *Research in Accounting in Emerging Economies, 8*(Special Issue), 409–454.

Hayes, R., & Jaikumar, R. (1988). Manufacturing's crisis: New technologies obsolete organisations. *Harvard Business Review* (September/October), 77–85.

Hopper, T., Tsamenyi, M., & Uddin, S. (2009). Management accounting in less developed countries: What is known and needs knowing. *Accounting, Auditing and Accountability Journal, 22*(3), 469–514.

Hoque, Z., & Hopper, T. (1994). Rationality, accounting and politics: A case study of management control in a Bangladeshi jute mill. *Management Accounting Research, 5*(1), 5–30.

Howell, R. A., & Soucy, S. R. (1987). Operating controls in the new manufacturing environment. *Management Accounting* (October), 25–31.

Johnson, H. T., & Kaplan, R. S. (1987). *Relevance lost: The rise and fall of management accounting.* Boston: Harvard Business School Press.

Kaplan, R. S. (1984). The evolution of management accounting. *The Accounting Review,* 390–418.

Kaplan, R. S., & Norton, D. (1996). Using the "Balanced Score Card" as a strategic management system. *Harvard Business Review* (January/February), 75–85.

Kattan, F., Pike, R., & Tayles, M. (2007). Reliance of management accounting environmental uncertainty: The case of Palestine. *Journal of Accounting and Organizational Change, 3*(3), 227–248.

Laughlin, R. C. (1988). Accounting in its social context: An analysis of the accounting systems of the Church of England. *Accounting, Auditing and Accountability Journal, 1/2*(2), 19–42.

Lord, B. R. (1996). Strategic management accounting: The Emperor's new clothes? *Management Accounting Research, 7*(3), 347–366.

Macintosh, N., & Scapens, R. (1990). Structuration theory in management accounting. *Accounting, Organisation and Society, 15*(5), 455–477.

Macintosh, N. B. (1995). The ethics of profit manipulation: A dialectic of control analysis. *Critical Perspectives on Accounting, 6*(4), 289–315.

Macintosh, N. B. (1996). *Management accounting and control systems: An organisational and behavioural approach.* Chichester: Wiley.

Miller, P., & O'Leary, T. (1993). Accounting expertise and the 'politics of the product': Economic citizenship and modes of corporate governance. *Accounting, Organisations and Society, 18*(2/3), 187–206.

Miller, P., & O'Leary, T. (1994). Accounting, economic citizenship and the spatial reordering of manufacture. *Accounting, Organisations and Society, 19*(1), 15–43.

Morse, W. J., & Roth, H. P. (1987). Why quality costs are important? *Management Accounting* (November), 42–43.

Otley, D. T., & Berry, A. J. (1994). Case study research in management accounting and control. *Management Accounting Research, 5*(1), 45–65.

Primrose, P. L. (1991). *Investment in manufacturing technology.* London: Chapman.

Roberts, J., & Scapens, R. (1985). Accounting systems and systems of accountability-understanding accounting practices in their organisational contexts. *Accounting, Organisation and Society, 10*(4), 443–456.

Roslender, R. (1995). Accounting for strategic positioning: Responding to the crisis in management accounting. *British Journal of Management, 6*, 45–57.

Roslender, R., & Hart, S. (2002). Integrating management accounting and marketing in pursuit of competitive advantage: The case for strategic management accounting. *Critical Perspectives on Accounting, 13*(2), 255–277.

Roth, H. P., & Morse, W. J. (1983). Let's help measure and report quality costs. *Management Accounting* (August), 50–53.

Scapens, R. W. (1990). Researching management accounting practice: The role of case study methods. *The British Accounting Review, 22*(3), 259–281.

Simmonds, K. (1981). Strategic management accounting. *Management Accounting, 59*(4), 26–29.

Smith, M. (1997). *Strategic management accounting: Text and cases.* Oxford: Butterworth, Heinemann.

Tayles, M., & Woods, M. (1998). The role of management accounting in quality initiatives, insights from case studies. *Journal of Applied Accounting Research, IV*(3), 63–107.

Tomkins, C. R., & Colville, I. (1984). The role of accounting in local government: Some illustrations from practice. In: A. G. Hopwood & C. R. Tomkins (Eds), *Issues in public sector accounting* (pp. 87–105). London: Philip Allan.

Uddin, S., & Hopper, T. (2001). A Bangladesh soap opera: Privatisation, accounting and regimes of control in a less developed country. *Accounting, Organisations and Society, 26*(7/8), 643–672.

Van Maanen, J. (1995). *Representation in ethnography.* Thousand Oaks, CA: Sage.

Whittington, R. (1992). Putting Giddens into action: Social systems and managerial agency. *Journal of Management Studies, 29*(6), 693–712.

Willmott, H. (1987). Studying managerial work: A critique and a proposal. *Journal of Management Studies, 24*(3), 249–270.

Yin, R. K. (1993). Applications of case study research. In: *Applied Social Research Methods Series* (Vol. 34). Thousand Oaks, London, New Delhi: Sage Publications.

A NEW INSTITUTIONAL ANALYSIS OF IFRSs ADOPTION IN EGYPT: A CASE STUDY OF LOOSELY COUPLED RULES AND ROUTINES

Ahmed Kholeif

ABSTRACT

Purpose – *This article examines a detailed case study of the symbolic use of International Financial Reporting Standards (IFRSs) in an Egyptian state-owned company (AQF Co.) that is partially privatized by drawing on new institutional sociology (NIS) and its extensions. It explains how the ceremonial use of IFRSs is shaped by the interplay between institutionalized accounting practices, conflicting institutions, power relations, and the role of information technology (IT) in institutionalizing accounting rules and routines.*

Methodology/approach – *The research methodology is based on an intensive case study informed by NIS, especially the interplay between conflicting institutions, power relations, and IT role in institutionalizing accounting practice. Data were collected from multiple sources, including interviews, discussions, and documentary analysis.*

Findings – *The findings revealed that the company faced conflicting institutional demands from outside. The Central Agency for Accountability required the company to use the Uniform Accounting System*

Research in Accounting in Emerging Economies, Volume 10, 29–55
Copyright © 2010 by Emerald Group Publishing Limited
All rights of reproduction in any form reserved
ISSN: 1479-3563/doi:10.1108/S1479-3563(2010)0000010007

(as a state-owned enterprise) and the Egyptian Capital Market Authority (CMA) required the company to use IFRSs (as a partially private sector company registered in the stock exchange). To meet these conflicting institutional demands, the company adopted loosely coupled accounting rules and routines and IT was used in institutionalizing existing Uniform Accounting System and preserving the status quo.

Research limitations *– This study has limitations associated with its use of the case study method, including the inability to generalize from the findings of a single case study and the subjective interpretation by the researcher of the empirical data.*

Practical implications *– This article identifies that the interplay between institutional pressures, institutionalized accounting practices, intra-organizational power relations, and the role of IT in institutionalizing accounting routines contributed to the ceremonial use of IFRSs in an Egyptian state-owned enterprise. Understanding such relationships can help other organizations to become more aware of the factors affecting successful implementation and internalization of IFRSs and provide a better basis for planning the introduction of IFRSs into other organizations worldwide.*

Originality/value of article *– This article draws on recent research and thinking in sociology, especially the development and application of NIS. In addition, this article is concerned with the symbolic use of IFRSs in a transitional developing economy, Egypt, and hence contributes to debate about exporting Western accounting practices and other technologies to countries with different cultures and different stages of economic and political development.*

Keywords: IFRSs, International Financial Reporting Standards; developing countries; Egypt; new institutional sociology.

1. INTRODUCTION

Supranational organizations such as the World Bank (WB) and International Monetary Fund (IMF) encourage and facilitate the diffusion and reproduction of specific accounting and accountability practices across time and space (Graham & Neu, 2003; Unerman, 2003; Lehman, 2005;

Nolke, 2005; Chand & White, 2007; Richardson, 2009). These international institutions exert pressures on developing and transitional countries to adopt International Financial Reporting Standards (IFRSs) as part of their reform programs as this is regarded necessary to command the confidence of investors (Points & Cunningham, 1998; Mir & Rahaman, 2005). However, the relevance of IFRSs to developing and transitional countries has been questioned by a growing number of scholars (e.g., Mensah, 1981; Ndubizu, 1984; Hove, 1989; Wallace, 1993; Larson & Kenny, 1995; Longden, Luther, & Bowler, 2001). For example, Wallace and Briston (1993, pp. 216–217) argue that:

> Developing countries continue to adopt foreign accounting and educational systems. This is often expensive, and the adopting country has little control over the relevance of imported accounting .... The biggest problem developing countries have is that of too many foreign "experts" marketing half-baked solutions to problems that neither they nor the recipient nations understand. Donor agencies should collaborate more closely with the recipient country to ensure that their assistance is delivered only in accordance with national accounting development plans.

The inappropriateness of IFRSs in developing and transitional countries has been reflected in the high level of noncompliance with these standards (Abayo, Adams, & Roberts, 1993; Hossain, Tan, & Adams, 1994; Solas, 1994; Street, Gray, & Bryant, 1999; Murphy, 1999; Street, Nichols, & Gray, 2000; Street & Gray, 2001; Abd-Elsalam & Weetman, 2003; Dahawy & Conover, 2007). For example, Solas (1994) examined the extent of financial information disclosure by Jordanian companies according to the requirements of IFRSs. He concluded that disclosure was not at an acceptable level. Street and Gray (2001) also found a significant extent of noncompliance with IFRSs in different countries around the globe.

In early 1990s, Egypt has undertaken a privatization program due to the external pressures from international donors (the WB and IMF). As part of this program, Egypt adopted IFRSs since 1997. A new Capital Market Law No. 95 of 1992 was issued and its Executive Regulations required adherence to IFRSs in 1993. After issuing an official Arabic translation of the standards by the Minister of Economy in 1997, the requirement to apply IFRSs became fully mandatory for the first time. The decision of the Egyptian government to mandate an immediate implementation of IFRSs allowed neither the listed companies nor the accounting profession adequate time to adapt to the "new" standards. This could result in low or noncompliance with IFRSs requirements (Abd-Elsalam & Weetman, 2003; Dahawy & Conover, 2007).

Seeking to locate the low or noncompliance with IFRSs in Egyptian sociopolitical contexts, this study aims to interpret a case study of an Egyptian state-owned company (AQF Co.) that has partially been privatized and became subject to the requirements of the Egyptian Capital Market Authority (CMA) to adopt IFRSs. However, state-owned companies are required to follow a Uniform Accounting System introduced since 1966 and closely monitored by the Central Agency for Accountability.[1] As a state-owned company, AQF Co. has to apply the Uniform Accounting System. Hence, AQF Co. has faced conflicting extra-organizational institutional pressures. How has the company responded to these conflicting regulatory requirements? To explain the response of the case organization, new institutional sociology (NIS) theory and its extensions are used in this article (DiMaggio & Powell, 1983; Modell, 2002; Lounsbury, 2006, 2008).

The NIS perspective explores the role of macroeconomic, political, and social institutions in shaping organizational structures, policies, and procedures (Scott, 2001). Organizations respond to such external macro-pressures to receive support and legitimacy (Modell, 2002). NIS has been adopted to explain homogeneity and persistence (Granlund & Lukka, 1998; Dacin, Goodstein, & Scott, 2002), conflicting institutional demands (Meyer & Rowan, 1977; D'Aunno, Sutton, & Price, 1991), the interplay between institutional pressures and intra-organizational power relations (Burns & Scapens, 2000; Modell, 2002; Tsamenyi, Cullen, & Gonzalez, 2006; Dambrin, Lambert, & Sponem, 2007; Lounsbury, 2008), and the role of information technology (IT) in institutionalizing organizational practices (Orlikowski, 1992; Soh & Sia, 2004; Kholeif, Abdel-Kader, & Sherer, 2007). This article draws on these recent developments in NIS to address the following research questions: how is the adoption of IFRSs in the case organization (AQF Co.) shaped by the interplay between institutionalized accounting practices, conflicting institutions, and power relations? And what is the role of IT in supporting this adoption of IFRSs in AQF Co.?

The remainder of this article is organized in six sections. In Section 2, we articulate the theoretical framework based on NIS and its extensions. This is followed by a background about the case organization and details of the research method employed in this study. The article then discusses how the adoption of IFRSs is shaped by the interplay between institutionalized accounting practices, conflicting institutions, power relations, and the role of IT. The final section provides a summary of the article and some conclusions.

2. THEORETICAL FRAMEWORK: NEW INSTITUTIONAL SOCIOLOGY AND ITS EXTENSIONS

In this section, NIS and its extensions are proposed as the theoretical framework informing the analysis of the case study. Initially, the concept of institutional isomorphism and its relationship with the adoption of IFRSs are discussed. Then, the implications of the interplay between intra-organizational power relation, conflicting institutions, and deinstitutionalization as well as IT for IFRSs adoption are examined. As mentioned in the previous section, this examination is necessary because the adoption of IFRSs is shaped by the institutional forces, intra-organizational power relations, conflicting institutions, and IT.

2.1. Institutional Pressures and the Adoption of IFRSs

The NIS perspective explores the role of extra-organizational institutions (the State, professionals, and public opinion) in shaping organizational structures, policies, and procedures (Scott, 2001). Organizations respond to such external macropressures to receive support and legitimacy (Covaleski, Dirsmith, & Samuel, 1996; Modell, 2002). Early institutionalists (e.g., Weick, 1976; Meyer & Rowan, 1977) argue that formal structures that are used to secure the legitimacy of extra-organizational institutions can become decoupled or loosely coupled from the technical aspects of organizations. This refers to minimal adoption of formal structures, that is, implementation without internalization. In the opposite case, when formal structures are tightly coupled to the technical aspects of organizations, this means active adoption of formal structures, that is, implementation (in behaviors and actions) and internalization are completed (Dambrin et al., 2007).

DiMaggio and Powell (1983) introduce the concept of organizational fields as a kind of extra-organizational institutions. They define it as the organizations that constitute a recognized area of institutional life such as suppliers, customers, and regulatory agencies. They argue that organizations within the field tend to make organizational changes and adopt similar formal structures in the search for legitimacy. There are three mechanisms through which institutional isomorphic change occurs: coercive isomorphism, normative isomorphism, and mimetic isomorphism. *Coercive isomorphism* is primarily related to the political influence exerted by institutions on which organizations depend for critical resources and long-term survival, such as the State laws and regulations. *Normative isomorphism* is the institutionalization of social practices as a result of professionalization by means of professional groups such as accounting associations. *Mimetic isomorphism* stems from the tendency of organizations to imitate each other in response to symbolic uncertainty.

Generally accepted accounting principles, such as IFRSs, are a kind of formal structure coming from outside the organization. Organizations adopt similar formal structures such as IFRSs under the pressures of extra-organizational institutions such as the State laws and regulations, the stock exchanges, and the accounting professions. IFRSs are often symbolically used for purposes of legitimization (Mir & Rahaman, 2005; Touron, 2005). This means that IFRSs are used because they are socially legitimized, independent of consequences in terms of efficiency. A number of accounting studies have documented the symbolic use of IFRSs in different countries. Cairns (2000) gives some evidence of the loose coupling between the spirit of the standards and the actual accounting practices of organizations in a number of countries.

Other studies observe similar behaviors in the adoption of IFRSs. Mir and Rahaman (2005) find that the decision to adopt IFRSs in Bangladesh is driven by the pressure exerted by the WB and IMF on the Bangladeshi government and professional accounting bodies. They argue that the perceived undemocratic nature of the IFRSs adoption process in Bangladesh creates and enhances conflict among various constituencies, resulting in a very low level of compliance with these standards. Dahawy and Conover (2007) argue that the imposition of IFRSs in Egypt creates resistance that is reflected in the selective compliance with the requirements of these standards. The NIS perspective gives little attention to how the process of institutionalization occurs or does not occur inside organizations (Tolbert & Zucker, 1996). To understand this outcome we need to examine intra-organizational dynamics and processes of accounting change and stability. Section 2.2 addresses this issue.

2.2. Institutional Pressures and Intra-Organizational Power Relations

A major criticism of NIS is related to its relative inattention to the role of proactive agency in constructing institutions (Carruthers, 1995; Dambrin et al., 2007; Lounsbury, 2008). For example, Barley and Tolbert (1997) argue that NIS has largely focused on the role of institutions in shaping and constraining the actions of actors. This criticism has been addressed in recent institutional studies that focus on the ability of actors to respond to institutional pressures (Oliver, 1991; Greenwood & Hinings, 1996; Barley & Tolbert, 1997; Burns & Scapens, 2000; Collier, 2001; Modell, 2002; Tsamenyi et al., 2006; Dambrin et al., 2007; Lounsbury, 2008; Hyvonen, Jarvinen, Pellinen, & Rahko, 2009). These studies have broadened NIS to include power relations.

In this article, the work of Burns and Scapens (2000) is drawn upon to study how institutions interact with the actions of organizational actors and the role of power relations in their interaction. Based on Giddens' (1984) structuration theory, Burns and Scapens (2000) describe the relationship between actions and institutions as the agency–structure relationship. They argue that although institutions constrain and shape action at a specific point in time, actions produce and reproduce institutions through their cumulative influence over time. They use such notions as "encoded," "enacted," "reproduced," and "institutionalized" to analyze both the synchronic and diachronic linkages of the major elements of their framework.

Burns and Scapens (2000) distinguish between accounting systems as rules and accounting practices as routines. The former refers to the formalized statement of procedures, whereas the latter refers to the procedures actually in use. Then, Burns and Scapens (2000) use the concept of rule-based behavior to link accounting rules to accounting routines. They argue that recursively following the rules may lead to a programmatic rule-based conduct. This programmatic behavior is what Burns and Scapens (2000) called routines. As such, accounting routines may not actually replicate the accounting rules, as there are different deliberate or unconscious modifications that could be introduced during implementing and using the rules in guiding day-to-day behavior. So, an organization's accounting routines might be largely ceremonial, and thereby preserve existing power structures. The adoption of IFRSs and its interaction with the Uniform Accounting System in the case organization draw mainly on Burns and Scapens' (2000) concepts of accounting rules and routines.

Burns and Scapens (2000) adopted the concept of power as articulated by Giddens (1984). In this regard, there are two main perspectives of power (Macintosh & Scapens, 1990). The first perspective is that power is best conceptualized as the transformative capacity of an actor to achieve his or her will, even at the expense of others who might resist him or her (power in the broad sense). It can be used to introduce new organizational rules or may be mobilized to resist such new rules. The second perspective is that power should be seen as a property of the society or social institutions or the medium for domination (power in the narrow sense). It is the power embedded in the institutionalized routines, which shape the actions and thoughts of organizational members. In Burns and Scapens' framework, the two perspectives of power are connected together as features of the duality of structure. Both perspectives of power are of particular interest to this article to interpret the adoption of IFRS by AQF Co., especially relating the structure level (macropressures for the adoption of IFRSs) to the action level (the response of AQF Co. at the microlevel to the pressures for the adoption of IFRSs).

2.3. The Role of Information Technology in Institutionalizing Accounting Rules and Routines

IT creators inscribe their view of the world in the technology that they create (Latour, 1992; Orlikowski, 1992; Soh & Sia, 2004; Kholeif et al., 2007). For instance, Hedberg and Jonsson (1978, p. 56) argue that:

> The way in which organizations' information (and accounting) systems reflect the world depends on the designers' assumptions about important characteristics of organizations and their environments.

Orlikowski (1992) has proposed a model, called "structurational model of technology," extending the concept of the "duality of structure" to the "duality of technology." She argues that "technology is created and changed by human action, yet it is also used by humans to accomplish some action" (p. 405). According to this view, technology is both the outcome and the medium of human action. The technology, on the one hand, is the product of human action as it is both physically constructed by designers and socially constructed by users at a certain time and organizational context. On the other hand, technology is the medium of human action, containing rules and resources that both enable and constrain different sorts of use.

Although defining technology as "material artifacts" (various configurations of hardware and software), Orlikowski (1992, p. 403) claimed that this does not imply an "exclusive focus on technology as a physical object." Rather, she argued that technology should be seen as "interpretively flexible." Orlikowski (1992) argues that the interpretive flexibility of technology works in both design and use stages. In design stage, designers build into technology certain interpretive schemes, certain facilities, and certain norms. In use stage, users interpret, appropriate, and manipulate the technology's embedded rules and resources to execute their tasks. This means that technology is potentially modifiable at any time, both through deliberate redesign and through use that, accidentally or otherwise, deviates from ways intended by the developers.

Orlikowski's (1992) model has some similarity to Burns and Scapens' (2000) model. It consists of four stages. The first stage describes the influence of institutional properties on humans' interactions with IT (encoding stage in Burns and Scapens' model). The second stage considers IT as a medium for human action, where IT facilitates and constrains human actions (enacting stage in Burns and Scapens' model). The third stage views IT as a product of human action (reproduction stage in Burns and Scapens' model). The final stage reflects the influence of interaction with technology on institutional properties (institutionalization stage in Burns and Scapens' model).

Of particular importance to this article is the Orlikowski's (1992) interpretive flexibility view of technology that is equivalent to the two-way relationship between rules and routines in Burns and Scapens' model. For example, according to Orlikowski (1992), custom software tends to reflect existing institutional properties of the organization and is easily modifiable during design and use stages. In Burns and Scapens' (2000) words, this means that the "new" IT-based rules could be a formalization of existing routines and reinforce the institutional status quo. The case organization, AQF Co., introduced custom developed accounting software in 1998/1999 to supposedly help it implement IFRSs. The interplay between the software implemented, the Uniform Accounting System, and IFRSs is interesting in AQF Co.

2.4. Conflicting Institutions and Deinstitutionalization

The use of power in this article is related to the issue of conflicting institutions. When organizations face conflicting extra-organizational institutional pressures, how they should respond? Meyer and Rowan (1977) argue that organizations adopt inconsistent, even conflicting, practice to gain legitimacy. However, D'Aunno et al. (1991) argue that organizations have limited ability to respond to conflicting institutional pressures and thus will confirm to them only partially. AQF Co., the case organization, has faced such conflicting institutional demands from the Egyptian Stock Exchange to adopt IFRSs and the Central Agency for Accountability to use the Uniform Accounting System. The response of AQF Co. represents the narrative of this case study.

Conflicting institutions exist because deinstitutionalization of "old" institutions does not occur. Deinstitutionalization[2] refers to "the processes by which institutions weaken and disappear ... the weakening and disappearance of one set of beliefs and practices is likely to be associated with the arrival of new beliefs and practices" (Scott, 2001, pp. 182, 184). Oliver (1992) identifies three major sources of pressures for deinstitutionalization: functional, political, and social sources. Functional pressures arise from perceived problems in performance levels or the perceived utility associated with institutionalized practices. Political pressures result primarily from shifts in the interests and underlying power distributions that have supported and legitimated existing institutional arrangements. Finally, social pressures are associated with the differentiation of groups, the existence of heterogeneous divergent or discordant beliefs and practices, and change in laws or social expectations that might hinder the continuation of a practice. A mix of these pressures, which supported the move toward IFRSs, exists in the case organization.

3. THE CASE ORGANIZATION: *AQF CO.*

AQF Co. is a leading company in nitrogenous fertilizer production based in Egypt. It was established by the Ministerial Decree No. 374 of 1976 as one of the public sector companies. It manufactures and sells a full line of nitrogenous fertilizers including prilled urea, granular urea, and ammonium nitrate. Currently, the AQF's local market share is 71% urea in both forms and 54% ammonium nitrate. As for the export market share, it has become 69% urea in both forms and 89% ammonium nitrate. However, the company started to perceive local competition from newly established local companies such as AlexF Co. and other competitors that entered the local market as a result of implementing GATT agreement in 2006. Sales and operating income of AQF have increased in recent years. In 2002/2003, AQF reported sales of L.E. 1,082.7 million and operating income of L.E. 421.5 million. Total assets of the company on June 30, 2003 were L.E. 3,756.6 million. AQF has about 2,992 employees as chemical engineers, technicians, and administrative staff. The organizational structure is shown in Fig. 1.

Currently, AQF operates in three factories: AQ I Plant, AQ II Plant, and AQ III Plant. AQ I Plant started manufacturing ammonia and urea in two

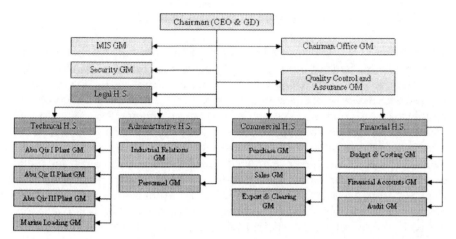

Fig. 1. The Management Structure of AQF.

production lines in September 1979. Its production capacity is 1,100 tons/day of ammonia and 1,550 tons/day of urea. In December 1990, AQF introduced marine loading to export its products to international markets. AQ II Plant was established in August 1991 to produce ammonia, nitric acid, and ammonium nitrate with capacity of 1,000 tons/day, 1,800 tons/day, and 2,400 tons/day, respectively. AQF continued its expansion and established AQ III Plant in October 1998. The capacity of this plant is 1,200 tons/day of ammonia and 2,000 tons/day of granular urea. In 2001, AQF introduced its most recent extension project, AQ IV, to be established on a private free zone basis. However, in 2003, the Egyptian government decided to establish this new project as a separate company known as AlexF Co., which started its production at the beginning of 2006.

According to Law No. 203 of 1991, AQF Co. has been supervised by the Holding Company for Chemical Industries to organize its gradual sale. In 1996, the government started the partial privatization of AQF by selling about 18% of its shares. Following its partial privatization in 1996, AQF started to improve its information systems. The company adopted IFRSs and was awarded ISO 9001:2000 certificate for the quality management system in 2001 as well as ISO 14001 certificate for the environment management system in 1999. As part of the preparation for ISO 9001:2000 certificate, the company renewed its IT infrastructure and introduced custom developed accounting software in 1998/1999 to supposedly help it implement IFRSs.

4. RESEARCH METHOD

The case study method was used to obtain a rich set of data surrounding the specific research issues and to capture the contextual complexity (Yin, 1994). Case study materials were gathered in 2001 and during 2003–2004. In 2001, the researcher was a member of a consultancy team to help the company establish an accounting system into the new plant, AQ IV. During 2003–2004, the researcher visited the company for research purposes only. The materials collected included unstructured and semi-structured interviews, site visits, and the collection of documentary evidence. To facilitate access to some confidential information, a formal written permission was obtained from the Central Agency for Public Mobilization and Statistics. Unstructured and semi-structured interviews were the main data collection methods to find out what participants do, think, or feel. The interviews were conducted with cost and financial accountants, IT staff, and line managers (see Table 1). Eighteen individual interviews[3] were face-to-face and lasted up to 2 h.

In addition to the interviews, other data collection methods were used. These methods include background questionnaires, documentary evidence, published accounts, and budgets. These multiple methods are deliberately selected as one method can complement others. This triangulation is essential for improving the validity and reliability of qualitative research or evaluation of findings. In this regard, Scapens (1990) suggests the triangulation of evidence by collecting different pieces of evidence on the same research issue, collecting other evidence from the same source, and working in teams to reach an agreed interpretation of a particular case. To acquire valid and reliable multiple and diverse realities, multiple methods

Table 1.   The Profile of Interviewees.

Accountants	Head of financial sector
	An accountant (A)
	An accountant (B)
	An accountant (C)
	General Manager of Financial Accounts
	General Manager of Cost Department
IT specialists	General Manager of MIS
	IT Specialist
Line managers	Head of Technical Sector (Factories)

such as the use of investigators, method and data triangulations to record the construction of reality is appropriate. As a consequence, the use of multiple sources of evidence in this case study is justifiable on the grounds of increasing the contextual validity of research evidence.

The case study materials were collected from AQF Co. This company was chosen because it demonstrates a case of the adoption of IFRSs in a highly conflicting institutional environment in a developing country (Egypt). There is a lack of research on the impact of highly conflicting institutional environments on the adoption of IFRSs. In addition, by comparison with previous research in developed countries intensive case study research on IFRSs adoption in developing countries can aid our understanding of the contextual and national differences on IFRSs implementations.

5. INSTITUTIONAL INTERPRETATION OF LOOSELY COUPLED ACCOUNTING RULES AND ROUTINES

In this section the adoption of IFRSs in AQF Co. is analyzed. Based on the theoretical framework, two separate, but related, reasons for the observed use of IFRSs are identified, knitting these reasons together through the new institutional perspective of the article. This section first focuses on conflicting coercive pressures exerted on AQF Co. from the regulatory environment, the Central Agency for Accountability, and the Egyptian Stock Exchange. The intra-organizational power relations and the role of IT in institutionalizing the Uniform Accounting System in AQF Co. are then addressed.

5.1. Conflicting Coercive Pressures: Introducing New Institutions Without Deinstitutionalizing Old Ones

5.1.1. The Nationalization Laws and the Central Agency for Accountability (1952–1990)

The defining period of modern Egypt is still the revolutionary socialist regime under President Nasser (1952–1970). After the revolution of 1952, the Egyptian government made a break with the past and moved the Egyptian economy from a free market-oriented economy to a massively state-controlled economy in few years. The nationalization laws and expropriation of various private enterprises became the expression of change in Egypt after the July Revolution in 1952. A series of nationalization decrees was issued in 1956, 1961, and 1963 to eliminate the dominant role of both foreign and large-scale, local private capital. In 1952, the private sector made about 76% of the total investment in the economy. The public sector very quickly established its dominance in the economy and for the next three decades was making between 80 and 90% of the investment in the economy and constituted around 37% of GDP annually (PCSU, 2002).

To control the finances of the public sector and auditing the books of public enterprises and government departments, the Egyptian government established the Central Agency for Accountability with the Law No. 129 of 1964. In describing the power of the Central Agency for Accountability, Kayed (1990, p. 262) states that:

> Because of the Central Agency for Accountability wide authority and responsibilities it is in a unique position to influence developments in accounting. Its influence arises from the nature of its activities, its size, and its role in the economy. Under the control of the Vice-President of the country, the Central Agency for Accountability has the authority to issue accounting and auditing instructions, which must be followed by organizations, whose financial statements and accounts have been audited by its members.

In view of the state's dependence on accounting information to prepare the National Plan, the Uniform Accounting System was introduced by the Central Agency for Accountability in 1966. It was compulsory for all state-owned enterprises in the public sector, with the exception of banks and insurance companies. In such an accounting system, accounts are classified in homogeneous classes in a manner that assists in preparing national accounts, as well as satisfying the needs of the traditional financial and cost accounting.[4]

Since its early beginnings in 1976, AQF Co. has adopted the Uniform Accounting System to both financial accounting and cost accounting because it has been owned by nonmanufacturing public enterprises. It also prepares traditional planning budgets such as a sales budget, a production budget, and a commodity and service requirements budget. The government's contributions in the ownership have been the main factor for using the Uniform Accounting System. In this regard, the Uniform Accounting System and planning budgets are imposed organizational formal structures. They are imposed and monitored by the coercive authority of the state agencies (the Central Agency for Accountability). The use of the Uniform Accounting System and planning budgets in AQF Co. has been routinized and institutionalized. They became part of day-to-day life and the way of doing things (Burns & Scapens, 2000). Accountants use the account codes as a way of communication with other organizational members in day-to-day interactions.

5.1.2. The Privatization Laws and the Egyptian Capital Market Authority (1991–Present)

In the early 1990s, a privatization program was undertaken because of the Egyptian government's dissatisfaction with the failure and losses of public sector enterprises and the external pressures from international donors (WB and IMF) in favor of privatization. The Egyptian government launched the privatization program with the Public Enterprise Law No. 203 of 1991 and its regulations, establishing the legal framework for sale of 314 public enterprises that earmarked for privatization. This law marked the start of public enterprise reform. It was designed to eliminate the difference in treatment between public and private enterprises.

Public holding companies were established in 1991. The ownership and management of 314 public enterprises, subjected to Law 203 of 1991, were transferred from the various ministries to 17 holding companies, which are held accountable to the Ministry of Public Enterprises. Holding companies are primarily responsible for organizing the sale of their constituent SOEs known as affiliated companies, with a mandate to maximize the present value of their affiliated companies on behalf of the state. According to this law, AQF Co. has been supervised by the Holding Company for Chemical Industries to organize its gradual sale.

Law No. 203 of 1991 solved several legal and institutional constraints that could have hindered the privatization program. Nonetheless, the legal and institutional frameworks were still incomplete even after Law No. 203 of 1991 was issued. The build up of the necessary legal and institutional frameworks demanded the enhancement of the capital market and its institutions. Historically, the Egyptian Capital Market has two locations: Alexandria and Cairo. The Alexandria Stock Exchange was officially established in 1888 followed by Cairo in 1903. The two stock exchanges were very active till the 1940s. However, the central planning and socialist policies, adopted since the 1950s, led to a drastic reduction in activity on the Egyptian stock exchanges for four decades. The Egyptian stock market till the late 1980s was not prepared to execute privatization transactions.

In the 1990s, capital market reform became mandatory with the move toward a free market economy and the privatization program. The Capital Market Law No. 95 of 1992 was promulgated in 1992 and came into effect in 1993 through the issuance of its Executive Regulations. The Law No. 95 of 1992 encourages establishing service institutions, intermediary companies such as brokerage companies, underwriters, portfolio managers, and depositories. It also introduced the idea of employee shareholders associations for public and private enterprises. Furthermore, all restrictions, which hinder easy entry to the market of foreign investors, were removed. International investors can easily invest in securities without limitations on capital mobility or foreign exchange restrictions. Furthermore, the listing rules governing the exchange allow for foreign securities to be listed and traded, meeting the same requirements as applicable to local securities.

According to Law No. 95 of 1992, the CMA was given sole control over supervising the securities market, including Alexandria and Cairo Stock Exchanges. It is charged with market development, supervision of trading, broker licensing, and market surveillance. The CMA, a government organization that reports to the Minister of Foreign Trade, was established in 1979. However, the Capital Market Law introduced new roles and functions for the CMA. These include monitoring the performance of exchanges and enforcement of listing and trading regulations. The CMA also monitors compliance by listed companies and directs exchanges to delist securities and to suspend listing or trading for noncompliance if the exchange fails to act promptly.

The Capital Market Law stipulates that listed companies comply with full disclosure of financial statements and all other relevant information requirements according to IFRSs, which were issued in September 1997. The law also requires that any prospectus must be approved by the CMA for both content and format prior to any public offering. In addition to the disclosure of information from the issuer's side, the stock exchange publishes daily bulletins containing market quotations, daily transactions, and other details of trading activities. The privatization program has stimulated the stock market activities.

The pace of privatization up to 1993 was slow because time was needed to introduce the necessary legislative and regulatory arrangements. Once the enabling mechanisms were in place the privatization program gained momentum in the second half of 1990s, after a favorable ruling by the constitutional court upholding the government's right to privatize the public sector. In early 1996, a list of 120 companies ripe for privatization was published and two of 120 others were released in 1997 (Khattab, 2007). They covered a wide range of activities – cement, metallurgy, textiles, pharmaceuticals, food processing, maritime transport, and tourism.

In 1996, the government started the partial privatization of AQF. In May 1996, 2.80% of the company shares was sold to private sector for L.E. 20 million through the stock market. As from August 1996, AQF becomes one of the joint stock companies running under the Companies Law No. 159 of 1981, which organizes the establishment of private sector companies. In 2002/2003, the company's shares that were sold to the public and employee share associations became 18.1%. The remaining shares are still owned by nonmanufacturing public enterprises, including National Banks Sector (39.4%), National Petroleum Authority (19.1%), General Organization for Industrialization (12.7%), and Insurance Sector (10.7%).

As the majority of the company's ownership (more than 80%) is still owned by public enterprises, the company continued using the Uniform Accounting System despite the registration in the stock exchange, which requires registered companies to adopt the Egyptian accounting standards, an Arabic translation of IFRSs. The general manager of Financial Accounts explained this apparent conflict as follows:

> We use the account chart (account codes and names) from the Uniform Accounting System but the company applies the Egyptian Accounting Standards. The company also uses some treatments of the Uniform Accounting System such as depreciation rates. This is because accounting standards are general principles and have not determined specific depreciation rates. In addition, we disclose the methods used in notes to financial statements. With respect to the matters that were in conflict with accounting standards, we applied the accounting standards. The company applies accounting standards and is subject to Law No. 159 of 1981 and its executive regulations.

As clearly evident from this comment, the disclosure requirements of the stock exchange were not able to overcome the institutionalized accounting rules and routines supported by control authorities and other government agencies. The extra-organizational institutions that dominated the centrally planned economy era still have the major influence on state-owned enterprises. Section 5.2 explains how accountants have used IT to create these loosely coupled accounting rules and routines.

5.2. The Role of IT to Reinforce the Institutional Status Quo and Preserve Existing Power Structures

Historically, the MIS Department in AQF has reported to the controller, the head of Finance Sector. It was part of Finance Sector. In 1989 custom accounting software based on the Uniform Accounting System was introduced to the Finance Sector in AQF. It was based on a mainframe-computerized system that used COBOL language. It had three applications: wages, inventories, and purchases. These applications were isolated from each other. Moreover, there was duplication in data entry. In 1998/99 AQF adopted "new" custom software, Oracle software. The decision to implement custom accounting software and renew IT infrastructure in 1998/99 was related to its gradual privatization. However, this decision was not influenced by the holding company.[5] It was an initiative launched by the ex-head of Quality Control and Assurance as part of the preparation for ISO 9001:2000 certificate and the adoption of IFRSs. So the introduction of the new custom software was seen as an internal decision rather than a mandatory order. It was not subjected to resistance from the company's organizational members as it did not challenge existing routines and institutions. The software was customized to be in full conformity with the Uniform Accounting System used by the company since its establishment in 1976.

Historical data were transferred into Oracle software and new applications have been introduced. The "new" software integrates and relates different databases. It has 28 applications that cover the most important systems of the company. Examples of these applications are wages, inventories, cost accounts, purchases, suppliers, and sales. However, almost all of these applications are based on the Uniform Accounting System. For example, the general manager of Financial Accounts stated that:

> Before adopting Oracle software, the work was manual in preparing financial statements, including documentary cycle and trial balance. In 1990s…the Uniform Accounting System has been programmed. The software currently prepares the trail balance. We still try to prepare financial statements by the software. We currently use Excel files to prepare financial statements.

Similarly, a cost accountant described the role of the Oracle software in determining product costs:

> Cost centres are divided into production (Account No. 5), production service (Account No. 6), marketing service (Account No. 7), and administrative and finance service (Account No. 8). Any journal entry recorded is also directed to the related cost centre. Account No. 3 (use of resources) is first allocated to cost centres as a first stage … The costs of service centres are next allocated to production centres. Then, we calculate the unit product cost … In past, the allocation process was manual. We were spending days to perform such allocation. Currently, the allocation is very fast and accurate. The software saves efforts and time and provides high degree of accuracy.

This comment clearly confirms the use of the Uniform Accounting System in AQF even after implementing the new software. According to the Uniform Accounting System (see Table 2), cost items (the uses of resources) are classified into wages, commodity requirements, service requirements, finished goods purchased for sale, current transferred expenses, and current transfer. Furthermore, the Uniform Accounting System divides responsibility centers

Table 2. Cost Items and Cost Centers in the Uniform Accounting System.

Analysis of Uses of Resources					
Three uses of resources	Five production centers	Six production service centers	Seven marketing service centers	Eight finance and administrative centers	Nine capital transaction centers
31 wages	531 wages	631 wages	731 wages	831 wages	931 wages
32 commodity requirements	532 commodity requirements	632 commodity requirements	732 commodity requirements	832 commodity requirements	932 commodity requirements
33 service acquired	533 service acquired	633 service acquired	733 service acquired	833 service acquired	933 service acquired
34 finished goods purchased for sale	534 finished goods purchased for sale	–	–	–	–
35 current transferred expenses	535 current transferred expenses	635 current transferred expenses	735 current transferred expenses	835 current transferred expenses	935 current transferred expenses
36 current transfer	–	–	–	–	–

This information is based on Briston and El-Ashker (1984).

into five cost centers, namely the production center, the production service center, the marketing service center, the finance and administrative center, and the capital transaction center. The latter center is used to analyze and show separately the cost of self-constructed fixed assets. Then, the Uniform Accounting System directly allocates the uses of resources to the five cost centers.

In fact, the Oracle software was fully customized to meet the information needs of the company. The customizability of the software was seen by the company's members as a major advantage. This is consistent with Burns and Scapens (2000) that it is easy to introduce change that does not conflict with existing routines and institutions. It is also in agreement with the interpretive flexibility of technology. The general manager of MIS Department explained the advantage of custom developed software over packaged software as follows:

> We conducted a feasibility study that compared between a number of packaged software to determine customisation efforts required in each one. We reached a decision that custom developed software is the best solution to the company's circumstances. We found that we would pay a large amount of money and we had to customise the

purchased package. Furthermore, we would not obtain the source code for the package because its price would be unreasonable ... In the case of package software, the company's organisational structure should be modified to fit the package.

He added:

Sometimes, we have to change or modify a module in response to a law or a governmental decision. There is no problem at all in the software's flexibility because we programmed the software. Each person responsible for a module is capable of modifying it at any time and under any circumstances.

Following the renewal of IT infrastructure and the introduction of custom Oracle software, the company's management decided to relocate the MIS Department to become under the direct supervision of the vice-CEO of Control and Commercial Affairs. The department has, therefore, become much closer to the office of the CEO. Despite the change in the MIS Department's location in the organizational structure, the department is still dominated by accountants. The general manager of the MIS Department and almost all its staff are accountants. This dominance of accountants over the MIS Department is the result of historical events. So, accountants are still the custodians/managers of custom Oracle software and the company's Intranet.

In sum, custom Oracle software was implemented in AQF to fit the requirements of the Uniform Accounting System used by the company as the majority of its shares are still owned by public sector enterprises. It has not challenged established accounting rules and routines. But the company claims that it does apply the IFRSs required by the Egyptian CMA. Then, how does the company apply IFRSs while it uses the Uniform Accounting System[6] and has software that was customized to meet the requirements of the Uniform Accounting System? This dilemma was resolved by adopting loosely coupled accounting rules and routines. The IFRSs are the ceremonial accounting rules claimed to be used by the company to meet the requirements of the Egyptian CMA but the Uniform Accounting System is the actual accounting routines used by the company to meet day-to-day activities. Accountants in AQF Co. use IT to reinforce their institutional status quo and preserve their existing power structures.

6. SUMMARY AND CONCLUSIONS

This article aimed at providing an institutional explanation to the low or noncompliance with IFRSs requirements in Egypt. Using NIS theory and its

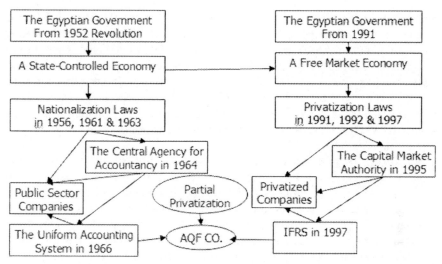

Fig. 2. The Impact of Conflicting Institutions on the Case Organization.

extensions to analyze a case study of an Egyptian state-owned enterprise, AQF Co., that has partially been privatized, this article interpreted the ceremonial use of IFRSs in this Egyptian company. The company faced conflicting institutional demands from outside the company (see Fig. 2). The Central Agency for Accountability required the company to use the Uniform Accounting System (as a state-owned enterprise) and The Egyptian CMA required the company to use IFRSs (as a partially private sector company registered in the stock exchange). To meet these conflicting institutional demands, the company adopted loosely coupled accounting rules and routines and IT was used in institutionalizing existing Uniform Accounting System and preserving the status quo. The company ceremonially used IFRSs, but it actually used the Uniform Accounting System to manage business transactions. It resisted the requirements of the Egyptian CMA by disguising its compliance with IFRSs. The Uniform Accounting System as institutionalized accounting routines acted as a barrier against change toward IFRSs implementation and internalization.

The macro and microinstitutional analyses were valuable in understanding the ceremonial use of IFRSs in the case organization. NIS theory at the macrolevel was used to explain coercive pressures exerted on the case organization before and after privatization. This extra-organizational analysis focuses on the role of institutions (such as laws and control agencies) in shaping and constraining the actions of actors (the case organizations). Change in laws (the requirements of new privatization laws and the Egyptian Stock Exchange) was not able to overcome institutionalized accounting practices, the Uniform Accounting System that is closely monitored by the Central Agency for Accountability. Institutions supporting the Uniform Accounting System have not disappeared. They are still in operation. This creates different conflicting institutional demands that the company should meet to continue gaining the support of the government, the public, and shareholders.

However, the macroinstitutional analysis was not enough to understand how organizational actors respond to extra-organizational institutional pressures. This macroanalysis should be complemented by microlevel analysis. Therefore, Burns and Scapens' (2000) framework as well as Orlikowski's (1992) model were used to understand the response of organizational actors to the change in extra-organizational institutional pressures due to the introduction of privatization program and related laws and regulations. In AQF Co., the decision to adopt IFRSs was mainly a response of the company to the requirements of the Egyptian Stock Exchange. Organizational members of AQF Co., especially accountants, resisted these requirements through mobilizing another power. Accountants draw on the power embedded in institutionalized accounting practices (the Uniform Accounting Systems).

The custom developed accounting software introduced by AQF Co. to support the adoption of IFRSs was customized to meet the requirements of the Uniform Accounting System used by the company since its establishment in 1976 but the company claims that it does apply the IFRSs required by the Egyptian Stock Exchange. This means that the company used the requirements of one institution (the Central Agency for Accountability) to resist the requirements of the other (the Egyptian Stock Exchange). In the end, loosely coupled accounting systems (rules) and practices (routines) were the outcome of these processes of resistance to accounting change. The loosely coupled rules and routines are not simply a specific organizational response to extra-organizational institutional pressures but, as described by Siti-Nabiha and Scapens (2005, p. 46), they "can arise through the working out of resistance to accounting change by the different groups within the organisation." This process view of loosely coupled rules and routines increases our understanding on how accounting change and stability can occur simultaneously (Lukka, 2007). With this integration between macro and microanalyses, it became possible to introduce a more complete and comprehensive explanation to the low or noncompliance with IFRSs in Egypt.

The article makes a contribution to the accounting literature on developing and transitional economies by specifically confronting the question of whether uniform systems of accounting technology, such as IFRSs, can be successfully introduced in countries with very different cultures and economic and political structures. Particularly, the findings of the case study presented in this article contribute to the literature addressing IFRSs in developing and transitional countries (e.g., Mensah, 1981; Ndubizu, 1984; Hove, 1989; Wallace, 1993; Larson & Kenny, 1995; Longden et al., 2001; Abd-Elsalam & Weetman, 2003; Mir & Rahaman, 2005; Dahawy & Conover, 2007). The ceremonial use of IFRSs in this article was an outcome that resulted from the processes of resistance to accounting change within the organization. In this regard, the existing institutional context acted as a barrier against change (Burns, 2000; Burns & Scapens, 2000). This article extends this literature by studying the introduction of IFRSs in a state-owned enterprise in Egypt (a developing country), focusing on the impact of conflicting institutional demands, identifying the role of IT in institutionalizing accounting routines, and describing intra-organizational power relations that contribute to the symbolic use of IFRSs.

Finally, there are several implications for future accounting research. The institutional framework can be applied to other problems in accounting, for example the introduction of new budgetary control systems. This framework is based on analyzing the interplay between institutional pressures, institutionalized accounting practices, conflicting institutions, intra-organizational power relations, and the role of IT in institutionalizing accounting routines. The use of such extended institutional analysis contributes to recent calls to broaden NIS (Oliver, 1992; Modell, 2002; Dillard, Rigsby, & Goodman, 2004; Tsamenyi et al., 2006; Dambrin et al., 2007; Lukka, 2007; Lounsbury, 2008). The proposed framework is valuable in explaining the origins of the ceremonial use of IFRSs and other accounting rules and routines.

Additional case studies of IFRSs adoption in other developing and transitional economies, perhaps with very different cultures and political structures, would test the reliability of the conclusions of this study. Imported information (and accounting) systems face a lot of difficulties in developing countries (e.g., Mensah, 1981; Ndubizu, 1984; Hove, 1989; Wallace, 1993; Larson & Kenny, 1995; Longden et al., 2001). It is assumed that organizations in different countries introducing IFRSs face similar difficulties and challenges identified in this article. However, new case studies should explore similar or other difficulties and challenges that companies working in developing countries face when trying to implement imported accounting technologies such as IFRSs.

NOTES

1. The Central Agency for Accountability is a control authority that reports to the Egyptian People's Assembly on the performance of all state-owned enterprises and government ministries and agencies.

2. The inclusion of deinstitutionalization into the analysis overcomes a major limitation of new institutional sociology theory.

3. Interviews were not tape-recorded because the interviewees preferred to talk in a more confidential way. However, extensive notes were taken during the interviews. Some interviewees were met more than once.

4. For more details about the Uniform Accounting System, see, for example, Briston and El-Ashker (1984).

5. AQF is a wealthy company. It controls the majority of Egyptian local market of fertilizers. Furthermore, it recently participated in establishing a new fertilizer company.

6. In fact, there were many conflicting areas between the Uniform Accounting System and IFRSs (Kholeif, 1997).

REFERENCES

Abayo, A., Adams, C., & Roberts, C. (1993). Measuring the quality of corporate disclosure in less developed countries: The case of Tanzania. *Journal of International Accounting, Auditing and Taxation, 2*, 145–158.

Abd-Elsalam, O. H., & Weetman, P. (2003). Introducing international accounting standards to an emerging capital market: Relative familiarity and language effect in Egypt. *Journal of International Accounting, Auditing & Taxation, 12*, 63–84.

Barley, S. R., & Tolbert, P. S. (1997). Institutionalization and structuration: Studying the links between action and institution. *Organization Studies, 18*(1), 93–117.

Briston, R. J., & El-Ashker, A. A. (1984). The Egyptian accounting system: A case study in western influence. *International Journal of Accounting, Education and Research, 19*(Fall), 129–155.

Burns, J. (2000). The dynamics of accounting change: Interplay between new practices, routines, institutions, power and politics. *Accounting, Auditing & Accountability Journal, 13*(5), 566–596.

Burns, J., & Scapens, R. W. (2000). Conceptualising management accounting change: An institutional framework. *Management Accounting Research, 11*, 3–25.

Cairns, D. (2000). The FT international accounting standards survey 1999. *Financial Times* (Management Report).

Carruthers, B. G. (1995). Accounting, ambiguity, and the new institutionalism. *Accounting, Organisations and Society, 20*, 313–328.

Chand, P., & White, M. (2007). A critique of the influence of globalization and convergence of accounting standards in FIJI. *Critical Perspectives on Accounting, 18*, 605–622.

Collier, P. (2001). The power of accounting: A field study of local financial management in a police force. *Management Accounting Research, 12*, 465–486.

Covaleski, M. A., Dirsmith, M. W., & Samuel, S. (1996). Managerial accounting research: The contributions of organizational and sociological theories. *Journal of Management Accounting Research, 8,* 1–29.

Dacin, M. T., Goodstein, J., & Scott, W. R. (2002). Institutional theory and institutional change: Introduction to the special research forum. *The Academy of Management Journal, 45*(1), 45–57.

D'Aunno, T., Sutton, R. I., & Price, R. H. (1991). Isomorphism and external support in conflicting institutional environments: A study of drug abuse treatment units. *The Academy of Management Journal, 34*(3), 636–661.

Dahawy, K., & Conover, T. (2007). Accounting disclosure in companies listed on the Egyptian stock exchange. *Middle Eastern Finance and Economics, 1,* 5–20.

Dambrin, C., Lambert, C., & Sponem, S. (2007). Control and change – Analysing the process of institutionalization. *Management Accounting Research, 18,* 172–208.

Dillard, J. F., Rigsby, J. T., & Goodman, C. (2004). The making and remaking of organizational context: Duality and the institutionalization process. *Accounting, Auditing & Accountability Journal, 17*(4), 506–542.

DiMaggio, P., & Powell, W. (1983). The iron cage revisited: Institutional isomorphism and collective rationality in organizational fields. *American Sociological Review, 48,* 147–160.

Giddens, A. (1984). *The constitution of society.* Cambridge: Polity Press.

Graham, C., & Neu, D. (2003). Accounting for globalisation. *Accounting Forum, 27*(4), 449–471.

Granlund, M., & Lukka, K. (1998). It's a small world of management accounting practices. *Journal of Management Accounting Research, 10,* 153–179.

Greenwood, R., & Hinings, C. R. (1996). Understanding radical organisational change: Bringing together the old and new institutionalism. *The Academy of Management Review, 21,* 1022–1054.

Hedberg, B., & Jonsson, S. (1978). Designing semi-confusing information systems for organisations in changing environments. *Accounting, Organisations and Society, 3*(1), 47–64.

Hossain, M., Tan, L., & Adams, M. (1994). Voluntary disclosure in an emerging capital market: Some empirical evidence from companies listed on the Kuala Lumpur stock exchange. *The International Journal of Accounting, 29*(4), 334–351.

Hove, M. R. (1989). The inappropriate uses of international accounting standards in less developed countries: The case of international accounting standards number 24 – Related party disclosures concerning transfer prices. *International Journal of Accounting, 24,* 165–179.

Hyvonen, T., Jarvinen, J., Pellinen, J., & Rahko, T. (2009). Institutional logics, ICT and stability of management accounting. *European Accounting Review, 18*(2), 241–275.

Kayed, M. (1990). *Accounting regulation in Egypt in relation to western influence.* Unpublished Ph.D. thesis, University of Hull, England.

Khattab, M. (2007). Constraints of privatisation in the Egyptian experience. Available at http://www.worldbank.org/mdf/mdf2/papers/partnerships/khattab.pdf. Accessed on December 1, 2007.

Kholeif, A., Abdel-Kader, M., & Sherer, M. (2007). ERP customization failure: Institutionalized accounting practices, power relations and market forces. *Journal of Accounting and Organizational Change, 3*(3), 250–269.

Kholeif, A. O. R. (1997). *Studying and evaluating international accounting standards and their applicability to practice in Egypt.* Unpublished M.Sc. thesis, Alexandria University, Faculty of Commerce, Egypt (in Arabic).

Larson, R. K., & Kenny, S. Y. (1995). An empirical analysis of international accounting standards, equity markets and economic growth in developing countries. *Journal of International Financial Management and Accounting, 6*(2), 130–157.

Latour, B. (1992). Where are the missing masses? The sociology of a few mundane artifacts. In: W. E. Bijker & J. Law (Eds), *Shaping technology building society* (pp. 225–258). Cambridge, MA: MIT Press.

Lehman, G. (2005). A critical perspective on the harmonization of accounting in a globalising world. *Critical Perspective on Accounting, 16*, 975–992.

Longden, S., Luther, R., & Bowler, D. (2001). *Management accounting in a society undergoing structural change: A southern African study*. London: CMIA.

Lounsbury, M. (2006). Accounting for institutions: New directions. *Conference Presentation, IPA 2006*, Cardiff, July 2006.

Lounsbury, M. (2008). Institutional rationality and practice variation: New directions in the institutional analysis of practice. *Accounting, Organizations and Society, 33*(4–5), 349–361.

Lukka, K. (2007). Management accounting change and stability: Loosely coupled rules and routines in action. *Management Accounting Research, 18*, 76–101.

Macintosh, N. B., & Scapens, R. W. (1990). Structuration theory in management accounting. *Accounting, Organisations and Society, 15*(5), 455–477.

Mensah, Y. W. (1981). Financial reporting model for dependent market economies. *Abacus, 17*, 161–170.

Meyer, J. W., & Rowan, B. (1977). Institutionalized organization: Formal structure as myth and ceremony. *American Journal of Sociology, 83*(2), 340–363.

Mir, M. Z., & Rahaman, A. S. (2005). The adoption of international accounting standards in Bangladesh. *Accounting, Auditing & Accountability Journal, 18*(6), 816–841.

Modell, S. (2002). Institutional perspectives on cost allocations: Integration and extension. *The European Accounting Review, 11*(4), 653–679.

Murphy, A. (1999). Firm characteristics of Swiss companies that uitlize international accounting standards. *The International Journal of Accounting, 34*(1), 121–131.

Ndubizu, G. A. (1984). Accounting standards and economic development: The third world in perspective. *International Journal of Accounting, 19*, 181–196.

Nolke, A. (2005). Introduction to the special issue: The globalization of accounting standards. *Business and Politics, 7*(3), 1–7.

Oliver, C. (1991). Strategic responses to institutional processes. *The Academy of Management Review, 16*(1), 145–179.

Oliver, C. (1992). The antecedents of de-institutionalisation. *Organisation Studies, 13*, 563–588.

Orlikowski, W. J. (1992). The duality of technology: Rethinking the concept of technology in organizations. *Organization Science, 3*(3), 398–429.

PCSU (Privatisation Coordination Support Unit) (2002). The Result and Impact of Egypt's Privatisation Program. *Privatisation in Egypt-Quarterly Review*, April–June, CARANA Corporation: Privatisation Coordination Support Unit. Available at http://www.carana.com/pcsu/monitor/Q2/Impacts%20and%20Results.pdf. Accessed on December 1, 2007.

Points, R., & Cunningham, R. (1998). The application of international accounting standards in transitional societies and developing countries. *Advances in International Accounting, 1*(Suppl.), 3–16.

Richardson, A. (2009). Regulatory networks for accounting and auditing standards: A social network analysis of Canadian and international standard-setting. *Accounting, Organizations and Society, 34*, 571–588.

Scapens, R. W. (1990). Researching management accounting practice: The role of case study methods. *British Accounting Review, 22*, 259–281.

Scott, W. R. (2001). *Institutions and organisations* (2nd ed.). London: Sage Publication.

Siti-Nabiha, A. K., & Scapens, R. W. (2005). Stability and change: An instituionalist study of management accounting change. *Accounting, Auditing & Accountability Journal, 18*, 44–73.

Soh, C., & Sia, S. K. (2004). An institutional perspective on sources of ERP package-organization misalignments. *Journal of Strategic Information Systems, 13*, 375–397.

Solas, C. (1994). Financial reporting practice in Jordan: An empirical test. *Advances in International Accounting, 7*, 43–60.

Street, D., & Gray, S. (2001). *Observance of international accounting standards: Factors explaining non-compliance*. ACCA Research Report no. 74. Association of Chartered Certified Accountants, London.

Street, D., Gray, S., & Bryant, S. (1999). Acceptance and observance of international accounting standards: An empirical study of companies claiming to comply with IASs. *The International Journal of Accounting, 34*(1), 11–48.

Street, D., Nichols, N., & Gray, S. (2000). Assessing the acceptability of international accounting standards: An empirical study of the materiality of US GAAP Reconciliations by Non-US companies complying with IASC standards. *The International Journal of Accounting, 35*(1), 27–63.

Tolbert, P. S., & Zucker, L. G. (1996). The institutionalization of institutional theory. In: S. R. Clegg, C. Hardy & W. R. Nord (Eds), *Handbook of organization studies* (pp. 174–190). London: Sage Publications.

Touron, P. (2005). The adoption of US GAAP by French firms before the creation of the international accounting standard committee: An institutional explanation. *Critical Perspective on Accounting, 16*, 851–873.

Tsamenyi, M., Cullen, J., & Gonzalez, J. (2006). Changes in accounting and financial information in a Spanish electricity company: A new institutional theory analysis. *Management Accounting Research, 17*(3), 409–432.

Unerman, J. (2003). Enhancing organizational global hegemony with narrative accounting disclosures: An early example. *Accounting Forum, 27*(4), 425–448.

Wallace, R., & Briston, R. (1993). Improving the accounting infrastructure in developing countries. *Research in Third World Accounting, 2*, 201–224.

Wallace, R. S. O. (1993). Development of accounting standards for developing and newly industrialized countries. *Research in Third World Accounting, 2*, 121–165.

Weick, K. E. (1976). Educational organizations as loosely coupled systems. *Administrative Science Quarterly, 21*, 1–19.

Yin, R. K. (1994). *Case study research, design and methods*. Beverly Hills, CA: Sage Publications.

THE RELATIONSHIP BETWEEN AUDITOR SIZE AND AUDIT FEES: FURTHER EVIDENCE FROM BIG FOUR MARKET SHARES IN EMERGING ECONOMIES

Stephan A. Fafatas and Kevin Jialin Sun

ABSTRACT

Purpose – *This study examines the relationship between Big Four audit firm country-level market shares and audit fees across a sample of nine emerging economies: Argentina, Brazil, Chile, Hong Kong, Israel, Korea, Mexico, South Africa, and Taiwan.*

Design/methodology/approach – *First, auditor market share is calculated as a percentage of client sales based on all publicly traded companies in each of the sample countries during the period 2002–2005. Next, Audit Analytics is used to obtain audit fee data for a set of foreign companies listed on a primary U.S. exchange. A final sample of 483 client-year observations is included in the audit fee regression analysis.*

Findings – *After controlling for other factors related to audit pricing, Big Four auditors with dominant country-level market shares earn a fee premium of approximately 27% over competitor firms.*

Research in Accounting in Emerging Economies, Volume 10, 57–85
Copyright © 2010 by Emerald Group Publishing Limited
All rights of reproduction in any form reserved
ISSN: 1479-3563/doi:10.1108/S1479-3563(2010)0000010008

Originality/value – *These results suggest that individual Big Four firm reputations, as measured by fee premiums, are not homogeneous across countries. Rather, it appears the largest audit firms are associated with quality-differentiated services and thus earn higher fees. Although accounting research tends to classify large international accounting firms into a pool of the "Big Four," these findings indicate that it is important to consider each firm's market share in specific geographic locations when examining questions related to auditor reputation and pricing.*

INTRODUCTION

How much variation is there among individual Big Four audit firm market shares across countries? Do these differences in relative market size reflect differences in firm reputation, as measured by audit fees? We explore these questions by evaluating the relationship between market share and audit fees for current Big Four firms Deloitte and Touche (DT), Ernst and Young (EY), KPMG, and PricewaterhouseCoopers (PWC) in a sample of nine emerging economies: Argentina, Brazil, Chile, Hong Kong, Israel, Korea, Mexico, South Africa, and Taiwan.[1] Following prior research, we use audit fees to measure auditor reputation under the theory that companies are willing to purchase more costly audit services presumably to receive a higher quality audit (e.g., Basioudis & Francis, 2007).

What are the key findings? First, we document significant variation among Big Four market shares across our sample countries during the years 2002–2005. For example, using revenues of publicly traded clients to measure market share, during 2002 PWC was by far the dominant firm in Brazil with a 65% market share, compared to a market share of 21% for the second largest firm, DT. In contrast, during that same year the difference between the first and the second largest firms in the United States was much smaller with PWC again leading the way at a 32% market share, but EY was a relatively close second at 26%.

Second, we find that auditors with dominant country-level market shares, defined as a country leader with at least a 10% advantage over the second largest firm, earn a fee premium over rival Big Four firms. The premium is both statistically and economically significant and reflects a fee increase of roughly 27%, ceteris paribus. This difference in fees suggests that auditors build country-specific reputations for quality-differentiated audit services, and the reputations of individual Big Four members are not homogenous across firms. Rather, auditor reputation, as captured by audit fees, varies based on the firm's relative size in each geographic market.

The results of this study extend prior research on the relationship between auditor size and audit fees. Although numerous studies find that, in general, a fee premium exists for services provided by the Big Four and, among these firms, by auditors that differentiate themselves as industry leaders, only recently have authors extended this research to include measures of geographic location as a determinant of audit fees. For example, recent studies document a significant relationship between measures of city-specific industry leadership and audit fee premiums (Ferguson, Francis, & Stokes, 2003; Francis, Reichelt, & Wang, 2005; Basioudis & Francis, 2007). In addition, in the United States, there is evidence that larger audit offices of Big Four firms provide higher quality audits as compared to smaller "local" offices and these quality differences are reflected in pricing differences across firm locations (Choi, Kim, Kim, & Zang, 2010). Our study adds to this body of research evaluating auditor size and quality in a geographic context by looking at the impact of Big Four *country-level* market shares on audit pricing.

Our research focuses on emerging economies, or *emerging markets*, as these countries represent a most interesting environment to analyze questions related to auditor reputation. The recent economic growth in these regions increases demand for high-quality auditors as companies require capital to fund developments and more reputable audit firms act as monitors for outside investors (Klapper & Love, 2004). As examples of audit firm growth in emerging markets, consider the recent performance of DT and KPMG. DT reported a 2008 revenue increase of 30.3% in the firm's Asia-Pacific region, which represented its fastest-growing geographic section (Deloitte Annual Review, 2008). Likewise, KPMG's revenue growth in 2008 was also led by the Asia-Pacific region with those member firms showing a 21.6% increase, compared to a 14.5% change in the firm's overall revenue and only an 8.8% change in the American region, which includes the United States (KPMG International Annual Review, 2008). KPMG in Brazil reported a 39.5% growth in revenues, leading all of the firm's locations in North and South America. Indeed, not only are the Big Four experiencing significant growth in emerging markets, but as shown in the KPMG case, growth among the member firms in these countries has outpaced average growth at the Big Four's global level. Given the recent increase in Big Four operations within emerging economies, this article provides a timely analysis of the current market for audit services in these countries.

The remainder of this article is organized as follows. The next section discusses previous literature and develops the hypothesis. A discussion of the specific research design is then presented, followed by a presentation of the results. The last section concludes with a summary of the findings and areas for future research.

BACKGROUND AND HYPOTHESIS DEVELOPMENT

Auditor Size and Audit Quality

Beginning with DeAngelo (1981), the relationship between audit firm size and audit quality represents a key subject of accounting academic research. DeAngelo (1981) defines audit quality as the joint probability that a given auditor will both discover a breach in the client's accounting system and report the breach. DeAngelo (1981) argues that this definition leads to a predicted relationship between audit firm size and audit quality. This argument is based on the theory that the value of an auditor's services will decline once it is revealed that an auditor failed either to discover or report a client's accounting breach. Since incumbent auditors earn client-specific rents, auditors with a greater number of clients stand to lose more in the event of an audit failure. Therefore, larger audit firms have stronger reputation incentives to provide high-quality audits. Further, the likelihood of reporting a client's accounting breach is closely linked to auditor independence. Large audit firms, with a smaller percentage of total wealth tied to any specific engagement, are more likely to resist the client's pressure to not report accounting breaches.

Following DeAngelo (1981), Watts and Zimmerman (1986) similarly posit that auditor size proxies for audit quality. They contend that an advantage of large audit firms stems from their enhanced monitoring abilities. Large firms are comprised of many partners, each with wealth and reputation incentives to guard against poor performance by other partners within the firm. This increased monitoring reduces the likelihood of a single partner succumbing to client pressures to not report an accounting breach. Thus, at both the firm- and partner-levels, reputation capital serves as a bonding mechanism that promotes higher audit quality at larger firms.[2]

Consistent with the theories of DeAngelo (1981) and Watt and Zimmerman (1986), empirical research shows that, when compared to smaller firms, Big Four auditors deliver higher quality audits. For example, Big Four firms are less likely to be sued as a result of audit failures (Palmrose, 1988), are more accurate with their going-concern modified reports (Geiger & Rama,

2006), and have clients who report lower discretionary accounting accruals, a measure of earnings management (Becker, DeFond, Jiambalvo, & Subramanyam, 1998). The benefits of audits provided by the Big Four include reduced information asymmetry and agency costs. Clients audited by Big Four firms report an increased stock market response to earnings announcements (Ettredge, Shane, & Smith, 1988; Teoh & Wong, 1993) and are associated with lower IPO share underpricing (Beatty, 1989).

Market Share and Fee Premiums

Given the quality reputations developed by the Big Four, a natural question to ask is whether these reputations lead to an audit fee premium for the largest accounting firms. To address this issue, we must first consider prior research in the marketing and industrial organization fields related to market share and pricing. Increased market share will impact firm pricing through its effects on quality perceptions of potential buyers. In an analytical study, Smallwood and Conslik (1979) illustrate how market share provides a signal to outsiders about brand quality. The authors claim that a new buyer may gain information about a product or service by looking at a display of brands in a store, through conversations with other people, or by looking at a list of dealers in the yellow pages (or online). In all cases, *a brand's increased market share is an indicator of high quality* as satisfied customers are likely to continue to buy from the same brand and dissatisfied customers will change brands.

In addition to signaling effects, market share may also increase perceived quality through positive externalities within a group of products or services (Katz & Shapiro, 1985). Positive externalities exist when the "utility of a product or service increases in the number of other individuals using that same product" (Hellofs & Jacobson, 1999, p. 16). Examples of positive externalities include firm accessibility through additional offices and the knowledge a company builds with specific products or service lines as sales increase. Hellofs and Jacobson (1999) present empirical support tying market share to perceived quality. Specifically, they investigate whether increases in the market share of firms offering differentiated products result in higher quality assessments by customers. Quality is measured from data obtained in customer surveys of 85 companies and product differentiation is defined using premium pricing amounts under the conjecture that customers are willing to pay a higher price for a product only if it is differentiated from its competition. Test results show a significant increase in perceived brand quality coinciding with growth in the market share of firms offering differentiated products.

Do quality products sell at a premium? This important question was examined by Shapiro (1983) who developed a theoretical schedule for the pricing of high-quality products. When sellers decide to offer high-quality products, they must first establish a reputation. Reputation requires investments (in production costs, advertising, etc.), and high-quality products should sell at a premium to cover these investments. Once their reputation is established, sellers have incentive to maintain their reputations for high-quality products in order to sustain their premium pricing. Accordingly, there is a theoretical link between high-quality products and premium pricing.

The links between market share and quality and between quality and pricing lead to the question of whether there is a positive relationship between market share and *profitability*. Indeed, this issue represents the focus of a considerable number of academic studies, and Szymanski, Bharadwaj, and Varadarajan (1993) include 276 market share–profitability findings from 48 empirical studies in their meta-analysis of the topic. Although some inconsistencies exist in the findings of these studies, the meta-analysis shows that increased market share is, on average, positively associated with higher firm profitability (measured as return on assets or return on equity). One challenge with the historical research cited in Szymanski et al. (1993) is that a majority of the papers implement an inter-industry approach which may introduce biases in comparing market share and profitability measures across firms. More recent research focused on the banking (Kurtz & Rhoades, 1992) and financial services (Chu, Chen, & Wang, 2008) sectors confirms a positive relationship between market share and profitability within these specific sets of service-related industries.

The discussion of key articles in marketing and industrial organization research takes us back to the earlier question of whether Big Four audits are associated with fee premium. Large auditors will earn a fee premium if they provide quality-differentiated products as compared to their smaller competitors. Simunic (1980, p. 170) claims that in the audit market "the principal differentiating characteristic of the service is likely to be the identity of the supplier," and it is the largest firms, "which enjoy visibility and brand name recognition among buyers."

While any licensed auditor is likely able to perform the statutory audit requirements, certain clients demand a higher level of expertise from their auditor and are willing to pay a premium for this expertise. Accordingly, the fact that some clients select to engage larger auditors and pay a premium for their services indicates that a quality-differentiated product is associated with that auditor (e.g., Francis & Stokes, 1986; Ferguson et al., 2003). It follows that differentiated audit quality is revealed by pricing differences and firms which have the highest quality reputations will earn fee premiums (Simunic, 1980).

Larger audit firms have greater resources to attract, train, and retain quality personnel. In addition to partner and staff assignments, larger auditors achieve high-quality audits by using updated technology, and implementing increased effort throughout the audit process. These firms use their resources to develop and maintain expertise for the latest accounting pronouncements and the rules and regulations within specific industries. Thus, as Francis (2004) states, "a higher audit fee implies higher audit quality, ceteris paribus, either through more audit effort (more hours) or through greater expertise of the auditor (higher billing rates)."

Several studies, beginning with Francis (1984) and Palmrose (1986), find evidence that Big Four firms command a fee premium for their brand name reputations, supporting the theory that these firms offer quality-differentiated products. On average, the premium ranges between 20% and 30% are documented in large economies such as the United States (e.g., Palmrose, 1986; Francis & Simon, 1987), the United Kingdom (e.g., Chan, Ezzamel, & Gwillman, 1993), and Australia (e.g., Francis, 1984; Francis & Stokes, 1986), as well as in developing nations like Bangladesh (Karim & Moizer, 1996) and Nigeria (Taylor & Simon, 2003).[3]

Results from more recent studies extend the measure of audit quality beyond the simple Big Four/non-Big Four paradigm. Most notably, researchers find that the largest auditors differentiate themselves from competitors through market share leadership in specific industries. Mayhew and Wilkins (2003) show that Big Four auditors with a dominant position (i.e., a 10% or greater lead in a specific industry's market share) earn a 29% fee premium on audits of firms going public (IPOs). Interestingly, the latest studies find that the premium for industry leadership is determined, in part, by city-based measures of auditor market share within an industry (Ferguson et al., 2003; Francis et al., 2005; Basioudis & Francis, 2007). These results show that broad measures of industry specialization may not generalize across time and firm offices (Ferguson & Stokes, 2002). Carson (2009, p. 356) extends the specialization literature by measuring industry market share at the global level since:

> (Large) audit firms have invested considerable resources in structuring their international operations as global networks of audit firms, with the intention of improving audit quality. Within such global networks, knowledge, staff, and resources, are shared on the basis of industry specialist groupings.

Importantly, Carson (2009) finds that both national and global industry specialization affect fee premiums earned by auditors. These results suggest that fee premiums of Big Four auditors are not homogeneous across network firms, but are affected by both national and global industry reputation measures. Collectively, the results from the most recent industry leadership research show that global, national, and city-specific measures of specialization affect audit fees. One important takeaway from this literature is that geographic-specific measures of auditor size are an important determinant of the market share/audit fee relationship.

Despite the recent academic interest in the role firm geography plays in audit quality, little is known about the effects of variation in individual Big Four market shares across countries. This is an important issue since Big Four auditors are structured as a network of "member" firms organized on an individual country basis where each member firm operates as a separate legal entity (Carson, 2009). Each member firm has a lead partner who oversees the partnership's operations within a specific country. The hybrid structure of these firms is beneficial given the existence of high litigation risk across countries. Although international firms strive to offer consistent audit quality throughout their international network, the recent high-profile audit failures at Enron, Adelphia, Tyco, and Parmalat show that this remains a challenging task. Investigating the relationship between auditor country-level market shares and audit pricing will help us gain a better understanding of firm characteristics that may cause variation in perceived audit quality across geographic markets.

Hypothesis

The link between Big Four firms' geographic market share and audit fee premiums is an empirical issue due to the organizational structure of international accounting firms. Each Big Four member firm is an independent entity and firm value is driven by reputation and their ability to attract clients in the local country's business environment. Firms that achieve a dominant presence have incentives to protect their reputations by offering higher quality audits.

To investigate the effect of Big Four audit firm size on audit pricing, we analyze auditor market shares in emerging economies. Emerging economies represent a unique setting to test theories related to auditor size and quality due to their volatile economic, geopolitical, and regulatory environments. Fan and Wong (2005) examine the role of auditors in East Asian countries and find evidence that external auditors play a governance role in these markets. The authors argue that the concentrated ownership (entrenchment) of corporations in Hong Kong, Indonesia, Malaysia, Philippines, Singapore, South Korea, Taiwan, and Thailand subject firms in these countries to greater agency costs. Results show that, in order to reduce these costs, firms with the greatest agency conflicts are more likely to hire Big Four auditors than firms with low agency conflicts. Further, firms that frequently raise equity capital in secondary markets are more likely to seek Big Four audits and the affiliation with Big Four firms (weakly) mitigates share price discounts created by agency conflicts.

As explained by the Fan and Wong (2005) study, an important role of the external auditor is to mitigate agency costs that arise from information asymmetries between client managers and outsiders. Auditors provide a level of assurance regarding the quality of financial reports and, accordingly, the auditor's value is greatest in settings where information asymmetries abound (Willenborg, 1999). It can be argued that the costs associated with information asymmetries, whether due to general macroeconomic risks, increased geopolitical uncertainty, more concentrated ownership structures (Fan & Wong, 2005), or the presence of more corrupt business practices and weaker judicial systems (La Porta, Lopez-de-Silanes, & Vishny, 1998), are greater in emerging economies as compared to more developed countries. Thus, the importance of external monitors is enhanced in emerging markets. For example, despite the size of the Brazilian economy (in 2008, it had the largest GDP in Latin America and the eighth largest in the world), the required governance practices of the country's public companies are relatively weak when compared to companies in more developed markets. According to Black, de Carvello, and Gorga (2010), Brazilian listings often have no independent directors, and audit committees are uncommon. Yet, while specific regulatory and disclosure laws for public companies are weaker in emerging markets, companies can partially compensate for this environment by establishing firm-level mechanisms to provide investor protection (Klapper & Love, 2004). Examples of these firm-level governance provisions include allowing outside analysts to have access to senior management, hiring a greater percentage of independent board members, and requiring the existence of an audit committee that monitors internal audit and accounting procedures.

As illustrated by the results of Fan and Wong (2005), another mechanism which companies in emerging markets may use to partially compensate for weak legal and regulatory policies is the use of a high-quality external auditor. Auditors with dominant market shares in these countries gain an understanding of the local business and regulatory environments. Their high market share signals quality-differentiated service to both clients and outside users of financial statements (Smallwood & Conslik, 1979). Auditors with these dominant country-level market shares have incentives to maintain their reputations for quality audits and enforce compliance with accounting standards and strengthen client disclosure policies (DeAngelo, 1981). We define a dominant auditor as a firm that has at least a 10% lead in the country's market share and posit that these auditors offer quality-differentiated audits in order to protect their reputations. The quality reputations developed by Big Four auditors with dominant country-level market shares should manifest in the form of higher audit fees charged to their clients. Accordingly, our hypothesis (stated in alternative form) is:

H$_a$. Big Four firms with dominant country-level market shares in emerging economies earn audit fee premiums, ceteris paribus.

Although we predict that higher market shares are associated with audit fee premiums, this is not an obvious relationship. Indeed, a scenario exists where no relation between the firm's relative size and audit pricing will emerge. While each individual member firm is independent at the country-level, Big Four auditors advertise an approach of consistent audit quality across engagements. For example, on PWC's website, the firm pushes a structure in which member firms work together to comprise a "vigorous global network."[4] This network of firms develops "a consistent application of common risk and quality standards by member firms." Firms that develop consistent knowledge sharing and control practices may not face reputation differences across geographic locations. Rather, these firms may experience reputation spillover effects and gains from positive network externalities such that overall audit quality is viewed at the global level as opposed to the national level. Accordingly, if the reputation of each member firm is homogenous across countries, we should not observe a fee premium due to dominant market positions. Thus, the issue of whether the relative size of Big Four auditors in emerging markets is associated with premium audit pricing is an empirical question.

RESEARCH DESIGN

Auditor Market Share

We begin with a sample of emerging markets identified through a search of prior research (e.g., Pasquariello, 2008) and listings in the financial press

(*The Economist*). We analyze only those countries that have sufficient audit fee data available to complete the related tests. After adjusting for audit fee data limitations our overall sample includes the following nine countries: Argentina, Brazil, Chile, Hong Kong, Israel, Korea, Mexico, South Africa, and Taiwan.

Following prior research (e.g., Krishnan, 2005), auditor market share is calculated using total client sales, obtained from Global Vantage.[5] Specifically, country market share (*CMS*) is equal to:

$$CMS_{ik} = \frac{\sum_{j=1}^{J_{ik}} SALES_{ijk}}{\sum_{i=1}^{I_K} \sum_{j=1}^{J_{ik}} SALES_{ijk}} \qquad (1)$$

where *SALES* is equal to client sales revenue, and the numerator is the sum of sales of all J_{ik} clients of audit firm i in country k. The denominator is the sales of J_{ik} clients in country k summed over all I_k audit firms operating in country k. We follow prior research (Mayhew & Wilkins, 2003) and use a 10% margin in market share to identify audit firm dominance in a given country. Specifically, we classify an auditor as a *LEADER* in a particular country if the firm is both the largest auditor in that country and has a market share that is at least 10% greater than that of the next largest firm.

Table 1A presents information on audit firm leadership across the nine emerging markets used in our sample. Instances of auditor leadership are distributed across the Big Four firms with PWC having the greatest number of dominant market shares. The breakdown of leadership classification across the country/year groupings in Table 1A is as follows (number of leadership positions in parenthesis): PWC (20), KPMG (13), EY (7), and DT (5). Note that the Global Vantage database does not specifically identify the auditor if the firm is not one of the Big Four. Rather, all firms outside of the Big Four are given a general "other" classification. Thus, it is not possible to calculate market shares of specific non-Big Four firms. While it is unlikely that a non-Big Four member would emerge as a market leader, as an additional sensitivity test we remove country-year observations where the largest auditor has less than a 25% market share (i.e., 1/4 of the total possible market share). These represent cases where it is more feasible that a non-Big Four firm may emerge as a leader. Removing these observations does not change the key results reported in later sections of the article.

Additional information on the market for audit services across the sample countries is presented in Table 1B. This table shows the percentage market

Table 1A. Audit Firm Leadership in Emerging Economies.

Country	2002	2003	2004	2005
Argentina ($\bar{n} = 22$)	–	DT (47%)	DT (42%)	–
Brazil (119)	PWC (65%)	PWC (42%)	–	EY (34%)
Chile (89)	–	PWC (44%)	PWC (41%)	PWC (47%)
Hong Kong (126)	–	PWC (42%)	PWC (46%)	PWC (28%)
Israel (30)	KPMG (27%)	–	–	KPMG (44%)
Korea (723)	PWC (34%)	PWC (28%)	PWC (29%)	–
Mexico (55)	–	–	–	EY (43%)
South Africa (73)	–	–	–	–
Taiwan (236)	–	KPMG (44%)	–	KPMG (45%)

Auditor market share is based on total client revenue and appears in parenthesis. Market share is calculated using the clients listed on Global Vantage (except for Korean market share, which is calculated using Worldscope due to missing data items). The *average* number of annual observations used in the calculation is listed in parenthesis next to each country (i.e., we obtained 89 total observations for Argentina across the four-year period which equates to an average of 22 observations per year to calculate the market share). A Big Four audit firm is denoted a "leader" if it is the largest auditor in a country and the firm has a 10% or greater market share advantage over the second largest firm. Country/year observations which do not indicate a leading auditor (–) reflect instances in which the largest audit firm has less than a 10% market share lead compared to the second largest firm.

share of the top two audit firms in each country between 2002 and 2005. For comparison purposes, we also list the U.S. data for the same time period. Note the striking consistency of the U.S. audit market – PWC leads each year with a little over 30% of the market and EY is a close second – as compared to the volatility of auditor size in many of the emerging markets. For example, PWC claims over 60% of the Brazil market in 2002, but just two years later is out of the top rankings. Much of these changes are likely associated with the rapid economic growth experienced in these countries during the sample period. In addition, a few of these countries may have implemented audit firm rotation policies to help ensure auditor independence. Indeed, this explains part of the dramatic drop in PWC's market share in Brazil where companies are required to hire new external audit firms every five years. PWC rotated off Petrobras, the third largest oil producer in the world, in 2004 and EY became the company's new auditor.[6] The volatility in the audit service markets as shown in Table 1B helps illustrate the importance of studying questions related to audit quality and pricing decisions in the emerging market segment of the global economy.

Table 1B. Leading Auditors in Emerging Economies.

	2002	2003	2004	2005
Argentina				
First	DT (43%)	DT (47%)[a]	DT (42%)[a]	DT (37%)
Second	EY (37%)	EY (27%)	EY (24%)	EY(36%)
			PWC (24%)	
Brazil				
First	PWC (65%)[a]	PWC (42%)[a]	EY (28%)	EY (34%)[a]
Second	DT (21%)	EY (26%)	DT (26%)	DT (23%)
Chile				
First	PWC (36%)	PWC (44%)[a]	PWC (41%)[a]	PWC (47%)[a]
Second	DT (31%)	DT (28%)	EY (30%)	EY (30%)
Hong Kong				
First	PWC (40%)	PWC (42%)[a]	PWC (46%)[a]	PWC (28%)[a]
Second	KPMG (32%)	KPMG (30%)	KPMG (28%)	EY (7%)
Israel				
First	KPMG (27%)[a]	KPMG (19%)	PWC (26%)	KPMG (44%)[a]
Second	EY (16%)	EY (16%)	KPMG (20%)	PWC (34%)
Korea				
First	PWC (34%)[a]	PWC (28%)[a]	PWC (29%)[a]	PWC (27%)
Second	DT (19%)	DT (18%)	KPMG (18%)	KPMG (19%)
Mexico				
First	EY (36%)	EY (37%)	EY (33%)	EY (43%)[a]
Second	PWC (29%)	PWC (31%)	PWC (29%)	PWC (26%)
South Africa				
First	DT (29%)	DT (25%)	DT (24%)	PWC (10%)
Second	KPMG (21%)	KPMG (24%)	KPMG (22%)	KPMG (4%)
Taiwan				
First	KPMG (21%)	KPMG (44%)[a]	KPMG (28%)	KPMG (45%)[a]
Second	PWC (16%)	DT (21%)	DT (20%)	DT (22%)
United States				
First	PWC (32%)	PWC (32%)	PWC (31%)	PWC (31%)
Second	EY (26%)	EY (28%)	EY (27%)	EY (28%)

[a]Denotes audit leadership if the auditor is the largest firm in a country and has a 10% or greater market share advantage over the second largest firm. As noted in Table 1A, market share appears in parenthesis and is based on total client revenues obtained from the Global Vantage or, as in the case of Korea, Worldscope databases. Information on the U.S. audit market is provided for comparison purposes.

Hypothesis Test

To test our hypothesis, we model audit fee determinants identified in prior research (e.g., Francis et al., 2005) and examine the relative difference in fees charged to clients of auditors classified as a country *LEADER*. We estimate the following pooled OLS regression for each observation included in our sample:

$$
\begin{aligned}
LNFEE_j = {} & \beta_1 + \beta_2 LNTA_j + \beta_3 NSEG_j + \beta_4 OPINION_j \\
& + \beta_5 CATA_j + \beta_6 LOSS_j + \beta_7 DEBT_j \\
& + \beta_8 CURRENT_j + \beta_9 NEW_j + \beta_{10} UTILITY_j \\
& + \beta_{11} BUSSERV_j + \beta_{12} MACHINERY_j \\
& + \beta_{13} LEADER_j + fixed\ effects + \varepsilon_j
\end{aligned}
\tag{2}
$$

where

LNFEE	= natural log of audit fees,
LNTA	= natural log of total assets,
NSEG	= the number of unique business segments,
OPINION	= 1 if client receives a modified audit report, 0 otherwise,
CATA	= the ratio of current assets to total assets,
LOSS	= 1 if client reports a loss in the current year, 0 otherwise,
DEBT	= total liabilities to assets,
CURRENT	= the ratio of current assets to current liabilities,
NEW	= 1 if company is a new client to the auditor, 0 otherwise,
UTILITY	= 1 if client is in an industry with SIC 4900–4999, 0 otherwise,
BUSSERV	= 1 if client is in an industry with SIC 7300–7399, 0 otherwise,
MACHINERY	= 1 if client is in an industry with SIC 3500–3599, 0 otherwise,
LEADER	= 1 if auditor has at least 10% more market share than the second largest auditor in a given country, and
fixed effects	= indicator variables for year (2003–2005) and country.

Model (2) includes variables to control for client size, audit complexity, and audit risk. For example, the variables *LNTA* and *NSEG* capture the effects of client size and audit complexity and their corresponding coefficients are expected to be positive. Higher fees are also expected for clients receiving a modified audit opinion (*OPINION*) as there is likely increased effort associated with these engagements. The variables *CATA,* *LOSS, DEBT,* and *CURRENT* are included to control for audit risk. We expect a negative relationship between the *CURRENT* variable and audit fees as a higher current ratio indicates the firm is more likely to meet short-term obligations and poses lower engagement risk. The remaining risk variables – *CATA, LOSS,* and *DEBT* – are all expected to be positively related to audit fees. A variable is also included to control for the impact of potential low-balling audit fees to attract new clients (*NEW*). An indicator variable for utilities (*UTILITY*) is included as these industries are often associated with increased government regulation which may reduce the role of the external auditor. As with prior studies (e.g., Carcello, Hermanson, Neal, & Riley, 2002), we expect a negative coefficient on the utility indicator variable. Additional indicator variables are included to control for two of the largest industries in the sample: business services (*BUSSERV*) and machinery (*MACHINERY*). Together, these industries provide 14% of the total observations. Finally, fixed-effect controls are included to capture year, and country-specific economic, legal, and regulatory characteristics.[7]

After controlling for these factors associated with audit fees, H_a predicts a positive coefficient on our variable of interest, *LEADER*. A positive coefficient on *LEADER* indicates that, ceteris paribus, Big Four auditors with a dominant market share in a given country earn a premium for their audit services beyond fees generated by other Big Four competitors. This result would suggest that quality reputation differences exist among the Big Four firms in emerging markets and these differences are priced in audit fees.

Sample Selection and Data

While we use the total sample of companies listed on the Global Vantage database, including both foreign- and domestic-listed firms, to calculate the auditor market shares reported in Tables 1A and B, we limit our sample in the specific audit fee analysis to firms that are (1) headquartered in an emerging market, (2) listed on a primary U.S. exchange (AMEX, NASDAQ, or NYSE), and (3) audited by a Big Four auditor in the same country as the company's headquarters. The condition that firms be listed on a U.S. exchange restricts the size of the audit fee sample; however, it is a valuable requirement for three primary reasons.

The first reason for focusing on firms listed on a U.S. exchange is that this approach offers a natural control for cross-country differences in variables associated with audit fee pricing. For example, firms in jurisdictions with weak investor protection laws can create a "bond" with investors by listing in the U.S. market and, thus, subject themselves to stronger U.S. liability standards and give investors the ability to apply relatively low-cost legal solutions such as class-action lawsuits (e.g., Coffee, 2002). A recent study by Choi, Kim, Liu, and Simunic (2009) shows that the strength of a country's legal regime influences Big Four audit fees as expected legal liability exposure is priced in audit engagements. By focusing on foreign firms that are listed in the United States, we add an additional control for the variation in auditor legal liability exposure across foreign jurisdictions.

Limiting the sample to firms listed on a U.S. exchange also controls for differences in accounting disclosure requirements in foreign markets. Fargher, Taylor, and Simon (2001) show audit fees are positively related to a country's accounting disclosure requirements as companies demand greater assurance from their auditors for higher levels of disclosure. The U.S. is typically associated with high disclosure requirements and companies which list on one of the primary U.S. exchanges must reconcile their financial statements with U.S. generally accepted accounting principles (GAAP).[8] Thus, each foreign firm that lists on the NYSE, NASDAQ, or AMEX must meet U.S. financial reporting standards and Securities and Exchange Commission (SEC) disclosure requirements.

The demand for audit quality provides the second primary reason for restricting our sample to those firms that list on a U.S. exchange. External auditors act as information intermediaries between outside investors and management. Accordingly, the demand for high-quality auditors is greatest in situations of increased information asymmetry (Willenborg, 1999). While one reason for listing on a foreign exchange is to access additional capital markets, U.S. shareholders will demand greater returns on their investments (i.e., increase a firm's cost of capital) when there is uncertainty about the accuracy of a company's past results or its ability to address local-country risk factors. The financial press, underwriters, and analysts all act as intermediaries which strengthen a firm's overall information environment. As such, foreign companies that list on a U.S. exchange have increased analyst coverage and forecast accuracy as compared to local-country firms which do not list abroad (Lang, Lins, & Miller, 2003). This increased coverage and accuracy is associated with higher firm valuations. Just as increased analyst coverage decreases information risk, the association with a high-quality external auditor helps outsiders understand the firm's operating environment. It is those companies in emerging markets which choose to list on a U.S. exchange that stand to receive the greatest benefit from the signaling effect of operating with a high-quality auditor that has experience in dealing with the local-country economic and business environment. Thus, focusing on this select group of firms provides a powerful setting to test theories related to auditor size and pricing as it presents a sample of companies which are most likely to demand high-quality audit firms.

Audit fee data availability marks the final advantage of focusing on U.S.-listed companies. The SEC requires filers to disclose audit fee information as part of their annual financial reporting process. Thus, a large sample of audit fee data is available for foreign firms which list on a U.S. exchange. In contrast, the availability of audit fee data for companies listed solely in an emerging market is sporadic. Disclosure of fee data is limited primarily to emerging markets that follow the British financial reporting system (e.g., Singapore, India, etc.). Further, the data that is available for these firms through large databases such as Global Vantage is often combined into a single amount, thus joining both audit and nonaudit fees into one value and clouding the implications of related test results.

On the down side, analyzing only those firms that are listed on a U.S. exchange means that it may be difficult to generalize our results to different environments. However, given that, to our knowledge, this is the first study to evaluate the relationship between Big Four market shares and fee premiums across emerging economies, our approach is to focus on a powerful setting in which to test the research hypothesis. We return to the issue of sample selection in the conclusion to the article and discuss implications for future research.

We obtain information on audit fees and auditor location for the nine emerging markets included in our sample from Audit Analytics. We begin with a sample of 924 observations which are listed on a U.S. exchange and audited by Big Four firms in the client's home country. From this initial sample, we remove 390 observations due to missing Compustat data for variables included in the audit fee model and an additional 51 observations from financial institutions, yielding a final sample of 483 observations during the period 2002–2005.[9] Descriptive statistics for this final sample are reported in Table 2. The country observations which make up the largest percentage of companies included in our sample are Israel (32%) and Brazil (18%). In contrast, South Africa and Korea all have fewer than 30 observations. The *LEADER* column reports the percentage of clients from each country in our audit fee sample that are audited by a corresponding leading auditor in Table 1B. Since our audit fee sample is comprised of foreign firms which are listed in the United States, this percentage does not equal the auditor's overall country-level market share, but rather that firm's percentage of clients in our

Table 2. Descriptive Statistics by Country.

Country	N	LEADER (Mean)	LNFEE (Mean)	LNTA (Mean)	NSEG (Mean)	OPINION (Mean)	CATA (Mean)	LOSS (Mean)	DEBT (Mean)	CURRENT (Mean)	NEW (Mean)
Argentina	31	0.129	13.040	7.810	3.419	0.581	0.197	0.290	0.662	0.921	0.032
Brazil	85	0.247	12.963	8.064	2.200	0.024	0.358	0.200	0.607	1.393	0.094
Chile	39	0.282	12.987	7.513	2.385	0.000	0.292	0.051	0.555	1.553	0.103
Hong Kong	45	0.333	12.052	5.021	2.733	0.000	0.529	0.467	0.327	3.260	0.111
Israel	155	0.097	11.855	4.697	1.387	0.000	0.613	0.432	0.431	3.074	0.013
Korea	26	0.231	13.477	8.621	2.692	0.000	0.364	0.115	0.464	1.645	0.038
Mexico	49	0.061	14.248	8.335	2.510	0.020	0.273	0.184	0.555	2.028	0.061
South Africa	22	0.000	14.390	8.234	1.773	0.000	0.231	0.273	0.549	1.270	0.000
Taiwan	31	0.097	13.067	7.752	2.548	0.000	0.369	0.290	0.373	2.138	0.000
Total	483	0.161	12.759	6.684	2.143	0.043	0.427	0.296	0.493	2.205	0.050

LEADER is the largest Big Four auditor in a country when the firm has a 10% or greater market share advantage over the second largest firm. *LNFEE* is the natural log of audit fees. *LNTA* is the natural log of total assets. *NSEG* is the number of business segments. *OPINION* equals 1 if the company received a going concern opinion, 0 otherwise. *CATA* is the ratio of current assets to total assets. *LOSS* equals 1 if earnings before extraordinary items are negative, 0 otherwise. *DEBT* is total liabilities divided by total assets. *CURRENT* is the ratio of current assets to current liabilities. *NEW* equals 1 if the client switched auditors that year, 0 otherwise.

final test sample. Average audit fees are highest in South Africa, Mexico, and Korea and lowest in Israel and Hong Kong. Not surprisingly, these countries have similar associations with average client size (*LNTA*).

Very few client observations received going-concern opinions during this time, with the exception of clients in Argentina. Almost 60% of the sample observations from Argentina (i.e., those clients listed in the United States) received going-concern opinions during 2002–2005, which is likely a by-product of the financial crisis faced by the country in 2001 and 2002. The relatively higher risk attributes of Argentine companies are also reflected in the *LOSS*, *DEBT*, and *CURRENT* variables, highlighting the importance of controlling for firm-specific characteristics in our audit fee model.

RESULTS

Primary Results

Table 3 presents the multivariate regression of model (2). Consistent with the results of prior literature, audit fees are higher for larger clients, clients with a greater number of unique business segments, and clients with relatively higher levels of current assets. In general, riskier clients pay higher audit fees as the coefficients on the *LOSS*, *DEBT*, and *CURRENT* variables are all significant. In addition, the results indicate that new clients are associated with relatively lower audit fees, which suggests that auditors may practice low-balling in these markets to attract new clients.

Turning to the variable of interest, the *LEADER* coefficient is positive and highly significant ($p < 0.01$), which indicates that Big Four firms with a dominant market share charge a fee premium for their audit services. This result supports our hypothesis and suggests that even within the Big Four, auditor reputation varies across countries based on the firm's relative size within a given market. To gain an economic interpretation of the results, we implement the procedure used in prior audit fee literature (e.g., Craswell, Francis, & Taylor, 1995; Francis et al., 2005) to evaluate the coefficient on *LEADER*. These prior studies show that the premium effect in an audit fee model equals the percentage change in the natural log of audit fees from the intercept change based on our variable of interest. This is calculated as $e^z - 1$, where z is the value of *LEADER* for auditors with a dominant market share. The *LEADER* coefficient equals 0.239 which, after controlling for other fee determinates, corresponds to an average premium of 27% across the four-year period earned by the top-ranked auditors in Table 1B.

Table 3. Audit Fees and Emerging Market Leadership.

$$LNFEE_j = \beta_1 + \beta_2 LNTA_j + \beta_3 NSEG_j + \beta_4 OPINION_j + \beta_5 CATA_j$$
$$+ \beta_6 LOSS_j + \beta_7 DEBT_j + \beta_8 CURRENT_j + \beta_9 NEW_j$$
$$+ \beta_{10} UTILITY_j + \beta_{11} BUSSERV_j + \beta_{12} MACHINERY_j$$
$$+ \beta_{13} LEADER_j + fixed\ effects + \varepsilon_j \tag{2}$$

Coefficient	Predicted Sign	Estimate	p-Value
Intercept	+	8.147	0.001
LNTA	+	0.511	0.001
NSEG	+	0.056	0.001
OPINION	+	−0.036	0.871
CATA	+	1.218	0.001
LOSS	+	0.178	0.005
DEBT	+	0.795	0.005
CURRENT	−	−0.070	0.001
NEW	−	−0.488	0.001
UTILITY	−	−0.542	0.001
BUSSERV	?	0.457	0.001
MACHINERY	?	−0.428	0.002
LEADER (H_a)	+	0.239	0.003
N		483	
Adj. R^2		0.767	

All p-values are based on one-tailed tests using White-adjusted t-statistics.
This table presents the results from estimating model (2) across nine emerging markets (see Table 1A) during 2002–2005. *UTILITY, BUSSERV,* and *MACHINERY* are 1/0 indicator variables measuring whether the company is in the utility (SIC 4900–4999), business services (SIC 7300–7399), or machinery (SIC 3500–3599) industries. Estimated coefficients for year and country fixed effects have been excluded for brevity. All other variables defined in Table 2.

Robustness Tests

As previous research indicates, audit fee premiums are impacted by investor protection regimes (e.g., Seetharaman, Gul, & Lynn, 2002; Choi, Kim, Liu, & Simunic, 2008). To help control for this issue, we limit our sample of observations to foreign firms that list in the Unites States and, in addition, include indicator variables for each country in model (2). Despite this requirement, it is possible that we are not fully controlling for the differences in legal liability across our sample of countries. To help alleviate this concern, we divide our sample of nine countries into two subsamples based on a general definition of legal origin. "Common Law" refers to countries with a legal regime based on the British common law system and includes Hong Kong, Israel, and South Africa. "Code Law" refers to those countries with a rule of law based on French or German civil law and includes Argentina, Brazil, Chile, Korea, Mexico, and Taiwan.

Prior research (e.g., La Porta et al., 1998) shows that common-law countries have stronger investor protection rights compared to countries with code-law origins. Further, the strength of a country's legal regime is a fee-increasing factor as auditors face greater risks in these countries (Seetharaman et al., 2002; Choi et al., 2008, 2009). To test whether the results in Table 3 are consistent across legal regimes, we reestimate model (2) for the two subsamples. The results, presented in Table 4, show that in both the common- and code-law samples the coefficient on *LEADER* remains positive and significant at the $p < 0.05$ level. Thus, after (1) including only those international firms which list on a U.S. exchange, (2) adding indicator variables for each country to the audit fee model, and (3) dividing the sample into two sections based on legal origin, it does not appear that investor protection differences are responsible for the finding that country-level market leadership is an important fee-increasing factor.

As a second robustness test, we investigate whether the results in Table 3 are driven by a particular time period. To accomplish this test, we reestimate model (2) annually for each of the years 2002–2005 and present the results in Table 5.[10] Despite the reduced sample size for each regression, the coefficient on *LEADER* is positive and significant at conventional levels ($p < 0.05$) in 2002 and 2005. In 2003 and 2004, *LEADER* remains positive, though only marginally significant ($p < 0.10$). Thus, even with the weaker power from using a smaller sample, the test results of separate annual regressions support the finding that audit market leadership at the geographic level is reflected in higher audit fees.

A number of additional tests were completed to assess the validity of the Table 3 results. First, to help ensure that results are not driven by naturally lower fees in the country/year observations which lack a leading audit firm, we drop all of the country/year observations in Table 1A that do not have an auditor classified as a *LEADER*. Second, we expand the *LEADER* variable to include the top *two* auditors when there is not a significant gap in market share between the first- and second-ranked firms, but there is a 10% difference between the second- and third-ranked firms (i.e., two auditors may be considered market "leaders" in a given country). Third, we augment

Table 4. Audit Fees and Market Leadership by Legal Environment.

$$LNFEEj = \beta_1 + \beta_2 LNTA_j + \beta_3 NSEG_j + \beta_4 OPINION_j$$
$$+ \beta_5 CATA_j + \beta_6 LOSS_j + \beta_7 DEBT_j + \beta_8 CURRENT_j$$
$$+ \beta_9 NEW_j + \beta_{10} UTILITY_j + \beta_{11} BUSSERV_j$$
$$+ \beta_{12} MACHINERY_j + \beta_{13} LEADER_j + fixed\ effects + \varepsilon_j \quad (2)$$

Coefficient	Predicted Sign	Common Law	Code Law
Intercept	+	8.086***	7.642***
LNTA	+	0.511***	0.527***
NSEG	+	0.108***	0.041**
OPINION	+	N/A	−0.129
CATA	+	1.546***	0.484*
LOSS	+	0.164**	0.144*
DEBT	+	0.589***	1.522***
CURRENT	−	−0.107***	−0.022***
NEW	−	−0.338*	−0.496*
UTILITY	−	N/A	−0.657***
BUSSERV	?	0.314***	1.462***
MACHINERY	?	−0.424**	−0.242**
LEADER (H$_a$)	+	0.308**	0.174**
N		222	261
Adj. R^2		0.767	0.706

This table presents the results from estimating model (2) across nine emerging markets (see Table 1A) during 2002–2005. "Common Law" refers to countries with a legal regime based on the British common law system and includes Hong Kong, Israel, and South Africa. "Code Law" countries include Argentina, Brazil, Chile, Korea, Mexico, and Taiwan. *UTILITY, BUSSERV,* and *MACHINERY* are 1/0 indicator variables measuring whether the company is in the utility (SIC 4900–4999), business services (SIC 7300–7399), or machinery (SIC 3500–3599) industries. See Table 2 for all other variable definitions. Estimated coefficients for year and country fixed effects have been excluded for brevity. N/A refers to instances where variables are excluded from a model due to missing data.
***, **, * Denote significance at the 0.01, 0.05, and 0.10 levels using one-tailed tests and White-adjusted *t*-statistics.

our leadership measure to represent total (rather than relative) size and identify an auditor as a *LEADER* if it has at least a 30% market share. In both of the expanded definitions of market leaders, the results in Table 3 are replicated as the coefficient on *LEADER* remains positive and significant at conventional levels. To assure our findings are not due to individual

Table 5. Audit Fees and Market Leadership by Year.

$$LNFEE_j = \beta_1 + \beta_2 LNTA_j + \beta_3 NSEG_j + \beta_4 OPINION_j$$
$$+ \beta_5 CATA_j + \beta_6 LOSS_j + \beta_7 DEBT_j + \beta_8 CURRENT_j$$
$$+ \beta_9 NEW_j + \beta_{10} UTILITY_j + \beta_{11} BUSSERV_j$$
$$+ \beta_{12} MACHINERY_j + \beta_{13} LEADER_j + fixed\ effects + \varepsilon_j \quad (2)$$

Coefficient	Predicted Sign	2002	2003	2004	2005
Intercept	+	7.752***	7.973***	8.750***	8.147***
LNTA	+	0.500***	0.533***	0.482***	0.511***
NSEG	+	0.058**	0.063**	0.067**	0.056*
OPINION	+	0.225	0.377*	−0.301	−0.036
CATA	+	1.098***	1.229***	1.016**	1.218***
LOSS	+	0.149	0.223**	−0.158	0.178**
DEBT	+	1.588***	1.133***	0.814**	0.795**
CURRENT	−	0.042	−0.023	−0.085**	−0.070***
NEW	−	N/A	−0.456**	−0.750***	−0.488**
UTILITY	−	−0.301	−0.338*	−0.628***	−0.542***
BUSSERV	?	0.197	0.186	0.457***	0.457***
MACHINERY	?	−0.805	−0.394*	−0.428	−0.428
LEADER (H$_a$)	+	0.339**	0.278*	0.287*	0.280**
N		90	129	129	135
Adj. R^2		0.800	0.786	0.773	0.747

This table presents the results from annual estimations of model (2) across individual years. *UTILITY, BUSSERV*, and *MACHINERY* are 1/0 indicator variables measuring whether the company is in the utility (SIC 4900–4999), business services (SIC 7300–7399), or machinery (SIC 3500–3599) industries. See Table 2 for all other variable definitions. Estimated coefficients for country fixed effects have been excluded for brevity. N/A refers to instances where variables are excluded from a model due to missing data.
***,**,* Denote significance at the 0.01, 0.05, and 0.10 levels using one-tailed tests and White-adjusted t-statistics.

auditors, we reestimate model (2) four times after dropping each of the audit firms one at a time. In all four cases, *LEADER* remains significantly positive ($p<0.05$), suggesting that no single firm is responsible for the overall findings that dominant firms earn a significant fee premium in emerging markets.

Finally, because a large percentage of the sample observations are from Brazil and Israel, we test whether our results are consistent across these two nations by running model (2) separately for each country. In each model, we are able to replicate the primary findings of the complete sample as presented in Table 3, with the coefficient on the *LEADER* variable positive and significant at the $p < 0.05$ level. These findings provide a preliminary indication that the results from this study are consistent across these two, relatively large, audit markets.[11]

CONCLUSION

We investigate the relationship between audit fees and auditor market share using a sample of companies from nine emerging markets (Argentina, Brazil, Chile, Hong Kong, Israel, Korea, Mexico, South Africa, and Taiwan) during 2002–2005. We consider only those international companies which are listed on a primary U.S. exchange, thus providing a more consistent measure of legal and disclosure environments and focusing on a group of companies most likely to demand high-quality auditors.

We find that during 2002–2005 the relative size among Big Four audit firms varies dramatically across our sample countries as compared to the U.S. audit market. Further, our results show that Big Four auditors with a dominant position in these countries earn a fee premium of approximately 27% compared to other Big Four firms. These results are consistent with an environment in which dominant individual Big Four audit firms build quality reputations and differentiate themselves from competitors. The value of this increased quality is priced in the form of higher audit fees charged to clients.

One implication of this study is that our results suggest there are economic incentives for Big Four network firms to build a dominant presence in emerging market countries. However, the economic benefits from establishing a significant presence in one of these markets extend beyond the member firm level. Rather, auditors that build country-specific experience and strong reputations in these locations benefit the entire firm network as worldwide offices are more likely to attract clients wishing to grow their international operations. For example, the 2006 Wynn Resorts Limited (WRL) switch from audit firms DT to EY was driven, in part, by WRL's growth in international operations and EY's geographic reputation. Specifically, WRL's May 19, 2006 form 8-K filed with the SEC states that its decision to switch from DT to EY was made by the audit committee in light of:

WRL's impending commencement of operations in Macau, SAR, People's Republic of China, and the relative strength of EY's commitment to its Asia-based gaming practice.

Thus, it appears that clients consider knowledge sharing across audit markets to be a product of both global industry reputation (Carson, 2009) *and* the individual country-level dominance that we document.

Our results also have implications for future audit research. We show that the effects of Big Four brand name reputation on audit pricing are not uniform across countries. Accordingly, as future studies continue to investigate issues related to auditor reputation and pricing, researchers should expand beyond the traditional Big Four/non-Big Four paradigm to incorporate audit firm size at the country-level.

This study uses audit fees to measure differences in auditor reputation across geographic markets. As such, we face the usual limitations from using publicly available data to make inferences about audit quality and pricing decisions. First, we include only public clients in our calculation of market share. It is possible that risk management strategies vary across firms such that some auditors will focus more or less heavily on private clients. To the extent that significant differences exist in the number and size of private clients across audit firms, our measure of country leadership may be incorrect. Further, using client-level data does not capture the audit firms' internal investments in quality. For example, our research design does not allow us to examine differences in firm resources such as the number of partners, the quality of employee education, or the firm-specific training resources, all of which are more direct measures of reputation as compared to audit fees.

In conclusion, the results from this study contribute to our understanding of the market for audit services in emerging economies. Specifically, our findings serve as initial evidence that the relative size of Big Four member firms at the country-level is associated with quality reputation as measured by fee premiums. However, important questions remain for future research. For example, do our results hold across a sample of foreign companies that do not list on a U.S. exchange and, thus, have a lower demand for high-quality auditors? Further, although we find evidence that the study's primary findings hold at the Brazilian and Israeli individual market levels, additional work may reveal whether these results generalize to other countries classified as emerging economies. This is a challenging task as audit fee data are either not required disclosures or are not captured in large databases such as Global Vantage for a majority of emerging markets countries. However, other research methods, such as distributing surveys to gather audit fees, may address this constraint. Expanding the initial analysis to a more rigorous investigation at the individual country-level presents an interesting extension to the current study's methodology and findings.

NOTES

1. Prior to the collapse of Arthur Andersen in 2002 and the merger of Price Waterhouse with Coopers & Lybrand in 1998, the current Big Four was known as the Big Six (or Big Eight depending on the time period). We refer to the set of the largest public accounting firms as the Big Four, regardless of the time period.

2. Dye (1993) offers a competing, but not mutually exclusive, explanation for the higher quality audits provided by the Big Four accounting firms. Dye models the quality of an audit as a function of auditor wealth. Wealthier (e.g., Big Four) auditors have more incentive to perform high-quality audits because they have more to lose from litigation arising from substandard audits. Thus, auditors provide value from both an *assurance* and *insurance* standpoint.

3. Francis (2004) cites an average Big Four premium of 20%, while Wallace (2004) indicates that prior literature estimates an average Big Four premium of around 30%. Although the findings of a Big Four premium are not consistent across all settings, a substantial meta-analysis of the audit fee literature performed by Hay, Knechel, and Wong (2006) confirms on average a highly significant relation exists between audit fees and auditor size.

4. See http://www.pwc.com/gx/en/corporate-governance/network-structure.jhtml (accessed on January 9, 2009).

5. Because Global Vantage does not report the auditor's name for Korea, we use Worldscope to obtain auditor market share information for this country. The large economies of China, Russia, and India do not have enough available data in Global Vantage and Audit Analytics to include in our study.

6. As of 2009 Petrobras had switched firms once again, this time to KPMG.

7. To avoid linear dependence, indicator variables for the year 2002 and the country Israel are excluded. The effects of these variables are captured in the intercept term.

8. In November 2007 the SEC voted to allow non-U.S. registrants to report under International Financial Reporting Standards (IFRSs) without reconciling with GAAP.

9. Including non-Big Four firms in the sample adds an additional 30 observations. Including these additional observations (and a Big Four dummy variable) does not materially change the study's reported findings.

10. The 90 observations in 2002 do not include a case where a client switched auditors, thus the *NEW* variable is excluded from the regression model.

11. As an additional test, we run two separate regressions on the overall sample after removing the Brazil and Israel observations. The *LEADER* variable remains positive and significant in both models, suggesting that our primary results are not due to the effects of a single country.

ACKNOWLEDGMENTS

We thank Jonathan Stanley, Monica Banyi, Roger Graham, Jared Moore, and participants at the 2010 American Accounting Association Southeast and Public Interest meetings for their comments and suggestions. Stephan Fafatas received support for this project from a Lenfest summer research grant through Washington and Lee University.

REFERENCES

Basioudis, I., & Francis, J. (2007). Big 4 audit fee premiums for national and office-level industry leadership in the United Kingdom. *Auditing: A Journal of Practice and Theory* (November), 143–166.

Beatty, R. P. (1989). Auditor reputation and the pricing of initial public offerings. *The Accounting Review, 64*, 693–709.

Becker, C., DeFond, M., Jiambalvo, J., & Subramanyam, K. R. (1998). The effect of audit quality on earnings management. *Contemporary Accounting Research* (Spring), 1–24.

Black, B., de Carvello, A. G., & Gorga, E. (2010). Corporate governance in Brazil. *Emerging Market Review, 11*, 21–38.

Carcello, J., Hermanson, D., Neal, T., & Riley, R. (2002). Board characteristics and audit fees. *Contemporary Accounting Research, 19*, 365–384.

Carson, E. (2009). Industry specialization by global audit firm networks. *The Accounting Review, 84*, 355–382.

Chan, P., Ezzamel, M., & Gwillman, D. (1993). Determinants of audit fees for quoted U.K. companies. *Journal of Business Finance and Accounting* (November), 765–786.

Choi, J.-H., Kim, C., Kim, J.-B., & Zang, Y. (2010). Audit office size, audit quality, and audit pricing. *Auditing: A Journal of Practice and Theory, 29*, 73–97.

Choi, J.-H., Kim, J.-B., Liu, X., & Simunic, D. (2008). Audit pricing, legal liability regimes, and Big 4 premiums: Theory and cross-country evidence. *Contemporary Accounting Research* (Spring), 55–99.

Choi, J.-H., Kim, J.-B., Liu, X., & Simunic, D. (2009). Cross-listing audit fee premiums: Theory and evidence. *The Accounting Review, 84*, 1429–1463.

Chu, W., Chen, C.-N., & Wang, C.-H. (2008). The market share-profitability relationships in the securities industry. *The Service Industries Journal, 28*, 813–826.

Coffee, J. (2002). Racing towards the top? The impact of cross-listings and stock market competition on international corporate governance. *Columbia Law Review, 102*, 1757–1831.

Craswell, A., Francis, J., & Taylor, S. (1995). Auditor brand name reputations and industry specializations. *Journal of Accounting and Economics, 20*, 297–322.

DeAngelo, L. (1981). Auditor size and audit quality. *Journal of Accounting and Economics, 3*, 183–199.

Dye, R. (1993). Auditing standards, legal liability, and auditor wealth. *Journal of Political Economy, 101*, 887–914.

Ettredge, M., Shane, P., & Smith, D. (1988). Audit firm size and the association between reported earnings and security returns. *Auditing: A Journal of Practice and Theory, 7*, 29–42.

Fan, J., & Wong, T. J. (2005). Do external auditors perform a corporate governance role in emerging markets? Evidence from East Asia. *Journal of Accounting Research, 43*, 35–71.

Fargher, N., Taylor, M., & Simon, D. (2001). The demand for auditor reputation across international markets for audit services. *International Journal of Accounting, 36*, 407–421.

Ferguson, A., Francis, J., & Stokes, D. (2003). The effects of firm-wide and office-level industry expertise on audit pricing. *The Accounting Review, 78*, 429–448.

Ferguson, A., & Stokes, D. (2002). Brand name audit pricing, industry specialization, and leadership premiums post-big 8 and big 6 mergers. *Contemporary Accounting Research, 19*, 77–110.

Francis, J. (1984). The effects of audit firm size on audit prices. *Journal of Accounting and Economics, 6*, 133–151.

Francis, J. (2004). What do we know about audit quality. *The British Accounting Review, 36*, 345–368.

Francis, J., & Simon, D. (1987). A test of audit pricing in the small-client segment of the U.S. audit market. *Accounting Review* (January), 145–157.

Francis, J., & Stokes, D. (1986). Audit prices, product differentiation, and scale economies: Further evidence from the Australian market. *Journal of Accounting Research, 24*, 383–393.

Francis, J. R., Reichelt, K., & Wang, D. (2005). The pricing of national and city-specific reputations for industry expertise in the U.S. audit market. *The Accounting Review, 80*, 113–136.

Geiger, M., & Rama, D. (2006). Audit firm size and going-concern reporting accuracy. *Accounting Horizons, 20*, 1–17.

Hay, D., Knechel, W. R., & Wong, N. (2006). Audit fees: A meta-analysis of the effect of supply and demand attributes. *Contemporary Accounting Research, 23*, 141–191.

Hellofs, L., & Jacobson, R. (1999). Market share and customers' perceptions of quality: When can firms grow their way to higher versus lower quality? *Journal of Marketing, 63*, 16–25.

Karim, A., & Moizer, P. (1996). Determinants of audit fees in Bangladesh. *International Journal of Accounting, 31*, 497–509.

Katz, M., & Shapiro, C. (1985). Network externalities, competition, and compatibility. *The American Economic Review, 75*, 424–440.

Klapper, L., & Love, I. (2004). Corporate governance, investor protection, and performance in emerging markets. *Journal of Corporate Finance, 10*, 703–728.

Krishnan, G. (2005). The association between big 6 auditor industry expertise and the asymmetric timeliness of earnings. *Journal of Accounting Auditing and Finance, 20*, 209–228.

Kurtz, R., & Rhoades, S. (1992). A note on the market share-profitability relationship. *Review of Industrial Organization, 7*, 39–50.

La Porta, R., Lopez-de-Silanes, F., & Vishny, R. (1998). Law and finance. *Journal of Political Economy, 106*, 1113–1155.

Lang, M., Lins, K., & Miller, D. (2003). ADRs, analysts, and accuracy: Does cross listing in the United States improve a firm's information environment and increase market value? *Journal of Accounting Research, 41*, 317–345.

Mayhew, B., & Wilkins, M. (2003). Audit firm industry specialization as a differentiation strategy: Evidence from fees charged to firms going public. *Auditing: A Journal of Practice and Theory, 22*, 33–52.

Palmrose, Z.-V. (1986). Audit fees and auditor size: Further evidence. *Journal of Accounting Research* (Spring), 97–110.

Palmrose, Z.-V. (1988). An analysis of auditor litigation and audit service quality. *The Accounting Review* (January), 55–73.

Pasquariello, P. (2008). The anatomy of financial crises: Evidence from the emerging ADR market. *Journal of International Economics, 76*, 193–207.

Seetharaman, A., Gul, F., & Lynn, S. (2002). Litigation risk and audit fees: Evidence from U.K. firms cross-listed on U.S. markets. *Journal of Accounting and Economics, 33*, 91–115.

Shapiro, C. (1983). Premiums for high quality products as returns to reputations. *Quarterly Journal of Economics, 98*, 659–679.

Simunic, D. (1980). The pricing of audit services: Theory and evidence. *Journal of Accounting Research* (Spring), 161–190.

Smallwood, D., & Conslik, J. (1979). Product quality in markets where consumers are imperfectly informed. *The Quarterly Journal of Economics, 43*, 1–23.

Szymanski, D., Bharadwaj, S., & Varadarajan, P. (1993). An analysis of the market-share profitability relationship. *Journal of Marketing, 57*, 1–18.

Taylor, M., & Simon, D. (2003). Audit markets in emerging economies: Evidence from Nigeria. *Research in Accounting in Emerging Economies, 5*, 165–175.

Teoh, S., & Wong, T. J. (1993). Perceived audit quality and the earnings response coefficient. *The Accounting Review, 68*, 346–366.

Wallace, W. (2004). The economic role of the audit in free and regulated markets: A look back and a look forward. *Research in Accounting Regulation, 17*, 267–298.

Watts, R. L., & Zimmerman, J. L. (1986). *Positive accounting theory.* Englewood Cliffs, NJ: Prentice Hall.

Willenborg, M. (1999). Empirical analysis of the economic demand for auditing in the initial public offerings market. *Journal of Accounting Research, 37*, 225–238.

FACTORS INFLUENCING CORPORATE DISCLOSURE TRANSPARENCY IN THE ACTIVE SHARE TRADING FIRMS: AN EXPLANATORY STUDY

Khaled Samaha and Khaled Dahawy

ABSTRACT

Purpose – *This study examines the factors influencing Corporate disclosure transparency as measured by the level of voluntary disclosure (VD) in the annual reports of the active share trading firms in Egypt.*

Design/methodology/approach – *The design and research method are empirical using archival data to collect information on the dependent variable (VD) and independent variables (corporate governance characteristics and company characteristics). A transformed multiple ordinary least squares (OLS) regression model was used to test the association between the dependent variable of VD and the independent variables.*

Findings – *The findings indicate that the extent of VD is affected by the highly secretive Egyptian culture. This implies that the introduction of a*

Research in Accounting in Emerging Economies, Volume 10, 87–118
Copyright © 2010 by Emerald Group Publishing Limited
All rights of reproduction in any form reserved
ISSN: 1479-3563/doi:10.1108/S1479-3563(2010)0000010009

new corporate governance code has not improved information symmetry as the overall level of VD is very low at just 19.38%. In addition, several corporate governance and company characteristics variables were found significant in explaining levels of VD by the sample companies.

Research limitations – *The findings have generalizability limitations as the study focuses only on the actively traded companies operating in the Egyptian stock market.*

Practical implications – *The results of this study should alarm the regulators and financial investors from the quality of financial information being provided in the Egyptian market. These results are more alarming since the investigated companies are the top 30 actively traded companies on the Egyptian Stock Exchange (EGX). It is logically expected that the status of disclosure would be lower in the other less actively traded companies on EGX.*

Originality/value – *This study provides evidence regarding three variables, for the first time in Egypt, namely "ownership structure" and "number of independent directors on the board" and "existence of audit committees" as explanatory variables of the level of VD. This research study will stimulate further research in understanding the importance of the role of corporate governance in promoting more transparency in other emerging economies and the need to build models that include country level factors to explain the level of VD.*

Keywords: Voluntary disclosure; secrecy; agency theory; signaling theory; active share trading firms; Egyptian Stock Exchange.

1. INTRODUCTION

International financial failures have alerted the business environment to the importance of corporate governance (Mitton, 2002; Bremmer & Elias, 2007). In several countries, securities regulators and other organizations have developed principles of good corporate governance as an important means for securing and improving investor protection and the efficiency of capital markets (e.g., Blue Ribbon Report, 2000). National regulators have introduced new mandatory requirements for corporate governance mechanisms (e.g., the Sarbanes–Oxley Act in the United States) or voluntary governance codes (e.g., in Asia; see Nowland, 2008). Nevertheless, the level of corporate governance still varies across firms and countries (Doidge, Karolyi, & Stulz, 2007).

Recently, Egypt has taken major strides in economic reform, improving investment climate and attracting local, regional, and foreign direct investments. The government has issued numerous procedures and undertaken actions to accelerate the rate of economic growth and to strengthen investors' confidence in Egypt's investment climate. One of the important steps taken in this direction has been the issuance of a code of corporate governance in 2005, which represents the general framework for corporate governance of Egyptian enterprises.[1] These rules are primarily applicable to joint stock companies listed on the stock market, especially those being actively traded. As a consequence, the economic indicators of the Egyptian market indicate a degree of success as market capitalization has increased dramatically reaching 45% by the end of 2006, and the number of investors increased from 25,000 in 1995 to 1.65 million in 2006. The number of registered companies in the Egyptian Stock Exchange (EGX) increased from 218 in 1991 to 800 in 2006 (EGX, 2007). In addition, the profile of EGX has advanced to be the leading market in the Middle East and North Africa (MENA) region. Foreign investors trading represented 31% of trade volume in 2006 rising from 17% in 2001 (CMA, 2006). These results indicate a degree of success of the economic reforms, preparing the Egyptian stock market for the competitiveness of the globalization era. Unfortunately, as seen in many transitional economies this rapid growth was not necessarily accompanied by an increase in the quality of corporate reporting.

Disclosure is regarded as a mechanism of accountability. A commitment to comprehensive and high-quality disclosure is expected to reduce information asymmetry. Several new regulations have increased the transparency of financial reporting, particularly the introduction of the International Financial Reporting Standards (IFRSs), which became mandatory for all publicly listed firms in many countries all over the world which aim at providing higher levels of transparency to investors. Disclosure outside financial statements is still to a large extent at the discretion of the management and varies widely across firms and countries (e.g., Baginski, Hassell, & Kimbrough, 2002; Francis, Khurana, & Pereira, 2005).

Traditionally publicly listed corporations in Egypt and the Middle East have a very low level of transparency and corporate disclosure (Samaha & Stapleton, 2008). This is often related to high financing costs and potential threats to competitiveness (Al-Shammari, Brown, & Tarca, 2008). From the late 1990s Egypt has dramatically reviewed and improved its regulatory frameworks, as special changes have occurred in the area of transparency and disclosure by the mandatory adoption of International Accounting Standards (IASs). However, Samaha and Stapleton (2008) indicate that the mandatory adoption of IASs starting from 1997 is not sufficient to resolve the transparency problem in Egypt, as they reported that there are large variations in compliance with IASs among a large sample of 281 listed companies in Egypt, but that the overall compliance level is very low at just 50%. Researchers have shown that the mandatory disclosure rules ensure equal access to basic information (Lev, 1992), but there is a need to augment this information by firms' voluntary disclosure (VD) and information production by intermediaries (Cheng & Courtenay, 2006). Furthermore, managers' attitudes to voluntarily disclose information are driven by market incentives and vary according to their perception of the involved costs and benefits (Healy & Palepu, 1995).

A number of papers address the relationship between corporate govern-ance characteristics, company characteristics, and firm's disclosure activities simultaneously.[2] Overall, previous research finds mixed results. The plausible reason for the mixed results might be that these studies focus on different countries, like the United States (Ajinkya, Bhojraj, & Sengupta, 2005; Chen, Chen, & Cheng, 2008; Kelton & Yang, 2008), the United Kingdom (Bassett, Koh, & Tutticci, 2007), Hong Kong (Chen & Jaggi, 2000; Ho & Wong, 2001; Chau & Gray, 2002), China (Wang & Cleiborne, 2008), Malaysia (Haniffa & Cooke, 2002), and Singapore (Chau & Gray, 2002; Eng & Mak, 2003; Cheng & Courtenay, 2006). However, the MENA region in general and specifically Egypt is absent from all these studies. The aim of this study is to fill this gap by examining a sample of the most actively traded firms in an Egyptian context.

One reason to investigate the Egyptian market is the rapid growth of Egypt as an emerging country with many foreign investment potentials. Another reason is that the business environment in Egypt experienced a dramatic reform over the past decade, as it has been dynamic, evolving through a new economic system that has led to partial convergence with IFRSs and setting of the Egyptian accounting standards (EASs). Egypt is characterized by a late move toward a market economy in 1991 when Egypt undertook an ambitious Economic Reform and Structural Adjustment Program (ERSAP), as advocated by the International Monetary Fund (IMF) and World Bank (Samaha & Stapleton, 2008). In addition, Egypt is always seen as a representative of the MENA region and studying itsfinancial market can shed light on the mechanisms and procedures of financial markets in the MENA region. The move toward a guided free market economy characterized by free trade and the working of a market pricing mechanism in the 1990s, in contrast to market imperfections and controls in the 1970s and 1980s, gives Egypt some of the characteristics of developing countries but in the context of moving toward a western type of market economy. After the launch of the government ERSAP in 1991, Egypt started to implement a privatization program that aims at increasing the role of the private sector in the development operation, while shrinking the role of the public sector, together with a reactivation of the stock exchange market. Consequently, the activities of the EGX have increased considerably, placing Egypt on the list of emerging markets (Samaha, 2005).

In addition, the Egyptian capital market development during the past few years has resulted in many important first steps (Samaha, 2005), as the EGX requires all listed companies to publish audited quarterly financial statements adhering to EASs. Companies are also required to make timely disclosure of all material news that may affect their business and earnings. As a result, more details are expected in the financial statements, leading to more transparency. Steps have been taken to improve stock market accessibility and transparency as well as to modernize and upgrade trading facilities and raise reporting and disclosure standards (EGX, 2007). This is expected to enhance the status of the Egyptian market in the global investment community.

The EGX has mandated the "Best Practices in Good Corporate Governance" in the year 2006 on all 30 actively traded listed companies (EGX 30). According to this Code, companies must publish a "governance statement" in their annual report. Additionally, nondisclosure as well as the extent of compliance with the Code needs to be disclosed as per the EGX listing requirements. The responsibility for good corporate governance is the responsibility of the board of directors. The Egyptian Code of Corporate Governance (ECCG) aims at having effective boards so that disclosures made are of a high quality, leading investors to a position of being able to make informed decisions in assessing a company's performance. Based on the previous discussion, actively traded firms, in Egypt, provide a suitable setting to examine voluntary corporate disclosure and factors influencing it.

This paper is organized as follows. Section 2 discusses the theoretical framework and identifies formal research hypotheses to be tested in the study. Section 3 describes the data and presents the research methodology employed along with an explanation of the regression model used in hypotheses testing. The discussion of empirical findings is provided in Section 4, with summary and limitations in Section 5.

2. THEORETICAL BACKGROUND, LITERATURE, AND HYPOTHESES

Theoretical justification for disclosure is based on concepts of information asymmetry (Akerlof, 1970), signaling theory (Ross, 1977), agency theory (Jensen & Meckling, 1976), litigation costs theory (Skinner, 1994), and disclosure-related costs (Ali, Ronen, & Li, 1994) that form the basis of information economics. These theories state that firm's disclosures are made to reduce information asymmetry between investors and managers, to signal the firm's superior quality compared to competitors, and to reduce agency and litigation costs. These theories sometimes provide conflicting views on how the extent of VD may be related to corporate governance and company characteristics, and this will be discussed by types of variables in the following subsections.

Applying agency and signaling theories, in this section we identify a number of potential attributes of corporate governance and company characteristics (the independent variables) that may influence the level of VD (the dependent variable). Having defined the dependent and independent variables, we outline their expected relations in the form of formal hypotheses.

2.1. The Dependent Variable – Voluntary Disclosure

VD presents an excellent opportunity to apply agency and signaling theories, in the sense that managers who have better access to the firm's private information can make credible and reliable communication to the market to optimize the value of the firm and to signal to the market that they are high-quality firms (Barako, Hancock, & Izan, 2006; Samaha & Stapleton, 2009). On the contrary, managers may, in quest of their personal goals, fail to make proper disclosure or nondisclosure of important information to the market, which may result in higher cost of capital and, consequently, shareholders may suffer a lower value for their investments.

VD is an issue of much concern for practitioners, policy makers, and financial regulators worldwide (Gul & Leung, 2004).[3] VD in annual reports has been the subject of a great deal of empirical research (see, e.g., Haniffa & Cooke, 2002; Eng & Mak, 2003; Gul & Leung, 2004; Leung & Horwitz, 2004; Cheng & Courtenay, 2006; Lim, Matolcsy, & Chow, 2007; Patelli & Prencipe, 2007).

The incentive to disclose in annual reports is that firm managers can reduce investors' concerns as to whether the management is acting in investors' best interests. Firms' annual report with nonmandatory or VD is aimed at convincing investors that firms' management are optimizing shareholder wealth. Such VD also promotes greater transparency to various stakeholders.

2.2. The Independent Variables

2.2.1. Corporate Governance Characteristics

Corporate governance mechanisms are involved in monitoring and determining a firm's overall information disclosure policy. The role of governance mechanisms in determining disclosure policy may be either complementary or substitutive (Ho & Wong, 2001). It is complementary when adoption of governance mechanisms strengthens the internal control of the firm and makes it less likely for managers to withhold information for their own benefits, leading to improvements in disclosure comprehensiveness and in the quality of financial statements. On the other hand, it is substitutive when governance mechanisms reduce information asymmetry and opportunistic behaviors in the firm, resulting in a decrease in the need for more monitoring and disclosure.

Following previous research, this study considers several corporate governance characteristics, namely, ownership structure, independent board members, and the existence of audit committees. These proxies of internal governance were considered in terms of how they impact on the extent of VD in actively traded Egyptian firms. We discuss each of these internal governance proxies and develop our hypotheses in turn.

Ownership structure – Agency theory suggests that in a more diffused ownership environment, companies will be expected to disclose more information to reduce agency cost and information diffusion (Jensen & Meckling, 1976). The potential for agency conflicts is greater for a company with diffused ownership because of the divergence of interests between contracting parties. As the number of shareholders increases, one would expect disclosure to increase if it can provide a solution to the additional monitoring problems associated with dispersion in ownership. Schipper (1981) proposed that monitoring problems that could be solved by issuing public accounting reports would increase with the number of owners. Cooke (1989) argued that companies with a larger number of shareholders are more likely to provide additional information to satisfy the information needs of diverse shareholders. Malone, Fries, and Jones (1993) found significant positive association between the number of shareholders and the extent of financial disclosure in the annual reports of U.S. companies in the oil and gas industry. Cooke (1989, 1991) also found the number of shareholders to be a significant factor influencing VD in the annual reports of Swedish and Japanese companies, respectively. Chau and Gray (2002) found that the coefficients for ownership structure were highly significant in Hong Kong and Singapore. Companies with a greater number of shareholders were found to provide more information in the annual reports. We expect a positive relationship between VD and the number of shareholders.

H1. There is a positive association between the number of shareholders and the level of voluntary disclosure by actively traded Egyptian firms.

Block holders – They refer to entities holding more than 5% of a firm's outstanding shares. When share ownership is diffused, additional monitoring is necessary (Eng & Mak, 2003). Prior research indicates a negative relationship between block ownership and disclosure (McKinnon & Dalimunthe, 1993; Mitchell, Chia, & Loh, 1995; Schadewitz & Blevins, 1998). Haniffa and Cooke (2002) suggest that the negative association implies that companies elect to disclose less to avoid loss of control. Hence it is expected that VD increases with decreases in block-holder ownership. We predict that the effect of block holders on VD to be substitutive, such that need for more monitoring and more transparent disclosure is decreased by a greater percentage of block-holder ownership.

H2. There is a negative association between block-holder ownership and the level of voluntary disclosure by actively traded Egyptian firms.

Managerial ownership – It reconciles the (potential) agency conflicts between managers and shareholders and thus reduces agency costs (Jensen & Meckling, 1976). Empirical studies find that managerial ownership overcomes the problem of managerial myopia, with high managerial ownership associated with an increase in innovation and productivity of firms and, in the long term, the value of these firms (Francis & Smith, 1995; Holthausen, Larcker, & Sloan, 1995). Because managerial ownership serves to align the interests of shareholders and managers, it reduces shareholders' demands for monitoring. Eng and Mak (2003) argue that when managerial ownership is low, there is a greater agency problem. That is, the manager has greater incentives to consume bonuses and reduced incentives to maximize job performance. In this instance, outside shareholders may need to increase monitoring of a manager's behavior to reduce the associated increase in agency costs (Ghazali & Weetman, 2006). However, monitoring by outside shareholders increases the costs of the firm. These costs associated with increased monitoring by outside shareholders can be reduced if managers can provide VD (e.g., see Eng & Mak, 2003; Leung & Horwitz, 2004). That is, VD is a substitute for monitoring.

Supporting a substitute relationship, Eng and Mak (2003) found managerial ownership to be negatively associated with VD in Singapore companies. Similarly, Ghazali and Weetman (2006) found that Malaysian companies with a higher proportion of shares held by executive directors disclose less voluntary information in their annual reports. Thus, we predict the effect of managerial ownership on VD to be substitutive, such that the need for more monitoring and more transparent disclosure is decreased by a greater percentage of managerial ownership.

H3. There is a negative association between managerial ownership and the level of voluntary disclosure by actively traded Egyptian firms.

Government ownership – Its role in determining disclosure policy may be either complementary or substitutive. Eng and Mak (2003) argued that agency costs are higher in government-owned companies because of conflicting objectives between pure profit goals of a commercial enterprise and goals related to the interests of the nation. Because of the conflicting objectives faced by these firms, there may be a greater need for communication with other shareholders of the firms leading to improvements in disclosure comprehensiveness and in the quality of financial statements. On the other hand, Ghazali and Weetman (2006) argued that companies with government ownership may not need to give extensive disclosure because of separate monitoring by the government leading to reduced information asymmetry and opportunistic behaviors in the firm, and thus less disclosure can be expected in government-controlled companies.

Of the most active companies that comprise the EGX 30 index, 22 are privatized companies (majority IPOs, minority IPOs, and sales to strategic, "anchor" investors), where the state retains its stake through a holding company structure, as the Ministry of Public Enterprises created 10 holding companies, each of which has 10–40 affiliates (EGX, 2007). It may be expected in a developing country like Egypt that government-controlled companies are strongly politically connected and these companies may disclose less information to protect their political linkages. Therefore, it is expected that companies with a higher proportion of government ownership will disclose less voluntary information.

H4. There is a negative association between government ownership and the level of voluntary disclosure by actively traded Egyptian firms.

Nonexecutive directors – They can be regarded as "professional referees whose task is to stimulate and oversee the competition among the firm's top management" (Fama, 1980, p. 294). A higher proportion of nonexecutive directors on corporate boards is likely to result in more effective monitoring of boards and thus enhances the monitoring of managerial opportunism and reduces the management's chance of withholding information (Cheng & Courtenay, 2006; Weir & Laing, 2003). Board independence is an important element in monitoring the corporate financial accounting process (Klein, 2002) and affecting the reliability of financial reports (Andersen, Deli, & Gillan, 2003).

Empirical evidence reports mixed results regarding the relationship between corporate disclosure and board independence. Several studies concluded the presence of a positive significant relationship (e.g., Beasly, 1996; Adams & Hossain, 1998; Chen & Jaggi, 2000; Leung & Horwitz, 2004; Ajinkya et al., 2005; Cheng & Courtenay, 2006). These findings suggest that independent directors play a complementary role to information disclosure. However, other studies did not find a significant relationship (e.g., Ho & Wong, 2001; Haniffa & Cooke, 2002; Ghazali & Weetman, 2006). Supporting a substitute relationship, other research reports the presence of a negative relationship (e.g., Eng & Mak, 2003; Gul & Leung, 2004; Barako et al., 2006). Our expectation is that with the introduction of the ECCG, independent directors will play a more proactive role in ensuring greater corporate transparency and accountability. This increased awareness may be partly discharged by more voluntary information disclosure in annual reports. The expectation is expressed in the following hypothesis:

H5. There is a positive association between the proportion of indepen-dent nonexecutive directors and the level of voluntary disclosure by actively traded Egyptian firms.

Audit committee – It has received increased attention in recent years (Mangena & Tauringana, 2008). Agency theory predicts that audit committees, which consist mainly of nonexecutive directors, can be viewed as a monitoring mechanism, which will be formed voluntarily in high agency cost situations to improve the quality of information flow between principal and agents (Mangena & Tauringana, 2008). In line with this, Collier (1993) argued that the existence of an audit committee should enhance the quality of financial reporting and act as a mechanism for controlling management.

Empirical evidence suggests that audit committees play a complementary role to information disclosure. Forker (1992) found a positive but weak relationship between the disclosure of the audit committee and the quality of share-option disclosure for U.K. companies. It is has been found that there is a strong association between the presence of an audit committee and more reliable financial reporting (McMullen, 1996). Barako et al. (2006) also found that the presence of an audit committee is positively and strongly associated with companies' VD practices in Kenya. Both ECCG and EGX listing rules in Egypt recommend the establishment of an audit committee, to enhance the level of information produced by companies. It is therefore hypothesized that:

H6. There is a positive association between the establishment of audit committees and the level of voluntary disclosure by actively traded Egyptian firms.

2.2.2. Company Characteristics
We introduce several company characteristics variables following the practice in prior research as possible determinants of VD (see, e.g., Raffournier, 1995; Meek, Roberts, & Gray, 1995; Ho & Wong, 2001; Eng & Mak, 2003; Ghazali & Weetman, 2006). These variables were considered in terms of how they impact on the extent of VD in actively traded Egyptian firms. We discuss each of these company characteristics and develop our hypotheses in turn.

Size – Positive association between size and disclosure was first hypothesized by Singhvi and Desai (1971), because of the expectation of larger companies' lower information generation costs, their greater interest in easier marketability of their securities, easier access to external financing, and lower adverse effect of disclosure. This line of reasoning is supported by agency theory according to which disclosure is related to the amount of outside financing (Jensen & Meckling, 1976), and as larger firm uses more outside capital, its incentive to disclose more should be bigger (Leftwich, Watts, & Zimmerman, 1981). Also bigger firms have incentive to disclose more, because potential litigation costs and net disclosure-related costs are an increasing function of firm size (Skinner, 1994; Ali et al., 1994; Eng & Mak, 2003). Considering these factors increased disclosure can be used as a protection against undesired pressures form the government (Buzby, 1975) and possible negative effects of misinterpretations by analysts due to lack of available information (Lang & Lundholm, 1993; McKinnon & Dalimunthe, 1993). Empirical support to these arguments is very strong with most studies confirming statistically significant positive association, whereas the results do not differ across different size proxies used. The expectation is expressed in the following hypothesis:

H7. There is a positive association between size and the level of voluntary disclosure by actively traded Egyptian firms.

Profitability – Akerlof (1970) stated that a well-run firm (with higher profitability and higher growth rates) would want to distinguish itself from a "lemon." It means that if the company is performing well its superiority can be signaled (Ross, 1977), information asymmetry between investors and managers reduced, and agency costs reduced (Jensen & Meckling, 1976) through increased disclosure. Authors like Meek et al. (1995) and Raffournier (1995) reveal that higher profitable companies disclose more information based on the argument that profitable firms need to reveal their superior performance. The expectation is expressed in the following hypothesis:

H8. There is a positive association between profitability and the level of voluntary disclosure by actively traded Egyptian firms.

Industry sector – Industry sector is an additional well-documented explanatory factor of VD. As Meek et al. (1995) points out "the relevance of selected items disclosure can vary across industries." Since manufacturing is of fundamental importance to Egypt and in part some industries are price controlled (i.e., high political visibility for manufacturing companies), it is possible that levels of VD in the corporate annual reports of manufacturing companies may be higher than those in other business sectors to reduce political costs. The expectation is expressed in the following hypothesis:

H9. There is a positive association between industry sector and the level of voluntary disclosure by actively traded Egyptian firms.

Extent of international activities – It has been suggested that as the firm becomes more international in its operations, the proportion of foreign stakeholders increases, leading to an increase in information asymmetry that in turn increases the demand for additional information leading to an increased level of disclosure (Malone et al., 1993; Meek et al., 1995). Half of the studies employing internationality variables have supported a significant positive association between internationalization and disclosure quality. Prior research (e.g., Zarzeski, 1996; Jaggi & Low, 2000; Archambault & Archambault, 2003; Samaha & Stapleton, 2009) argues that firms tend to expand their financial and accounting disclosure when competing for foreign resources, as bonding for resource providers. In this context expanded disclosure reduces resource providers' uncertainty about transactions with the firm and, in turn, lowers the costs that the firm has to endure to obtain resources. The expectation is expressed in the following hypothesis:

H10. There is a positive association between the extent of international activities and the level of voluntary disclosure by actively traded Egyptian firms.

Leverage – According to agency theory higher monitoring costs would be incurred by firms that are highly leveraged. To reduce these costs, firms are expected to disclose more information to improve the communication and transparency with their creditors (Meek et al., 1995), that is, the relationship between leverage and the extent of disclosure is expected to be positive (Jensen & Meckling, 1976). Results from the meta-analysis technique of Ahmed and Courtis (1999) reveal a positive association between leverage and disclosure. The expectation is expressed in the following hypothesis:

H11. There is a positive association between leverage and the level of voluntary disclosure by actively traded Egyptian firms.

Auditor choice – Auditor choice has been considered a significant explanatory factor of VD in most prior studies. Inchausti (1997) argue that signaling theory predicts that managers of successful companies will wish to signal their success and strength to potential investors and justify their compensation. The signaling can be achieved by disclosing more information and choice of external auditor. Signaling literature suggests that positive signals are sent when the firm chooses large multinational auditor because they have greater incentives to resist clients' pressure for limited disclosure to avoid adverse economic consequences to their reputation (Titman & Trueman, 1986; Craswell & Taylor, 1992; Samaha & Stapleton, 2009). The expectation is expressed in the following hypothesis:

H12. There is a positive association between auditor choice and the level of voluntary disclosure by actively traded Egyptian firms.

Liquidity – Firms with weak liquidity ratios may wish to disclose more information to explain the reasons for such situation and to assure investors of its short-term nature (signal their better status). This is in line with agency theory according to which higher leverage is associated with higher agency costs. Regulatory bodies, debt holders, and shareholders are particularly concerned with the going-concern status of companies (Wallace & Naser, 1995), and the Egyptian Capital Market Authority (CMA) refers to companies' liquidity ratios to assess their ability to meet short-term commitments (Samaha & Stapleton, 2009). Demand for company information by the CMA and shareholders is expected to increase when liquidity is lower. As a result, a company with a lower liquidity ratio is more likely to disclose additional information to reduce agency costs and assure shareholders and the CMA that its financial position is sufficient to meet short-term commitments. The expectation is expressed in the following hypothesis:

H13. There is a negative association between liquidity and the level of voluntary disclosure by actively traded Egyptian firms.

3. RESEARCH DESIGN

3.1. Data

Despite the increased market capitalization of the Egyptian stock market, trades remain concentrated in a few companies that exhibit real strong fundamentals (EGX, 2007). In 2006, the EGX had 800 listed companies of which 30 are the most actively traded companies as measured by the EGX 30 index.

The EGX 30 companies were selected for this study because these companies are considered the leading and most active in the Egyptian market. EGX 30 is the most commonly used index to measure the performance of the Egyptian capital market. It is a price index that includes the top 30 companies with respect to their liquidity and activity. This index is measured by market capitalization and adjusted by the free float that must be at least 15% for a company to be listed on EGX 30. Companies constituting the EGX 30 for 2006 represent a range of industries, as indicated in Table 1.

The number of sample companies might be seen low compared to other empirical studies reported in the literature. However, it has to be considered given several important factors: (1) the novelty of the idea of corporate governance in the Egyptian context, (2) the secretive environment that controls the Egyptian financial markets in general (Samaha & Stapleton, 2008), and (3) lack of electronic venues to access data which makes the only means for data collection is manual analysis of the information. The interaction of these factors makes it more realistic to study the most active companies first as they are the ones who would have the highest propensity to offer VD and apply corporate governance requirements. In case that this

Table 1. EGX 30 Industry Sector Classification.

Sector	Number of Companies
Financial services	5
Textiles and clothing	6
Housing and real estate	4
Building materials and construction	4
Communication	3
Entertainment	2
Holding companies	2
Mining and gas	2
Information technology	1
Media	1
Total	30

research finds promising results, future research will be done to improve the generalizability of the results by increasing the sample size to include the less actively traded companies.

3.2. Variables

3.2.1. Dependent Variable

The VD checklist was constructed based on the ones used by Chau and Gray (2002) in Hong Kong and Singapore, and Ghazali and Weetman (2006) in Malaysia. This provides a useful yardstick for comparison with earlier research.[4]

We calculated three partial scores for the disclosure items in line with Ghazali and Weetman (2006) and Meek et al. (1995). These are financial (FN), strategic (ST), and corporate social reporting (CSR). In addition to having partial scores, one overall score for VD was calculated. VD assigned an equal weighting to each item of disclosure in the checklist.

Scoring was based on an unweighted index, which is considered an appropriate method for a study that is not focusing on the information needs of any specific groups (Chau & Gray, 2002; Cooke, 1989). A dichotomous procedure was applied, whereby a company is awarded 1 if an item included in the disclosure checklist is disclosed and 0 if it is not disclosed. One of the major issues of adopting this dichotomous procedure is the applicability of the item concerned, that is, the determination of whether the information disclosure item is not disclosed (0) or not applicable (N/A) when that particular item is not included in the annual report. To tackle this problem, an information disclosure item was coded as N/A only after having investigated the entire annual report and ensuring that no similar information could be found in any part of the report. This approach has been used in prior studies (e.g., Samaha & Stapleton, 2009; Ghazali & Weetman, 2006).

Once all the items of the information have been scored, an index is created to measure the relative level of disclosure by a company. The scores for each item were then added and equally weighted to derive a final score for each company. The total VD score a company can earn varies:

$$VD = \sum_{i=1}^{n} d_i$$

$d = 1$ if the item d_i is disclosed and 0 if the item d_i is not disclosed.
$n =$ the number of items that the company is expected to disclose.

3.2.2. Independent Variables

A multiple ordinary least squares (OLS) regression model was used to test the association between the dependent variables of VDs and the independent variables. The hypotheses to be tested are summarized in Table 2, whereas in all cases the dependent variable is the disclosure level proxy (VD, FN, ST, and CSR). The main VD model estimated for our OLS regression is as follows:

$$VD = \beta 0 + \beta 1 \text{ SHAR} + \beta 2 \text{ BOWN} + \beta 3 \text{ MOWN} + \beta 4 \text{ GOWN}$$
$$+ \beta 5 \text{ IND} + \beta 6 \text{ AC} + \beta 7 \text{ ASSET} + \beta 8 \text{ PRO} + \beta 9 \text{ IT1} + \beta 10 \text{ IT2}$$
$$+ \beta 11 \text{ IT3} + \beta 12 \text{INT} + \beta 13 \text{ LEV} + \beta 14 \text{ AUD} + \beta 15 \text{ LIQ} + e$$

where VD represents overall voluntary disclosure index, $\beta 0, ..., \beta 15$ represent regression coefficients, independent variables are defined in Table 2, and e represents the error term.

4. RESULTS AND DISCUSSION

4.1. Descriptive Statistics

Descriptive statistics of the independent variables are presented in Table 3. The descriptive statistics imply that ownership structure is highly concentrated in listed Egyptian companies with number of shareholders ranges between 3 and 99 with an average of 28 shareholders. The mean

Table 2. Summary of Hypotheses.

Hypotheses	Measure	Proxy	Expected Sign	Source of Information
H1	Number of shareholders (SHAR)	In line with Ghazali and Weetman (2006), it is calculated as the number of the owners holding the total number of shares issued	+	Ownership structure information (EGID)
H2	Block-holder ownership (BOWN)	In line with Eng and Mak (2003), it is calculated as the percentage of shares owned by the block-holders–shareholders whose ownership equal to or exceeds 5% to the total number of shares issued	–	Ownership structure information (EGID)
H3	Managerial ownership (MOWN)	In line with Eng and Mak (2003), it is calculated as the percentage of shares owned by the CEO and executive directors to the total number of shares issued	–	Ownership structure information (EGID)
H4	Government ownership (GOWN)	Percentage of the shares owned by the public sector (holding companies, companies, banks, insurance companies and other institutions) to the total number of shares issued	–	Ownership structure information (EGID)
H5	Independent nonexecutive directors on the board (IND)	In line with Ghazali and Weetman (2006), it is calculated as the ratio of the number of nonexecutive directors to the total number of the directors	+	• Board of directors' report (EGID) • http://www. egyptwatch.com
H6	Existence of Audit Committees (AC)	Dichotomous, 1 or 0	+	• Board of directors' report (EGID) • http://www.egypt watch.com
H7	Size (ASSET)	Natural logarithm of total assets	+	Annual report: Financial statements

Table 2. (*Continued*)

Hypotheses	Measure	Proxy	Expected Sign	Source of Information
H8	Profitability (PRO)	Return on equity defined as net income before tax to the total stockholders' equity	+	Annual report: Financial statements
H9	Industry type (IT1, IT2, IT3)	Categorized into the following: Manufacturing IT1, trade/service IT3, and financial IT2	+	EGX Bulletin (December 2006)
H10	Internationality (INT)	In line with Zarzeski (1996), a firm is defined as international based on the following: foreign business transactions (foreign sales or exports), or being an MNC affiliation, trading of firm's shares on foreign stock exchanges (however, this is very rare in listed Egyptian companies)	+	• Annual report: Footnotes • Board of directors' report (EGID)
H11	Leverage (LEV)	Defined as total debt to total stockholders' equity	+	Annual report: Financial statements
H12	Type of Auditor (AUD)	Dichotomous, 1 for big 4 or 0 otherwise	+	Annual report: Auditor report section
H13	Liquidity (LIQ)	Is a quick ratio and defined as current asset – after deducting the inventory – to the current liabilities	–	Annual report: Financial statements

Table 3. Descriptive Statistics of the Independent Variables.

Code in SPSS	Minimum	Maximum	Mean	SD
Panel A: Continuous independent variables				
SHAR	3	99	27.66	23.64
BOWN	.00	1.00	.4210	.4078
MOWN	.00	.66	.0894	.1764
GOWN	.00	.86	.3189	.3269
IND	.00	.95	.4140	.3402
LEV	.00	7.66	.8206	1.2674
ASSET	188349534	38274231487	7160662662	11069624391
PRO	−.01	1.18	.2599	.2775
LIQ	.07	14.21	1.8103	1.9902
Panel B: Categorical independent variables				
AC	.00	1.00	.37	.4901
AUD	.00	1.00	.70	.4660
IT1	.00	1.00	.43	.5040
IT2	.00	1.00	.17	.3790
IT3	.00	1.00	.40	.4982
INT	.00	1.00	.76	.4302

percentage of independent directors on the board is 41%. Long-term debt seems to constitute a substantial portion of the capital structure of the sample firms with the mean leverage variable being 82%. Firms are widely distributed in terms of size ranging from 188 million EGP to 38 billion EGP (currently the 1 USD = 5.5 EGP). The sample firms seem to be dominated by the big 4 audit firms as indicated by the mean of the type of auditor variable (70%). The statistics show that 76% of the sample firms have foreign connections. Only 11 companies (37%) have an audit committee. The sample is divided into 13 manufacturing companies, 12 trade/services companies, and 5 financial companies.

Table 4 reports descriptive statistics of the overall VD, partial and subindices. The table is divided into two panels. Panel A shows the overall and partial VD, while Panel B shows the subindices scores. Panel A shows that overall VD ranges from 4% to 58% with a mean score of 19.38%. This indicates the presence of large variations in VD levels between the companies. However, it also indicates a low level of VD. The low levels of VD ratio implies that analysts in Egypt may search for information outside of annual reports (e.g., via investor relations department).

Analysis of the partial indices indicates that FN information has the highest score followed by ST and CSR at the lowest end. This result is

Table 4. Descriptive Statistics of the Dependent Variable.

	Overall Voluntary Disclosure (VD)
Panel A: Overall voluntary disclosure index	
Mean (%)	19.38
Minimum (%)	4
Maximum (%)	58
K–S significance	.041**

Score (%)	Number of Companies	%
Above 80	0	0
60–79.9	1	3.3
40–59.9	3	10
Below 40	26	86.7
Total	30	100

	Financial Information Partial Index (FN)		Strategic Information Partial Index (ST)		Corporate Social Responsibility Partial Index (CSR)	
Panel B: Voluntary disclosure partial indices						
Mean (%)	26.16		15.72		6.8	
Minimum (%)	7		3		0	
Maximum (%)	52		72		46	
K–S significance	.051*		.046**		.006***	

Score (%)	Number of Companies	%	Number of Companies	%	Number of Companies	%
Above 80	0	0	0	0	0	0
60–79.9	0	0	1	3.3	0	0
40–59.9	2	6.7	1	3.3	2	6.7
Below 40	28	93.3	28	93.3	28	93.3
Total	30	100	30	100	30	100

*Significant at the 10% level; **Significant at the 5% level; ***Significant at the 1% level.

different from the results reported by other researchers. Ghazali and Weetman (2006) reported voluntary mean disclosure varying from 20.2% in the case of CSR information to 39.3% for ST information, with FN information in between at 35.6%. The total VD scores in Malaysia range from 6.3% to 74.0% with a mean score of 31.4%. Chau and Gray (2002) reported that the voluntary mean disclosure for Singapore in 1997 varied from 10.68% for FN to 16.76% for CSR, with ST in between at 16.00%. The overall mean disclosure in 1997 was at 13.83%. For the Hong Kong companies, the voluntary mean disclosure in 1997 varied from 9.77% in the case of FN to 18.49% for ST, with CSR in between at 10.45%. The overall mean disclosure in 1997 was 12.23%.

Table 4 also shows that no company has a disclosure score higher than 80%. Only one company (3.3%) disclosed between 60% and 80%, while three companies obtained a disclosure score between 40% and 60%. The remaining 26 companies (87%) scored below 40%. These results are below the Malaysian results (Ghazali & Weetman, 2006) which indicated that 26 companies out of 87 (30%) disclosed more than 40% of the items included in the index. These results show that even among the most actively traded stocks on the EGX, there is considerable variability in the amount of information voluntarily disclosed in annual reports and only one company can be said to be "good discloser" according to the classification of Samaha and Stapleton (2008). Table 4 also shows that the scores are not normally distributed as indicated by the nonparametric Kolmogrov–Smirnov test (or K–S Lilliefors).

4.2. Multivariate Regression Robustness Tests

For the multivariate analyses, four regressions were estimated, one for each of the four main dependent variables (VD, FN, ST, and CSR). Prior to performing the multivariate analysis, a multicollinearity test was performed using Pearson's product moment correlations (not reported). The results show that MOWN and BOWN are not correlated with one another. BOWN is negatively related to AC ($r = -.625$), SHAR ($r = -.521$), and IND ($r = -.594$). Finally, AC is positively related to IND ($r = .571$). These correlations are well below the .8 level for concern (Field, 2009). Therefore, the problem of multicollinearity is minimal, giving support to the appropriateness of multivariate analysis.[5]

The Kolmogrov–Smirnov Z-test with Lilliefors correction for each independent and dependent variable (not reported) indicated that some of the independent variables are not normally distributed; thus, following Cooke (1998), the continuous independent and dependent variables were transformed into normal scores before running the regression analysis. The normal scores are based on the Van der Waerden approach to avoid violating the regression assumptions (a method proposed by Cooke, 1998).

4.3. Multivariate Regression Results

The multivariate results from testing the association between the VD scores and the independent variables are reported in Table 5. The regression model for the overall level of VD is reported in Table 5 and has reported an F-value of 13.313 (significant at the .0001 level). The adjusted R^2 is 75.6 and is considered high for this type of study and gives confidence in the explanatory power of the model used. The explanatory power of this model is higher than studies conducted in other developing countries: Eng and Mak (2003) [20.61%] in Singapore, Chau and Gray (2002) in respect of Hong Kong [42.7%], Ghazali and Weetman (2006) [36.1%] in Malaysia, Ho and Wong (2001) [31.4%] in Hong Kong, Cheng and Courtenay (2006) [22.9%] in Singapore, Barako et al. (2006) [53.4%] in

Table 5. Results of Transformed OLS Regression.

			Overall Voluntary Disclosure Model (VD)
Adjusted R^2			75.6
F statistic			13.313
Significance			.000**
Durbin–Watson test			1.314
Independent Variables	Beta	t	Significance (P-Value)
Intercept		−2.627	.014*
SHAR	.132	1.731	.104
BOWN	−.201	−2.249	.040*
MOWN	−.367	−3.292	.005**
GOWN	.092	1.129	.277
IND	.219	2.328	.034*
AC	.171	2.136	.045*
AUD	.399	3.755	.002**
IT1	.205	2.267	.039*
IT2	−.012	−.322	.752
IT3	.007	.357	.822
INT	−.040	−.633	.536
LEV	−.112	−1.468	.163
ASSET	.098	1.157	.265
PRO	−.033	−.624	.542
LIQ	.417	4.063	.001***

*Significant at the .05 level; **Significant at the .01 level; ***Significant at the .001 level.
$N = 30$.

Kenya, Haniffa and Cooke (2002) [47.9%] in Malaysia, and Chau and Gray (2002) in respect of Singapore [72.5%] companies. This conclusion will have theory implications that will be discussed in the "Summary and Limitations" section.

This study also assessed three subcategories of VD, namely, strategic information, financial information, and corporate social responsibility information. These subcategories of VD were also regressed (results not reported). The amount of explained variation in these three subcategories of VD ranges from 54.3% in the case of FN information to 69.8% for CSR information and 65.6% for ST information.

Of the corporate governance variables, lower MOWN and BOWN, greater IND, and existence of AC are related to greater VD. However, we find no significant relationship between VD and SHAR and GOWN.

MOWN is the most important predictor of the extent of overall VD, with the highest estimated coefficient of 3.292 significant at less than the .0001 level and in the predicted direction. Therefore, Hypothesis 3 supported in that lower managerial ownership was associated with increased VD. This is consistent with Eng and Mak (2003) and Ghazali and Weetman (2006) in Singapore and Malaysia, respectively. This is consistent with a substitute relationship between MOWN and disclosure in that the increase in MOWN reduces the need for monitoring by outside shareholders. This seems to suggest that the level of information asymmetry increases as executive directors own a higher proportion of shares in the firm. This may have implications of concern for investors and accounting standard setters, given that remuneration packages often allow for managers to hold shares in the firm.

The positive sign for IND provides support for Hypothesis 5 in that companies with a higher proportion of independent directors on the board disclose more voluntary information in their annual reports. Again, IND is significant at the 5% level in explaining all types of information disclosure (FN, ST, and CSR) and in the predicted direction (not reported). Information disclosure is likely to be high in companies with a higher proportion of independent directors on the board. This is consistent with a complement relationship between IND and disclosure in that IND is likely to actively press the company to disclose more nonmandatory information. This result supports the intuition that greater board independence is linked to more transparency and better monitoring. The result for IND is inconsistent with Haniffa and Cooke (2002), Ho and Wong (2001), and Ghazali and Weetman (2006), who found the ratio of independent directors to total directors on board to be insignificant. This significance of the presence of IND may reflect a similarity between de jure and de facto independence. In contrast, Eng and Mak (2003) found a significant negative association in Singapore companies. Similarly, Barako et al. (2006) found a significant negative association in Kenyan companies. The results suggest that external directors in Egypt play a complementary monitoring role to disclosure, whereas in Eng and Mak (2003) Singapore sample and in Barako et al. (2006) Kenyan sample, they play a substitute role to disclosure.

The next most significant variables are BOWN and AC (with a p-value .040 and 045, respectively). Both are in the predicted direction. The negative sign for the BOWN provides support for Hypothesis 2 in that VD increases with decreases in block-holder ownership. However, BOWN is significant at the 5% level in explaining one type of information disclosure (CSR) and in the predicted direction (not reported). Information disclosure is likely to be high in companies with a lower proportion of block-holder ownership. This is inconsistent with Eng and Mak (2003) who found that the level of VD to be not significantly related with BOWN.

The positive sign for AC provides support for Hypothesis 6 in that companies with an audit committee disclose more voluntary information in their annual reports. Furthermore, the existence of audit committees is significant at the 5% level in explaining two types of information disclosure (ST and CSR) and in the predicted direction (not reported). This is consistent with a complement relationship between AC and disclosure in that the existence of audit committees is likely to actively press the company to disclose more nonmandatory information. The result for AC is consistent with Ho and Wong (2001) and Barako et al. (2006) who found the existence of AC to be positively significant.

SHAR is neither significant in explaining overall VD nor any partial category of disclosure (except social disclosure), indicating that SHAR is not influencing VD levels. Thus, Hypothesis 1 that companies with a larger number of shareholders are likely to have a higher extent of VD is not supported. This is consistent with Ghazali and Weetman (2006) who found it to be not statistically significant in explaining any type of information disclosure in Malaysia.

The results show that GOWN is not related to VD. Thus, Hypothesis 4 that VD increases with decreases in government ownership is not supported. The result is consistent with Ghazali and Weetman (2006) who found that GOWN is not influencing disclosure levels. However, the result is inconsistent with the findings of Eng and Mak (2003) who found that Singapore firms are less likely to provide voluntary information as GOWN increases.

Of the company characteristics variables, manufacturing companies (IT1) and AUD are related to greater VD and in the predicted direction. Thus,

Hypotheses 9 and 12 are supported. The results further indicate that high LIQ is related to greater VD which is not in the predicted direction. Thus, Hypothesis 13 is not supported. However, we find no significant relationship between VD and INT, ASSET, LEV, and PRO, as they were not statistically significant in any of the models. Thus, Hypotheses 7, 8, 10, and 11 are not supported.

In relation to the significance of manufacturing companies in the overall model, this is perhaps not surprising given the size of this sector in the Egyptian economy. For example, Cooke (1991) noted that Japan's manufacturing sector discloses more information than all other sectors, because it is a major sector of that economy. In the Egyptian context, manufacturing is the most important sector contributing more than 40% of the GDP (EGX, 2007), and the high level of disclosure may be attributable to its role in the Egyptian economy. The significance of high liquidity in the overall model indicates companies having high liquidity ratios disclose more to signal to the market that they are superior firms according to the signaling theory.

The insignificance of the size variable is inconsistent with prior research by Ho and Wong (2001) and Ghazali and Weetman (2006) who indicated that larger companies seek to satisfy the information demands of investors to attract prospective investors to the company and to compete for international funding. Large companies are also expected to have better governance structure with clear separation between owners and managers. This could occur because large firms need more financing capital than smaller firms. The general lack of influence of size on VD may be related to the fact that the EGX 30 companies are the highest in terms of market capitalization, so that all sample companies have reacted similarly.

5. SUMMARY AND LIMITATIONS

This paper examines the factors influencing voluntary disclosures by the active share trading firms in Egypt. Building upon agency and signaling theories, the accounting disclosure research literature suggests that the amount of VD made by a company in its annual report may be influenced by the presence of sound corporate governance mechanisms and other firm-specific factors. In this article, we examine this phenomenon using data collected from the annual reports of the 30 most actively traded listed Egyptian firms.

The results strongly indicate low VD. The companies investigated scored only 19.38% of the indicated index. These results should alarm the regulators and financial investors from the quality of financial information being provided in the Egyptian market. The positive impact of the immense efforts taken by the Egyptian government to set a corporate governance code is not visible yet. These results are more alarming since the investigated companies are the top 30 actively traded companies on EGX. It is logically expected that the status of disclosure would be a lot lower in the other less actively traded companies on EGX.

Low disclosure might be due to the novelty of the idea of corporate governance and the fact that the market operators have not yet understood what is required and appreciated the positive impact that can be achieved from increased transparency. It is worth noting that low level of VD is not a strange phenomena in the Egyptian market only, but also found in several other studies: Eng and Mak (2003) in Singapore, Cheng and Courtenay (2006) in Singapore, Ho and Wong (2001) in Hong Kong, and Ghazali and Weetman (2006) in Malaysia.

The ECGC recommends the actively traded companies to have an audit committee and utilize the experience of independent board members. The findings of this study indicate that these new provisions to enhance corporate governance are statistically significant in explaining VD in Egyptian annual reports. However, the introduction of new corporate governance code has not improved information symmetry as the overall level of VD is very low. This suggests that the efforts of regulators have not brought significant improvement in the transparency of information.

From these findings four policy implications are evident. First, the Egyptian regulators need to take steps to enhance the enforceability of the recommended corporate governance procedures to ensure its implementation and put harsh penalties on nonimplementers, as it is not enough to regulate but it is more important to follow-up on the implementation of the regulation. Second, the next revision of the code could include enforcement for independent nomination and audit committees and an expansion of the role of the audit committee. Third, actively traded companies should be required to include a minimum number of independent directors on board committees dealing with potential conflict of interest issues. Finally, there should be efforts to explain and educate the preparers and users of financial information of the benefits of corporate governance and its positive impact on securing transparency via increased disclosure. The results of this research may be useful for regulators in Egypt as they continue to endorse the appropriate corporate governance requirements.

It is important to note that when comparing the results of this study to other papers that studied developing countries there are major variances that require further understanding. The differences in results indicate the need for theorizing about disclosure at the country level. The variation in the disclosure level that is reported in the recent studies that examined the developing nations indicates that the socioeconomic factors present in the local environment of every country have a strong impact on the level of disclosure. Furthermore, the large variance in the explanatory powers of the models that were used in these studies indicates that the contribution of the other factors that are not captured in these models (e.g., legal, political, economic ... , etc.) have different degrees in explaining levels of VD. These findings imply that company level factors (proxied by the agency and signaling theories in this paper) may not be sufficient to explain the level of VD. There is a need to build models that include country-level factors to better explain the level of VD.

In conclusion, the study of the variables that affect the level of VD in Egypt is in its infancy. There is a need to study the variables that affect the degree of disclosure within the context of culture. The variables in developed nations are different than those in developing nations. Accounting research needs to pay more attention to accounting as it is practiced in developing nations because as this study and several prior researches has shown, there are major differences between accounting in developing and developed nations.

The results presented in this study are subject to all of the usual limitations associated with accounting disclosure research plus two additional ones. First, findings from this study suffer from an external validity problem in that they come only from the actively traded listed firms in Egypt. That is, these results may not be able to be extended across samples in all countries. Second, as only firms with the highest trading were included in the sample, the results may not extend across all companies in Egypt. With no financial analyst followings in Egypt, the consideration of disclosure quality presents challenges for future research. Finally, this study uses data from a single country only and as a result do not take the interaction of country-level factors into account. Therefore, the findings should be interpreted with care because of these limitations. Future studies in this area should address these specific issues directly.

NOTES

1. In preparing this Code, the special nature of Egyptian companies and the lessons learnt from the experience of other countries have been taken into account.

The preparation process started with a review of the guidelines on corporate governance in the OECD. Subsequently, a team of Egyptian experts drafted the initial Code, which was then subjected to in-depth examination and extended discussions on the part of the leadership of the holding companies of the public enterprise sector, the heads of administrative and legal departments in these enterprises, and the leadership of some private sector companies. At the end, the Code was reviewed by experts from the OECD, the IFC, and the World Bank. These code principles are divided into six groups: (1) ensuring the existence of an effective regulatory and legal framework for the enterprise sector, (2) the State acting as the owner, (3) equitable treatment of shareholders (owners), (4) relationships with stakeholders, (5) transparency and disclosure, and (6) responsibilities of the board of directors.

2. For example, Chen and Jaggi (2000), Ho and Wong (2001), Chau and Gray (2002), Haniffa and Cooke (2002), Eng and Mak (2003), Gul and Leung (2004), Eng and Mak (2003), Leung and Horwitz (2004), Ajinkya et al. (2005), Cheng and Courtenay (2006), Cerbioni and Parbonetti (2007), Bassett et al. (2007), Chen et al. (2008), Kelton and Yang, (2008), and Wang and Cleiborne (2008).

3. Voluntary disclosure can be defined as "disclosure in excess of requirements, representing free choices on the part of company managements to provide accounting and other information deemed relevant to the decision needs of users of their annual reports" (Meek et al., 1995).

4. The items on the checklist were checked against the mandatory disclosure requirements of Egypt that are based on the EASs to make sure that there are no mandatory items. Four items in the Chau and Gray (2002) checklist relating to acquisitions and disposals were found to be mandatory by the new EASs issued in mid-2002, which apply to the financial year starting 2003. Therefore these four items were excluded. In addition, four items about segmental information were excluded as they were found to be mandatory by the new EASs. In addition all items relating to fixed assets, intangibles, and foreign currency were also excluded as they are mandatory by the EASs. In addition, we sought expert opinions from an investment analyst and a senior official from the Egyptian stock exchange to refine the list so that it would reflect voluntary items that were considered important for disclosure in an Egyptian corporate annual report. The final list consisted of 80 items of which 29 were strategic, 27 were financial, and 24 represented corporate social responsibility information.

5. OLS regression is based on the assumptions of no significant multicollinearity between the explanatory variables and conditions of linearity and normality. Our tests showed only low coefficients in the correlation matrix suggesting that the problem of multicollinearity was minimal, although it can still exist even when none of the bivariate correlation coefficients is very large, since one independent variable may be an approximate linear function of a set of several independent variables. Another effective means of testing multicollinearity is to compute the variance inflation factor (VIF). VIF measures the degree to which each explanatory variable is explained by the other explanatory variables, and very large VIF values indicate high collinearity. VIFs were generated by SPSS for each of the independent variables. A review of the tolerance and variance inflation factor statistics provides no evidence of pro-significant multicollinearity in the regression model. VIFs did not

exceed 5 and are thus well below the common cutoff threshold of 10 (Field, 2009), indicating that multicollinearity did not exist in the multiple regression model. Furthermore, the lowest tolerance value in the models is .407 which is far from the cutoff threshold .2 (Field, 2009). This means that each predictor in the OLS models has at least 41% of its variation independent of the other predictors. This confirms the VIF statistic that there is no multicollinearity in the models. The results of the regression analysis can, therefore, be interpreted with a greater degree of confidence.

REFERENCES

Adams, M., & Hossain, M. (1998). Managerial discretion and voluntary disclosure: Evidence from the New Zealand life insurance industry. *Journal of Accounting and Public Policy*, *17*, 245–281.

Ahmed, K., & Courtis, J. K. (1999). Associations between corporate characteristics and disclosure levels in annual reports: A meta-analysis. *British Accounting Review*, *31*(1), 35–61.

Ajinkya, B., Bhojraj, S., & Sengupta, P. (2005). The association between outside directors, institutional investors and properties of management earnings forecasts. *Journal of Accounting Research*, *43*(3), 343–376.

Akerlof, G. A. (1970). The market for "lemons": Quality uncertainty and the market mechanism. *Quarterly Journal of Economics*, *84*(3), 488–500.

Ali, A., Ronen, J., & Li, S-H. (1994). Discretionary disclosures in response to intra-industry information transfers. *Journal of Accounting, Auditing and Finance*, *9*(2), 265–283.

Al-Shammari, B., Brown, P., & Tarca, A. (2008). An investigation of compliance with international accounting standards by listed companies in the Gulf Co-Operation Council member states. *The International Journal of Accounting*, *43*(4), 425–447.

Andersen, K. L., Deli, D. N., & Gillan, S. L. (2003). *Boards of directors, audit committees, and the information content of earnings*. Working Paper. John L. Weinberg Center for Corporate Governance, University of Delaware, Newark, DE.

Archambault, J. J., & Archambault, M. E. (2003). A multinational test of determinants of corporate disclosure. *The International Journal of Accounting*, *38*(1), 173–194.

Baginski, S. P., Hassell, J. M., & Kimbrough, M. D. (2002). The effect of legal environment on voluntary disclosure: Evidence from management earnings forecasts issued in U.S. and Canadian markets. *The Accounting Review*, *77*(1), 25–50.

Barako, D. G., Hancock, P., & Izan, H. Y. (2006). Factors influencing voluntary corporate disclosure by Kenyan companies. *Corporate Governance: An International Review*, *14*(2), 107–125.

Bassett, M., Koh, P.-S., & Tutticci, I. (2007). The association between employee stock option disclosures and corporate governance: Evidence from an enhanced disclosure regime. *British Accounting Review*, *39*(4), 303–322.

Beasly, M. S. (1996). An empirical analysis of the relation between the board of director composition and financial statement fraud. *The Accounting Review*, *71*, 443–465.

Blue Ribbon Report. (1999). *Report and recommendations of the Blue Ribbon Committee on improving the effectiveness of corporate audit committees*. New York: New York Stock Exchange and the National Association of Securities Dealers.

Bremmer, J., & Elias, N. (2007). Corporate governance in developing economies: The case of Egypt. *International Journal of Business Governance and Ethics, 3*(4), 430–445.

Buzby, S. L. (1975). Company size, listed versus unlisted stocks, and the extent of financial disclosure. *Journal of Accounting Research, 13*(1), 16–37.

Cerbioni, F., & Parbonetti, A. (2007). Exploring the effects of corporate governance on intellectual capital disclosure: An analysis of European Biotechnology companies. *European Accounting Review, 16*(4), 791–826.

Chau, G. K., & Gray, S. J. (2002). Ownership structure and corporate voluntary disclosure in Hong Kong and Singapore. *The International Journal of Accounting, 37*, 247–265.

Chen, C. J. P., & Jaggi, B. (2000). Association between independent non-executive directors, family control and financial disclosures in Hong Kong. *Journal of Accounting and Public Policy, 19*, 285–310.

Chen, S., Chen, X., & Cheng, Q. (2008). Do family firms provide more or less voluntary disclosure? *Journal of Accounting Research, 46*(3), 499–536.

Cheng, C. M. E., & Courtenay, S. M. (2006). Board composition, regulatory regime and voluntary disclosure. *The International Journal of Accounting, 41*, 262–289.

CMA. (2006). *Economic bulletin-stock exchange.* Cairo: Capital Market Authority Information Center.

Collier, P. (1993). Factors affecting the formation of audit committees in major UK listed companies. *Accounting and Business Research, 23*, 421–430.

Cooke, T. E. (1989). Voluntary corporate disclosure by Swedish companies. *Journal of International Financial Management and Accounting, 1*(2), 171–195.

Cooke, T. E. (1991). An assessment of voluntary disclosure in the annual reports of Japanese corporations. *The International Journal of Accounting, 26*(3), 174–189.

Cooke, T. E. (1998). Regression analysis in accounting disclosure studies. *Accounting and Business Research, 28*(3), 209–224.

Craswell, A. T., & Taylor, S. L. (1992). Discretionary disclosure of reserves by oil and gas companies: An economic analysis. *Journal of Business Finance and Accounting, 19*(2), 295–308.

Doidge, C., Karolyi, G. A., & Stulz, R. M. (2007). Why do countries matter so much for corporate governance? *Journal of Financial Economics, 86*, 1–39.

EGX, D. (2007). Cairo and Alexandria stock exchange. *Fact Book*, December, pp. 1–61, Cairo (in Arabic).

Eng, L. L., & Mak, Y. T. (2003). Corporate governance and voluntary disclosure. *Journal of Accounting and Public Policy, 22*, 325–345.

Fama, E. F. (1980). Agency problems and the theory of the firm. *Journal of Political Economy, 88*, 88–307.

Field, A. (2009). *Discovering statistics using SPSS for windows* (3rd ed.). London: Sage publications.

Forker, J. J. (1992). Corporate governance and disclosure quality. *Accounting and Business Research, 22*, 111–124.

Francis, J., & Smith, A. (1995). Agency costs and innovation: Some empirical evidence. *Journal of Accounting and Economics, 19*, 383–409.

Francis, J. R., Khurana, I. K., & Pereira, R. (2005). Disclosure incentives and effects on cost of capital around the world. *Accounting Review, 80*(4), 1125–1162.

Ghazali, N. A. M., & Weetman, P. (2006). Perpetuating traditional influences: Voluntary disclosure in Malaysia following the economic crisis. *Journal of International Accounting, Auditing and Taxation, 15*, 226–248.

Gul, F. A., & Leung, S. (2004). Board leadership, outside directors' expertise and voluntary corporate disclosures. *Journal of Accounting and Public Policy, 23,* 1–29.

Haniffa, R. M., & Cooke, T. E. (2002). Culture, corporate governance and disclosure in Malaysian corporations. *Abacus, 38,* 317–349.

Healy, P. M., & Palepu, K. G. (1995). The challenges of investor communication: The case of CUC International, Inc. *Journal of Financial Economics, 38*(2), 111–140.

Ho, S. M. S., & Wong, K. R. (2001). A study of the relationship between corporate governance structures and the extent of voluntary disclosure. *Journal of International Accounting, Auditing and Taxation, 10,* 139–156.

Holthausen, R. W., Larcker, D. F., & Sloan, R. G. (1995). Business unit innovation and the structure of executive compensation. *Journal of Accounting and Economics, 19,* 279–313.

Inchausti, B. G. (1997). The influence of company characteristics and accounting regulation on information disclosed by Spanish firms. *The European Accounting Review, 6*(1), 45–68.

Jaggi, B., & Low, P. Y. (2000). Impact of culture, market forces, and legal system on financial disclosures. *The International Journal of Accounting, 35*(4), 495–519.

Jensen, M. C., & Meckling, W. H. (1976). Theory of the firm: Managerial behavior, agency costs and ownership structure. *Journal of Financial Economics, 3*(3), 305–360.

Kelton, A. S., & Yang, Y. (2008). The impact of corporate governance on internet financial reporting. *Journal of Accounting and Public Policy, 27,* 62–87.

Klein, A. (2002). Audit committee, board of director characteristics, and earnings management. *Journal of Accounting and Economics, 33,* 375–400.

Lang, M., & Lundholm, R. (1993). Cross-sectional determinants of analyst ratings of corporate disclosures. *Journal of Accounting Research, 31*(2), 246–271.

Leftwich, R. W., Watts, R. L., & Zimmerman, J. L. (1981). Voluntary corporate disclosure: The case of interim reporting. *Journal of Accounting Research, 19*(Suppl.), 50–77.

Leung, S., & Horwitz, B. (2004). Director ownership and voluntary segment disclosure: Hong Kong evidence. *Journal of International Financial Management and Accounting, 15,* 235–260.

Lev, B. (1992). Information disclosure strategy. *California Management Review, 34,* 9–32.

Lim, S., Matolcsy, Z., & Chow, D. (2007). The association between board composition and different types of voluntary disclosure. *European Accounting Review, 16*(3), 555–583.

Malone, D., Fries, C., & Jones, T. (1993). An empirical investigation of the extent of corporate financial disclosure in the oil and gas industry. *Journal of Accounting, Auditing and Finance, 8*(3), 249–273.

Mangena, M., & Tauringana, V. (2008). Audit committees and voluntary external auditor involvement in UK interim reporting. *International Journal of Auditing, 12*(1), 45–63.

McKinnon, J. L., & Dalimunthe, L. (1993). Voluntary disclosure of segment information by Australian diversified companies. *Accounting and Finance, 33*(1), 33–50.

McMullen, D. A. (1996). Audit committee performance: An investigation of the consequences associated with audit committee. *Auditing, 15,* 87–103.

Meek, G. K., Roberts, C. B., & Gray, S. J. (1995). Factors influencing voluntary annual report disclosures by U.S., U.K. and Continental European multinational corporations. *Journal of International Business Studies, 26*(3), 555–572.

Mitchell, J. D., Chia, C. W. L., & Loh, A. S. (1995). Voluntary disclosure of segment information: Further Australian evidence. *Accounting and Finance, 35*(2), 1–16.

Mitton, T. (2002). A cross-firm analysis of the impact of corporate governance on the East Asian financial crisis. *Journal of Financial Economics*, *64*(2), 215–241.

Nowland, J. (2008). The effect of national governance codes on firm disclosure practices: Evidence from analyst earnings forecasts. *Corporate Governance: An International Review*, *16*(6), 475–491.

Patelli, L., & Prencipe, A. (2007). The relationship between voluntary disclosure and independent directors in the presence of a dominant shareholder. *European Accounting Review*, *16*(1), 5–33.

Raffournier, B. (1995). The determinants of voluntary financial disclosure by Swiss listed companies. *European Accounting Review*, *4*(2), 261–280.

Ross, S. A. (1977). The determination of financial structure: The Incentive-signalling approach. *The Bell Journal of Economics*, *8*(1), 23–40.

Samaha, K. (2005). *International accounting standards in an emerging capital market: A study of compliance and factors explaining compliance in listed Egyptian companies*. Unpublished Ph.D. thesis, University of Manchester, UK.

Samaha, K., & Stapleton, P. (2008). Compliance with international accounting standards in a national context: Some empirical evidence from the Cairo and Alexandria stock exchanges. *Afro-Asian Journal of Finance and Accounting*, *1*(1), 40–66.

Samaha, K., & Stapleton, P. (2009). Firm specific determinants of the extent of compliance with International Accounting Standards in the Corporate annual reports of companies listed on the Egyptian stock exchange: A positive accounting approach. *Afro-Asian Journal of Finance and Accounting*, *1*(3), 266–294.

Schadewitz, H. J., & Blevins, D. R. (1998). Major determinants of interim disclosures in an emerging market. *American Business Review*, *16*(1), 41–55.

Schipper, K. (1981). Discussion of voluntary corporate disclosure: The case of interim reporting. *Journal of Accounting Research*, *19*(3), 85–88.

Singhvi, S. S., & Desai, H. B. (1971). An empirical analysis of the quality of corporate financial disclosure. *Accounting Review*, *46*(1), 129–139.

Skinner, D. J. (1994). Why firms voluntarily disclose bad news. *Journal of Accounting Research*, *32*(1), 38–60.

Titman, S., & Trueman, B. (1986). Information quality and the valuation of new issues. *Journal of Accounting and Economics*, *8*(4), 159–172.

Wallace, R. S. O., & Naser, K. (1995). Firm-specific determinants of comprehensiveness of mandatory disclosure in the corporate annual reports of firms on the stock exchange of Hong Kong. *Journal of Accounting and Public Policy*, *14*(4), 311–368.

Wang, K. O. S., & Cleiborne, M. C. (2008). Determinants and consequences of voluntary disclosure in an emerging market: Evidence from China. *Journal of International Accounting, Auditing and Taxation*, *17*(1), 14–30.

Weir, C., & Laing, D. (2003). Ownership structure, board composition and the market for corporate control in the UK: An empirical analysis. *Applied Economics*, *35*, 1747–1759.

Zarzeski, M. T. (1996). Spontaneous harmonization effects of culture and market forces on accounting disclosure practices. *Accounting Horizons*, *10*(1), 18–37.

ANALYSIS OF THE DETERMINANTS OF CORPORATE SOCIAL RESPONSIBILITY DISCLOSURE IN THE ANNUAL REPORTS OF TUNISIAN LISTED FIRMS

Souhir Khemir and Chedli Baccouche

ABSTRACT

Purpose – *This study's purpose is twofold. First, we assess the extent of corporate social responsibility disclosure. Second, we investigate the determinants of the decision to disclose social responsibility information.*

Methodology/approach – *This research focuses on analyzing corporate social responsibility disclosure through the annual reports of 23 Tunisian listed firms over a four-year period from 2001 to 2004. A multivariate analysis of social responsibility disclosure is employed to test the factors influencing this type of disclosure.*

Findings – *The findings in this study suggest that corporate social responsibility disclosure did increase from 2001 to 2004 and disclosure was primarily literal and regarding products. Results also suggest that a firm's internationalization degree, their debt level, and the degree of their*

Research in Accounting in Emerging Economies, Volume 10, 119–144
Copyright © 2010 by Emerald Group Publishing Limited
All rights of reproduction in any form reserved
ISSN: 1479-3563/doi:10.1108/S1479-3563(2010)0000010010

political visibility are the significant factors influencing the decision of corporate social responsibility disclosure.

Research limitations and implications – *This study is subject to the usual limits of the content analysis method use. The small size of the sample, its composition, and its choice in a nonrandom way may make it suffer from selectivity bias.*

Originality/value – *This study contributes to the analysis of corporate social responsibility disclosure practices in an emerging country context by analyzing the nature of the trends in social responsibility disclosure practices and examining the impact of certain firm characteristics on such practices.*

Keywords: Corporate social responsibility disclosure; annual reports; determinants; Tunisian listed firms.

1. INTRODUCTION

The environmental and social degradations the world has seen these last decades are strengthening the emergence and the spread of the notion of corporate social responsibility. Such a notion has echoed in the business circle and has become an important stake. It means that companies are obliged, besides offering profits, to integrate the sociopolitical environment into their strategic steps, to manage their ethical and philanthropic responsibilities, as well as their economic activities. This implies an ability to answer to pressures both external and internal and to improve the company image in the eyes of its diverse stakeholders.

Conscious of the importance of this stake in assuring their long-term sustainability, several companies considered necessary the commitment to a social responsibility approach. One of the dimensions of this commitment is social responsibility disclosure in the same way as accounting and financial disclosure. Such a disclosure will allow the firms to defend their reputation and to account for their impact on the society and environment, to their various stakeholders. The number of companies which report on their social responsibility performance has considerably increased in past years. Using a European website[1] which identifies sustainability reporting companies, Igalens (2009) states that over the period 2004–2008, 20,000 reports were issued by 5,000 companies from 115 countries. Moreover, according to the GRI[2] website, more than 1,000 companies in the world have published sustainability reports based on the G3 guidelines in 2008, that is to say an increase of 26% from 2007. However, despite the importance of this particular disclosure type and the existence of some attempts at national and international standardization (like NRE law[3] in France, GRI guidelines), this one is voluntary and not subject to specific and obligatory standardization in different countries. Disparities exist between companies as regards the nature of the published information and its disclosure manner, and this is what attracted the researcher's interest in the accounting discipline. To that end, research by several different people concerning various corporate social responsibility disclosure aspects has been led. Some have tried to analyze and describe the nature and the extent of social responsibility information disclosed in a specific country during a definite period (Ernst & Ernst, 1978; Zeghal & Ahmed, 1990). Others have attempted to examine the explanatory factors, in absence of binding standardization, and succeeded in demonstrating that social responsibility disclosure depends on certain firm characteristics such as size, activity, sector, debt level, profitability (Cowen, Ferreri, & Parker, 1987; Patten, 1991, 1992; Roberts, 1991, 1992). The majority of these studies have focused on developed countries especially the United States and European countries (Ernst & Ernst, 1978; Patten, 1992; Gray, Kouhy, & Lavers, 1995a, 1995b; Oxibar, 2003, 2009; Dammak-Ayadi, 2004; Brammer & Pavelin, 2008; Reverte, 2009). Very little research has been led in emerging countries (Hackston & Milne, 1996; Hall, 2002; Haniffa & Cooke, 2005; Naser, Al-Hussaini, Al-Kwari, & Nuseibeh, 2006), in particular those of the Maghreb. Like these last ones, our study contributes to the analysis of corporate social responsibility disclosure practices in the Tunisian context. It consists of an explanatory descriptive study which seeks to assess the emergence level and the social responsibility information nature in the annual reports of Tunisian firms and tries to decline the explanatory factors. The choice of this context is justified by the desire to enrich the previous literature which was mainly based on Western countries. Thus, the studies that treated the determinants of social responsibility disclosure in the Maghreb countries were very rare or virtually absent. However, in Tunisia, these last years were marked by a growing interest on behalf of the state for environmental protection, conservation of the workers' rights, etc. Consequently, it will be interesting to examine the determinants of corporate social responsibility disclosure in this context in order to compare it with other countries. This study is organized as follows: in the first section, we present the theoretical framework and develop our hypotheses; the second section looks at the methodology pursued to test empirically the proposed hypotheses.

The results of statistical tests and their interpretations will be the object of the third section.

2. THEORETICAL FRAMEWORK AND HYPOTHESES DEVELOPMENT

2.1. Theoretical Framework

Given its discretionary character, corporate social responsibility disclosure was the subject of a multitude researches since the 1980s (Mathews, 1995). However, the most researches have been led in developed countries (Ernst & Ernst, 1978; Zeghal & Ahmed, 1990; Oxibar, 2003, 2009). Few studies have dealt with this theme in the emerging countries (Hackston & Milne, 1996; Haniffa & Cooke, 2005; Naser et al., 2006). The literature recognizes that social responsibility disclosure practices differ from country to country (Adams, Hill, & Roberts, 1998), particularly between developed and emerging ones (Imam, 2000 cited in Gao, Heravi, & Xiao, 2005).

Through their study, Ernst & Ernst (1978) examined the social responsibility information disclosed in the annual reports of US Fortune 500 companies. To measure social responsibility disclosure level, they used the content analysis method with the following categories: environment, energy, human resources, product, community involvement, ethical, and other, by making the distinction between monetary quantitative information, nonmonetary quantitative information, and qualitative information. This study has served as basis for many subsequent studies.

Zeghal and Ahmed (1990) led a multi-supports analysis to examine the social responsibility disclosure of 80 Canadian companies belonging to the petroleum and banking sector during 1981 and 1982. They referred to social responsibility information categories proposed by Ernst & Ernst (1978) and adapted them to the Canadian context and selected industries. By establishing an interindustry and intersupports comparison, they observed that the information concerning the human resources is the first theme of disclosure for both sectors, coming after the information on products, loyal business practices for banks, and implication in the civil society and environment for the oil companies. They concluded that advertising does not constitute a major vehicle of social responsibility disclosure while brochures are widely used for such disclosure by banks and oil companies.

In order to analyze and to identify the determinants of social responsibility disclosure in the annual reports as well as in the websites, Oxibar (2003, 2009) has developed an analysis grille with the following categories: environment, human resources, product, civil society, ethical business relationships, and others. The application of the grille on a sample of 49 French listed companies during the year 2000 shows that the social responsibility disclosure level seems low, that the environment is the major theme disclosed, and that the information communicated is essentially literal. The results of the multiple regressions indicate that the degree of political visibility positively influences environmental and civil society disclosures in the annual reports. However, the debt level and the capital dilution are negatively related to the environmental disclosure in the annual reports, while the presence of a structure for social responsibility positively affects the disclosure relative to civil society and ethical business relations.

In the New Zealand context, Hackston and Milne (1996) examined the social responsibility disclosure practices in the annual reports of 47 large companies and tried to identify potential determinants. They concluded that firm size, activity sector, and listing status are determinants of the social responsibility disclosure strategies in New Zealand.

Haniffa and Cooke (2005) studied the social responsibility disclosure extent in the annual reports of Malaysian nonfinancial listed companies and its association with culture and corporate governance. Consistent with previous studies, they used the content analysis method to measure social responsibility disclosure in annual reports by defining the following categories: environment, human resources, product, community, and added value. They find significant differences in the social responsibility disclosure extent during 1996 and 2002. The results indicate a significant relationship between the social responsibility disclosure and boards dominated by Malay directors, boards dominated by executive directors, chairs with multiple directorships, and foreign ownership. Firm size, profitability, multiple listings, and activity sector are significantly related to corporate social responsibility disclosure.

To test the validity of the theories used by previous researches in explaining variations in the voluntary disclosure extent and more specifically in the social responsibility disclosure, Naser et al. (2006) conducted an analysis of the social responsibility information contained in the annual reports of 21 Qatarian listed companies. Their findings lend a partial support to the agency theory, to the political economy theory, and to the legitimacy theory. They conclude that these theories gain more support in developed than in developing economies. The stakeholder theory seems for them the most relevant approach. They indicate that the change in the corporate social responsibility disclosure is associated with firm size, business risk, and the corporate growth. However, the proportion of institutional investors, dispersion of individual investors, and government property has a little impact on the social responsibility disclosure of Qatarian companies.

2.2. Hypotheses Development

We propose to refer to the positive accounting theory and to the stakeholder theory for the formulation of our research hypotheses. According to the positive accounting theory, social responsibility disclosure constitutes a mean used by managers to reduce agency costs (Jensen & Meckling, 1976). It allows them to defend their interests and to demonstrate to the shareholders their management effectiveness. This is a positive response to the social pressures and is likely to prevent the regulatory authorities' intervention in the conduct of corporate activities. The stakeholder theory considers social responsibility disclosure as a means to answer the pressures of a varied set of individuals who are related to the company via explicit or implicit contracts, and therefore allowing the transfer of social, political, and economic message to divers recipients. Previous studies have shown that social responsibility disclosure may be explained by a variety of firm characteristics. The hypotheses of the present study concern the association between social responsibility disclosure and five characteristics of the firm, namely the economic performance, the capital structure, the internationalization degree, the debt level, and the political visibility.

2.2.1. Economic Performance Hypothesis
Several studies have analyzed the relationship between economic performance and corporate social responsibility disclosure. However, their findings are mixed. Indeed, Cowen et al. (1987), Belkaoui and Karpik (1989), Patten (1991), Hackston and Milne (1996), and Oxibar (2003, 2009) do not succeed in establishing a relationship between social responsibility disclosure and economic performance. Freedman and Jaggi (1998), by analyzing the relationship between social responsibility disclosure and economic performance for different sizes of companies working in industries related to the environment, find a positive and significant relation. Using the same kind of idea, Roberts (1992) demonstrated that social responsibility disclosure made by American firms is strongly influenced by the average of the annual changes of returns on equity (ROE). Similarly, Cormier and Magnan (1999)

found a significant positive relationship between ratio of return on assets (ROA) and environmental disclosure of Canadian companies subject to the regulation on water pollution. Hence, it is assumed that

H₁. There is an association between the firm's economic performance and its social responsibility disclosure practices.

2.2.2. Capital Structure Hypothesis

Some capital characteristics such as its level of dispersion or concentration were correlated with corporate social responsibility disclosure level. Indeed, conflicts of interests appear between shareholders and managers due to the separation of ownership and management of the company. Roberts (1992) supposes the existence of a positive association between corporate owner-ship dispersion and social responsibility disclosure practices. He predicted that when the ownership becomes more dispersed, stakeholder's pressure for social responsibility disclosure increases. However, no significant effect was detected by the results which he found. Oxibar (2003, 2009) obtained a negative relationship between capital dispersion, environmental disclosure, and product disclosure in annual reports. Yet, no relationship was identified with the disclosure on the human resources and the civil society. Therefore, we anticipate that

H₂. There is an association between the firm's capital dispersion and its social responsibility disclosure practices.

2.2.3. Internationalization Degree Hypothesis

Social responsibility disclosure varies across business locations (Pelle Culpin, 1998; Belkaoui & Karpik, 1989). Indeed, a company operating worldwide does not have the same interlocutors as a company operating on the national level. Thus, the presence in the foreign markets leads companies to consider the needs of various stakeholders which differ according to country. Branco and Rodrigues (2008) supposed the existence of a positive relationship between the firm's internationalization degree activities and its social responsibility disclosure practices. Dammak-Ayadi (2004) tested the existence of a positive relationship between the internationalization degree and the social reports publication. Thus, it is expected that

H₃. There is a positive association between the firm's internationalization degree activities and its social responsibility disclosure practices.

2.2.4. Debt Level Hypothesis

By examining the relationship between the ratio of total debt to total assets and social responsibility disclosure, Belkaoui and Karpik (1989) succeeded in demonstrating that the more the company is indebted, the less it discloses social responsibility information. The results which they have found support the hypothesis that a high debt ratio is negatively associated with social responsibility disclosure. Cormier and Magnan (1999) showed that the debt ratio has a significant negative influence on the environmental disclosure. Oxibar (2003, 2009) found a negative relationship between the company's debt level and environmental disclosure in annual reports. On the other hand, Roberts (1992) considers that the debt can encourage companies to lead social activities and to be positive as regards the information disclosed to satisfy the creditors' expectations in terms of its social role. He suggests a positive relationship between the company's debt level and its social responsibility disclosure level. In this regard, we think that

H_4. There is an association between the firm's debt level and its social responsibility disclosure practices.

2.2.5. Political Visibility Hypothesis

The variables related to firm size are frequently used as of political visibility. Cowen et al. (1987) succeed in demonstrating that a firm's size significantly impacts its disclosure about the environment and energy. They consider that large companies are usually the subject of big attention from the public; this exposes them to a higher pressure with regard to social responsibility disclosure. Similarly, Hackston and Milne (1996) obtained a significant positive association between firm size and social responsibility disclosure level in the New Zealand context. Also, Belkaoui and Karpik (1989) and Patten (1991) showed that firm size has a positive and significant influence on social responsibility disclosure. Oxibar (2003, 2009) demonstrates that political visibility apprehended by the total assets has a positive influence on disclosure about the environment and civil society in annual reports. Dammak-Ayadi (2004) has examined the firm size influence on the social reports publication, however, she could not specify the sign of its influence. Branco and Rodrigues (2008) stipulate that big companies consider social responsibility disclosure as a means to improve their reputation. They demonstrate that firm size has a positive influence on social responsibility disclosure in annual reports and websites. Thus, these studies have shown a positive relationship between firm size and social responsibility disclosure.

Consequently, it is assumed that

H₅. There is a positive association between the degree of a firm's political visibility and its social responsibility disclosure practices.

3. METHODOLOGY

3.1. Sample Selection

To better understand the determinants of social responsibility disclosure in the Tunisian context, we used a sample of 23 nonfinancial firms listed on the Tunisian Stock Exchange covering the period 2001–2004, and totaling 92 firm-year observations. Listed firms are supposed to be more attentive to their disclosures in annual reports. We have not considered banks and leasing and insurance companies, since they have an atypical financial structure. To get variety in disclosure level, a large sample is preferable. Nevertheless, at the time of study, only 24 nonfinancial companies are listed on the Tunisian Stock Exchange. Moreover, combining cross-sectional and time series observations, panel data, used in several studies (Gao et al., 2005; Aerts, Cormier, & Magnan, 2006), provide more information and less collinearity among variables. The purpose of using panel data is to increase the number of the observations and to better analyze the trends of corporate social responsibility disclosure over time.[4]

Table 1 lists the number of firms by activity sector.

The data used for our empirical study was collected from the annual reports of selected companies. This choice is justified by the desire to be consistent with the previous studies which makes comparisons relatively easy.

3.2. Measuring of Variables

3.2.1. Measuring of the Variable to Explain

Like previous studies (Ernst & Ernst, 1978; Abbott & Monsen, 1979; Guthrie & Mathews, 1985; Zeghal & Ahmed, 1990; Hackston & Milne, 1996; Oxibar, 2003, 2009), the content analysis method is used to approximate the nature and the level of social responsibility disclosure contained in annual reports of Tunisian listed firms. The different categories used for the social responsibility disclosure analysis are the environment,

Table 1. Distribution of Firms by Activity Sector.

Activity Sector	Number of Firms
Agro-food	3
Automobiles and equipment	4
Building and building materials	3
Industrial goods and services	3
Chemistry	3
Oil and gas	1
Household products and personal care	2
Health	1
Telecommunication	1
Air transport	2
Total	23

human resources, product, and community involvement. Those are extracted from the categories list developed by Ernst & Ernst (1978) and the one adapted by Hackston and Milne (1996) in the New Zealand context. At the same time, sentences are selected as a measure unit of social responsibility disclosure. This choice is justified by the fact that they can be counted with more accuracy than words, and they can overcome the problem of size, margin, and graphics inclusion that are inherent in the use of pages portions (Hackston & Milne, 1996). Finally, we propose to retain the following forms of social responsibility information: literal, monetary quantitative, and nonmonetary quantitative as analysis dimensions of social responsibility disclosure according with previous researches (Guthrie & Parker, 1990; Hackston & Milne, 1996; Hall, 2002; Oxibar, 2003, 2009).

3.2.2. Measuring of Explanatory Variables
Table 2 shows the measures of explanatory variables.

3.3. The Study Model

To analyze the relationship between firm characteristics mentioned above and social responsibility disclosure level, we will test the following empirical model:

$$\text{DIVS}_{it} = \beta_{it} + \beta_1(\text{ROE})_{it} + \beta_2(\text{ROA})_{it} + \beta_3(\text{STRC})_{it} + \beta_4(\text{DIT})_{it}$$
$$+ \beta_5(\text{END})_{it} + \beta_6(\text{VA})_{it} + \beta_7(\text{VCA})_{it} + \varepsilon_{it}.$$

Table 2. Measures of Explanatory Variables.

Explanatory Variable	Measures Proposed in the Previous Literature	Measures Selected
Economic performance	• Return on equity (ROE) (Patten, 1991; Roberts, 1992; Oxibar, 2003, 2009; Dammak-Ayadi, 2004) • Return on assets (ROA) (Patten, 1991; Dammak-Ayadi, 2004; Brammer & Pavelin, 2008; Branco & Rodrigues, 2008; Reverte, 2009) • Net income/sales (Dammak-Ayadi, 2004)	ROE and ROA
Capital structure	• 1 – percentage of 5% or more of capital held by shareholders • STRC = [1 − $\sum$(percentage of capital held by institutional investors (ACTINS), percentage of capital held by the state (ACTETAT), percentage of capital held by employees (ACTSAL), percentage of capital held by family shareholders (ACTFAM))] (Oxibar, 2003, 2009)	STRC = [1 − $\sum$(ACTINS, ACTETAT, ACTSAL, ACTFAM)]
Degree of Internationalization	• Number of host country • Part of sales made abroad (Dammak-Ayadi, 2004; Branco & Rodrigues, 2008)	Part of sales made abroad
Debt level	• Financial debt/total assets (Oxibar, 2003, 2009) • Total debt/total assets (Belkaoui & Karpik, 1989; Brammer & Pavelin, 2008; Branco & Rodrigues, 2008)	Total debt to total assets ratio
Political visibility	• Total assets (Hackston & Milne, 1996; Branco & Rodrigues, 2008) • Sales (Belkaoui & Karpik, 1989; Hackston & Milne, 1996) • Market capitalization (Hackston & Milne, 1996) • Number of employees, logarithm of number of employees ...	Logarithm of total assets and logarithm of sales

where:

DIVS: the number of sentences of total social responsibility disclosure including all information relating to the environment (ENVT), the human resources (HR), the product (TDP) and community involvement (IMPL);
β_{it} and β_i: coefficients;
ROE: net income/average stockholders' equity;
ROA: net income/average total assets;
STRC: $[1-\sum(ACTINS, ACTETAT, ACTSAL, ACTFAM)]$;
DIT: sales realized in the foreign countries/total sales;
END: total debts/total assets;
VA: logarithm of total assets;
VCA: logarithm of sales;
ε_{it}: error term.

The indices i and t correspond, respectively, to the company and to the period of study.

4. PRESENTATION AND ANALYSIS OF THE RESULTS

4.1. The Results of Descriptive Analysis

4.1.1. Description of Social Responsibility Disclosure Level
In what follows, we proceed to describe the volume, the themes, and the forms of social responsibility disclosure. Table 3 below presents the themes of social responsibility disclosure in number of sentences and in percentage of total social responsibility disclosure.

Table 3. Corporate Social Responsibility Disclosure by Themes.

Theme	2001		2002		2003		2004	
	NP	%	NP	%	NP	%	NP	%
Environment	27	11.20	34	10.49	39	12.42	38	13.87
Human resources	83	34.44	115	35.49	111	35.35	96	35.04
Product	93	38.59	154	47.53	128	40.76	121	44.16
Community involvement	38	15.77	21	6.48	36	11.46	19	6.93
Total	241	100	324	100	314	100	274	100

NP, number of sentences; %, percentage of total social responsibility disclosure.

It appears that the social responsibility disclosure level via annual reports registers an increase of 33 sentences in 2004 compared to 2001. However, the comparison of this disclosure level through the four years reveals disparities. An increase was registered during 2002, and it is also the largest gain registered during the period of study. This level was almost maintained during 2003, while in 2004, we observed a decrease of 40 sentences. Fig. 1 shows the evolution of the social responsibility disclosure for four years.

Differences in the disclosure practices appear through the years and according to companies. While some companies are aware of the potential importance of the social responsibility disclosure, others are not and are rather reluctant to disclose. Figs. 2 and 3 give an overview of the disclosure trends for the various categories of social responsibility information, respectively, in number of sentences and in percentage of total disclosure.

Product is the main theme of social responsibility disclosure. It represents 38.59% of the total social responsibility disclosure in 2001 and 44.16% in 2004, followed by the themes related to human resources with 34.44% of the total social responsibility disclosure in 2001 and 35.04% in 2004, succeeded by the environment with 11.20% of the total volume of social responsibility information disclosed in 2001, and 13.87% in 2004. The information relative to community involvement represents only 6.93% of social responsibility information disclosed in annual reports in 2004.

Table 4 shows the forms of social responsibility information disclosed in number of sentences and in percentage of total social disclosure.

According to this table, we note the essentially literal nature of the social responsibility information disclosed. It represents 63.49% and 68.25% of total social responsibility disclosure, in 2001 and 2004 respectively. The

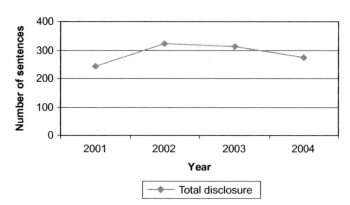

Fig. 1. Corporate Social Responsibility Disclosure Level in Number of Sentences.

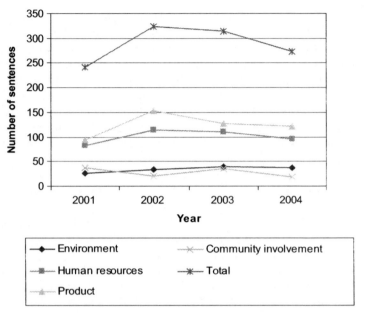

Fig. 2. Corporate Social Responsibility Disclosure by Themes in Number of Sentences.

firms rarely employ the monetary quantitative form in their disclosures; this form represents only 11.62% and 12.04% of the total social responsibility disclosure in 2001 and 2004, respectively. Social responsibility disclosure levels under the nonmonetary quantitative form are relatively low; they represent 24.90% and 19.71% of the social information disclosed, in 2001 and 2004 respectively. Figs. 4 and 5 show the trends of social responsibility disclosure by forms measured in terms of number of sentences disclosed and by percentage of the total social responsibility disclosure.

Thus, we observe that the studied companies seem to privilege the literal form compared to two other forms of social responsibility disclosure. These observations are consistent with those of the previous studies. These studies emphasized the predominance of literal form compared to the other monetary and nonmonetary quantitative form (Zeghal & Ahmed, 1990; Hackston & Milne, 1996; Oxibar, 2003, 2009).

4.1.2. Descriptive Statistics for the Variables of the Model
The sample shows the distribution characteristics summarized in Table 5.

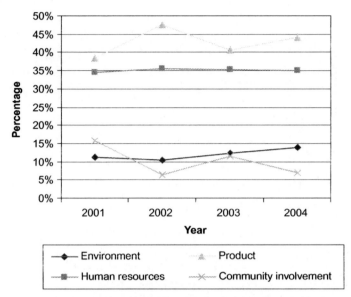

Fig. 3. Corporate Social Responsibility Disclosure by Themes in Percentage of Total Social Responsibility Disclosure.

Table 4. Corporate Social Responsibility Disclosure by Forms of Information.

Form	2001		2002		2003		2004	
	NP	%	NP	%	NP	%	NP	%
Literal	153	63.49	218	67.28	202	64.33	187	68.25
Nonmonetary quantitative	60	24.90	75	23.15	70	22.29	54	19.71
Monetary quantitative	28	11.62	31	9.57	42	13.38	33	12.04
Total	241	100	324	100	314	100	274	100

NP, number of sentences; %, percentage of total social responsibility disclosure.

The results from the table of the descriptive statistics show that companies disclose on average 12.28 sentences about social responsibility information in their annual reports from 2001 to 2004 including 1.5 sentences about their environmental actions, 4.15 sentences on their human resources, 5.39 sentences on their products, and 1.23 sentences on their community involvement. At the least they do not disclose any information, while at

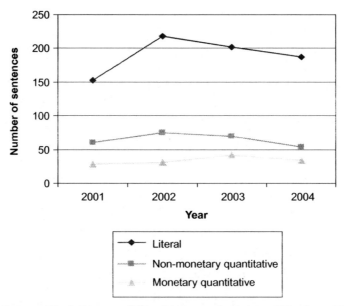

Fig. 4.   Forms of Social Responsibility Disclosure in Terms of Number of Sentences
Disclosed.

the maximum, they communicate 49 sentences about total social responsibility disclosure, 12 sentences about environment, 24 sentences about human resources, 39 sentences about product, and 18 sentences about community involvement. This indicates that the social responsibility disclosure level is generally even lower. On average, the ROE is equal to −0.2160, varying between −30.88 and 1.917. Moreover, the average of the ROA is equal to 0.018, varying between −24.92 and 18.01. Thus, the selected companies have low performance. The capital structure presents a minimum of 0.010, a maximum of 0.860, and an average of 0.432; this points to the variability of the ownership structures of the firms of the sample. On average, the internationalization degree is equal to 0.11; the lowest value is 0 because of the existence of certain companies whose activities do not exceed the Tunisian territory. The maximum value is 0.861; this is due to the presence of some others who invest more in activities oriented toward other countries. The average of debt to total assets ratio is equal to 0.663, and it is relatively high. At the lowest it is equal to zero and at most, it is 8.622. Finally, the two political visibility variables VA and VCA are high; their respective averages are 7.62 and 7.45.

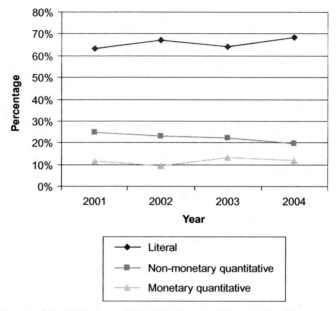

Fig. 5. Forms of Social Responsibility Disclosure Measured in Percentage of Total Social Responsibility Disclosure.

Table 5. Descriptive Statistics.

Variables	Mean	Standard Deviation	Minimum	Maximum
DIVS	12.282	12.991	0	49
ENVT	1.5	2.906	0	12
RH	4.152	5.745	0	24
PDT	5.391	6.801	0	39
IMPL	1.239	2.806	0	18
ROE	−0.216	3.245	−30.880	1.917
ROA	0.018	3.541	−24.921	18.013
STRC	0.432	0.232	0.010	0.860
DIT	0.110	0.210	0	0.861
END	0.663	1.120	0	8.622
VA	7.622	0.455	6.076	9.128
VCA	7.459	0.512	5.811	8.916

DIVS, total social responsibility disclosure; ENVT, environmental disclosure; RH, human resources disclosure; PDT, product disclosure; IMPL, community involvement disclosure; ROE, return on equity; ROA, return on assets; STRC, capital structure; DIT, internationalization degree; END, debt level; VCA, logarithm of sales; VA, logarithm of total assets.

4.2. The Results of Multivariate Analysis

4.2.1. The Test's Results on the Quality of the Model

To estimate our model, we use econometric estimation techniques of the panel data applied to the Poisson distribution. This estimation method, in addition to the fact that it takes into account the dependent variable nature (discrete variable, variable of counting), allows us to specify whether the observed individual effect for each firm is fixed or random. As indicated by the estimation results presented in Table 6 below, the fixed effect model provides statistically better results than the random effect model, according to the Hausman test (1978).

Indeed, for the total social responsibility disclosure as well as for its different categories, the test probabilities are lower than 10% implying that the fixed effect model is preferable to the random effect model (this interpretation is specific to the results provided by the software).

4.2.2. Results of the Multiple Regression Tests

Table 7 below reports the results of multiple regression procedure used to study the association between the total social responsibility disclosure level (DIVS) and its different categories, namely the environmental disclosure (ENVT), the human resources disclosure (RH), the product disclosure (PDT), the community involvement disclosure (IMPL), and some firms' characteristics that are supposed to influence them.

Table 6. Hausman Test Results.

Dependent Variable	Hausman Test
DIVS	Chi-square $= 19.76$ p-value $= 0.0053$
ENVT	Chi-square $= 13.59$ p-value $= 0.0932$
RH	Chi-square $= 15.83$ p-value $= 0.0448$
PDT	Chi-square $= 27.46$ p-value $= 0.0006$
IMPL	Chi-square $= 30.02$ p-value $= 0.0002$

DIVS, total social responsibility disclosure; ENVT, environmental disclosure; RH, human resources disclosure; PDT, product disclosure; IMPL, community involvement disclosure.

Table 7. Results of Multiple Regression Relative to the Societal Disclosure and its Various Categories.

Variables	Expected Sign	DIVS	ENVT	RH	PDT	IMPL
ROE	+	0.485	0.708	−0.460	0.616	6.943*
ROA	+	−0.065	−0.151	−0.2**	−0.054	0.506*
STRC	+	−0.229	0.633	0.073	−1.873**	4.570**
DIT	+	8.282***	11.698**	11.127***	6.865***	28.003**
END	±	0.575***	1.282*	0.814**	0.448*	−0.640
VCA	+	3.445***	9.785***	2.243	3.682**	−4.699
VA	+	0.382	0.721	1.549**	0.299	−3.508*
2 log-likelihood		−182.171	52.309	−89.752	−152.380	−45.192
Value of chi-square		79.82	22.45	22.00	39.67	16.54
Significance		0.0000	0.0041	0.0049	0.0000	0.0352

DIVS, total social responsibility disclosure; ENVT, environmental disclosure; RH, human resources disclosure; PDT, product disclosure; IMPL, community involvement disclosure; ROE, return on equity; ROA, return on assets; STRC, capital structure; DIT, internationalization degree; END, debt level; VCA, logarithm of sales; VA, logarithm of total assets.
***Significant at a 1% level, **Significant at a 5% level, *Significant at a 10% level.

Interpretation of Multiple Regression Tests Results by Social Responsibility Disclosure Categories. As mentioned in the table above, all chi-square values with the exception of the one relating to community involvement disclosure are significant at a 1% level, allowing us to conclude that the different models contribute in explaining the total social responsibility disclosure and its different categories.

• Total social responsibility disclosure
  The model concerning the total social responsibility disclosure is strongly significant, it presents a very important explanatory power, and it has the highest chi-square value of 79.82. The results of the multiple regression showed that the total social responsibility disclosure level is significantly influenced by the firm's degree of internationalization activities, its debt level, and its degree of political visibility. In contrast, neither the variables used for the operationalization of economic performance nor for the capital structure are significant; consequently, the total social responsibility disclosure of Tunisian firms does not depend either on their economic performance or their capital structure.

• Environmental disclosure
  By reasoning in terms of explanatory power, the model concerning the environmental disclosure is classified third with a relatively low chi-square

value (22.45). As it has been obtained for the total social responsibility disclosure, economic performance and capital structure do not present significant impact on the environmental disclosure in annual reports of Tunisian companies. However, the firm's degree of internationalization activities is significantly associated with the environmental disclosure at a 1% level. This is in compliance with the predictions. Similarly, the debt ratio is significantly and positively related to the environmental disclosure at a 10% level. Finally, only one of the two measures proposed to approximate the political visibility which is the logarithm of sales (VAC) presents a significant and positive impact on the environmental disclosure level to a risk level of 1%.

- Human resources disclosure
  By comparing it to those obtained for the total social responsibility disclosure and the environmental disclosure, the chi-square value of the human resources model seems the weakest (22.00). However, it is significant at a 1% level. The results of the multiple regression analysis underline that the economic performance measures are negatively correlated to the human resources disclosure level. The ROA is significant at a 5% level. As for the total social responsibility disclosure and for the environmental disclosure, capital structure has no significant influence on the human resources disclosure. According to the results found for the environmental disclosure, the human resources disclosure appears higher for firms with an important degree of internationalization and debt level.

- Product disclosure
  This model comes just after the total social responsibility disclosure model with a chi-square value of 39.67. For this social responsibility disclosure category, we find that economic performance does not seem to be an explanatory factor. However, in addition to internationalization degree, debt level and a firm's degree of political visibility which affect positively and significantly the product disclosure, we have obtained that the capital structure also affects the disclosure relating to the product but in the opposite sense to what was expected.

- Community involvement disclosure
  While the model presents the lowest explanatory power compared to the other models with a chi-square value of 16.54, it is significant at a 5% level. It also has the best adjustment quality (the lowest maximum likelihood value (45.22)). Contrary to what has been previously found,

community involvement disclosure does not seem affected by debt level. On the contrary, it appears positively and significantly influenced by the degree of internationalization, economic performance, and capital structure. Finally, we notice that the two political visibility measures present negative correlation coefficients with the community involvement disclosure. The negative relationship found is significant for the variable logarithm of total assets (VA) at a 10% level.

Interpretation of Multiple Regression Tests Results by Hypotheses. The results of multiple regression tests showed that the internationalization degree, the debt level, and the political visibility degree are determinants of social responsibility disclosure in the annual reports of Tunisian firms. On the other hand, the impact of economic performance and the capital structure have not been demonstrated. Thus, only hypotheses H3, H4, and H5 are validated.

- Internationalization degree hypothesis
  This hypothesis has been validated at a 1% level. Contrary to Dammak-Ayadi (2004) and Branco and Rodrigues (2008) who do not demonstrate the influence of the degree of internationalization on the social responsibility disclosure decisions, it was found that the firm's degree of internationalization activities positively influences its social responsibility disclosure practices with its different categories. Indeed, the Tunisian listed firms having developed their activities abroad are interested in improving their reputation and their image in the international market. They must satisfy the expectations of foreign investors who often present increased demands for social responsibility information compared to local investors. This pushes them to consider these different expectations during the establishment of their annual reports.

- Debt level hypothesis
  Debt level is an explanatory factor of the total social responsibility disclosure and all its categories with the exception of community involvement. Indeed, in Tunisia, firms with high debt level disclosed social responsibility information to appear as corporate citizens and to attract present and potential creditors. Thus, in order to give a good image among fund providers, Tunisian firms are incited to disclose more information about their social responsibility actions. Consequently, more firms have appealed to the debt to finance their projects, and more managers are brought to disclose information about their social

responsibility, in order to satisfy the creditors' expectations. The findings differ with those of Belkaoui and Karpik (1989), Cormier and Magnan (1999), and Oxibar (2003, 2009) who obtained a negative association.

- Political visibility hypothesis
  This hypothesis was verified at a 1% level. Consistent with the results of Cowen et al. (1987), Belkaoui and Karpik (1989), Patten (1991), Hackston and Milne (1996), Oxibar (2003, 2009), and Branco and Rodrigues (2008), we can conclude that the political visibility level seems determinant of the total social responsibility and all its categories. Previous studies conducted in developed and developing countries demonstrate the influence of political visibility on corporate social responsibility disclosure practices. In general, large firms are exposed to greater attention from the public than the smaller ones and therefore are exposed to greater pressure for social responsibility disclosure. Also, this type of disclosure seems less costly for them. Thus, managers rationalize the allocation of space within annual reports for the various categories of social responsibility information according to the rival pressures which direct their disclosure choices. In Tunisia, large firms use the stock exchange to consolidate their presence in the financial market. They will receive special attention from various stakeholders who wish to invest, therefore, they make use of corporate social responsibility disclosure to develop their notoriety.

- Economic performance hypothesis
  The hypothesis relative to the economic performance has not been validated either for the total social responsibility disclosure or for two of its categories, namely environmental and product disclosure. Cowen et al. (1987), Belkaoui and Karpik (1989), Patten (1991), Hackston and Milne (1996), and Oxibar (2003, 2009) also have not demonstrated the impact of economic performance on corporate social responsibility disclosure. This may come from methodological deficiencies relating to the operationalization of economic performance.

  However, this hypothesis was verified in a negative sense for the human resources disclosure and in a positive sense for the community involvement disclosure. Thus, we can maintain that economic performance has no significant impact on the social responsibility disclosure practices of Tunisian firms; this means that in Tunisia, the social responsibility disclosure policies are conducted independently of economic performance.

- Capital structure hypothesis

  As in Roberts (1992) and Oxibar (2003, 2009), the hypothesis relative to the capital structure has not been confirmed either for the total social responsibility disclosure or for the environmental and the human resources disclosure. However, we find that capital structure is negatively correlated with product disclosure and positively associated with community involvement disclosure. Thus, we can argue that capital structure has no significant influence on the social responsibility disclosure decisions in the annual reports of Tunisian firms. Consequently, we reject the hypothesis H2, which stipulates that the firms with diluted capital are supposed to be confronted to increased social information demands, and that is why they make corporate social responsibility disclosures.

5. CONCLUSION

The main objective of this study is to analyze empirically the nature of the trends in the social responsibility disclosure practices in the annual reports of a sample of Tunisian listed firms during the four years from 2001 to 2004, and to examine the impact of certain firm characteristics on such practices. This analysis shows that social responsibility disclosure in Tunisia is still in a precarious state. Although it has been marked by an increase from 2001 to 2004, its level remains low in any given year. The most disclosed theme is the product, followed by human resources, environment, and community involvement. Disclosures are mainly literal. The status of these practices can be explained by the voluntary character of social responsibility disclosure in Tunisia, which depends essentially only on the diligence of managers who are generally unaware of its importance. The study results support a significant positive association between social responsibility disclosure level and firm's degree of internationalization activities, its debt level and its degree of political visibility. Such an association is found for different social responsibility disclosure categories with the exception of community involvement. The findings also indicate that neither the economic performance nor capital structure is considered as explanatory factors of the total social responsibility disclosure. These results converge in part with those found in developed countries and do not reveal specific trends in emerging countries. This study is subject to the usual limits of the content analysis method use. Indeed, the subjective nature of this method's results has been widely criticized in previous researches. Also, the use of only annual reports for analyzing the social responsibility disclosure constitutes another limit. Finally, the small size of the sample, its composition, and its choice in a nonrandom way may make it suffer from selectivity bias. In future researches, we suggest conducting similar studies on large samples selected randomly and including listed and unlisted companies belonging to sectors more sensitive to social responsibility issues. Large samples provide the opportunity for examining other determinants of social responsibility disclosure such as internal determinants to the company and specific determinants to emerging countries. We also suggest the use of disclosure means other than annual reports such as brochures, leaflets, articles published in the press, websites, etc., in order to obtain a more complete vision of the corporate social responsibility disclosure strategies.

NOTES

1. www.sustainabilityreporting.eu/uk/index.htm
2. The Global Reporting Initiative (GRI) is an international institution created in 1997 by the Coalition of Environmentally Responsible Economics (CERES) with the United Nations Environment Programme (UNEP) to formulate principles and indicators that firms may use to report about their economic, environmental, and social performances. Three versions of its guidelines have been published: the first one in 2000, the second in 2002, and the third one called G3 in 2006.
3. The law on New Economical Regulations, published on May 15, 2001, requires a disclosure on social environmental issues in the annual reports of firms listed on the French Stock Exchange.
4. El-Bannany (2007, p. 120) says that "disclosing social information changes through time and using just one year is not long enough to understand changes in the social disclosure level and the determinants of these changes. This can only be achieved by conducting a longitudinal study."

REFERENCES

Abbott, W. F., & Monsen, R. J. (1979). On the measurement of corporate social responsibility: Self-reported disclosures as a method of measuring corporate social involvement. *Academy of Management Journal* (September), 501–515.

Adams, C. A., Hill, W. Y., & Roberts, C. B. (1998). Corporate social reporting practices in Western Europe: Legitimating corporate behavior? *British Accounting Review, 30*, 1–21.

Aerts, W., Cormier, D., & Magnan, M. (2006). Intra-industry imitation in corporate environmental reporting: An international perspective. *Journal of Accounting and Public Policy, 25*, 299–331.

Brammer, S., & Pavelin, S. (2008). Factors influencing the quality of corporate environmental disclosure. *Business Strategy and the Environment, 17*, 120–136.

Branco, M. C., & Rodrigues, L. L. (2008). Factors influencing social responsibility disclosure by Portuguese companies. *Journal of Business Ethics, 84,* 497–527.

Belkaoui, A., & Karpik, P. (1989). Determinants of the corporate decision to disclose social information. *Accounting, Auditing and Accountability Journal, 2*(1), 36–51.

Cormier, D., & Magnan, M. (1999). Corporate environmental disclosure strategies: Determinants, costs and benefits. *Journal of Accounting, Auditing and Finance, 14*(3), 429–451.

Cowen, S., Ferreri, L., & Parker, L. D. (1987). The impact of corporate characteristics on social responsibility disclosure: A typology and frequency based analysis. *Accounting, Organizations and Society, 12*(2), 111–122.

Dammak-Ayadi, S. (2004). *La publication des rapports sociétaux par les entreprises françaises. Doctorat en Sciences de Gestion.* Paris, France: Université de Paris Dauphine.

El-Bannany, M. (2007). A study of determinants of social disclosure level in UK banks. *Corporate Ownership and Control, 5*(1), 120–130.

Ernst & Ernst. (1978). 1977 Survey of Fortune 500 Annual Reports. Ernst & Ernst Cleveland, OH.

Freedman, M., & Jaggi, B. (1998). An analysis of the association between pollution disclosure and economic performance. *Accounting, Auditing and Accountability Journal, 1*(2), 43–58.

Gao, S., Heravi, S., & Xiao, J. Z. (2005). Determinants of corporate social and environmental reporting in Hong Kong: A research note. *Accounting Forum, 29,* 233–242.

Gray, R., Kouhy, R., & Lavers, S. (1995a). Social and environmental reporting. *Accounting, Auditing and Accountability Journal, 8*(1), 44–77.

Gray, R., Kouhy, R., & Lavers, S. (1995b). Methodological themes: Constructing a research database of social and environmental reporting UK companies. *Accounting, Auditing and Accountability Journal, 8*(2), 78–101.

Guthrie, J., & Mathews, M. R. (1985). Corporate social accounting in Australasia. *Research in Corporate Social Performance and Policy, 7,* 251–277.

Guthrie, J., & Parker, L. D. (1990). Corporate social disclosure practice: A comparative international analysis. *Advances in Public Interest Accounting, 3,* 159–175.

Hackston, D., & Milne, M. (1996). Some determinants of social and environmental disclosure in New-Zealand companies. *Accounting, Auditing and Accountability Journal, 9*(1), 77–108.

Hall, J. A. (2002). *An exploratory investigation into the corporate social disclosure of selected New Zealand companies.* Discussion paper series, 211. Massey University School of Accountancy, Palmerston North, NZ.

Haniffa, R. M., & Cooke, T. E. (2005). The impact of culture and governance on corporate social reporting. *Journal of Accounting and Public Policy, 24,* 391–430.

Igalens, J. (2009). La reddition de comptes en matière de RSE. *Journal des sociétés* (69), 34–40.

Imam, S. (2000). Corporate social performance reporting in Bangladesh. *Managerial Auditing Journal, 15*(3), 133–141.

Jensen, M. C., & Meckling, W. H. (1976). Theory of the firm: Managerial behavior, agency costs and ownership structure. *Journal of Financial Economics, 3,* 305–360.

Mathews, M. R. (1995). Social and environmental accounting: A practical demonstration of ethical concern? *Journal of Business Ethics, 14,* 663–671.

Naser, K., Al-Hussaini, A., Al-Kwari, D., & Nuseibeh, R. (2006). Determinants of corporate social disclosure in developing countries: The case of Qatar. *Advances in International Accounting, 19,* 1–23.

Oxibar, B. (2003). *La diffusion d'informations sociétales dans les rapports annuels et les sites internet par les entreprises françaises. Doctorat en Sciences de Gestion.* Paris, France: Université Paris Dauphine.

Oxibar, B. (2009). *Communication sociétale: Théories et pratiques.* Paris, France: l'Harmattan.

Patten, D. M. (1991). Exposure legitimacy and social disclosure. *Journal of Accounting and Public Policy, 10,* 297–308.

Patten, D. M. (1992). Intra-industry environmental disclosures in response to the Alaskan oil spill: A note of legitimacy theory. *Accounting, Organization and Society, 17*(5), 471–475.

Pelle Culpin, I. (1998). *Du paradoxe de la diffusion d'information environnementale par les entreprises européennes. Doctorat en Sciences de Gestion.* Paris, France: Université Paris Dauphine.

Reverte, C. (2009). Determinants of corporate social responsibility disclosure ratings by Spanish listed firms. *Journal of Business Ethics, 88,* 351–366.

Roberts, C. B. (1991). Environmental disclosures: A note on reporting practices in mainland Europe. *Accounting, Auditing and Accountability Journal, 3,* 62–71.

Roberts, R. W. (1992). Determinants of corporate social responsibility disclosure: An application of stakeholder theory. *Accounting, Organization and Society, 17*(6), 595–612.

Zeghal, D., & Ahmed, S. A. (1990). Comparison of social responsibility information disclosure media used by Canadians firms. *Accounting, Auditing and Accountability Journal, 3*(1), 38–53.

CORPORATE ENVIRONMENTAL AND CLIMATE CHANGE DISCLOSURES: EMPIRICAL EVIDENCE FROM BANGLADESH

Ataur Rahman Belal, Md. Rezaul Kabir,
Stuart Cooper, Prasanta Dey, Niaz Ahmed Khan,
Taiabur Rahman and Mohobbot Ali

ABSTRACT

Purpose – *In this article, we examine the nature and the extent of corporate environmental and climate change disclosures in Bangladesh.*

Design/methodology/approach – *For this purpose, we have undertaken a content analysis of annual reports related to the year 2008 and websites of the 100 largest companies (according to market capitalization) listed on the Dhaka Stock Exchange. We have used 24 content analysis categories to capture the relevant disclosures related to climate change and other environmental issues.*

Findings – *Key findings of our analysis suggest that the level of environmental and climate change disclosures is very low in Bangladesh.*

Research in Accounting in Emerging Economies, Volume 10, 145–167
Copyright © 2010 by Emerald Group Publishing Limited
All rights of reproduction in any form reserved
ISSN: 1479-3563/doi:10.1108/S1479-3563(2010)0000010011

Although 91% of companies made disclosures in at least one category, most companies disclosed information only on the "energy usage" category, which is a mandatory requirement. Even fewer companies made disclosures in the specific areas of climate change. No disclosure was made in the significant categories such as GHG emissions. The second most popular category related to climate change was adaptation measures. Among the other environmental disclosures, a significant finding is that only 5% of (website 6%) companies disclosed that they had an effluent treatment plant. Closer examination of the nature of disclosures suggests that most of the disclosures are positive and descriptive in nature.

Originality/value – *As far as we are aware, this is the first study of its kind in Bangladesh which systematically examines corporate climate change disclosures as a particular focus of research.*

Keywords: Corporate environmental disclosures; climate change disclosures; developing countries; Bangladesh.

1. INTRODUCTION

Of late, the issue of climate change has come to the forefront of discussion and attention among the government, business, and nongovernment quarters. Interests on this issue have been heightened even further by the Copenhagen Conference on Climate Change held in December 2009. The business sector, in addition to national governments, has begun to respond to it (ACCA & GRI, 2009; CIMA, 2010; Eberlein & Matten, 2009; Kolk, Levy, & Pinkse, 2008). As the engines of economic growth, it is argued that business activities result in significant environmental and climate change effects (ACCA, 2007a, 2007b). In an increasingly carbon-constrained world, therefore, it is expected that firms will address this issue in a comprehensive, transparent, and accountable manner. One of the corporate responses could be the systematic measurement and reporting of their environmental and climate change impact (Hopwood, 2009). Accounting and reporting practices need to "move beyond the conventional accounting toolbox" if they are to reflect climate change risks (Bebbington & Larrinaga-González, 2008, p. 705). Further, they suggest that nonfinancial reporting is necessary to provide relevant information about the risks associated with global climate change in order to reflect a "true and fair view" of corporate performance. They continue that there is a need for further research into how organizations' "carbon position and carbon management is disclosed" (p. 708). Such research should, they argue, help to unveil some of the risks and uncertainties associated with climate change. From the Bangladeshi context in this article, we examine the nature and the extent of corporate environmental disclosure in general and climate change disclosures in particular.

Bangladesh is considered as one of the worst victims of climate change although its contribution to greenhouse gas (GHG) emissions is minimal (Ali, 1996; MoEF, 2008; Pachauri, 2009; Venema & Cisse, 2004). MoEF of the government of Bangladesh (2008, p. xv) argues that Bangladesh should prepare now to "adapt to climate change and safeguard the future well-being of her people." The country's premier national document on the subject, The Bangladesh Climate Change Strategy and Action Plan (BCCSAP) 2008, notes the involvement of the private sector in meeting the challenges of climate change. In this context, it may be quite topical and useful to find out the extent and nature of the actual responses of the private sector so far. For this purpose, we have undertaken a stocktaking exercise of corporate environmental and climate change disclosures by the Bangladeshi firms. As far as our knowledge goes, this study, although modest in its scope, is the first which systematically examines corporate climate change disclosures in Bangladesh.

Most of the previous studies in this area have concentrated on environmental disclosures. Some of the recent studies (ACCA, 2007a, 2007b; Bebbington & Larrinaga-González, 2008; Jeswani, Wehrmeyer, & Mulugetta, 2008; Johnston, Sefcik, & Soderstrom, 2008; Kolk et al., 2008; Stanny & Ely, 2008) which deal with climate change disclosures and corporate responses to climate change have tended to mainly concentrate on developed country firms and their efforts. In this study, we examine corporate environmental and climate change disclosures from an emerging economy perspective in general and Bangladesh in particular. Thus, the study addresses a clear gap in the literature in this area.

After this general introduction, the article proceeds with a review of prior research related to corporate environmental disclosures in general and climate change disclosures in particular. The third section provides the context of climate change in Bangladesh. The fourth section of the article explains the methodological procedures. The penultimate section presents the main findings of this study, while the final section summarizes the key observations, recapitulates the main arguments, and offers some concluding thoughts and remarks.

2. PRIOR RESEARCH

Given the growing importance of environmental and climate change issues, a fundamental question arises as to how firms are responding. One possible response is to account for and report on these issues (Hopwood, 2009). Academic and professional interest in environmental accounting and reporting has increased dramatically since the early 1990s (Gray, 2002; Mathews, 1997; Owen, 2008; Parker, 2005).

Previous studies have documented and discussed levels of social and environmental disclosure and considered the reasons why such disclosure has been undertaken (Owen, 2008; Parker, 2005). The vast majority of these studies have focused upon large companies that are domiciled in developed countries (Belal & Owen, 2007). Although less prevalent, there are now a number of studies that have considered social and environmental disclosures by companies domiciled in developing countries, and previous studies in Bangladesh have indicated an increase in corporate environmental disclosure, albeit from a very low base (see Belal, 1997, 2000; Imam, 1999, 2000).

Given the growing importance of climate change, more specific accounting and reporting standards have been developed, such as the Climate Disclosure Standards Board's Reporting Framework and the Greenhouse Gas Protocol's Corporate Accounting and Reporting Standard. These standards focus exclusively upon climate change mitigation, GHG emissions, and adaptation rather than broader environmental issues (such as biodiversity, effluents, waste, water, material use, and non-GHG emissions, as GRI's broader sustainability guidelines do).

There have also been recent surveys on corporate practices related to climate change disclosures published in the United Kingdom and other countries (ACCA, 2007a, 2007b; ACCA & GRI, 2009). KPMG (2008) suggests that on average, 69% of "the 100 largest companies by revenue" in each of 22, both developed and developing, countries do not disclose information about climate risks. They further report that 68% do not address the business risks of climate change and 62% do not report on their carbon footprint. There was considerable variation by country with only 4% of companies from the Czech Republic providing any carbon footprint disclosure compared to 75% of companies in the United Kingdom (KPMG, 2008, p. 52). Rather optimistically perhaps, the report states:

> We would expect climate to be a fully managed issue by 2011, including strategy, risk management, disclosure on carbon footprint by the company and its wider value chain, and business opportunities and innovations afforded by climate change. (p. 109)

To the best of our knowledge, there is no previous study available on climate change disclosures in Bangladesh and only a handful of academic studies are available from other countries' perspectives. One of the earliest studies on disclosures of pollution and GHG emissions was by Freedman and Jaggi (2005). Their study focused on reporting by a sample of 120 very large firms from a number of developed countries in industries that have particular climate change risks. Their results suggested that only 45% disclosed information pertaining to their CO_2 emissions. The study did show that firms from countries that ratified the Kyoto Protocol had higher disclosure indexes and that larger firms disclose more detailed pollution information.

There are also a number of papers that study the voluntary corporate disclosures made within the carbon disclosure project (CDP). The CDP was launched in 2000 and acts "on behalf of 534 institutional investors, holding $64 trillion in assets under management and some 60 purchasing organizations such as Cadbury, PepsiCo and Wal-Mart" (https://www.cdproject.net/en-US/WhatWeDo/Pages/overview.aspx; accessed on August 7, 2010). It operates by surveying organizations about their carbon disclosure, and the number of responses received has increased dramatically from 235 organizations in 2003 to 2,456 organizations in 2009. Kolk et al. (2008) confirmed the "impressive and growing" response rates, but questioned the value of the current disclosures to "investors, NGOs or policy makers" (p. 719). When considering the motivations for disclosing information to CDP, Stanny and Ely (2008) found that for US S&P 500 firms in 2007 size, previous disclosures, and foreign sales were important, whereas Reid and Toffel (2009) concluded that disclosing information to CDP was more likely when the firm or other firms in their industry had "already been targeted by a shareholder resolution on a related issue" (p. 1171).

Finally, there is one study that does compare corporate responses to climate change in developing and developed countries (Jeswani et al., 2008). Focusing on the nine most energy-intensive and GHG-emitting industrial sectors, this study compares corporate responses to climate change in Pakistan and the United Kingdom. The findings suggest that firms' responses depend on the location, sector, size, and type of ownership. This study finds that there is a higher propensity for Pakistani companies to be indifferent or at the beginner level when responding to climate change issues and only 5% of Pakistani companies were actively responding (compared to 30% of UK companies). The study identified a number of barriers to climate change responses and these included their perceived "high cost," a "lack of awareness," and the "absence of governmental policies," which they suggest are similar in other developing countries.

There is an emerging call for a corporate response to climate change issues and this includes demands for related corporate disclosure (see Stanny & Ely, 2008, p. 338). Some initial progress has been made, but corporate climate change reporting is still very much in the early stages and there is considerable scope for improvement (ACCA, 2009). What we can also see is that there is a small, but growing, academic research interest in the area of corporate climate change reporting and disclosures. To date, this research is formative in nature and uses different sources to consider the related issues, but almost all of the research to date focuses on large international companies from developed countries. This article attempts to address this gap in the literature through our study of corporate environmental reporting in general and climate change reporting in particular from the context of Bangladesh.

3. THE CONTEXT OF CLIMATE CHANGE AND CORPORATE INVOLVEMENT IN BANGLADESH

In this section, by way of setting the broader scene, we briefly review the context of climate change and vulnerability in Bangladesh together with an examination of key national policy pronouncements on the role of the private/business sector.

Climate change is not just an environmental issue, but it directly affects many other social and economic phenomena such as poverty, health, and economic development in a wider context (ACCA, 2009). Erratic floods, cyclones, and droughts are causing significant interruption to Bangladeshi agriculture. The Intergovernmental Panel on Climate Change Report (IPCC, 2007) estimates that by 2050, rice production in Bangladesh could decline by 8% and wheat by 32% (against a base year of 1990). Bangladesh also regularly faces the challenges of riverbank erosion, landslides, soil degradation, and deforestation. UNDP (2004) has identified Bangladesh to be "the most vulnerable country" in the world to tropical cyclones and the sixth most vulnerable country to floods. The exposure to such risks is further enhanced by Bangladesh's very high population, abject poverty, geography, reckless industrial pollution, poor environmental governance, and ineffective implementation of regulatory policies (Belal, Khan, & Alam, 1998).

The characteristics of the climate of Bangladesh have been changing over the decades. The temperature is generally increasing in the monsoon season (June, July, and August). The mean annual rainfall of the country is about

2,300 mm, but there exists a wide spatial and temporal distribution. MoEF (2005) states that the duration of the rainy season has decreased, but the total annual rainfall remains more or less the same. It implies that heavy rainfall is taking place within a short period of time and this affects the agriculture sector and other livelihood systems. The SAARC Meteorological Research Council (SMRC, 2003) revealed that the rate of sea level rise during the last 22 years is significantly higher than the mean rate of global sea level rise over 100 years. Salinity and its seasonal variations are adversely affecting coastal ecosystems and associated fisheries and agriculture production. Extreme weather conditions and natural disasters such as riverine and flash flood, tropical cyclones, tornados, and droughts are on the rise. It is reported that between 1991 and 2000, 93 major disasters occurred in Bangladesh, resulting in nearly 200,000 deaths and causing US $5.9 billion in damages with high losses in agriculture and infrastructure (MoEF, 2008).

Bangladesh has developed an elaborate policy and planning framework for facing the challenges of climate change and associated adversities. The government is an active signatory to the United Nations Framework Convention on Climate Change (UNFCCC). The key relevant policy documents include the Bangladesh National Adaptation Programme of Action, BCCSAP, Bangladesh Capacity Development Action Plan (CDAP) for Sustainable Environmental Governance, Millennium Development Goals Progress Framework (Reports), Bangladesh National Capacity Self-Assessment for Global Environmental Management (NCSA), and National Conservation Strategy. Besides, the country also has a number of sectoral (e.g., forestry, environment, agriculture, and energy) policies.

Within the limits of its meager resources, Bangladesh has invested more than $10 billion over the last 35 years to make the country less vulnerable to natural disasters. In 2009, the government allocated $100 million from its own source to take up 44 different climate change related projects under various ministries (The Daily Prothom Alo, November 18, 2009). In addition, different voluntary organizations and NGOs are taking various awareness programs regarding the effects of climate change (The Daily Prothom Alo, November 20, 2009). The government has also recently established a National Climate Change Fund, with an initial capitalization of $45 million – mainly focusing on adaptation.

In these policy and programmatic efforts, however, the role and significance of the private sector and business community remain marginal. Except for cursory and superficial references and mentions of the private sector in a few of the above policy documents, the treatment of the private sector's role in environmental management and climate change regime is strikingly limited. The NCSA document, for example, calls for the "sensitization of the private sector" for various issues concerning the Multilateral Environmental Agreements (MEA) ratified by the government. The CDAP for Sustainable Environmental Governance suggests engagement of the private sector under a broad theme of "participation of concerned stakeholders" in selected activities such as "renewable energy for rural areas" and "extraction of bio-diesel." In the BCCSAP, "capacity development of the private sector" is proposed under one of its six "pillars" titled "capacity building and institutional strengthening"; there is no further elaboration on the proposed action.

A recent report on the emerging issues in the Asian CSR predicts that climate change is going to be the "number one stakeholder concern" which needs to be addressed by the companies in Asia (CSRAsia, 2009). Accordingly, it is argued that in order to achieve long-term success in an increasingly carbon-constrained world, the Bangladeshi companies will need to respond to the challenges of climate change with appropriate strategies. The above review of the broader climate change context and policy and programmatic frameworks, however, does not seem to reflect and corroborate the above vision and prediction for the corporate role and involvement in Bangladesh.

4. RESEARCH METHODOLOGY

In this article, we have adopted content analysis procedures for analyzing the annual reports and websites of top 100 companies listed on the Dhaka Stock Exchange. The top 100 companies (see Appendix A for a list) were chosen on the basis of their market capitalization and together they represent nearly 87% of the total market capitalization of all listed companies in Bangladesh. The sample represents a wide variety of different industrial sectors. The literature on social and environmental accounting (see, e.g., Adams, Hill, & Roberts, 1998; Jeswani et al., 2008; Stanny & Ely, 2008) suggests that the largest companies are more likely to make disclosures on social and environmental issues because of their political visibility and resources at their disposal. We have analyzed annual reports related to the year 2008 because this is the latest report available in the public domain at the time of writing this article. In the previous literature, the annual report was predominantly used for the examination of social and environmental disclosures (Belal & Momin, 2009). In addition to the annual reports, we have also analyzed the corporate websites (where a functioning website was available) of the top 100 companies, as some companies might use this media for environmental and climate change disclosures. We believe this has made our study more comprehensive.

On the basis of the literature review, relevant guidelines, and our knowledge of the Bangladeshi context, we have developed a content analysis framework consisting of 24 categories (see Appendix B) to capture environmental and climate change disclosures made via annual reports and websites. For this purpose, a disclosure indexing approach was used, whereby each company disclosing a category received a score of 1 otherwise 0. An individual company index was calculated by dividing the number of categories disclosed by each company by the total number of possible categories, that is, 24. In addition to that, we have measured the volume of disclosures in number of sentences. As compared to other measurement units (such as number of words and pages), sentences give us a better under-standing of the disclosures made. Out of the 24 categories, 11 categories (including disclosure on energy) belonged to the climate change theme and the remaining 13 categories captured disclosures on other environmental issues. In order to understand the nature and quality of disclosures in each category, and in line with previous studies, we have examined their attributes such as descriptive, monetary, and quantitative disclosures. We have also examined whether the news content of each disclosure is good, bad, and neutral.

In order to increase the reliability of our analysis, we have used a well-developed instrument with explicit rules. Three researchers were involved in the coding process. At the beginning, all three researchers coded five annual reports independently and reconciled the differences to achieve consistency in the coding procedures. Then the remaining coding work was carried out by one of the authors in a large spreadsheet. To avoid "coder fatigue" (Neuendorf, 2002), sufficient breaks were taken by the main coder in this time-consuming and onerous coding process. Differences were resolved on the basis of agreements by the three authors who were involved throughout the coding process. This rigorous process ensured that a reliable analysis is achieved. The results of this process are reported in the following section.

5. RESULTS AND ANALYSIS

In this section, we present and analyze the findings of this study highlighting the extent and nature of environmental and climate change disclosures by the top 100 companies in Bangladesh. The overall disclosure profiles of the companies are reported in Table 1.

Table 1 shows that 91% of companies are making environmental and climate change disclosures in at least one category in their annual reports. However, only 40% of companies made such disclosures in their websites. One reason for less website disclosure could be attributed to lower internet usage and poor IT (information technology) literacy in Bangladesh.

It must be noted here that the above percentage of disclosers might appear high. In fact, most of the companies have disclosed in the environmental categories other than climate change. Only 28% and 16% of companies made disclosures in at least one of the climate change related categories in the annual reports and websites, respectively.

From the disclosure index exhibited in Table 2, it appears that overall level of disclosure is very low with companies scoring 11.5% and 3.38% of total possible scores for annual reports and websites, respectively. This

Table 1. Overall Environmental and Climate Change Disclosure Profiles.

Description	Annual Reports	Websites
Total percentage of companies with disclosures in at least one category	91	40
Total percentage of companies with no disclosures	09	60
Total	100	100

Table 2. Overall Environmental and Climate Change Disclosure Index.

Description	Annual Reports ($N = 100$)			Websites ($N = 100$)		
	Climate change	Other environmental	Combined	Climate change	Other environmental	Combined
Total possible scores for all companies	1,100	1,300	2,400	1,100	1,300	2,400
Total scores achieved for all companies	144[a]	132	276	27	54	81
Overall index (%)	13.09	10.15	11.50	2.45	4.15	3.38

[a]This figure includes a score of 88 for energy related category.

provides clear empirical evidence that environmental and climate change disclosures by the Bangladeshi companies is very low.

There are at least two reasons for the low take up of environmental and climate change disclosures by the Bangladeshi companies. First, we believe that inadequate articulation of the corporate role in the mitigation and adaptation of climate change (see Section 3 of this article) is one of the reasons for lesser corporate enthusiasm on this subject. In other words, it can be attributed to the lack of appropriate policy incentives which is consistent with the study by Jeswani et al. (2008). Second, it could be indicative of the poor performance of the Bangladeshi companies in this area.

Table 3 shows the performance of top five companies on the basis of their individual disclosure index.

If we look at the individual rankings of the companies in Table 3, we see that BRAC Bank and ACI Limited topped the list with an annual report disclosure index of 37.50% in both cases. However, it was Heidelberg Cement Bangladesh Ltd. and Square Textiles Limited who topped the list with a website disclosure index of 29.17% in both cases. As compared to this maximum score, the minimum score was zero for both media. Closer observation of Panel A data indicates the dominance of the banking sector, as three out of eight companies in Panel A are from the banking sector. ACI Limited features on both panels.

Table 3. Top Five Companies.

Companies	Index (%)	Ranks
Panel A: Annual report index		
BRAC Bank Ltd.	37.50	1
ACI Limited	37.50	1
Prime Bank Ltd.	33.33	3
Glaxo SmithKline Bangladesh Ltd.	33.33	3
Lafarge Surma Cement Ltd.	29.17	5
Dutch-Bangla Bank Ltd.	29.17	5
British American Tobacco Bangladesh Ltd.	29.17	5
Beximco Textiles Ltd.	29.17	5
Panel B: Website index		
Heidelberg Cement Bangladesh Ltd.	29.17	1
Square Textiles Ltd.	29.17	1
ACI Limited	25.00	3
Mercantile Bank Ltd.	25.00	3
Square Pharmaceuticals Ltd.	20.83	5

In addition, we have also measured the volume of disclosures for each company in terms of number of sentences. For the annual reports, the average number of sentences was 6 (for website 4), while the maximum and minimum were 61 (for website 45) and 0 (for website 0), respectively. These figures indicate an insignificant amount of environmental and climate change disclosures by the Bangladeshi companies. Here, it is to be noted that the sentence count did not include the mandatory disclosure of energy costs in the notes to the accounts which is expressed in monetary terms.

We now turn our attention to the analysis of the various categories used in this study. Table 4 shows the percentage of companies with disclosures in the relevant categories.

In terms of popularity of the categories, it appears that in the annual reports, the top three categories were energy usage, environmental policy, and climate change adaptation. For website disclosure, the top three categories were environmental policy, climate change adaptation, and disclosure of other environmental issues. The least popular category mainly included various climate change related categories.

Table 4 shows that 88% of companies provided energy usage data in their annual reports. Only 3% of companies provided their energy usage data in the website in a descriptive form. Only 4% (website disclosure 1%) of companies made some kind of brief policy statements related to climate change (on the average, three sentences only), whereas 10% of companies identified climate change as an important factor which might affect their future business settings. Some examples are given below.

> MBL is concerned with conservation and preservation of the environment. There is a rising level of awareness and demand to address the issue of sustainability of the environment because the whole world is increasingly experiencing the devastating effects of environmental changes for Green House effects due to Global Warming. The Bank is mindful of its responsibilities to the future generations by playing its part in promoting environmental awareness and in the conservation of the environment. (Website, Mercantile Bank Ltd.)

> Given the increase in the number, cost, and variability of catastrophic losses, some insurers, re-insurers, and their trade associations now view climate change as a "strategic factor" in charting their future. Particularly vulnerable are the emerging insurance markets in the developing world. Insurers see this as the future of their industry, yet these regions are also particularly unprepared and vulnerable to climate change. (Annual Report 2008, Green Delta Insurance Company)

13% (website disclosure 4%) and 28% (website disclosure 16%) of companies disclosed various mitigation (e.g., tree plantation) and adaptation measures (e.g., community engagement to help the victims of cyclone

Table 4. Percentage of Companies Disclosing in Each Category.

Categories	Percentage of Companies (Annual Report, $N = 100$)	Percentage of Companies (Websites, $N = 100$)
1. Climate change governance information	0	0
2. Climate change policy statement	4	1
3. Emissions reduction target	0	0
4. GHG emissions data	0	0
5. Energy usage data	88	3
6. Mitigation measures	13	4
7. Product impacts on climate change	1	3
8. Adaptation measures	28	16
9. Assurance of climate change disclosures	0	0
10. Reference to standards/ protocols	0	0
11. Other climate change issues	10	0
12. Environmental governance information	0	0
13. Environmental policy statement	45	18
14. Targets and performance data	1	1
15. Environmental audit	3	0
16. Spills and waste	6	4
17. Financial elements of environmental issues	2	0
18. Sustainability and sustainable development	13	5
19. Installation of effluent treatment plants	5	6
20. Product impacts on environment	21	5
21. Reference to standards/ guidelines/compliance	15	5
22. Environmental awards	1	0
23. Negative environmental disclosures	1	0
24. Other environmental issues	19	10

SIDR) undertaken by them. Some examples of mitigation and adaptation related disclosures are given below.

> We also use comprehensive energy conservation program. This feeds back all recyclable energy into our various systems, especially for our air-conditioning purpose. Our investment in this program has made us energy efficient and environmentally conscious entity. (Website, Square Textiles Ltd.)

> DBH provides assistance to HFHIB for building shelters for the Cyclone Aila affected families. Delta BRAC Housing Finance Corporation Ltd. (DBH), the specialist in housing finance, has provided financial assistance to the project of Habitat for Humanity International-Bangladesh (HFHIB) for building shelters to the Cyclone Aila affected families of Shyamnagar and Ashashuni upazilas of Satkhira. (Website, Delta BRAC Housing Finance Corporation Ltd.)

It is noteworthy that none of the companies provided disclosures on important climate change issues such as GHG emissions target and performance, climate change governance, assurance and reference to carbon accounting standards.

A significant number of companies (45%; website disclosure 18%) made brief policy statements on the environment. However, the length of disclosures barely exceeded an average of three sentences. Among the environmental disclosures, a significant finding is that only 5% (website 6%) of companies disclosed that they had an effluent treatment plant (ETP), although the establishment of ETPs has been made mandatory in Bangladesh. Some examples of disclosures in this area are given below.

> There are new requirements that are going to be enforced shortly; necessary preparations for this are also in the process. The most important one amongst those is fixing of treatment plant onboard, which will come into practice by 27th September 2008. BSC is trying its best to comply with regulations in time and keep our fleet up-to-date as far as the international regulations are concerned. (Annual Report, 2008, Bangladesh Shipping Corporation Limited)

> The Tannery is equipped with a high-tech effluent treatment plant ensuring a pollution free environment for both workers and locality where we operate. (Website, Bata Shoe Company)

Finally, we have examined the nature and the quality of disclosures made by the companies. Table 5 exhibits the nature of disclosures.

Table 5 indicates that most of the disclosures in the annual reports are positive and descriptive in nature while all of the website disclosures are of the same nature. The monetary disclosures are mainly related to the energy category and they are located in notes to the accounts. There is hardly any attempt to quantify the disclosures made.

Table 5.　Nature of Disclosures.

	Annual Report (%)	Website (%)
Panel A		
Monetary	32.97	0.00
Quantitative	0.36	0.00
Descriptive	66.67	100.00
Total	100.00	100.00
Panel B		
Good	63.41	100.00
Bad	1.81	0.00
Neutral	34.78	0.00
Total	100.00	100.00

6. DISCUSSION AND CONCLUSION

Based on the preceding analysis, a number of conclusions can be drawn:

First, the above analysis shows that the level of environmental and climate change disclosures is very low. Although 91% made disclosures in at least one category, most companies disclosed information only on the "energy usage" category, which is a mandatory requirement. Even fewer companies made disclosures in the specific areas of climate change. This indicates that although there is a degree of corporate awareness of climate change issues, disclosures were made in some selected and restricted categories only. No disclosure was made in the significant categories such as GHG emissions. Here, however, we must acknowledge that in the context of Bangladesh, the total country level GHG emissions are low, perhaps one could say insignificant, relative to those in developed countries. The second most popular category within the climate change theme was adaptation measures and this is an interesting finding. We could perhaps say that GHG emission is not the key issue in Bangladesh, but the effect of severe weather events, which are expected to worsen with climate change, are real and apparent. Much of the adaptation disclosure that we found was actually related to actions taken in response to severe weather events. Thus, they are reactive rather than a proactive measure to better enable greater resilience to severe weather events in the future. The disclosures we found are not discussing measures that will enable its populace to adapt to and cope with climate change in the future and this is disappointing.

It is clear that there are significant differences in the extent of environmental and climate change disclosures in the annual reports and websites. Annual reports still appear to be the most popular media at least in the context of Bangladesh. This echoes the findings of Belal and Momin (2009) and stands in sharp contrast to the observation made by Bebbington and Unerman (2008) from the developed countries' context that separate sustainability reports and internet reports have become much more popular for this kind of disclosures. The empirical evidence provided in this article does not support that assertion.

Second, closer examination of the nature of disclosures suggests that most of the disclosures are positive and descriptive in nature. There is hardly any reference to negative news or difficulties faced by the companies in this regard. This finding raises questions about the credibility of disclosures as we are aware that the government (Department of Environment) served "notice" and summoned explanation on a number of noncompliant companies on the issue of ETP and other environmental matters (personal communication with DoE, 2009). Lack of independent assurance information further undermines the credibility of the disclosures made.

The disclosure exercise, as the study findings suggest, remains essentially superficial; substance is often superseded by rhetoric. There has been little practical action towards translating the high-blown statements into reality, which is evidenced by the small number of companies (5%) disclosing information on the installation of ETPs. The issue of noncompliance requires urgent attention of the policy makers.

Finally, we would like to close this article with a number of policy recommendations:[1]

(i)   The current policy framework (articulated in Section 3 of this article) does not adequately provide for specific role of companies in minimizing environmental and climate change impact. It is imperative to provide for a better articulation of the corporate sector's role in these policy documents. In particular, the Bangladeshi corporate sector should be encouraged to undertake a more proactive role in preparation for adaptation of the future risks arising from climate change.

(ii) The relevant mandatory legal requirements (e.g., the obligation to establish ETPs or report environmental impact on the part of the corporate institutions) need to be effectively monitored by the relevant government agencies. This in turn will call for capacity building efforts for these oversight agencies to enable them to perform their role.

(iii) There needs to be policy-level incentives for the few relatively better performing companies in this regard. In the absence of an effective "reward and punishment" mechanism, compliant companies may eventually lose the zeal in the face of unhealthy competition from their noncompliant peers and free riders.

NOTE

1. Some of these suggestions were explored elsewhere on a popular forum (see *The Financial Express*, February 23, 2010, and *The Daily Star*, February 27, 2010).

ACKNOWLEDGMENTS

This article is an output from the INSPIRE Project funded by the British Council for the benefit of the Bangladesh Higher Education Sector and the UK Higher Education Sector. The views expressed are not necessarily those of the British Council. An early version of the article was presented at the International Conference of Bangladesh Environment Network (ICBEN), January 2–3, 2010, Dhaka, Bangladesh; the British Accounting Association Conference, March 30–April 1, 2010, Cardiff, UK; and a workshop at Rouen Business School, May 31, 2010, France.

REFERENCES

ACCA. (2007a). *Climate change: UK corporate reporting*. London: Association of Chartered Certified Accountants (ACCA).

ACCA. (2007b). *Disclosures on climate change: Australia*. London: Association of Chartered Certified Accountants (ACCA).

ACCA. (2009). *Carbon accounting: Too little too late?* London: Association of Chartered Certified Accountants (ACCA).

ACCA & GRI. (2009). *High impact sectors: The challenge of reporting on climate change*. London: Association of Chartered Certified Accountants (ACCA).

Adams, C., Hill, W., & Roberts, C. (1998). Corporate social reporting practices in Western Europe: Legitimating corporate behaviour? *British Accounting Review, 30*(1), 1–21.

Ali, A. (1996). Vulnerability of Bangladesh to climate change and sea level rise through tropical cyclones and storm surges. *Water, Air, & Soil Pollution, 92*(1–2), 171–179.

Bebbington, J., & Larrinaga-González, C. (2008). Carbon trading: Accounting and reporting issues. *European Accounting Review, 17*(4), 697–717.

Bebbington, J., & Unerman, J. (2008). Editorial. *Social and Environmental Accountability Journal, 28*(1), 1–2.

Belal, A. (2000). Environmental reporting in developing countries: Empirical evidence from Bangladesh. *Eco-Management and Auditing, 7*(3), 114–121.

Belal, A., & Momin, M. (2009). Corporate social reporting (CSR) in emerging economies: A review and future direction. *Research in Accounting in Emerging Economies, 9,* 119–143.

Belal, A. R. (1997). Green reporting practices in Bangladesh. *The Bangladesh Accountant* (January–March), 107–115.

Belal, A. R., Khan, N. A., & Alam, S. A. (1998). Industrial pollution and the environment in Bangladesh: An overview. *Asian Journal of Environmental Management, 6*(2), 115–124.

Belal, A. R., & Owen, D. (2007). The views of corporate managers on the current state of, and future prospects for, social reporting in Bangladesh: An engagement based study. *Accounting, Auditing & Accountability Journal, 20*(3), 472–494.

CIMA, T. (2010). *Accounting for climate change.* London: Chartered Institute of Management Accountants (CIMA).

CSRAsia, T. (2009). *The future of CSR 2009 Report.* Hong Kong, China: CSR Asia.

Eberlein, B., & Matten, D. (2009). Business responses to climate change regulation in Canada and Germany: Lessons for MNCs from emerging economies. *Journal of Business Ethics, 86*(Suppl. 2), 241–255.

Freedman, M., & Jaggi, B. (2005). Global warming, commitment to the Kyoto protocol, and accounting disclosures by the largest global public firms from polluting industries. *The International Journal of Accounting, 40*(3), 215–232.

Gray, R. (2002). The social accounting project and accounting, organisations and society: Privileging engagement, imaginings, new accountings and pragmatism over critique? *Accounting, Organisations and Society, 27*(7), 687–708.

Hopwood, A. G. (2009). Accounting and the environment. *Accounting, Organizations and Society, 34*(3–4), 433–439.

Imam, S. (1999). Environmental reporting in Bangladesh. *Social and Environmental Accounting, 19*(2), 12–14.

Imam, S. (2000). Corporate social performance reporting in Bangladesh. *Managerial Auditing Journal, 15*(3), 133–141.

IPCC. (2007). *Climate change 2007: Physical science basis. Working group I contribution to the Intergovernmental Panel on Climate Change (IPCC) Fourth Assessment Report: Summary for policymakers.* Cambridge, UK: Cambridge University Press.

Jeswani, H. K., Wehrmeyer, W., & Mulugetta, Y. (2008). How warm is the corporate response to climate change? Evidence from Pakistan and the UK. *Business Strategy and the Environment, 17*(1), 46–60.

Johnston, D. M., Sefcik, S. E., & Soderstrom, N. S. (2008). The value relevance of greenhouse gas emissions allowances: An exploratory study in the related United States SO_2 market. *European Accounting Review, 17*(4), 747–764.

Kolk, A., Levy, D., & Pinkse, J. (2008). Corporate responses in an emerging climate regime: The institutionalization and commensuration of carbon disclosure. *European Accounting Review, 17*(4), 719–745.

KPMG, T. (2008). *KPMG International survey of corporate responsibility reporting 2008.* Amsterdam, The Netherlands: KPMG.

Mathews, M. (1997). Twenty-five years of social and environmental accounting research. *Accounting, Auditing & Accountability Journal, 10*(4), 481–531.

MoEF. (2005). *National Adaptation Programme of Action (NAPA)*. Dhaka, Bangladesh: Ministry of Environment and Forests (MoEF), Government of the People's Republic of Bangladesh.

MoEF. (2008). *Bangladesh climate change strategy and action plan 2008*. Dhaka, Bangladesh: Ministry of Environment and Forests (MoEF), Government of the People's Republic of Bangladesh.

Neuendorf, K. A. (2002). *The content analysis guidebook*. London: Sage.

Owen, D. (2008). Chronicles of wasted time? A personal reflection on the current state of, and future prospects for, social and environmental accounting research. *Accounting, Auditing and Accountability Journal, 21*(2), 240–267.

Pachauri. (2009). Welcome speech by Dr. R. Pachauri at Copenhagen Climate Change Summit, December 7, 2009, Copenhagen, Denmark.

Parker, L. D. (2005). Social and environmental accountability research: A view from the commentary box. *Accounting, Auditing and Accountability Journal, 18*(6), 842–860.

Reid, E. M., & Toffel, M. W. (2009). Responding to public and private politics: Corporate disclosure of climate change strategies. *Strategic Management Journal, 30*(11), 1157–1178.

SMRC, T. (2003). *The vulnerability assessment of the SAARC coastal region due to sea level rise: Bangladesh case*. Dhaka, Bangladesh: SAARC Meteorological Research Council (SMRC).

Stanny, E., & Ely, K. (2008). Corporate environmental disclosures about the effects of climate change. *Corporate Social Responsibility and Environmental Management, 15*(6), 338–348.

UNDP. (2004). *Reducing disaster risk: A challenge for development*. New York: United Nations Development Programme (UNDP).

Venema, H. D., & Cisse, M. (2004). *Seeing the light: Adapting to climate change with decentralized renewable energy in developing countries*. Winnipeg, Canada: International Institute for Sustainable Development.

APPENDIX A. LIST OF COMPANIES SURVEYED

Sl. No.	Company Name	Market Capitalization on May 7, 2009, in BDT (Millions)	Industry
1	Titas Gas Transmission and Distribution Co. Ltd.	45906.745	Fuel and Power
2	Square Pharmaceuticals Ltd.	33790.200	Pharmaceuticals and Chemicals
3	Summit Power Ltd.	25366.770	Fuel and Power
4	Lafarge Surma Cement Ltd.	24911.462	Cement
5	Islami Bank Bangladesh Ltd.	23676.840	Bank
6	Power Grid Co. of Bangladesh Ltd.	22435.350	Fuel and Power
7	Investment Corporation of Bangladesh	20430.000	Investment
8	Dutch-Bangla Bank Ltd.	19661.250	Bank
9	Beximco Pharmaceuticals Ltd.	19170.769	Pharmaceuticals and Chemicals
10	Dhaka Electric Supply Company Ltd (DESCO)	16287.332	Fuel and Power
11	Uttara Bank Ltd.	16092.983	Bank
12	Arab Bangladesh Bank Ltd.	15742.285	Bank
13	Bangladesh Export Import Co. Ltd.	15203.129	Miscellaneous
14	IFIC Bank Ltd.	12629.577	Bank
15	Prime Bank Ltd.	12619.141	Bank
16	British American Tobacco Bangladesh	12360.000	Food and Allied
17	National Bank Ltd.	12140.478	Bank
18	Pubali Bank Ltd.	9834.300	Bank
19	Renata Ltd.	9083.959	Pharmaceuticals and Chemicals
20	Summit Alliance Port Ltd.	9047.500	Services and Real Estate
21	Export Import Bank of Bangladesh Ltd.	8046.627	Bank
22	BEXTEX Ltd.	8020.925	Textile
23	BRAC Bank Ltd.	7413.120	Bank
24	ACI Limited	7308.840	Pharmaceuticals and Chemicals
25	BSRM STEEL	7170.250	Engineering
26	Heidelberg Cement Bangladesh Ltd.	6708.390	Cement
27	Southeast Bank Ltd.	6631.360	Bank
28	Jamuna Oil Company Ltd.	6471.000	Fuel and Power
29	Dhaka Bank Ltd.	6324.523	Bank
30	Bank Asia Ltd.	6081.328	Bank

APPENDIX A. (*Continued*)

Sl. No.	Company Name	Market Capitalization on May 7, 2009, in BDT (Millions)	Industry
31	Berger Paints Bangladesh Ltd.	5945.644	Miscellaneous
32	LankaBangla Finance Ltd.	5744.200	Bank
33	Al-Arafah Islami Bank Ltd.	5701.299	Bank
34	ICB Islami Bank Ltd.	5445.574	Bank
35	Eastern Bank Ltd.	5433.181	Bank
36	Square Textiles Ltd.	5153.153	Textile
37	Green Delta Insurance Co. Ltd.	5057.583	Insurance
38	Trust Bank Ltd.	5016.564	Bank
39	Shahjalal Islami Bank Ltd.	4969.231	Bank
40	IDLC Finance Ltd.	4677.750	Bank
41	National Credit & Commerce Bank Ltd.	4512.678	Bank
42	Eastern Housing Ltd.	4500.669	Services and Real Estates
43	Mercantile Bank Ltd.	4435.540	Bank
44	Standard Bank Ltd.	4225.034	Bank
45	Delta BRAC Housing Finance Corporation Ltd.	4149.698	Services and Real Estate
46	Bata Shoe Co. (Bangladesh) Ltd.	4075.272	Tannery Industries
47	BOC Bangladesh Ltd.	3777.177	Fuel and Power
48	One Bank Ltd.	3717.654	Bank
49	National Housing Finance and Investment Ltd.	3708.900	Services and Real Estate
50	Glaxo SmithKline Bangladesh Ltd.	3665.734	Pharmaceuticals and Chemicals
51	S. Alam Cold Rolled Steels Ltd.	3664.788	Engineering
52	Singer Bangladesh Ltd.	3626.081	Engineering
53	Atlas Bangladesh Ltd.	3454.000	Engineering
54	Jamuma Bank Ltd.	3421.056	Bank
55	Mutual Trust Bank Ltd.	3409.144	Bank
56	Premier Bank Ltd.	3388.439	Bank
57	Bangladesh Shipping Corporation (BSC)	3380.000	Miscellaneous
58	Pragati Insurance Ltd.	3179.209	Insurance
59	Bangladesh Online Ltd.	3129.072	IT Sector
60	Social ISLAMI Bank Ltd./Social Investment Bank	3004.208	Bank
61	Aftab Automobiles Ltd.	2938.315	Engineering

APPENDIX A. (*Continued*)

Sl. No.	Company Name	Market Capitalization on May 7, 2009, in BDT (Millions)	Industry
62	Union Capital Ltd.	2690.960	Bank
63	Beximco Synthetics Ltd.	2555.420	Pharmaceuticals and Chemicals
64	Industrial Promotion and Development Co. of Bd. Ltd.	2342.841	Bank
65	Reckitt Benckiser (Bangladesh) Ltd.	2085.143	Pharmaceuticals and Chemicals
66	Uttara Finance and Investment Ltd.	2082.960	Bank
67	National Tubes Ltd.	2036.921	Engineering
68	Apex Adelchi Footwear Ltd.	1905.188	Tannery Industries
69	Pragati Life Insurance Ltd.	1674.188	Insurance
70	Prime Islami Life Insurance Co. Ltd.	1588.000	Insurance
71	Reliance Insurance Ltd.	1571.850	Insurance
72	Keya Cosmetics Ltd.	1529.280	Pharmaceuticals and Chemicals
73	International Leasing and Financial Services Ltd.	1501.555	Bank
74	Prime Finance & Investment Ltd.	1498.950	Insurance
75	Apex Tannery Ltd.	1438.656	Tannery Industries
76	MIDAS Financing Ltd.	1419.069	Bank
77	Phoenix Finance and Investments Ltd.	1368.283	Bank
78	United Leasing Co. Ltd.	1355.393	Bank
79	Sandhani Life Insurance Co. Ltd.	1318.221	Insurance
80	Peoples Insurance Co. Ltd.	1308.000	Insurance
81	National Tea Co. Ltd.	1278.750	Food and Allied
82	Eastern Cables Ltd.	1245.000	Engineering
83	Golden Son Ltd.	1181.296	Engineering
84	Bangladesh General Insurance Co. Ltd.	1180.836	Insurance
85	Olympic Industries Ltd.	1107.700	Engineering
86	Progressive Life Insurance Co. Ltd.	1085.813	Insurance
87	Bangladesh Thai Aluminum Ltd.	1084.285	Engineering
88	Eastland Insurance Co. Ltd.	1073.618	Insurance
89	Aramit Ltd.	1071.200	Miscellaneous
90	Quasem Drycells Ltd.	1050.240	Engineering
91	Usmania Glass Sheet Factory Ltd.	1047.922	Miscellaneous
92	United Insurance Co. Ltd.	1044.250	Insurance
93	Fidelity Assets & Securities Co. Ltd.	938.553	Bank
94	AGNI Systems Ltd.	920.837	IT Sector
95	Bangladesh Industrial Finance Co. Ltd.	901.176	Bank

APPENDIX A. *(Continued)*

Sl. No.	Company Name	Market Capitalization on May 7, 2009, in BDT (Millions)	Industry
96	Bangladesh Finance and Investment Co. Ltd.	897.515	Bank
97	Monno Fabrics Ltd.	836.625	Textile
98	National Polymer Industries Ltd.	826.914	Engineering
99	Pioneer Insurance Co. Ltd.	802.125	Insurance
100	Phoenix Insurance Co. Ltd.	794.915	Insurance

APPENDIX B. CONTENT ANALYSIS FRAMEWORK

A. Climate Change Disclosure Category (11)
1. Governance information
2. Climate change policy statement
3. Emissions reduction target
4. GHG emissions data
5. Energy usage data
6. Mitigation measures
7. Product impacts on climate change
8. Adaptation measures
9. Assurance of climate change disclosures
10. Reference to standards/protocols
11. Other climate change issues

B. Environmental Disclosure Category (13)
12. Governance information
13. Environmental policy statement
14. Targets and performance data
15. Environmental audit
16. Spills and waste
17. Financial elements of environmental issues
18. Sustainability and sustainable development
19. Installation of effluent treatment plants
20. Product impacts on environment
21. Reference to standards/guidelines/compliance
22. Environmental awards
23. Negative environmental disclosures
24. Other environmental issues

THE ADOPTION OF IPSASs IN SOUTH ASIA: A COMPARATIVE STUDY OF SEVEN COUNTRIES

Pawan Adhikari and Frode Mellemvik

ABSTRACT

Purpose – *This empirical article aims at studying whether, how, and to what extent the South Asian countries have or are planning to move in the International Public Sector Accounting Standards (IPSASs) direction.*

Design/methodology/approach – *By applying the institutional perspectives, the article seeks to explore the roles and contributions of international financial institutions in the dissemination of public sector accounting reform ideas, particularly IPSASs ideas in South Asia. Document search represents the major method of collecting data for this study.*

Findings – *The present article demonstrates that the majority of the South Asian countries have envisaged the adoption of the cash basis IPSAS as a way forward in order to implement accrual accounting. International financial institutions have seemingly created a myth in the region that accrual accounting cannot be introduced without first complying with the cash basis IPSAS. However, the countries' efforts are to a large extent directed at adapting rather than adopting IPSASs in all material respects. In relation to this, the article suggests that the acceptance of IPSASs in South Asia is better understood in terms of legitimacy.*

Research in Accounting in Emerging Economies, Volume 10, 169–199
Copyright © 2010 by Emerald Group Publishing Limited
All rights of reproduction in any form reserved
ISSN: 1479-3563/doi:10.1108/S1479-3563(2010)0000010012

Research limitations/implications – *It is beyond the scope of this article to cover the ongoing public sector accounting reforms in South Asia other than IPSASs reforms as well as to reveal accounting changes at other levels than central government level.*

Practical implications – *The article raises doubts as to whether and to what extent the cash basis IPSAS will help public sector management reforms in South Asia.*

Originality/value – *Given the paucity of consistent research efforts on the topic in Western English language literature, the present article strives to bring ongoing IPSASs reforms in South Asia into the international arena. The article also contributes to the growing body of the comparative public sector accounting research by presenting the similarities and differences in government accounting reforms, particularly IPSASs reforms, in South Asia.*

Keywords: Accrual basis IPSASs; cash basis IPSAS; institutional theory; international financial institutions; South Asia.

1. INTRODUCTION

The wave of new public management (NPM) has led to many developments in the public sector during the last three decades. Accounting change, which primarily deals with the adoption of accrual accounting, has been central to public sector reforms, particularly in Western countries (Christiaens & Peteghem, 2007; Guthrie, Humphey, & Olson, 1998, 1999; Ellwood & Newberry, 2007; Carlin, 2005; Mellett & Ryan, 2008; Lapsley, Mussari, & Paulsson, 2009). Accrual accounting has been perceived as a means of realizing the intended benefits of NPM in actual practice (Guthrie, 1998; Timoshenko & Adhikari, 2009). In recent years, this trend toward streamlining the public sector has extended beyond the boundaries of developed countries and has increasingly gained ground in developing countries and countries in transition. Many developing countries have initiated structural changes in the provision of public services, reflecting the NPM trend, albeit their efforts have not been widely represented in mainstream research (World Development Report, 2000; Economic Commission for Africa (ECA), 2003; Alawattage, Hopper, & Wickramasinghe, 2007; Mimba, Helden, & Tillema, 2007). These structural changes have created the need for new accounting and accountability, providing the impetus for accounting reforms in developing countries (Broadbent & Guthrie, 2008).

However, what is striking is that, unlike developed countries where the trend is to shift away from the cash to the accrual basis of accounting, developing countries seem to be much focused on improvements in the standards and procedures that regulate the accounting system (Chan, 2005). To illustrate this, the IPSASB (2008) has reported that the majority of the International Public Sector Accounting Standards (IPSASs) adopters are either developing nations or those in transition. As many of these developing countries and transitional economies adhere to cash accounting, the cash basis IPSAS has become the centerpiece of their government accounting reforms (Chan, 2005; Sutcliffe, 2009; Parry & Wynne, 2009). The cash basis IPSAS requires, among other things, general-purpose financial statements, general considerations, correction of errors, consolidated financial statements, foreign currency treatments, other transitional provisions, presentation of budget information, and recipients of external assistance (International Federation of Accountants (IFAC), 2008). Unlike the general-purpose financial statements under the accrual basis accounting, consisting of the statement of financial position, the statement of financial performance, the cash flow statement, and the statement of changes in net equity/assets, the statement of cash receipts and payments is the core of the general-purpose financial statements under the cash basis accounting.

Notably, widespread use of IPSASs, particularly the cash basis IPSAS in the developing world is twofold (Chan, 2005). First, the IPSASs have the advantage of being supported by powerful international financial institutions, namely the World Bank (WB), the International Monetary Fund (IMF), and the Asian Development Bank (ADB). Next, the IPSASs ideas are being increasingly recommended as the best government accounting alternatives that the global accountancy profession can offer to the public sector. This support of international financial institutions and professional accountants has made the IPSASs a de facto benchmark for improving, evaluating, and harmonizing the government accounting systems of developing nations.

Representing the group of developing nations, the South Asian countries no longer form an exception to the IPSASs trend. Subramanian (2008) states that all South Asian countries, namely Bangladesh, Bhutan, India, Maldives, Nepal, Pakistan, and Sri Lanka, have either initiated or are contemplating initiating public sector accounting reforms aimed at introducing IPSASs. Moreover, the South Asian Federation of Accountants (SAFA), a forum of professional accounting bodies for the South Asian countries, has constituted a working group to help governments in the region implement accrual accounting using the IPSASs (SAFA, 2006). However, little is know about the process and manner in which the IPSASs are being implemented in South Asia. Given the paucity of consistent research efforts on the topic in Western English language literature, the present article aims at studying whether, how, and to what extent the South Asian countries have or are planning to move in the IPSASs direction. A growing body of literature in recent years has attempted to examine the phenomenon of comparative public sector accounting (Humphrey & Guthrie, 1996; Humphrey, Miller, & Scapens, 1993; Pine & Torres, 2003; Guthrie et al., 1999; Lüder & Jones, 2003; Bourmistrov & Mellemvik, 2005; Chan & Jianfa, 2005; Benito, Brusca, & Montesinos, 2005, 2007; Jorge, 2008). This literature has provided a better basis to understand the varied development paths and attitudes toward public sector accounting reforms around the world – in both strategy and content. Moreover, the findings of these studies have allowed transfer of good practice and prevented mistakes being repeated elsewhere (Broadbent & Guthrie, 2008). The present article also intends to contribute to this growing body of comparative public sector accounting research by presenting similarities and differences in government accounting reforms, particularly the IPSASs reforms in South Asia.

The article draws on so-called "new institutional theory" or "new institutionalism," as it helps explain how and why organizations interact with their operating environments and how this interaction would impact upon their accounting choice and practice (Bergevärn, Mellemvik, & Olson, 1995; Carpenter & Feroz, 2001; Rahaman, Lawrence, & Roper, 2004; Tsamenyi, Cullen, & Gonzalez, 2006). The empirical material for this study is based on a collection of official documents, mainly the World Bank's assessment framework of 2008 and its individual country study reports on public sector accounting and auditing. Moreover, documents incorporating accounting laws, regulations, and other types of accounting guidance in each specific country have also been widely collected and assessed throughout the research. However, it is worth noting that, by mainly focusing on the adoption of IPSASs in the South Asian countries, this article has limitations of scope. It is beyond the scope of this study to cover the ongoing public sector accounting reforms in South Asia other than the IPSASs reforms as well as to reveal the accounting changes at other levels than central government level.

The remainder of the article is organized as follows. Section 2 incorporates institutional perspectives that have provided a theoretical setting for this research. In Section 3, a short introduction to the socioeconomic context of South Asia is presented. A case study of individual countries, with details of the extent to which they are now adopting IPSASs, particularly the cash basis IPSAS is discussed in Section 4. Section 5 looks comparatively at the adoption of IPSASs in the region. The article ends with a discussion of the concerned countries' efforts in the direction of IPSASs in the light of the theoretical perspectives applied as well as setting out some concluding remarks.

2. INSTITUTIONAL PERSPECTIVE

A central aspect of institutional theories, especially so-called "new institutionalism" as propagated by Meyer and Rowan (1977) and DiMaggio and Powell (1983), is that organizational structures and procedures tend to become more alike (i.e., isomorphic) with those structures and procedures in their environment that are socially accepted. The socially acknowledged structures and procedures profoundly impact upon organizational choice regardless of their actual usefulness. A plethora of studies is currently available demonstrating how the search for legitimacy enforces organizations to interact with their institutional environments and comply with the external requirements (DiMaggio & Powell, 1983; Scott, 1987; Oliver, 1991; Carruthers, 1995; Meyer & Rowan, 1977; Carpenter & Feroz, 2001).

DiMaggio and Powell (1983) state that organizations create institutions or become isomorphic by way of three mechanisms, that is, coercive, mimetic, and normative mechanisms. These three institutional mechanisms are regarded as the primary causal factors influencing and shaping organizational structures and practices (Scott, 1987). Many researchers have applied these mechanisms in order to give an understanding of how accounting changes are endeavored institutionalized (Carmona & Macias, 2001; Carmona & Donoso, 2004; Collin, Tagesson, Andersson, Cato, & Hansson, 2009; Adhikari & Mellemvik, 2009; Timoshenko & Adhikari, 2009). The coercive mechanism of creating an institution is linked to resource scarcities, meaning that organizations lacking resources tend to adhere to the rules and practices proposed by the institutions upon whom they are dependent (Fein & Mizruchi, 1999; Oliver, 1991; Tolbert & Zucker, 1997). On the other hand, resource abundance provides some organizations with the opportunity to exercise power as they could enforce the recipient organizations to comply with the established social patterns (Fein & Mizruchi, 1999). The mimetic way of creating an institution is linked to "environmental uncertainties," stemming from ambiguous causes or unclear solutions.

Such ambiguities lead organizations to guise themselves as analogous organizations by adopting similar structures and models (Carpenter & Feroz, 2001). In doing so, organizations are regarded as legitimate, as they can then act in accordance with other successful organizations' expectations (Granlund & Lukka, 1998). The normative mechanism concerns with creating an institution through adopting ideas and requirements disseminated by professional organizations, consultants, and experts. Professional bodies, as carriers of knowledge, set specific guidelines and procedures in their attempts to justify the rational way of managing organizations within their autonomy (Czarniawska & Joerges, 1996; Czarniawska & Sevon, 1996; Sahlin-Andersson, 2001). Compliance with professional requirements is expected to provide organizations with a number of benefits, including increased resources and social accreditation (Oliver, 1991, p. 153).

In recent years, a number of studies, conducted particularly in Scandinavia, have, however, striven to broaden the underlying ideas and scope of this new institutionalism (Czarniawska & Sevon, 1996; Andersson & Engwall, 2002). These studies have endeavored to offer a broader understanding of how organizational or structural changes are carried out within a particular context. Indeed, organizations do not institutionalize the rules and practices in an exact format or in a planned way as they are evolved. This means that they select the most relevant ideas from a myriad of ideas circulating in institutional environments and mold them differently by taking into account their specific organizational contexts. Moreover, it is worth noting that organizations are likely to encounter a number of social and cultural restrictions during the process of institutional transformation. These contextual limitations force organizations to search for some kind of consensus – rather than complying with the original ideas and practices. As a result, the ideas and practices institutionalized in a particular context tend to absorb many specific "flavors" and local qualities (Czarniawska & Sevon, 1996; Andersson & Engwall, 2002).

A growing body of literature applies the ideas derived from the domain of institutional theory to shed light on the causes and consequences of accounting change and the factors exerting impacts upon the change (Bergevärn et al., 1995; Carpenter & Feroz, 2001; Scapens & Siti-Nabiha, 2005; Dambrin, Lambert, & Sponem, 2007). This study, focusing on the South Asian countries' journey toward the IPSASs, intends to make a contribution to this literature. Moreover, by applying the aforementioned institutional perspectives, we strive to explore the roles and contributions of international financial institutions in dissemination of public sector accounting reform ideas, particularly IPSASs ideas in the region. Several researchers have in their studies emphasized the dominant role and influence of international financial institutions, especially the World Bank and the IMF, in facilitating accounting reforms in developing nations (Uddin & Hopper, 2001, 2003; Mir & Rahaman, 2005; Neu, Ocampo, Graham, & Heincke, 2006; Alawattage et al., 2007). These studies have attempted to demonstrate how accounting changes have become an important centerpiece of lending conditions for the developing world. Continuing in this vein, it is worth exploring where the IPSASs ideas have evolved in the region? Have they stemmed from the national governments in order to streamline their accounting systems? Or perhaps from international financial institutions presenting recommendations about how to improve the public financial management system in the region? Moreover, the institutional perspectives will allow us to study whether the IPSASs are being implemented in the region as in the form presented by the IPSASB to avoid "reinventing the wheel" or with some modifications in order to meet the specific local contexts.

3. THE SOCIOECONOMIC CONTEXT OF SOUTH ASIA

South Asia mainly consists of seven nations, namely Bangladesh, Bhutan, India, the Maldives, Nepal, Pakistan, Sri Lanka, and some British Indian Ocean Territories. These seven countries are also the founding members of the South Asian Association for Regional Cooperation (SAARC).[1] On many occasions and in many texts, Iran, Afghanistan, and Myanmar have also been included in South Asia. However, in our study, the term "South Asia" mainly refers to the aforementioned seven founding members of the SAARC. The South Asian countries have used the SAARC as a means of promoting and sustaining mutual trade and economic cooperation among them (Ali, Ahmed, & Henry, 2006). One of the goals of the SAARC has been the removal of existing trade barriers in order to transform the region into a free trade zone, the so-called "South Asia Free Trade Area (SAFTA)."

Geographically, South Asia is a huge landmass accommodating almost one-fifth of the world's population and is home to half the world's poor. The region consists of countries as small as the Maldives with an area of 298 km^2 and a population of about 200,000 and countries as big as India with an area of 3.3 million km^2 and a population of 1 billion (Haque, 2001; World Bank,

2009). Although the South Asian countries are different in terms of their historical roots and cultural and religious beliefs, they share more or less similar social and governance problems ranging from a low level of literacy and poor health services to corruption (Haque, 2001). What is striking is that the majority of the South Asian countries have in recent years enjoyed significant progress in human development as a result of the rapid economic growth. This growth has led to a substantial reduction in poverty in many parts of the region and visualized the potentials for achieving development (World Bank, 2009). However, at the same time, the failure of some countries to achieve this reduction in poverty has widened the income gap between the countries, characterizing the region no longer as a uniformly low-income region. While Bhutan, the Maldives, parts of Sri Lanka, and several Indian states have achieved middle-income status among developing nations, the human development indicators and incomes in Bangladesh, Nepal, most of Pakistan, and the lagging regions of India and Sri Lanka still correspond to that of low-income countries (Table 1).

One commonality of the South Asian countries is perhaps their dependency on international aid and loans for pursuing development activities. In 2006, the South Asian countries received average international aid worth 4.91% of GNI (World Bank, 2009; ADB, 2007a). At the same time, the average total external debt of the countries stood at about 46.98%

Table 1. The Socioeconomic Indicators of South Asia.

Country Indicator	Bangladesh	Bhutan	India	Maldives	Nepal	Pakistan	Sri Lanka
Population 2007 (millions) (see World Bank, 2009)	158.6	0.66	1123.3	0.31	28.1	162.4	19.9
Population living below USD 2 per day (2006) (see ADB, 2007a)	82.8	–	81.3	–	65.3	73.6	41.4
GNI per capita 2007 (Atlas method, US$) (see World Bank, 2009)	470	1770	950	3510	340	870	1540
GDP 2007 (US$ billions) (see World Bank, 2009)	67.7	1.1	1171.0	1.1	10.2	143.6	32.4
Average annual GDP growth 2007 (see World Bank, 2009)	6.5	19.1	9.0	22.5	2.5	6.4	6.8
Foreign aid 2006 (% of GNI) (see ADB, 2007a)	2.1	11.1	0.2	9.2	5.2	1.5	5.1
Total external debt 2006 (% of GDP) (see ADB, 2007a)	33.2	78.5	15.3	49.1	38.1	28.4	86.3

of GDP. Indeed, this dependency on international resources has raised concern about public accountability and governance in the region and provided the countries with a stimulus to introduce some elements of market-driven governance into their public administration (Haque, 2001). Mimba et al. (2007) state that the majority of the South Asian countries have in recent years initiated NPM reforms aiming to reduce bureaucratic power, streamline administrative efficiency, modernize public expenditure management, and reinforce accountability of public resources. Improvements to the existing accounting systems and the capacity enhancement of the national accounting and auditing institutions have become central to governance reforms in the region. Subramanian (2008) states that the prevailing accounting thought in the region has changed direction toward adopting and implementing IPSASs, which is also widely promoted by international financial institutions. The following sections address whether, how, and to what extent the countries in the region have made progress toward implementing IPSASs.

4. IPSASs REFORMS IN SOUTH ASIA

This section is meant to study existing government accounting regulations and ongoing IPSASs reforms in the South Asian countries. It commences with government accounting in Bangladesh and continues by presenting the case of Bhutan, India, the Maldives, Nepal, Pakistan, and Sri Lanka, respectively.

4.1. The Case of Bangladesh

Government accounting and reporting in Bangladesh is mainly regulated by the account code and a number of laws and instructions, including Parts 7 and 8 of the Constitution, the 1974 Comptroller and Auditor General (CAG) Act, the 1984 CAG (additional functions) Amendment Ordinance, the General Financial Rules and Regulations (GFRR), and the Treasury Regulations and Audit Code. The account code has set out the detailed rules for maintaining the cash basis of accounting. Volume 1 of the account code has introduced the form in which and the general principles and methods according to which the accounts of government should be kept. Similarly, volumes II and III of the account code have accommodated the directions regarding the form of initial and subsidiary accounts to be kept in the district and thana accounts offices and by the officers of public works and forest departments. The Controller General of Accounts (CGA) is a central unit for the general government budget sector under the Ministry of Finance. The office has prescribed a 13-digit code for all government transactions with a view to enabling the analysis of accounting data in different ways and at different levels.

There is no prescription for the adoption of international accounting standards in the prevailing accounting regulations. This also means that the accounts and annual financial statements of the government of Bangladesh are to a large extent prepared without considering the requirements laid down in the cash basis IPSAS. To illustrate this, controlled entities have not been clearly defined, which has led the government budget sector to perform both as a reporting and an economic entity. In fact, full consolidation of all entities controlled by central government is central to the cash basis IPSAS. The annual financial statements of the CGA do not correspond with general-purpose financial statements to be used under the cash basis IPSAS, as they exclude a summary statement of cash receipts and payments recognizing the cash controlled by a reporting entity; the cash balances available for use; and the cash balances that are subject to external restrictions, undrawn borrowings, and comparative information of previous years (World Bank, 2007a). Moreover, the statements lack disclosures on the nature of accounting errors and the amount of correction, as explained in the cash basis IPSAS. Along with this, the audited financial statements exclude disclosures on applied accounting policies, assumptions, and explanatory notes – one of the key requirements of the cash basis IPSAS.

The World Bank (2001, 2007a) has further pointed out a number of institutional weaknesses, including the slow computerization of government accounts, the lack of professional accountants and trainers at the Financial Management Academy (FIMA) imparting accounting knowledge and conducting training for government accountants, and an underdeveloped code of ethics and continuing education for government accountants, extending the gaps between the accounting system and the IPSAS requirements. However, the Ministry of Finance has recently announced the forming of a committee to suggest improvements in the education and training of government accountants and auditors. The ministry has also declared broader financial management reform programs in cooperation with international financial institutions, prioritizing improvements in public expenditure management and the computerization of government accounting. As part of reforms, the IPSAS-based statements for the core ministries (excluding specialized organizations) and the specialized organizations are intended to be published by the financial year 2009/2010 (World Bank, 2007a). Moreover, a committee has been formed in order to work on the action plan to adopt accrual accounting in the long run. The government of Bangladesh considers the adoption of the cash basis IPSAS to be a point of departure for implementing accrual accounting.

4.2. The Case of Bhutan

Government accounting in Bhutan is mainly regulated by the 2001 Financial Rules and Regulations (FRR) and the 2007 Public Finance Act (PFA). The 2001 FRR incorporates the financial management manual (FMM) and six other technical documents including the finance and account manual, the budget manual, the aid and debt management manual, the property management manual, the procurement manual, and the revenue manual. The FMM has set out the basic rules for maintaining cash accounting using double-entry bookkeeping (MoF, 2001). In addition to this, it consists of the provision for recognizing the value of goods and services received and applied in kinds and recording the supplementary memorandum for the government's financial commitments and debts. An accounts division, one of six divisions and sections operating within the Department of Public Accounts (DPA), subordinated to the Ministry of Finance, is charged with maintaining common public expenditure accounts and preparing the consolidated annual financial statements of the government. The PFA of 2007 has further mandated the preparation and presentation of the annual audited financial statements reflecting the financial positions of the government of Bhutan.

As is the case in Bangladesh, the FRR and the PFA have not prescribed the use of international accounting standards for government accounting. Albeit the DPA prepares the statement of cash receipts and payments, it excludes the additional information on the subclassification of cash receipts and payments into total cash receipts, total cash payments, and opening and closing balances, as demanded by the cash basis IPSAS. The World Bank (2007b) states that the FRR and the PFA have provided both the scope and flexibility to comply with a number of key reporting requirements laid down in the cash basis IPSAS. This also means that a modification in the reporting formats would allow the government of Bhutan to prepare and present the consolidated financial statements disclosing third-party settlement of government obligations, restrictions on the issue of available cash balances by the government, foreign currency transactions, and comparative information up to one year in accord with international standards. However, a substantial change in the existing accounting system has been called for in order to adjust to many of the requirements of the cash basis IPSAS, including presentation of accounting policies, demonstration of prior period adjustments and errors, and incorporation of the cash out of control, among other matters.

In the case of Bhutan, the lack of education and training of public sector accountants is seen as a major hindrance in fully complying with the cash basis IPSAS (World Bank, 2007b). Having acknowledged this capacity constraint, the DPA has in recent years attempted to carry out the training need assessment of accounting personnel and develop the relevant in-country and in-service training model by cooperating with regional accounting bodies and international financial institutions (ADB, 2007b). The World Bank (2007b) claims that the government of Bhutan has expressed its commitment to developing public sector accounting standards in line with the cash basis IPSAS and to studying the feasibility of gradually moving toward accrual accounting. More recently, the DPA has published its government accounting reform agenda prioritizing the e-release of government funds, the development of Royal Government of Bhutan Accounting Standards, and issuance of the code of ethics for finance personnel, among other things (DPA, 2009). The department has emphasized the importance of accounting standards corresponding to the cash basis IPSAS in order to promote sound financial and other management practices throughout the Bhutanese public sector.

4.3. The Case of India

The 1990 Government Accounting Rules (GAR), framed under the Article 150 of the Constitution, and the 2006 General Financial Rules (GFR) are the two main regulatory frameworks for Indian government accounting. The CGA in the Ministry of Finance is charged with prescribing the accounting forms for the union and states, and framing, or revising, the rules and manuals relating to government accounting (GoI, 2005). The Institute of Government Accounts and Finance (INGAF), a training arm of the CGA, is authorized to impart in-service training and continuing education to government accountants.

Indian central government accounting uses cash accounting and single-entry bookkeeping (Khumawala, 1997; Srinivas, 2006). However, the accounting system has mandated the preparation of a number of financial statements covering some information on assets, liabilities, and noncash transactions (Kaushik, 2006; GASAB, 2008). The Indian central government accounting system can be seen as a combination of two types of accounts: the appropriation account and the finance accounts. While the appropriation accounts, which are mainly focused on budgetary control, record the original budget estimates, supplementary grants, surrenders, reappropriations, actual expenditures, and the excess of savings under the heads, the finance accounts present the classified and consolidated accounts of all government transactions incurred under the consolidated fund, contingency fund, and public accounts (Kaushik, 2006; GASAB, 2008).

Albeit developed on the cash principle, the Indian central government accounting is yet to be harmonized with the cash basis IPSAS. A recent research report issued by the GASAB, constituted by the CAG of India to facilitate government accounting reform, delineates the prevailing gaps between Indian government accounting and the cash basis IPSAS. The report clarifies that a number of requirements laid down in the cash basis IPSAS, for instance, presenting the details of the external assistance received, demonstrating the date when the financial statements were authorized and who gave that authority, reporting the cash balance which is actually available for use, separating the third-party payments in government accounts, and including the comparative information of previous years, among others, are either missing in the Indian system or are not treated in accordance with the IPSAS (GASAB, 2008). In addition to this, Indian regulations lack a provision for the preparation of the consolidated financial statements covering all controlled and controlling entities – one of the main requirements of the cash basis IPSAS. Presently, the consolidated financial statements of India recognize only its own cash flows and not those of the entities it controls, for instance, parastatals such as government companies, corporations, and autonomous bodies (GASAB, 2008).

In the context of India, the cash basis IPSAS has been seen as a generic standard compared to the GASB's Indian Government Accounting Standards (IGASs), on account of its inability to address many of the existing accrual items in the accounting system. Despite the fact that the GASB had initially agreed to revise some of its IGASs in order to increase compliance with the cash basis IPSAS, the Board has greatly emphasized the development of Indian Government Financial Reporting Standards, which are claimed to be in line with the accrual basis IPSAS. In fact, following the recommendation of the Twelfth Finance Commission in late 2004, accrual accounting has become a key accounting reform agenda in India (Kaushik, 2006). A number of departments, including the departments of Post across the country have already embarked on pilot studies on accrual accounting with the financial support of the World Bank (The Hindu, 2009; SAFA, 2006). Moreover, the recent announcement of the CAG of India to move toward the accrual basis of accounting within the next five years, that is, by 2014, has further accelerated the transition process (The Hindu Business Line, 2009; The Economic Times, 2009).

4.4. The Case of the Maldives

The 2002 government financial regulations and the 2006 Public Finance Law (PFL) are the main regulatory frameworks for public finance, including government accounting in the Maldives. The law, which is one of the key components of the ongoing public accounting system (PAS) project, financed and managed by the World Bank and the European Community, has introduced a number of legislative changes, impacting upon the overall financial management system of the country (Ministry of Finance and Treasury (MoFT), 2007). Some of the striking features of this law include the requirement of a single treasury account, the enforcement of a commitment management system in order to ensure that actual plus commitments do not exceed budgets, the establishment of a fixed asset register, and the introduction of a mechanism to control and manage contracts and commitments, among others. The law obliges all public entities to produce comprehensive financial statements in a form and manner prescribed by the Auditor General.

As is the case in Bangladesh, Bhutan, and India, government accounts in the Maldives are maintained on a cash basis. The accounting system can, however, be referred to as modified cash, in that it does recognize some forms of assets, liabilities, and contingent liabilities. The Financial Comptroller prepares the annual financial statements, which mainly incorporate a statement of the estimated revenue and expenditure of each public fund included in the appropriation act; a statement of the actual revenue and expenditure of each public fund; and a statement of the assets, liabilities, and contingent liabilities of the country as a whole at the end of the financial year (MoFT, 2009). The World Bank (2007c) states that albeit the Audit Act allows IPSASs to be followed, the PFL has not mandated the use of international standards in public sector accounting. This also means that the prevailing accounting system in the government of the Maldives does not correspond to the requirements of both the cash and the accrual basis IPSASs. To illustrate this, the annual financial statements exclude disclosures on the impact of events occurring after the reporting date, the consolidation of controlled entities, the actual cash balances available for use, the comparative cash information, the authorization date, and the accounting policies and notes, which are some of the key features of the cash basis IPSAS. Similarly, the financial statements also do not fulfill the requirements of the accrual basis IPSASs, as they lack disclosures on assets, liabilities, net equity, revenues and expenses by major class, net surplus or deficits, and cash flows separating operating, investing, and financing activities, to name a few matters (World Bank, 2007c).

Similarly to other small countries in the region, the lack of education and training of public sector accountants and an absence of a code of ethics are regarded to be the other factors widening the gulf between the present accounting system and IPSASs requirements. The World Bank (2007c), however, states that the country has renewed its commitment to comply with the cash basis of IPSAS, while also maintaining a note for additional information on assets, liabilities, and contingent liabilities, as required by the PFL. The MoFT emphasizes the implementation of an integrated financial management computer package, the development of a code of ethics for public sector accountants, and the launch of distance learning accounting education (World Bank, 2007c; MoFT, 2007). In addition to this, attempts are being made to introduce IPSAS formats for the statements, explanatory notes, and disclosures within the financial year 2009, as part of the public sector accounting project. Progression toward the accrual basis of accounting has been prioritized in the long run after the country fulfills the requirements of the cash basis IPSAS and strengthens use of information technology (MoFT, 2007).

4.5. The Case of Nepal

The 2007 Interim Constitution, the 1999 Financial Procedures Act, and the 2007 Financial Procedures Regulations are the three main norms regulating government accounting in Nepal. While the Constitution mainly focuses on the operation of the consolidated fund and the presentation of annual budget, the accounting procedures are codified in the act and regulations. The Financial Comptroller General Office (FCGO), an independent organ for government accounting within the Ministry of Finance, is charged with enacting government accounting acts and regulations, facilitating accounting practices, preparing annual financial statements, and mobilizing government accountants, among other things. The FCGO is represented at district levels by the "District Treasury and Control Offices" (DTCOs).

Nepalese government accounting uses a cash basis system with double-entry methodology to record expenditures (FCGO, 2008). Although the act and regulations have allowed government entities to separate outstanding staff advances and suppliers not paid until the next fiscal year from the cash transactions, the accounting system does not recognize these obligations and commitments (Agrawal & Bista, 1981; Chitrakar & Macmillan, 2002; World Bank, 2003a, 2007d; IMF, 2007). In fact, advance payments and inventories are treated as expenditures for the fiscal year in which they are procured and as revenues of the year in which they are recovered. The World Bank (2007d) has further pointed out a number of weaknesses in the Nepalese cash basis system, including the omission of "off budget" transactions and the lack of provisions to recognize direct payments and commodity grants offered by donors.

Notably, the operation of Nepalese cash basis accounting has not been in accordance with the cash basis IPSAS (Adhikari & Mellemvik, 2008). For instance, the accounting statements and reports are prepared on an annual basis without addressing many of the IPSAS requirements, including the cumulative expenditures incurred or incomes generated for more than a year, transactions made by third parties, receipts and payments on foreign currencies, correction of errors, and undrawn external assistance, among other things (World Bank, 2007d). The FCGO prepares and presents the summary consolidated statements incorporating only the cash receipts and payments of the ministries and departments excluding other controlled entities such as public corporations, boards, and local bodies. In addition to this, the audited statements have yet to include the accounting policies, assumptions, and explanatory notes, as prescribed by the cash basis IPSAS.

The Nepalese case shows that the adoption of accrual accounting had been on the government accounting reform agenda for more than two decades (Adhikari & Mellemvik, 2008). However, the failure to introduce accrual accounting has in recent years led to a focus on improvements in prevailing cash accounting by using the cash basis IPSAS. International financial institutions, particularly the World Bank, have recommended the government to consider the immediate implementation of the cash basis IPSAS as part of a longer term program to adopt accrual accounting (Adhikari & Mellemvik, 2008). As recommended by these institutions, a public sector accounting technical committee consisting of representatives from the Auditor General's Office, the Ministry of Finance, and the FCGO has recently been set up within the Accounting Standards Board, an autonomous body to pronounce standards for the private sector in order to facilitate the IPSAS project in Nepal (Guragain, 2008). The committee has developed Nepal public sector accounting standards corresponding to the cash basis IPSAS and submitted these to the government for approval (Accounting Standards Board, 2009). Attempts are now being made to develop the code of ethics and continuing education for government accountants in cooperation with the Institute of the Chartered Accountants of Nepal and incorporate the cash basis IPSAS in the coursework of state-owned, in-service training institutions, that is, the revenue administration training center and the staff college (Government of Nepal, 2008).

4.6. The Case of Pakistan

The government accounting system in Pakistan is regulated by the 1973 Constitution of Pakistan, the 2001 Auditor General's Ordinance, and the 2001 CGA Ordinance. The Constitution contains articles covering the national budget and government accounts, which consist of the consolidated fund accounts and public accounts (Narayan & Godden, 2000; GoP, 1999). Moreover, it has provided the Auditor General with the authority to prescribe the forms, principles, and methods of accounts of the federation and provinces. Two ordinances issued in 2001 have transferred the responsibilities for the preparation and maintenance of the accounts of the federation, the provinces, and districts from the Auditor General to the CGA (World Bank, 2003b; MeKendrick & Yousafzai, 2008).

Cash accounting using the single-entry bookkeeping system was used in the government of Pakistan until recently (Mehboob, 2008). However, in recent years, the project for Improvement to Financial Reporting and Auditing (PIFRA), launched in 1997 with the support of the World Bank, has led to substantial changes in government accounting practice. Presently, the New Accounting Model (NAM), based on the IFAC's guidelines for government financial reporting, particularly Study 11 "Government Financial Reporting: Accounting Issues and Practices" is being implemented with the use of SAP/R3 applications (SAFA, 2006; Narayan & Godden, 2000). The guidelines aim to assist governments in the preparation of their financial reports and present a description of the common bases of accounting used by governments, varying from the cash to the accrual basis and modifications to the cash and accrual basis. To be more specific, the NAM is anchored on the then modified cash basis of accounting standard discussed by the IFAC prior to the issuance of the cash and the accrual basis of IPSASs (World Bank, 2007e).

The NAM has introduced the new chart of accounts incorporating some accrual elements as stated by the IMF's GFSM 2001 (World Bank, 2003b).

Some of the key features of the NAM include the introduction of the concept of double-entry bookkeeping and the enforcement of commitment, physical, and financial assets and liabilities accounting (Mehboob, 2008). However, despite relying on the IFAC's guidelines, the general-purpose financial statements of the government of Pakistan exclude a range of accounting disclosures laid down in the cash basis IPSAS (World Bank, 2007e). The absence of information on the applied accounting policies and notes, the payments made by third parties on behalf of the entity, and the correction of errors are some of the examples. Moreover, the financial statements lack information on all cash receipts, cash payments, and cash balances controlled by the entity and the consolidated accounting information from all consolidated entities.

The World Bank (2007e) states that the government of Pakistan has expressed its commitment to complying with the cash basis IPSAS, while, at the same time, maintaining the modified cash system, as required by the NAM. The announcement of the Auditor General to adopt the IPSAS-2 cash flow reporting format, as part of the overall reporting requirements of the government, can be seen as an initial step in this respect. The CGA claims that the full-fledged implementation of the NAM would provide the office with the reporting opportunity that generally complies with the cash basis IPSAS. Moreover, the progressive implementation of the NAM has also been envisaged as a means of presenting full accrual information in the future. The SAFA (2006) has claimed that the NAM is capable of conversion into accrual-based accounting system with some modifications.

In the context of Pakistan, special focus has therefore been given to the training and capacity development of government accountants in recent years. Both government accountants and auditors have now been mandated to adhere to the INTOSAI code of conducts and to undertake a course on IPSASs, offered by the Audit and Accounts Training Institute (AATI), a national institute for training government accountants and auditors. More recently, the government, in support of the World Bank, has launched the second round of the PIFRA project, the so-called PEFRA II. The PIFRA II has particularly emphasized capacity building of the CGA, the Auditor General's Office, and the agencies preparing the accounts at each level of government (Ceesay, 2004).

4.7. The Case of Sri Lanka

Public sector accounting in Sri Lanka is regulated by a number of laws, including the 1978 Constitution of Sri Lanka, the 1992 Financial

Regulations, the 1971 Financial Act, the 1987 Financial Responsibility Act, and a number of other local government acts and ordinances. For accounting purposes, government organizations in Sri Lanka are categorized into three groups: ministries, departments, and constitutional bodies; non-revenue earning statutory bodies and public enterprises; and revenue-earning statutory bodies and public enterprises (ADB, 2002). The first two groups are regulated by the 1992 Financial Regulations, meaning they are required to prepare cash-based budgets and financial reports. The latter group is required to report in accordance with Sri Lankan Accounting Standards (SLASs), promulgated by the Institute of Chartered Accountants of Sri Lanka. The department of state accounts, one of the treasury departments functioning under the umbrella of the Ministry of Finance and Planning, is charged with preparing the consolidated accounts of the state, which mainly comprise the monthly, quarterly, and annual accounts of the cash receipts and payments, loan granted, and outstanding loan obligations, among other things (World Bank, 2003c).

The use of accounting standards has not been codified in the existing Sri Lankan accounting laws and regulations (Kuruppu & Adhikari, 2008). The World Bank (2007f), however, claims that the state accounts department has prepared annual accounts in accordance with the cash basis IPSAS since 2002. The government has also endeavored to simplify accounting procedures and systems, signaling an emphasis on outputs and results. Despite these efforts, it is clear that there are a number of inconsistencies between the cash basis IPSAS and the general-purpose financial statements of the Sri Lankan government. These gaps stand out in the following areas: consolidating noncommercial public enterprises and statutory boards, presenting the third-party payments, and disclosing restrictions on the cash balances. Moreover, the prevailing code of ethics for government accountants has not been revised in accordance with the IFAC's requirements. As is the case in other small South Asian countries, the human resource constraint is envisaged in preparing the financial statements to confirm with the cash basis IPSAS (Ministry of Finance and Planning (MoFP), 2009). The major training institutions for public sector accountants, that is, the Institute of Public Finance and Accountancy (IPFDA) and the INGAF, are still in the process of offering continuing professional education to government accountants (ADB, 2002; World Bank, 2007f).

The Sri Lankan government has stated its intention to tackle the aforementioned institutional weaknesses in order to fully comply with the cash basis IPSAS and to move progressively toward the accrual basis of accounting using IPSASs, one of the key demands of its development partners (World Bank, 2007f). An initial step toward the accrual basis accounting has been undertaken in 2005 by incorporating the additional disclosures on financial performance and results. More precisely, the accounts of the fiscal year 2005 have been presented by including the statements of financial performance, cash flows, financial position, and contingent liabilities. Moreover, the treasury has mandated all ministries and government entities to maintain accounts of their fixed assets and allowed the Institute of Charted Accountants of Sri Lanka (ICASL) to begin the process of developing the Sri Lankan versions of the accrual basis IPSASs (World Bank, 2007f).

A public sector accounting standards committee within the ICASL has now started to lay down the accrual basis Sri Lanka public sector accounting standards, corresponding to the accrual basis IPSASs (Adhikari, Kuruppu, & Mellemvik, 2009). In addition to this, the MoFP (2009) has, in its updated action plan for 2009, clarified that it will include disclosures on movable assets purchased after January 1, 2004, and outstanding liabilities. The introduction of these accrual elements in the financial statements is seen as a step forward toward the adoption of accrual accounting for the government of Sri Lanka (Adhikari et al., 2009).

5. COMPARING THE ADOPTION OF IPSASs IN SOUTH ASIA

This study demonstrates that government accounting in all South Asian countries is undergoing a period of transition and modernization. While some countries have already commenced reforms, others are in the process of streamlining their government accounting. The majority of ongoing government accounting reform projects in the region have been recommended and, in many cases, financed by international financial institutions, particularly the World Bank. To begin with, Bangladesh has an ongoing financial management reform program, which includes the standardization and computerization of government accounting. Bhutan has passed a new PFA emphasizing the development of public sector accounting standards and the accounting profession, among other things. The Indian GASAB has pronounced both the cash and the accrual basis accounting standards for central and state governments and is facilitating a pilot project on accrual accounting in a number of states. The public sector accounting project in the Maldives aims at introducing IPSAS formats for statements, explanatory notes, and disclosures within the fiscal year 2009. The Accounting Standards Board, Nepal, has developed Nepal Public Sector Accounting Standards in line with the cash basis IPSAS (ASB, 2009). The NAM, developed on the modified cash basis, is being implemented in Pakistan. And Sri Lanka has been attempting to pronounce the accrual basis accounting standards and to disclose addition accrual information in the financial statements, signaling a move toward the accrual basis of accounting.

Notably, the cash basis accounting is being pursued in all South Asian countries, albeit in varied forms. This also means that the prevailing accounting systems in the region are much focused on ensuring due control over and reporting compared to budget appropriations. However, the accounting systems in India, Pakistan, Sri Lanka, and Maldives can be referred to as modified cash, as they include some noncash and accrual transactions. Interestingly, none of these countries fully comply with the cash basis IPSAS. In terms of compliance with the cash basis IPSAS, the South Asian countries can be categorized into three groups. Sri Lanka is probably at the forefront, as it prepares the general-purpose financial statements by referring to the cash basis IPSAS. The World Bank's suggestion to Nepal to learn from the experience of Sri Lanka in adopting the cash basis IPSAS further reinforces this assertion (World Bank, 2007d). The next group consists of India, Pakistan, the Maldives, and Bhutan. Seemingly, the financial statements of these countries can be changed to be compatible with the cash basis IPSAS by including some additional disclosures on, for example, cash balances, comparative information, prior period adjustments and errors, third-party transactions, accounting policies and explanatory notes, and authorization dates, among other things. Moreover, Bhutan and Bangladesh are further required to improve the education and training of their government accountants prior to the implementation of the cash basis IPSAS. Nepal and Bangladesh can probably be placed in the last group. The financial statements of these two countries are largely inconsistent with requirements laid down in the cash basis IPSAS in major aspects – a situation requiring significant changes in formats and contents. However, ongoing government accounting reforms in Bangladesh and Nepal delineate the fact that these two countries have placed much emphasis on the adoption of the cash basis IPSAS as compared to other countries in the region.

It is worth pointing out that no single country in the region has so far prescribed the use of IPSASs in its prevailing accounting regulations. Albeit the majority of countries have expressed their intention to comply either with the cash or the accrual basis IPSASs, their efforts are to a large extent directed at adapting rather than adopting the IPSASs in all material respects. For instance, Pakistan, the Maldives, and Sri Lanka have clarified that they are willing to both comply with the requirements of the cash basis IPSAS and maintain the accounts of assets, liabilities, and other accrual items, as demanded by their national regulations. Notably, all South Asian countries have expressed their intentions to shift away from cash to accrual accounting in the long run. Most of them have envisaged the adoption of the cash basis IPSAS as a way forward to implementing accrual accounting. It has been argued that the adoption of the cash basis IPSAS would help these countries ratify many of the existing deficiencies and elevate their capacity to practice accrual accounting (Subramanian, 2008). However, India is the only country that has so far developed a clear transition plan including a timetable for the adoption of accrual accounting. Albeit Pakistan and Sri Lanka have extended the scope of their financial statements by including a number of accrual elements, they have yet to set up a detailed plan and timetable for the possible transition toward accrual accounting. Despite willingness, the SAFA (2006) has, however, expected a delay in the possible transition toward the accrual basis of accounting in the region due to a relatively small number of professional accountants, the lack of accrual accounting knowledge in the government sector, lower computer literacy, and the control-oriented mentality of the governments, among other factors.

6. DISCUSSION AND CONCLUSIONS

This article seeks to explore the adoption of IPSASs, particularly the cash basis IPSAS in South Asia using institutional perspectives as a theoretical setting. This study shows that the ongoing IPSASs project and the capacity development of government accountants and training institutions in the South Asian countries have been supported and financed by international financial institutions, namely the World Bank and the ADB. International financial institutions have been the carrier and disseminator of IPSASs ideas in the region, meaning that a reform policy toolkit is no longer solely the product mix of national governments. The acceptance of IPSASs has become a means for the South Asian countries to assure these institutions and other donors the effective and efficient use of resources, a key precondition for approving development aid and loans. In this regard, the present study can be seen as an extension of existing literature demonstrating the dominant role of international financial institutions in facilitating accounting reforms in developing countries.

However, what is striking is that none of the countries have declared convergence with IPSASs in material aspects. In other word, each country is attempting to translate IPSASs ideas in their own way so as to ensure compliance with their specific local requirements. Indeed, this effort seemingly thwarts the wish of the IPSASB, urging governments around the world to avoid "reinventing the wheel." The IPSASB emphasizes that countries should spend their time and energy in developing IPSASs implementation guidance and elevating the accounting education and training opportunities, rather than amending the standards to cope with their local regulations. In the light of this, the acceptance of IPSASs in the region as a means of improving governance and accountability can be classified a symbol of legitimacy, intended to bolster the image of the South Asian countries as "modern" or "rational" in the view of international financial institutions, donors, and others.

The evidence presented in the study leads us to argue that normative and coercive pressures have been more influential in driving the South Asian countries' journey toward IPSASs implementation. This means that the studies, recommendations, and projects conducted by international financial institutions, particularly the World Bank and the ADB, and the accounting professionals in the region, have forced the countries involved to undertake a move in the IPSASs direction. As stated previously, IPSASs have become a benchmark for international financial institutions to evaluate the quality, transparency, and comparability of accounting information in developing countries. Moreover, the reform ideas widely propagated by these institutions and professional bodies (in the context of this study, the adoption of IPSASs) have a tendency to possess legitimacy based on the supposition that they are rationally effective (Meyer & Rowan, 1977). Indeed, this has made it difficult, if not impossible, for national policy makers in the region to defy IPSASs ideas while reforming their public sector accounting. In the context of South Asia, the importance of IPSASs has been further linked to the facilitation of the SAFTA, leaving the countries no other alternatives than IPSASs (SAFA, 2006).

Along with the normative pressure, the existing of the coercive pressure cannot be denied in driving the South Asian countries in the IPSASs direction. This is probably due to the financial dependency on international financial institutions, leading many countries to accept the cash basis IPSAS, despite the fact that some of them are already on their way toward the accrual basis of accounting. The cases of the Maldives, Pakistan, and Sri Lanka can serve as examples. This also means that international financial institutions have seemingly created a myth in the region that accrual accounting cannot be introduced without first complying with the cash basis of IPSAS. However, the degree of the coercive pressure varies across countries, depending on their reliance on resources. For example, India seems to depend less on international aid and debts, as compared to other South Asian countries (see, e.g., Table 1). India has declared its intention to shift away from the cash to the accrual basis of accounting within the next five years and has embarked on pilot studies on accrual accounting, referring to the cash basis IPSAS as a set of generic standards insufficient to meet the information needs of the government and other stakeholders (GASAB, 2008). On the other hand, it could be argued that the high ratio of external debt, as compared to other South Asian countries, has probably given Sri Lanka the impetus to comply with the cash basis IPSAS, prior to other countries in the region (see, e.g., Table 1). Whatever, the case of South Asia reinforces the claim that the deepest economic crisis often initiates the profoundest reform measures, elevating the influence and dominance of international financial institutions (Batley, 1999). Moreover, the case of South Asia is a stark contrast to the ongoing public sector accounting reforms in many European countries, which are apparently less dependent on international resources and expertise. For instance, a number of studies have shown that IPSASs are yet to be acknowledged in the majority of developed countries, particularly European central governments (Christiaens & Reyniers, 2008; Benito et al., 2007; Pine & Torres, 2003).

DiMaggio and Powell (1983) state that it may not always be possible to distinguish between three different forms of institutional pressure. In fact, two or more of these institutional pressures may be operating simultaneously, making it difficult to determine which form of pressure is more potent at any given time. In this regard, it is not easy to ignore the presence of the mimetic pressure in the region, acting in concert with the normative and coercive ones. However, the mimetic pressure seems to be more potent in the context of small countries. To illustrate this, the Accounting Standards Board in Nepal has clarified that it has used the Sri Lankan financial statements as a model while designing the financial statements for the Government of Nepal (Guragain, 2008). It could therefore be argued that all three types of the institutional pressure have acted in concert to move the South Asian countries in the IPSASs direction, with normative and coercive pressures presumably being the most potent pressures, even though it is impossible to distinguish their effects empirically.

Indeed, the initiatives of the South Asian countries in the direction of the cash basis IPSAS (except India) have envisaged the possibility of updating their accounting so as to reflect the internationally agreed minimum benchmarks of best practice in cash accounting and reporting (Subramanian, 2008). However, given the requirements of the cash basis IPSAS, which are closer to current practice and are less costly to implement, a risk can also be envisaged that the cash basis IPSAS may become the de facto standard in the region, undermining the countries' both desire and ongoing efforts to adopt accrual accounting. Chan (2005) argues that a simpler form of accrual accounting, disclosing at least current fiscal resources and current liabilities, is a basic necessity for developing countries in order to discharge their accountability to a wider group of stakeholders. Moreover, the ECA (2003) has in its study indicated that those countries in Africa, which have already adopted accrual accounting, are at the forefront of public management reforms. In conclusion, this study raises doubts as to whether and to what extent the adoption of cash basis IPSAS will then help the South Asian countries translate the rhetoric of improved governance and accountability into actual practice. At the same time, it is also interesting to follow the extent of pressure toward the cash basis IPSAS and its implementation in other developing countries. Further studies can look into these matters.

NOTE

1. The South Asian Association for Regional Cooperation (SAARC) is an economic and political organization, established on December 8, 1985, by Bangladesh, Bhutan, India, the Maldives, Nepal, Pakistan, and Sri Lanka. In 2007, Afghanistan became the eighth member of the organization.

REFERENCES

Accounting Standards Board. (2009). *Nepal public sector accounting standard*. Kathmandu, Nepal: Himalaya Printing Offset Press.

Adhikari, P., Kuruppu, C., & Mellemvik, F. (2009). *Public sector accounting reforms in two South Asian countries: A comparative study of Nepal and Sri Lanka*. Working Paper no. 6. Bodø Graduate School of Business, Norway.

Adhikari, P., & Mellemvik, F. (2008). Changing ideology in Nepalese central government accounting reform. In: S. Jorge (Ed.), *Implementing reforms in public sector accounting* (pp. 183–199). Coimbra, Portugal: Imprensa da Universidade de Coimbra.

Adhikari, P., & Mellemvik, F. (2009). Nepalese governmental accounting development in the 1950s and early 1960s: An attempt to institutionalize expenditure accounting. *Accounting Historians Journal, 36*(1), 112–133.

Agrawal, G., & Bista, B. (1981). *Government accounting in Nepal*. Kathmandu, Nepal: Centre for Economic Development and Administration, Tribhuvan University.

Alawattage, C., Hopper, T., & Wickramasinghe, D. (2007). Introduction to management accounting in less developed countries. *Journal of Accounting and Organizational Change*, *3*(3), 183–191.

Ali, M. J., Ahmed, K., & Henry, D. (2006). Harmonization of accounting measurement practices in South Asia. *Advances in International Accounting*, *19*, 25–58.

Andersson, K. S., & Engwall, L. (2002). *The expansion of management knowledge: Carriers, flows and sources*. Stanford, CA: Stanford University Press.

Asian Development Bank (ADB). (2002). *Diagnostic study of accounting and auditing practices in Sri Lanka*, Manila, Philippines.

Asian Development Bank (ADB). (2007a). *Key Indicators 2007* (Vol. 38), Manila, Philippines.

Asian Development Bank (ADB). (2007b). *Kingdom of Bhutan: Strengthening public financial management*. Project No. 41152, Technical Assistance Report, Manila, Philippines.

Batley, R. (1999). The new public management in developing countries: Implications for policy and organizational reform. *Journal of International Development*, *11*(5), 761–765.

Benito, B., Brusca, I., & Montesinos, V. (2005). Local government accounting: An international empirical analysis. In: A. Bourmistrov & F. Mellemvik (Eds), *International trends and experiences in government accounting* (pp. 80–97). Oslo, Norway: Cappelen Akademisk Forlag.

Benito, B., Brusca, I., & Montesinos, V. (2007). The harmonization of government financial information systems: The role of the IPSASs. *International Review of Administrative Sciences*, *73*(2), 293–317.

Bergevärn, L., Mellemvik, F., & Olson, O. (1995). Institutionalization of accounting – A comparative study between Sweden and Norway. *Scandinavian Journal of Management*, *11*(1), 25–41.

Bourmistrov, A., & Mellemvik, F. (2005). *International trends and experiences in government accounting*. Oslo, Norway: Cappelen Akademisk Forlag.

Broadbent, J., & Guthrie, J. (2008). Public sector to public services: 20 years of "contextual" accounting research. *Accounting, Auditing & Accountability Journal*, *21*(2), 129–169.

Carlin, T. M. (2005). Debating the impact of accrual accounting and reporting in the public sector. *Financial Accountability and Management*, *21*(3), 309–336.

Carmona, S., & Donoso, R. (2004). Cost accounting in early regulated markets: The case of the royal soap factory of Seville (1525–1692). *Journal of Accounting and Public Policy*, *23*(2), 129–157.

Carmona, S., & Macias, M. (2001). Institutional pressures, monopolistic conditions, and the implementation of early cost systems: The case of the royal tobacco factory of Seville (1820–1887). *Abacus*, *37*(2), 139–165.

Carpenter, V., & Feroz, E. (2001). Institutional theory and accounting rule choice: An analysis of four US state governments' decisions to adopt generally accepted accounting principles. *Accounting, Organization and Society*, *26*(7/8), 565–596.

Carruthers, B. (1995). Accounting, ambiguity, and the new institutionalism. *Accounting, Organizations and Society*, *20*(4), 313–328.

Ceesay, I. B. (2004). Public financial accountability in Pakistan: The impact of PIFRA on capacity. *Capacity Enhancement Briefs*, No. 4, April, World Bank Institute.

Chan, J. (2005). Government accounting reform in developing countries: Connecting MDG, PRS and IPSAS. Paper presented at the 10th Biennial CIGAR Conference, May 26–27, Poitiers, France.

Chan, J. L., & Jianfa, L. (2005). Government accounting standards in China, U.S., and U.K. In: A. Bourmistrov & F. Mellemvik (Eds), *International trends and experiences in government accounting* (pp. 15–27). Oslo, Norway: Cappelen Akademisk Forlag.

Chitrakar, K., & Macmillan, G. (2002). *The road map for accounting reform in the neal public sector*. Report Prepared for ADB TA 3580-Corporate and Financial Governance Cluster – Improving Accounting and Auditing Standards in the Public Sector, Kathmandu, Nepal.

Christiaens, J., & Peteghem, V. (2007). Governmental accounting reform: Evolution of the implementation in Flemish municipalities. *Financial Accountability and Management, 23*(4), 375–399.

Christiaens, J., & Reyniers, B. (2008). Accrual accounting in Europe: To what extent and why are reforms based on IPSAS? Paper presented at the 5th EIASM International Conference on Accounting, Auditing and Management in Public Sector Reforms, September 3–5, Amsterdam, The Netherlands.

Collin, S. Y., Tagesson, T., Andersson, A., Cato, J., & Hansson, K. (2009). Explaining the choice of accounting standards in municipal corporations: Positive accounting theory and institutional theory as competitive or concurrent theories. *Critical Perspectives on Accounting, 20*, 141–174.

Czarniawska, B., & Joerges, B. (1996). Travels of ideas. In: B. Czarniawska & G. Sevon (Eds), *Translating organizational change*. Berlin, Germany: Walter de Gruyter.

Czarniawska, B., & Sevon, G. (1996). *Translating organizational change*. Berlin, Germany: Walter de Gruyter.

Dambrin, C., Lambert, C., & Sponem, S. (2007). Control and change – Analysing the process of institutionalization. *Management Accounting Research, 18*, 172–208.

Department of Public Accounts. (2009). Future plans of DPA/activities under 10th plan. Available at http://www.mof.gov.bt/index.php?deptid=4. Accessed on August 3, 2009.

DiMaggio, P., & Powell, W. W. (1983). The iron cage revisited: Institutional isomorphism and collective rationality in organizational fields. *American Sociological Review, 48*, 147–160.

Economic Commission for Africa (ECA). (2003). *Public sector management reforms in Africa*. Addis Ababa, Ethiopia: Development Policy Management Division (DPMD).

Ellwood, S., & Newberry, S. (2007). Public sector accrual accounting: Institutionalising neo-liberal principles? *Accounting, Auditing & Accountability Journal, 20*(4), 549–573.

FCGO. (2008). *Government of Nepal: Consolidated financial statements fiscal years: 2006/2007*. Kathmandu, Nepal: Government of Nepal.

Fein, L., & Mizruchi, M. (1999). The social construction of organizational knowledge: A study of the uses of coercive, mimetic, and normative isomorphism. *Administrative Science Quarterly, 44*(4), 653–683.

Government Accounting Standards Advisory Board (GASAB). (2008). *A study on gap analysis of Indian government accounting with international standards*. New Delhi, India: Comptroller and Auditor General of India.

Government of India (GoI). (2005). *General financial rules* (Available at http://finmin.nic.in/the_ministry/dept_expenditure/GFRS/GFR2005.pdf. Accessed on August 3, 2009). Ministry of Finance, Department of Expenditure.

Government of Nepal (GoN). (2008). *An assessment of the public financial management performance measurement framework (As of FY 2005/06)*. Kathmandu, Nepal: Financial Comptroller General Office.

Government of Pakistan (GoP). (1999). *Accounting policies and procedures manual*, Islamabad, Pakistan.

Granlund, M., & Lukka, K. (1998). Towards increasing business orientation: Finnish management accountants in a changing cultural context. *Management Accounting Research, 9*(2), 185–211.

Guragain, M. (2008). An important of IPSAS cash basis in Nepalese perspective. *The Nepal Chartered Accountant* (June), 10–11.

Guthrie, G. (1998). Application of accrual accounting in the Australian public sector – Rhetoric or reality. *Financial Accountability and Management, 14*(1), 1–19.

Guthrie, J., Humphey, C., & Olson, O. (1998). *Global warming: Debating international developments in new public financial management*. Oslo, Norway: Cappelen Akademisk Forlag.

Guthrie, J., Humphey, C., & Olson, O. (1999). Debating developments in new public financial management: The limits of global theorising and some new ways forward. *Financial Accountability and Management, 15*(3/4), 209–228.

Haque, A. S. (2001). Governance and public management: The South Asian context. *International Journal of Public Administration, 24*(12), 1289–1297.

Humphrey, C., & Guthrie, J. (1996). Trends and contradictions in public sector financial management developments in Australia and Britain. *Research in Governmental and Nonprofit Accounting, 9*, 283–302.

Humphrey, C. G., Miller, P., & Scapens, R. W. (1993). Accountability and accountable management in the UK public sector. *Accounting, Auditing & Accountability Journal, 6*(3), 7–29.

International Federation of Accountants (IFAC). (2008). *Handbook of international public sector accounting pronouncements* (Vol. 1). New York: IFAC.

International Monetary Fund. (2007). *Nepal: Report on observance of standards and codes-fiscal transparency module*. Washington, DC: IMF.

IPSASB. (2008). IPSAS adoption by government, September. Available at http://web.ifac.org/download/IPSASB_Adoption_Governments.pdf. Accessed on April 21.

Jorge, S. (2008). *Implementing reforms in public sector accounting*. Portugal: Imprensa da Universidade de Coimbra.

Kaushik, K. P. (2006). Government accounting: Recent trends and direction for India. *The Chartered Accountant* (January), 1018–1029.

Khumawala, S. (1997). Public sector accounting in India: A historical review and an analysis since independence to the economic reforms of the nineties. *Journal of Public Budgeting, Accounting & Financial Management, 9*(2), 305–330.

Kuruppu, G. C. J., & Adhikari, P. (2008). Reforms for public accountability: A comparative study of Nepal and Sri Lanka. Paper presented at the12th Biennial CIGAR Conference, May 28–29, Modena, Italy.

Lapsley, I., Mussari, R., & Paulsson, G. (2009). On the adoption of accrual accounting in the public sector: A self-evident and problematic reform. *European Accounting Review, 18*(4), 719–723.

Lüder, K., & Jones, R. (2003). The diffusion of accrual accounting and budgeting in European governments – A cross-country analysis. In: K. Lüder & R. Jones (Eds), *Reforming governmental accounting and budgeting in Europe* (pp. 13–58). Frankfurt am Main, Germany: Fachverlag Moderne Wirtschaft.

Mehboob, K. (2008). Upgrading government financial reporting, Dawn (The Internet Edition), November 3. Available at http://www.dawn.com/2008/11/03/ebr10.htm. Accessed on April 21.

Mekendrick, J., & Yousafzai, S. (2008). Assessment of the recent reforms in the public sector of Pakistan. Paper presented at the 5th EIASM International Conference on Accounting, Auditing and Management in Public Sector Reforms, September 3–5, Amsterdam, The Netherlands.

Mellett, H., & Ryan, C. (2008). Special issue on public sector reform and accounting change: Guest editorial note. *Journal of Accounting and Organizational Change, 4*(3), 217–221.

Meyer, J., & Rowan, B. (1977). Institutional organizations: Formal structures as myth and ceremony. *American Journal of Sociology, 83*(2), 340–363.

Mimba, N. S. H., Helden, G. J., & Tillema, S. (2007). Public sector performance measurement in developing countries. *Journal of Accounting and Organizational Change, 3*(3), 192–208.

Ministry of Finance (MoF). (2001). *Financial Management Manual*, Bhutan.

Ministry of Finance and Planning (MoFP). (2009). Action plan for the year 2009. Department of State Accounts. Available at http://www.treasury.gov.lk/EPPRM/sad/pdfdocs/actionplan2009.pdf. Accessed on August 3.

Ministry of Finance and Treasury (MoFT). (2007). *The government of Maldives Public Accounting System (PAS): Contract signing.* PAS Press Release, December 13.

Ministry of Finance and Treasury (MoFT). (2009). *Law on Public Finance*, Law no. 3/2006. Available at http://www.finance.gov.mv/index.php?page = treasury. Accessed on August 3.

Mir, M. Z., & Rahaman, A. S. (2005). The adoption of international standards in Bangladesh. *Accounting Auditing & Accountability Journal, 18*(6), 816–841.

Narayan, F. B., & Godden, T. (2000). *Financial management and governance issues in Pakistan.* Manila, Philippines: The Asian Development Bank.

Neu, D., Ocampo, E., Graham, C., & Heincke, M. (2006). Information technologies and the World Bank. *Accounting, Organizations and Society, 31*(7), 635–662.

Oliver, C. (1991). Strategic responses to institutional processes. *The Academy of Management Review, 16*(1), 145–179.

Parry, M., & Wynne, A. (2009). The cash basis IPSAS – An alternative view. *International Journal on Government Financial Management, 9*(2), 23–29.

Pine, V., & Torres, L. (2003). Reshaping public sector accounting: An international comparative view. *Canadian Journal of Administrative Sciences, 20*(4), 334–350.

Rahaman, A. S., Lawrence, S., & Roper, J. (2004). Social and environmental reporting at the VRA: Institutionalized legitimacy or legitimation crisis? *Critical Perspectives on Accounting, 15*, 35–56.

Sahlin-Andersson, K. (2001). National, international and transnational constructions of new public management. In: T. Christensen & P. Lægreid (Eds), *New public management: The transformation of ideas and practice.* Aldershot, UK: Ashgate Publishing Limited.

Scapens, R. W., & Siti-Nabiha, A. K. (2005). Stability and change: An institutional study of management accounting change. *Accounting, Auditing & Accountability Journal, 18*(1), 44–73.

Scott, R. (1987). The adolescence of institutional theory. *Administrative Science Quarterly, 32*(4), 493–511.

South Asian Federation of Accountants (SAFA). (2006). A study on accrual-based accounting for governments and public sector entities in SAARC countries, September.

Srinivas, G. (2006). Harmonization of accounting standards: An auditor's reflections. *Asian Journal of Government Audit*, April. Available at http://www.asosai.org/journal_archives.htm. Accessed on August 3.

Subramanian, P. K. (2008). Public sector accounting and auditing diagnostic tools for comparing country standards to international standards. *International Journal on Governmental Financial Management, VIII*(1), 1–14.

Sutcliffe, P. (2009). International public sector accounting standards board review the cash basis IPSAS: An opportunity to influence developments. *International Journal on Government Financial Management, 9*(2), 15–22.

The Economic Times. (2009). India to change format of government accounting, May 6. Available at http://economictimes.indiatimes.com/articleshow/4490761.cms?prtpage = 1. Accessed on July 30, 2009.

The Hindu. (2009). India to change format of government accounting: CAG. May 6. Available at http://www.hindu.com/thehindu/holnus/002200905061551.htm. Accessed on August 3, 2009.

The Hindu Business Line. (2009). Govt may migrate to accrual accounting in 5 years. May 7. Available at http://www.thehindubusinessline.com/2009/05/07/stories/2009050752091500.htm. Accessed on August 3, 2009.

Timoshenko, K., & Adhikari, P. (2009). Exploring Russian central government accounting in its context. *Journal of Accounting and Organizational Change, 5*(4), 490–513.

Tolbert, P., & Zucker, L. (1997). The institutionalization of institutional theory. In: S. Clegg, C. Hardy & W. Nord (Eds), *Handbook of organizational studies* (pp. 173–190). London: Saga.

Tsamenyi, M., Cullen, J., & Gonzalez, J. M. G. (2006). Changes in accounting and financial information system in a Spanish electricity company: A new institutional theory analysis. *Management Accounting Research, 17*, 409–432.

Uddin, S., & Hopper, T. (2001). A Bangladeshi soap opera: Privatisation, accounting, and regimes of control in a less developed country. *Accounting, Organizations and Society, 26*(7/8), 643–672.

Uddin, S., & Hopper, T. (2003). Accounting for privatisation in Bangladesh: Testing World Bank claims. *Critical Perspectives on Accounting, 14*(7), 739–774.

World Bank. (2001). *Bangladesh country financial accountability assessment report*. Bangladesh Country Management Unit, Financial Management Unit, South Asia Unit.

World Bank. (2003a). *Financial accountability in Nepal – A country assessment*, Washington, DC.

World Bank. (2003b). *Islamic republic of Pakistan: Country financial accountability assessment*. Report No. 27551-PAK. Financial Management Unit, South Asia Region.

World Bank. (2003c). Sri Lanka Country Financial Accountability Assessment (CFAA) study. South Asia Regional Financial Management Unit.

World Bank. (2007a). *Bangladesh public sector accounting and auditing: A comparison to international standards*. Report no. 39175-BD, South Asia Region Financial Management Unit.

World Bank. (2007b). *Bhutan public sector accounting and auditing: A comparison to international standards*. Country Report 39621-BT, South Asia Region Financial Management Unit.

World Bank. (2007c). *Maldives public sector accounting and auditing: A comparison to international standards.* Country Report (40089-MV), South Asia Region Financial Management Unit.

World Bank. (2007d). *Nepal public sector accounting and auditing: A comparison to international standards.* Country Report (39701-NP), South Asia Region Financial Management Unit.

World Bank. (2007e). *Pakistan public sector accounting and auditing: A comparison to international standards.* Country Report (39699-PK), South Asia Region Financial Management Unit.

World Bank. (2007f). *Sri Lanka public sector accounting and auditing: A comparison to international standards.* Country Report (39176-LK), South Asia Region Financial Management Unit.

World Bank. (2008). Public sector accounting and auditing: A framework for comparison to international standards. South Asia Regional Financial Management Unit.

World Bank. (2009). South Asia: Data, project, and research. Available at http://web.worldbank.org/WBSITE/EXTERNAL/COUNTRIES/SOUTHASIAEXT/0,menuPK: 158937~pagePK:158889~piPK:146815~theSitePK:223547,00.html. Accessed on July 27, 2009.

World Development Report 1999/2000. (2000). *Entering the 21st century.* Oxford: Oxford University Press for the World Bank.

THE ROLES OF DEGREE OF COMPETITION AND TYPES OF BUSINESS STRATEGIES IN ADOPTING MULTIPLE PERFORMANCE MEASUREMENT PRACTICES: SOME REFLECTIONS FROM BANGLADESH

Md. Habib-Uz-Zaman Khan, Rafiuddin Ahmed
and Abdel Karim Halabi

ABSTRACT

Aim – *This empirical study explores the association between competition, business strategy, and the uses of a multiple performance measurement system in Bangladesh manufacturing firms.*

Design/methodology – *The study uses a questionnaire survey of 50 manufacturing companies. Data were analyzed using multiple regression analysis and other descriptive statistics.*

Findings – *The results suggest that greater emphasis on multiple measures for performance evaluation is associated with businesses that*

Research in Accounting in Emerging Economies, Volume 10, 201–232
Copyright © 2010 by Emerald Group Publishing Limited
All rights of reproduction in any form reserved
ISSN: 1479-3563/doi:10.1108/S1479-3563(2010)0000010013

are facing high competition. The practices of multiple performance measures are also significantly related to the types of business strategy being followed. Specifically, firms pursuing a prospector strategy have relied more on multiple performance measures to rate business performance than the firms pursuing a defender strategy.

Practical implications – *The article notes that the designers of performance measurement systems need to consider contingent factors that affect an organizations' control system.*

Originality/value – *Substantiating the connection between contingent variables and the use of multiple performance measures in manufacturing firms facilitate a better acceptance of firms' tendency toward new measurement tools. The study contributes to the performance measurement and contingency literature since it presents empirical evidence of the state of multiple performance measures with organizational contingent variables using a developing country's manufacturing sector data.*

Keywords: Multiple performance measures; market competition; firms' strategy; manufacturing sector; Bangladesh.

INTRODUCTION

The adoption of performance measures to capture qualitative dimensions of organizational performance, commonly known as nonfinancial indicators in the academic circle, has gained prominence in recent times (Kaplan & Norton, 1992; Horngren, Datar, Foster, Rajan, & Ittner, 2009). The use of nonfinancial indicators has become a necessity for firms trying to succeed in a fiercely competitive market. Commentators argue that the introduction and continued use of nonfinancial performance measures have become popular primarily because of the shortcomings of financial performance measures (Lynch & Cross, 1991; Kaplan & Norton, 1992, 1993, 1996a, 1996b; Ittner & Larcker, 1998a, 1998b; Otley, 1999; Banker, Potter, & Srinivasan, 2000; Hoque & James, 2000). In order to overcome the shortcomings of traditional financial performance measures, and to devise a measurement system incorporating all dimensions of the value chain of a business, academics and practitioners have endeavored to use a more comprehensive measurement system. The rationale for the adoption of comprehensive performance measures is that these are assumed to offer continuous indications with regard to what is most indispensable for the day-to-day operations and where efforts must be directed for continuous business growth and success (Hoque & James, 2000; Ittner & Larcker, 1998a, 1998b; Otley, 1999).

Kaplan and Norton (1992, 1996a, 1996b) posit that the use of a multiple performance measurement system promotes a balance between outcome measures (the results from past efforts) and measures that will drive future performance. Earlier studies also noted that the role of the contextual variables might influence the use and effectiveness of performance evaluation systems (Govindarajan & Gupta, 1985; Simons, 1987). These contextual variables include firm size, strategic priority, market competition, and computerized manufacturing systems (Ittner & Larcker, 1998a, 1998b; Hoque, 2004; Hoque, Mia, & Alam, 2001). In his study on 52 New Zealand manufacturing firms, Hoque (2004), for example, found a significant and positive association between strategy and management's use of nonfinancial measures for performance evaluation, although a positive relationship between environmental uncertainty and organizational performance through use of nonfinancial performance measures was not found. In another study on 71 New Zealand manufacturing units, Hoque et al. (2001) noted that greater emphasis on multiple measures for performance evaluation is associated with businesses facing high competition and making greater use of computer-aided manufacturing processes.

Little is known about the impact of various contingent factors on multiple performance measures in developing and emerging countries setting, and this motivates the present study based on Bangladesh manufacturing firms. Overall, the evidence on the correlation between multiple performance measures and contingent variables in developing countries is rare. The Bangladesh manufacturing sector is very dynamic, having experienced very strong growth in total value added and exports since the 1990s, and since 2000, manufacturing exports have represented more than 90% of exports (Fernandes, 2008). Further, the sector contributed 29.77% of gross domestic product (GDP) for the financial year 2006–2007 (Bangladesh Economic Review, 2007). Likewise, owing to better diversity and complication in several areas (e.g., product markets, industrial processes, and cost composition, being mainly overhead cost), manufacturing companies in Bangladesh need to put greater emphasis on their performance measurement systems. In recent years, some initiatives regarding the use of some nonfinancial measures in performance evaluation in manufacturing sector of Bangladesh have emerged (Mossaraf & Ahmed, 2008; Hossain, 2008; Akhter, 2007; Begum, Hoque, & Shill, 2001; Sharkar, Sobhan, & Sultana, 2006). The current study is therefore an endeavor to empirically study the relationships among an organization's market competition, types of strategy organizations adopted, and the multiple performance measurement practices in Bangladesh. This study provides original evidence on the contingency factors affecting the adoption of the multiple performance measures for manufacturing firms in a developing country context, and to document a specific association between multiple performance measures, market competition, and business strategy using the Miles and Snow (1978) typology.

Taken as a whole, this article addresses following research issues that have so far not been addressed:

(1) Are relationships among an organization's market competition, types of strategy organizations adopted, and multiple performance measurement practices a global trend?

(2) Can analogous measurement scales be utilized to measure strategy and market competition in a developing country's (i.e., Bangladesh) setting?

(3) What is the nature of the strategy–performance measurement practices relationship in a developing country's context when multiple performance measures are employed?

The remainder of the article is organized in the following sequence. The next section describes the prior literature and this is followed by the research hypotheses. The article then outlines the research methodology used. The empirical results appear in the results section followed by a discussion, and the article's conclusion then follows.

LITERATURE REVIEW AND HYPOTHESES DEVELOPMENT

Use of Multiple Performance Measures

The performance management literature is replete with discussions about the inadequacy of accounting numbers particularly since they are historic in nature, lack strategic focus, and do not have an innovative outlook (see Bourne, Mills, Wilcox, Neelly, & Platts, 2000; Schoenfeld, 1986; Dearden, 1987; Emmanuel & Otley, 1995; Kaplan & Norton, 1996a; Ishtiaque, Khan, Akhter, & Fatima, 2007; Ittner & Larcker, 1998a, 1998b; Chenhall, 1997; Dixon, Nanni, & Vollman, 1990; Keegan, Eiler, & Anania, 1989; Lynch & Cross, 1991; McNair & Mosconi, 1987). The use of nonfinancial measures was initiated after the 1990s with the advent of a popular performance measurement tool – the balanced scorecard (BSC). The architects of the BSC model – Kaplan and Norton (1992, 1993) – designed this performance measurement tool combining both financial and nonfinancial measures with a view to assist business enterprises measuring performance in a more balanced manner. Multiple measures include a combination of the following multidimensional performance measures (Kaplan & Norton, 1996a):

Financial perspective – The main intention of this perspective is to ensure proper utilization of shareholders' investment. According to Jusoh, Ibrahim, and Zainuddin (2008), financial measures provide the ultimate outcome or bottom-line improvement of the organization where it measures the economic consequences of actions already taken in the learning and growth, internal business process, and customer perspectives. Financial measures usually narrate the firms' profitability such as operating income, return on investment and economic value added (EVA), sales growth, cost control, and cash flow. Financial consequences of a firm are viewed as the "fruits" of the trees and thought of as a lagging indicator (Langfield-Smith, Thorne, & Hilton, 2009; Mazumder, 2007).

Customer perspective – This perspective envelops a firm's capability to provide quality products and services, the effectiveness of its delivery, and attaining overall customer service and satisfaction. This perspective assists an organization to look after its internal business processes with a view to progress toward financial outcomes. Under this perspective, notable measures are customer satisfaction, customer response time, market share, and on-time delivery.

Internal business process perspective – This perspective focuses on the internal processes (departments or processes) that the organization must excel to gain customer satisfaction and make financial returns to shareholders. This perspective is as comparable as the "stem" of the "trees." Kaplan and Norton (1992, p. 134) note, "... failure to convert operational performance, as measured in the scorecard, into improved financial performance, should send executives back to their drawing boards to rethink the company's strategy or its implementation plans." The main performance measures under this perspective may include manufacturing efficiency, quality, defect rate, and cycle time.

Learning and growth perspective – This perspective takes into account how an organization learns and makes changes and improvements so that long-term value formation can be recognized (Jusoh et al., 2008). It mainly focuses on the competences of people (employees), systems, and procedures applied in attaining advance performance in internal processes, making customers satisfied and eventually benefiting financial performance, and measures such things as training and development, employee satisfaction, employee retention, and employee productivity. This perspective is considered as comparable as the "roots" of the "trees."

Hoque and James (2000) advocates that the use of multiple performance measures might motivate breakthrough improvements in critical activity areas such as products, processes, customers, and market developments. Kaplan and Norton (1996a, 1996b) suggest that while traditional financial measures report on what happened during the last periods without indicating how managers can improve performance in the next, a multidimensional approach to performance evaluation functions as the cornerstone of a company's current and future success. Similar view has been also widely shared in academic environment in recent years (see, e.g., Atkinson et al., 1997; Dixon et al., 1990; Lynch & Cross, 1991; Nanni, Dixon, & Vollmann, 1992; Shields, 1997; Simons, 1995, 2000). Hemmer (1996) reports how nonfinancial performance measures can be best combined with financial measures to obtain the best measurement of performance in a competitive situation (see also Kaplan & Atkinson, 1998; Shields, 1997; Hoque & James, 2000; Ittner & Larcker, 2001).

Contextual Factors and Performance Measures: A Contingency View

This study uses a contingency-based approach that has extensively been applied in management accounting research (Otley, 1980; Donaldson, 2001; Chenhall, 2003). The contingency approach to management accounting is established on the foundation that there is no universally suitable accounting system that fits all organizations. Rather, the particular features of an appropriate accounting system are subjected to specific circumstances in which an organization finds itself (Thompson, 1967; Woodward, 1965; Otley, 1980). Accordingly, it is said that the effective design of management control and/or accounting systems depends on a firm's ability to accept changes in external environments and internal factors such as organizational size, structures, companies' strategies, top management leadership, and corporate cultures (Khandwalla, 1972; Waterhouse & Tiessen, 1978; Merchant, 1981, 1984; Dunk, 1992; Miles & Snow, 1978; Gupta & Govindarajan, 1984; Simons, 1987; Hoque, 2004; Hoque et al., 2001; Langfield-Smith, 1997). Furthermore, the contingency approach is the only one which states that organizational performance depends on the existence of a fit (match) between the uniqueness of a firm and the condition in which it operates (Gerdin & Greve, 2004; Donaldson, 2001).

This study considers two important contextual factors, namely competition and business strategy, and their impact on the use of multiple performance measures in Bangladeshi manufacturing companies. These two factors are deemed important as their role in designing organizational performance measures has been emphasized in earlier performance measurement literatures (see Hoque, 2004; Mia & Clarke, 1999; Hoque et al., 2001; Langfield-Smith, 1997; Jusoh et al., 2008; Miles & Snow, 1978). In the following paragraphs, the relationship among competition, business strategy, and use of multiple performance measures are thus discussed in turn.

Market Competition
It has been widely acknowledged that to compete in the universal field, firms must put increased effort into improving products and process-related activities on a continuous basis (Mossaraf & Ahmed, 2008; Lynch & Cross, 1991; Kaplan & Norton, 1996a, 1996b). With the improvements of such activities, firms benefit in the form of either augmenting companies' value through shareholders wealth or entering into the new markets (Ishtiaque et al., 2007; Hoque, 2004). These endeavors may lead to a positive impact on a company's financial results as well as escalates value for customers and operating efficiencies. Lambert (1998) argues that customer purchasing behavior is influenced by characteristics of the economic environment such as the level of competition. McNair and Mosconi (1987) advocate that a performance measurement system within a firm ought to scrutinize changes in market demands to make sure and review progress toward business objectives and ensure accomplishment of performance goals. Furthermore, to attain a competitive advantage, organizations are required to keep an eye on many market issues (such as competition for price and market share, marketing and product competition, competitors' numbers, actions of competitors). As a result, there must be a measurement system that entails both financial and nonfinancial facets of performance. Different factors, however, might have an association with the firms' increased use of multiple performance measures. According to Hoque et al. (2001), one likely determinant of the use of multiple performance measures is competition confronted by the firms in the marketplace where they operate. Lynch and Cross (1991) and Hoque et al. (2001) found an association between firms' usage of multiple performance measures with competition. Lynch and Cross (1991) note that such measures advance competitiveness through clearly examining the organization's static competencies such as efficient production, meeting deadlines, and acquiring dynamic competencies.

The extant performance measurement literature states that competition in an industry expedites businesses to set up analogous performance measures. In other words, a firm has to offer the best product quality and present customers with value for money if it wishes to be a leader in the competitive industry (Cooper, 1995; Defond & Park, 1999; Hoque et al., 2001; Hoque, 2004). This is achieved only in the event of an integrated and coordinated organizational effort (Nanni et al., 1992). Organizational standing in offering superior customer service and better product quality, coupled with constant products or service innovation, thus necessitates shared as well as synchronized initiatives by all parts of the organization. The more the integration and coordination of efforts, the greater the need for a sophisticated control tool such as the multiple performance measurement system, which can provide firm-wide models (or benchmarking) of performance (Hoque et al., 2001). Performance measures encompassing both the financial and nonfinancial performance of firms that address customer satisfaction, innovation, and quality production on top of financial results are crucial to achieve competitive advantage (Jusoh & Parnell, 2008; Kaplan & Norton, 1996a, 1996b; Ittner & Larcker, 1998a, 1998b; Hoque et al., 2001; Miles & Snow, 1978; Merchant, 1984; Simons, 1995). Kaplan and Norton (1996a, 1996b) argue that multiple performance evaluation not only emphasizes on achieving economic objectives such as return on investment, net earnings, and sales growth, but also includes the performance drivers such as customer satisfaction, innovation and efficiency, and employee satisfaction of the financial objectives.

The intensity of using multiple measures however might be driven by the degree of competition a firm confronts over time (Hoque et al., 2001; Simons, 1991). Hoque et al. (2001) note that the use of multidimensional performance measurement systems changes according to the degree of competition, not the mere presence of information across multiple dimensions. Kaplan and Norton (1996a, 1996b) emphasize that the integration (or balance) between financial and nonfinancial measures in the performance measurement system is believed to be indispensable for the firm's long-term success. Moreover, the use of multiple measures of performance can at the same time be designed to fulfill the owner's most pressing concerns and keep the operating company protected from the consequences of irrepressible events (Kaplan & Norton, 1996a, 1996b; Mia & Clarke, 1999).

The preceding discussion provides the theoretical basis for our first hypothesis in relation to the relationship between multiple performance measures and market competition. There are many reasons relating the premise of applying multiple performance measures and market competition to Bangladeshi firms. In Bangladesh, the manufacturing sectors, particularly textile and clothing, ready made garments (RMG), food processing, and the pharmaceutical sector, have been experiencing rising demand both locally and internationally (Mahmud, Ahmed, & Mahajan, 2007). Over the past few years, for example, Bangladesh was able to gain a strong foothold in a quota-driven global apparel market, which led to rapid growth in this sector (Khundker & Nasreen, 2002; World Bank, 2005a, 2005b). The rise of free trade and the subsequent elimination of the quota system at the end of 2004, however, meant Bangladeshi firms faced acute competition from other Asian countries such as China, India, Indonesia, and Thailand (Mlachila & Yang, 2004). According to Rahman and Anwar (2006), distortions in the global apparel market in the form of entry restrictions and quota premiums were hereafter to be replaced by competition and competitive price. The pharmaceutical sector, on the other hand, is very technological intensive and more innovative in new products compared with low-technology sectors such as textiles (Gehl Sampath, 2007). Bangladesh also has adopted a number of macroeconomic measures such as the policy of economic liberalization, structural adjustment, and privatization to create and improve the competitiveness of local industries and encourage these industries to look for international business opportunities. In order to promote the attractiveness of industries producing internationally competitive products, the Bangladesh government established special export processing zones (EPZ) where foreign investors were given access to well-developed infrastructure, lower taxes, repatriation of profits in foreign currencies, and other privileges. Firms operating in EPZ together with the strong presence of multinational companies (MNCs) have underpinned a more competitive situation for local manufacturing firms. Many domestic firms, which have long enjoyed tariff protection, thus now find it difficult to adjust to the changed competitive situation resulting from the reduction or removal of tariff and other nontariff barriers. Consequently, local Bangladeshi firms have tended to play a key role in production efficiency, product quality, and retaining customers by fulfilling their demand on time. In such circumstances, there is an urgency to use multiple performance measures in the organizational control system.

In view of the discussions above, our first hypothesis in relation to the relationship between multiple performance measures and market competition is stated as follows:

H1. A firm facing an intense market competition is likely to make greater use of multiple measures than financial measures of performance alone.

Business Strategy

Performance measurement and management researchers suggest that accounting performance measures should be planned in line with the firm's business strategy (Langfield-Smith, 1997; Dent, 1990; Simons, 1987; Otley, 1980). While the importance of business strategy as a contingency variable has been explored for other management control systems (Zahra & Pearce, 1990; Govindarajan & Fisher, 1990; Simons, 1987; Gosselin, 1997), it has yet to be examined with the uses of multiple performance measures. The performance measurement literature suggests that although a performance measurement system is essential in all companies, different manufacturing environments demand different measures to assess firms' effectiveness (Abernethy & Lillis, 1995; Bruggeman & Slagmulder, 1995; Duncan, 1972; Khandwalla, 1972; Mia & Chenhall, 1994). The related literature advocates that organizations use those types of measures that fit with their strategy, their organizational structure, and the environmental uncertainty. The type of strategy employed by a firm should influence the design of the performance measurement system.

In examining the business strategy contingency variable, the current study utilizes Miles and Snow's (1994, 1978)[1] four strategic types of firms: defenders, prospectors, analyzers, and reactors.[2]

Defenders operate within a narrow product–market domain characterized by high production volume and low product diversity, and compete aggressively on price, quality, and customer service. They engage in little or no product/market development and stress efficiency of operations. *Prospectors* frequently search for market opportunities and repeatedly experiment with potential responses to emerging environmental trends. They compete through new products and market development. Product lines change over time as new market opportunities are sought. *Analyzers* share characteristics of both prospectors and defenders as they operate in two types of product–market domains, one relatively stable and the other changing. *Reactors* do not follow a conscious strategy and are viewed as a dysfunctional organizational type. According to Miles and Snow (1978), reactors lack a consistent strategy–structure relationship and therefore seldom make adjustments of any sort until environmental pressures force them to do so.

From these discussions, it can be inferred that the selection (or type) of multiple measures for performance evaluation is determined by the strategy being followed by an organization. We speculate that a firm following a *prospector* strategy will benefit more than a firm using a *defender* strategy. The reasoning behind this is that the firm following the *prospector* strategy searches persistently for market opportunities and they will be more likely to adapt their performance measurement systems to their strategy and focus on nonfinancial measures pertaining to customers, products, employees, and quality. Firms following a *defender* strategy, in contrast, will be more inclined toward financial measures.

Recent research has demonstrated that some Bangladeshi organizations have introduced a broader scope of financial and nonfinancial information with a view to assist strategic decision making. Mossaraf and Ahmed (2008), for example, noted that Bangladeshi firms that are pursuing customer strategies are more likely to use a broader range of performance information relating to internal and external factors and financial and nonfinancial measures. This leads to the possibility of the manufacturing sector leading growth for some time. Manufacturing organizations, and in particular the pharmaceutical sector, are responding to rising customer demands of quality, flexibility, and reliability of supply through the investment and implementation of superior manufacturing technology (Mossaraf & Ahmed, 2008). It follows then that to unleash the full potential of the sector and in order to attain greater diversification, the type of strategies managers follow should be integrated with market potentials and performance. In view of the discussion and theoretical argument presented above, the second hypothesis of the study is posited as follows:

H2. Firms pursuing a prospector strategy tend to be associated with a greater use of multiple performance measures than firms pursuing a defender strategy.

RESEARCH DESIGN

The methodologies adopted for confirming or refuting the hypotheses involved both primary and secondary data. Primary data were collected via a questionnaire survey. The draft questionnaire was developed from a review of the relevant literature, and then circulated to a group of prominent academics, management accounting consultants, and Chief Accountants and Finance Officers (CAFOs). After feedback was received, the questionnaire was revised. The questionnaire[3] was mailed to the Chief Executive Officers (CEOs) of 148 Bangladeshi's manufacturing companies[4] selected from the Dhaka Stock Exchange (DSE). The official web addresses of all sample firms were collected from the "companies profile section" maintained by DSE.

We have chosen manufacturing industry as a sample unit of extant study for numerous reasons. First, manufacturing firms in Bangladesh are considered highly competitive and might have more aptitude to explore new market domains continuously (Industrial Policy of Bangladesh, 2005). Moreover, manufacturing industry is an important engine of growth to Bangladesh's GDP as this sector contributes 29.77% of GDP at constant prices for financial year 2006–2007 (Bangladesh Economic Review, 2007). Consistent with earlier studies, a mail survey was adopted since it collects detailed information from a broad cross-section of firms at a low cost (Chenhall, 2003; Gosselin, 1997; Shields, 1995). Questionnaires (with a covering letter and a postage-paid self-addressed envelope) were mailed during February 2008. Two reminder letters were also sent (each 3 weeks apart) for follow-up. Surveys are burdened with problems linked to measurement error and bias. This problem however may be aggravated when the survey is written in the respondents' second language. The concern of language is conceivably less important in the Bangladeshi manufacturing perspective where fluency and writing in English is very common, especially among top managers due to their high academic background and professional attainment (see Ishtiaque et al., 2007; Khan & Halabi, 2009).

A total of 50 completed questionnaires were returned, which represents a response rate of 33.78%; this response rate is rather low compared with Hoque's rate of 59.2%. The relevant statistics of respondent companies in terms of employees, annual sales, and assets are attached (see Appendix). To detect the nonresponse bias and likely response bias owing to early and late responses, the study employed t-tests which showed no significant differences between the respondents and nonrespondents in terms of size and varied sectors. The organizations that made up the sample are shown in Table 1.

Table 1.   Sample Size and Respondent Types.

Manufacturing Firms	Sample Size	Sample Percentage
Cement and construction	1	2.00
Ceramic	1	2.00
Food and allied	15	30.00
Pharmaceuticals and chemicals	18	36.00
Engineering	9	18.00
Tannery (leathers)	2	4.00
Textile	3	6.00
Paper and printing	1	2.00
Total (N)	50	100

VARIABLES MEASUREMENT

Multiple Performance Measures Usage

To evaluate multiple performance measures usage, the study employs 40 items (10 that relate to financial and 30 nonfinancial) which comprise the four-dimensional BSC model. Each element of the performance measure consists of multiple items that have been drawn from prior research (Hoque et al., 2001; Gosselin, 2005; Speckbacher, Bischof, & Pfeiffer, 2003; Jusoh et al., 2008; Silk, 1998; Kaplan & Norton, 2001; Karathanos & Karathanos, 2005; Malmi, 2001; Ismail, 2007; Halachmi, 2005). In addition, a small number of items were self-constructed. These were the contribution margin, the EVA, the number of new customers, the unit product cost, research and development (R&D) costs, human resources development cost, company cost per employees, and total training hours for employees. The contribution margin is commonly used for managerial decision making, and although it has some limitation, the EVA has been included as it evaluates performance in a conventional sense. Three employee-related measures have been added to the learning and growth perspective as these emphasize the importance of employee and human resources–related measures in improving the business process, and have a consequential impact on bottom line (Kaplan & Norton, 1996a, 1996b). These items were pretested in the pilot phase.

The respondents were asked to indicate, on a five-point Likert-type scale ranging from 1 (not at all) to 5 (to a great extent), the extent of their organization's use of each indicator across the four perspectives.

Descriptive statistics (mean and standard deviation) for each performance indicator are presented in Table 2. A principal components analysis (PCA) with varimax rotation was performed for those measures to determine their dimensionality among groups. Prior to performing the PCA, the suitability of data for factor analysis was assessed. An inspection of the correlation matrix revealed the presence of many coefficients above 0.30, signifying that factor analysis was appropriate (Pallant, 2001). The Bartlett Test of Sphericity (BTS) and the Kaiser–Meyer–Olkin (KMO) measure of sampling adequacy were also used to assess the factorability (Bartlett, 1954). The results show that the BTS reached statistical significance (chi-square = 767.95, $p < 0.01$) and the KMO was 0.88, exceeding the recommended value of 0.60 (Kaiser, 1974). These results suggest that the factorability of the data was appropriate and also indicate that factor analysis shows that the items of each dimension are unidimensional as they

Table 2. Descriptive Statistics for the Multiple Performance
Measurement Items ($N = 50$).

Multiple Performance Measures	Mean	Standard Deviation
Financial perspective		
Gross profit margin	4.88	0.03
Operating margin	4.96	0.01
Return on assets	4.76	0.08
Current ratio	3.76	1.08
Inventory turnover ratio	4.74	0.10
Cost versus budgets	4.50	0.34
Residual income	3.14	1.28
Contribution margin	3.02	1.56
Daily working capital	3.41	1.57
Economic value added	1.97	1.98
Learning and growth perspective		
Human resources development cost	3.54	1.17
Number of new employees	3.25	1.41
Employees' performance (sales per employees)	4.54	0.56
Total training hours for employees	4.65	0.45
R&D expansion cost	2.94	1.78
Wastage and scrap rate	3.01	1.73
Sales proportion from new product	2.98	1.69
Company's cost per employees	3.82	1.12
Employees' satisfaction	2.97	1.74
Percentage of key stuff turnover	3.10	1.22
Internal business process perspective		
Unit of output (per labor hours)	4.54	0.28
Measuring defects in units (per million)	4.33	0.34
Quantity of energy consumed	4.13	0.91
Unit of output (per machine hours)	4.60	0.23
Unit product cost	4.80	0.08
Number of product lines or products	4.01	0.98
Number of machine hours used	3.98	1.02
Total number of workers injured	3.02	1.56
Rate of incidence of injury	2.23	1.89
Level of absenteeism	2.37	2.73
Time to launch new products and services	3.74	1.52
Customer perspective		
Number of customer complaints	3.01	1.45
Number of new customers	3.25	1.32
Market share	4.67	0.84
After-sales service	3.82	1.02

Table 2. (*Continued*)

Multiple Performance Measures	Mean	Standard Deviation
On-time delivery of product/service	3.16	1.45
Number of customer orders received	4.18	0.95
Number of customer suggestions	2.02	1.68
Customer satisfaction survey	2.95	1.47
Organization image and brand	2.56	1.54

Here, theoretical range, 1–5; 1: not at all; 5: to a very great extent. $N = 50$.

loaded adequately on a single factor. Table 3 presents the results of the factor analysis.

Intensity of Market Competition

Several models in measuring the intensity of market competition are accessible in the literature (see, e.g., Khandwalla, 1972; Gordon & Naryanan, 1984; Hoque & Hopper, 1997; Hoque et al., 2001; Libby & Waterhouse, 1996; Merchant, 1984). The Khandwalla (1972) model has been extended by incorporating other competition factors such as new entrants in the market, competitors' strategies and actions, number of competitors, and the strength of a company's market position (see, e.g., Cooper, 1995). Based on related studies, Hoque et al. (2001) conceptualized the intensity of market competition under six different areas: price, new product development, marketing or distribution channels, market (revenue) share, competitors' actions, and number of competitors in the market. The current study adapted the competition factors used by Hoque et al. (2001). For the purpose of this study, the intensity of market competition is the degree of competition confronted by a business organization on each of the above six factors. Moreover, this instrument is also believed to be significant and relevant to market competition. Respondents were asked to indicate, on a five-point Likert-type scale ranging from 1 (not at all) to 5 (to a very great extent), the intensity of their business units' market competition with respect to the above competition factors. A factor analysis extracted a single factor with eigenvalue greater than 1.0. Table 4 presents the factor loadings, eigenvalue, and the percentage of the variance explained. The Cronbach alpha was 0.85 which indicates consistency and reliability.

Table 3. Results of Factor Analysis for Performance Measurement
Dimensions ($N = 50$).

Factor	Items	Factor Loading	Eigenvalue	Percentage of Variance Explained
1	Financial perspective	0.87		
	Gross profit margin	0.84		
	Operating margin	0.79		
	Return on assets	0.71		
	Current ratio	0.69		
	Daily working capital	0.67	2.84	67.23
	Inventory turnover ratio	0.65		
	Cost versus budgets	0.64		
	Residual income	0.54		
	Contribution margin	0.56		
	Economic value added	0.52		
2	Learning and growth perspective			
	Human resources development cost	0.82		
	Number of new employees	0.76		
	Employees' performance (sales per employees)	0.75		
	Total training hours for employees	0.69		
	R&D expansion cost	0.67	2.96	69.01
	Wastage and scrap rate	0.54		
	Sales proportion from new product	0.51		
	Company's cost per employees	0.49		
	Employees' satisfaction	0.48		
	Percentage of key stuff turnover	0.45		
3	Internal business process perspective			
	Unit of output per labor hours	0.82		
	Measuring defects units (per million)	0.78		
	Quantity of energy consumed	0.73		
	Unit of output per machine hours	0.68		
	Unit product cost	0.64		
	Number of product lines or products	0.57	3.12	64.76
	Number of machine hours used	0.55		
	Total number of workers injured	0.54		
	Rate of incidence of injury	0.48		
	Level of absenteeism	0.45		
	Time to launch new products and services	0.45		

Table 3. (*Continued*)

Factor	Items	Factor Loading	Eigenvalue	Percentage of Variance Explained
4	Customer perspective			
	Number of customer complaints	0.88		
	Number of new customers	0.79		
	Market share	0.76		
	After-sales service	0.64		
	On-time delivery of product/service	0.61	3.54	71.32
	Number of customer orders received	0.59		
	Customer suggestion	0.54		
	Customer satisfaction survey	0.51		
	Organization image and brand	0.48		

Table 4. Results of Factor Analysis for the Intensity of Market Competition ($N = 50$).

Items	Factor Loading	Eigenvalue	Percentage of Variance Explained
Competition for price	0.76		
Competition for new product development	0.71		
Competition for marketing or distribution channels	0.69		
		2.98	67.56
Competition for market (revenue) share	0.65		
Number of competitors in the industry	0.62		
Competitors' actions or strategies	0.59		

Business Strategy

A number of research studies have used the measurement instruments of organizational strategy to confirm the impact of strategy on organizational control (see, e.g., Abernethy & Guthrie, 1994; Chong & Chong, 1997; Ittner, Larcker, & Rajan, 1997; Hoque et al., 2001). The present study measures strategy in relation to the two extreme strategic positions (i.e., prospectors and defenders) of the Miles and Snow's (1978) typology. Respondents were provided short descriptions of these strategic priorities, and then requested to specify the degree of importance that their firms had given to the priorities over the past 3 years on a five-point Likert-type scale, ranging from 1 (defender strategy) to 5 (prospector strategy).[5] The higher scores symbolize firms that are closer to the prospector end of the strategy continuum and vice versa. The mean score for the construct was 4.34 and the standard deviation 0.44.

RESULTS

Descriptive Statistics and the Correlation Matrix

Descriptive statistics and correlation matrix for all variables are shown in Tables 5 and 6, respectively. All the Cronbach alpha coefficients exceed the lower limit of acceptability (considered to be 0.70; Nunnally, 1978; Cronbach, 1951). As can be seen in Table 6, consistent with our expectation, the use of multiple measures of performance is positively and significantly correlated with the force of market competition ($r = 0.57$, $p = 0.000$) and the business unit strategy ($r = 0.69$, $p = 0.000$). Table 6 also shows that both the business unit strategy and intensity of market competition are positively and significantly associated with all of the four performance dimensions. In addition, results show that the business strategy and market competition are positively and significantly related with each other, implying possible multicollinearity problems. However, subsequent to examining tolerance and variation inflation factor (VIF), none of these tests have identified multicollinearity among the variables (VIF, 10, 16), which indicates no major problems for regression analysis.

Table 5.   Descriptive Statistics.

Variables	No. of Items	Theoretical Range	Actual Range	Mean	SD	Cronbach Alpha
Market competition	6	6–30	12–30	19.45	4.3	0.87
Strategic priorities	1	1–5	1–5	4.34	0.44	N/A
Multiple performance measures	40	40–200		89.96	8.49	0.93
Financial perspective	10	10–50	10–50	17.04	1.45	0.76
Learning and growth perspective	11	11–55	11–55	24.55	2.12	0.83
Internal business perspective	10	10–50	10–50	30.18	3.67	0.71
Customer perspective	9	9–45	9–45	18.20	1.89	0.88
Firm size (Tk.[a] m revenues)	N/A	N/A	Tk. 1–500m	Tk.265m	672.6	N/A

[a]Tk. (Taka) represents Bangladeshi currency. (100 paisa = 1 Taka.)

Table 6. Pearson Correlations ($n = 50$).

Code	Variables	MC	SP	MPM	FP	ILP	IBP	CP	FS
MC	Market competition	1							
SP	Strategic priorities	0.45**	1						
MPM	Overall multiple performance measures	0.57**	0.69**	1					
FP	Financial perspective	0.78**	0.76**	0.81**	1				
ILP	Learning and growth perspective	0.53*	0.49**	0.54**	0.34**	1			
IBP	Internal business perspective	0.47**	0.44**	0.22*	0.46**	0.42**	1		
CP	Customer perspective	0.53**	0.65**	0.44**	0.56**	0.53**	0.43**	1	
FS	Firm size (Tk.m revenues)	0.02	0.04	−0.07	0.07	−0.05	−0.06	0.01	1

*Correlation is significant at the 0.05 level (two-tailed).
**Correlation is significant at the 0.01 level (two-tailed).

Hypotheses Testing

To test the hypotheses, the regression model was run using SPSS 14.0 with the following regression equation:

$$Y = b_0 + \beta_1 X_1 + \beta_2 X_2 + \beta_3 X_3 + e \tag{1}$$

where Y is the performance measures usage (dependent variable), X_1 the market competition, X_2 the types of strategy followed, X_3 the firm's size (logarithm of sales revenues of ith firm), b_0 the intercept, e the error term, and β_1, β_2, and β_3 the regression coefficients for the contingent variables.

Consistent with Hoque et al. (2001), organization size is added to the model to control for the opportunity that multiple performance measures usage may differ with business unit size (sales revenue being a proxy for business unit size). The regression equation is shown as follows:

$$Y = 8.234 + 0.497X_1 + 0.194X_2 + 0.00X_3 + e \tag{2}$$

The results presented in Table 7 indicate that the coefficients β_1 (intensity of market competition) and β_2 (types of strategy followed) are both positive and significant $(\beta_1 = 0.497, \ t = 4.995, \ p = 0.000; \ \beta_2 = 0.194, \ t = 1.783, \ p = 0.025)$. Thus, these results provide sufficient evidence to support the proposition that greater multiple performance measures usage is connected with increasing intensity of market competition and types of strategies followed by manufacturing firms. That is, management of Bangladeshi manufacturing firms has a greater tendency to use comprehensive

Table 7. Regression Coefficients of Overall Performance and Other Performance Dimensions of Balanced Scorecard.

Performance Measures	Constant (b_0)	$\beta_1 X_1$	$\beta_2 X_2$	$\beta_3 X_3$
Overall	8.234	0.497	0.194	0.004
	(0.955)	(4.995)*	(1.783)*	(0.478)
Financial	4.563	0.453	0.346	0.001
	(2.453)	(4.450)*	(0.054)*	(1.458)
Customer	6.872	0.513	0.167	−0.003
	(1.769)	(3.990)	(1.561)	(0.004)
Internal business process	2.562	0.399	0.345	0.013
	(1.349)*	(4.557)*	(1.541)*	(0.358)
Learning and growth	3.988	0.552	0.610	−0.025
	(1.450)	(5.231)*	(2.563)*	(0.031)

*t-Value significant at 5% level of significance (two-tailed).

performance measures based on competition. These findings are in line with performance measurement literature using contingent theory applied in developed countries (Hoque et al., 2001; Gordon & Naryanan, 1984; Mia & Clarke, 1999). The study thus extends performance measurement literature by offering an explanation for the relationship between the intensity of market competition and diversity of organizational performance measures in developing countries. However, while earlier studies (e.g., Hoque et al., 2001) investigated the effect of market competition on the use of multiple performance measures at the business unit level, the current study has been carried out in corporate firms. Furthermore, this study's evidence on the use of multiple performance measures based on the types of strategies an organization pursues is also in accordance with earlier studies applying Miles and Snow (1978) typology (Abernethy & Guthrie, 1994; Chong & Chong, 1997; Ittner et al., 1997). Table 7 also shows that firm size is not significantly associated with multiple performance measures usage. The whole model is significant ($F = 16.531$; $p = 0.000$) and explains 53.08% of the performance variance.

Supporting Regression Analysis

The analysis conducted up to this point focuses on the linkage of all perspectives of the multiple performance measurements with two contingent variables. The question now is whether each performance measure used has the same effects on firm variables compared with those of the overall multiple performance measures? To investigate this question and the relationship predicted in the regression model, analysis was also performed using each of the four performance dimensions. The results presented in Table 8 indicate that both types of strategies followed and the intensity of market competition are associated significantly with each of the

Table 8. Adjusted R^2, F-Value, p-Value of Variables, Financial Perspective, Learning and Growth Perspective, Internal Business Perspective, and Customer Perspective.

Dimensions	R^2	Adjusted R^2	F-Value	Significance (p)
Financial perspective	0.315	0.299	9.555	0.000
Learning and growth perspective	0.349	0.345	14.250	0.000
Internal business perspective	0.449	0.437	34.459	0.000
Customer perspective	0.375	0.364	19.233	0.000

performance dimensions. Again, business unit size does not appear to be an important predictor of a performance measurement system usage. Overall, the results for the financial, innovation and learning, internal business process, and customer perspective (panel E) explain 29.9%, 34.5%, 43.7%, and 36.4% of the variances, respectively.

To add further rigor to the analysis of the association between multiple performance measures and uses of business strategy (i.e., if businesses pursue a prospector strategy, will they be more inclined to use multiple performance measures), a two-way analysis of variance (ANOVA) test was undertaken. To perform the ANOVA, strategy was split on the basis of the median scores to form two different groups: prospector (above median) and defender (below median). Multiple performance measures usage was also split at the median to form two groups: multiple performance measures (above median) and traditional performance measures (below median).[6] The mean scores for multiple performances measures shown in Table 9 indicate that firms pursuing a prospector strategy have greater propensity to rely on multiple performance measures to measure business performance than the firms pursuing defender strategy. Likewise, it has also shown that the frequency of multiple measures usage is lowest when it fits with defender strategy (mismatch). In other words, firms following a defender strategy emphasize more on financial measures The results of the F-test suggest significant variations (as derived probability $(p) <$ significant level (0.01)) between these two groups of firms in terms of their use of multiple performance measures. Consequently, it is acknowledged that within the firms studied, the more the firms pursuing prospector strategy, the more is the use of multiple performance measures. As a result, this finding is consistent with that of Bouwens and Abernethy (2000) and Abernethy and Lillis (1995) who argue that prospector strategies need sophisticated accounting systems in order to meet the uncertainty and market demand.

Table 9. ANOVA Results: Mean Performance Scores.

	Firms Pursuing Prospector Strategy (Mean Score)	Firms Pursuing Defender Strategy (Mean Score)	F-Value (p^*)
Higher use of multiple performance measures	75.87	71.34	−8.75 (0.000)
Traditional performance measures (less uses)	73.78	72.45	

$^*p$, two-tailed test.

Simons (1987) also finds that prospector firms seem to place more emphasis on forecast and broad ranges of accounting data in control systems.

CONCLUSION, IMPLICATIONS, AND LIMITATIONS

This article empirically examines the effect of market competition and the types of strategy on use of multiple measures of performance of 50 Bangladeshi manufacturing firms. Results suggest a positive and significant relationship between the intensity of market competition and use of multiple measures for performance evaluation. In other words, the results reveal that business enterprises operating in Bangladesh rely on multiple measures of performance because these firms operate in an extremely competitive atmosphere. These results thus confirm earlier contingency research on the effect of competition on management accounting practice (e.g., Hoque et al., 2001; Ezzamel, 1990; Simons, 1990, 1991; Govindarajan, 1984; Hemmer, 1996; Libby & Waterhouse, 1996; Khandwalla, 1972; Merchant, 1984), and are also in agreement with those of Khandwalla (1972), Hayes (1977), Gordon and Naryanan (1984), and Chenhall and Morris (1986) who reported the tendency on the use of nonaccounting data in situations of intense competition.

The study also disclosed that multiple performance measures are positively and significantly associated with the organizational choice regarding types of strategy followed. That is to say, the business strategies are perceived to play as a key predecessor of firms' multiple measures practices. This evidence is to a great extent consistent with the other studies noting a congruent (good fit) matching of strategic priorities, and the choice of performance measures in performance evaluation is indispensable to augment organizational performance (e.g., Hoque, 2004; Govindarajan & Gupta, 1985; Ittner et al., 1997; Lynch & Cross, 1991; Simons, 1987, 1995; Kaplan, 1983; Perera, Harrison, & Poole, 1997). There is, however, no evidence that multiple performance measures are related to the firm size. Results also indicate that all four performance dimensions are important for today's competitive environments in Bangladeshi manufacturing firms. The two-way ANOVA analysis supports the use of multiple performance measures for firms pursuing a prospector strategy. These findings are noteworthy from a practical standpoint and consistent with other studies on the broader performance evaluation system (Kaplan & Norton, 1996a,

1996b; Hemmer, 1996; Shields, 1997; Atkinson et al., 1997; Ittner & Larcker, 1998a, 1998b; Hoque & James, 2000; Otley, 1999; Young & Selto, 1991). A combination of both financial and nonfinancial performance indicators is needed in the measurement process. The use of multiple measures for performance assessment is generally underpinned with the presence of various contextual factors (two factors considered in this study).

The present study makes a number of contributions both in performance measurement theory and in practice. At the practical level, designers of performance measurement systems must emphasize variables that are essential to the accomplishment of a firms' effort in relation to the design of control and measurement systems in developing countries. Additionally, the findings convey to top-level executives of developing countries who are in charge of formulating and implementing business strategy, as the findings have offered a better insight into the relationship between business strategy, market competition, and performance practices. At a theoretical level, the key significance of this study is its extension and application of the contingency theory to developing countries. Aligning multiple performance measures to contingent variables contributes to knowledge and contingency theory and the relationships with organizational measurement and management system. Furthermore, by exploring this under-researched area, the study has substantiated the role of contingent variables in the design of multiple performance measurement system broadly in developed countries setting. There is however still a need for further research to try to explore the effects of competition and business strategy on the use of contemporary performance measurement systems (as evidenced here) not only in Western countries, but also in other emerging countries.

The above results are not free from limitations, yet these limitations can be used for further research. Specifically, the study is confined only to manufacturing organizations listed on the DSE. Therefore, generalizing our results to other unlisted manufacturing sector or to nonmanufacturing organizations is to be done after controlling for the differences in industry types and their attributes. Likewise, the small sample size coupled with lower response rate restricts the finding of the study. Future research can then be undertaken with a larger sample size and with maximizing more responses beyond the listed manufacturing sector firms. The garments sector, for instance, would be useful to analyze as this accounts for 40% of manufacturing and is largely unlisted. In addition, the findings of the study might change over time, and, therefore, a longitudinal study in different settings using "softer" methodologies such as case studies may add more rigors. The current study has used size as a control variable; yet there might be other variables such as delegation, environmental uncertainty, and employee experience that may influence the projected relationship between the dependent and the independent variables. Disregarding these variables in the present study is thus recognized as a likely limitation. Lastly, there are limitations in relation to variable measurement "strategy." Although consistent with other studies (e.g., Naranjo-Gil, 2004; Hoque et al., 2001), the instrument taken for measuring business strategy consists only of a single item which poses difficulties to establish the construct validity of the item.

Future studies then are imperative using time-series data (as suggested by Ittner & Larcker, 1998b). This research can extend this study by investigating how and why performance measurement systems change over time (Libby & Waterhouse, 1996). This study considered only two contingent variables leaving other variables unattended. Thus, the examination of how multiple performance measures could be useful to organizations operating in diverse industries with the application of computerized manufacturing operation, firms' investment in intangibles, and the product (or organization) life cycle could be other areas for further research. Future research may also be directed to examine any connection between single items of "market competition" and the construction of the performance measurement. Hoque et al. (2001) noted that performance measures might have a varied level of competition in each item of competition. Further, a study incorporating multiple items in capturing strategic priorities (see Chenhall & Langfield-Smith, 1998) using Miles and Snow typology could lead to refinement of priorities of business strategy with respect to several dimensions such as providing high-quality products, low production costs, low prices, and fast deliveries, and introducing new products quickly.

NOTES

1. Miles and Snow (1978) proposed a comprehensive, business-level strategic typology interrelating organizational strategy, structure, and process. Their typology provides a useful framework for distinguishing distinct firm strategies vis-à-vis the competitive environments in which firms operate.

2. The key benefit of the Miles and Snow typology is the strong and steady support for its validity in the literature (e.g., James & Hatten, 1995; Simons, 1987; Hambrick, 1983; Snow & Hrebiniak, 1980), and its conceptual and theoretical implication to the field of strategic management literature (Ghoshal, 2003; Hambrick, 2003; Chakravarthy & White, 2002).

3. A copy of the survey questionnaire may be obtained from the corresponding author.

4. The companies surveyed consist of 8 from cement, 4 from ceramic industry, 34 from food and allied, 25 from pharmaceuticals and chemicals, 23 from engineering, 8 from tannery industry, 39 from textile industry, and 8 from paper and printing sector.

5. For a use alike, see Hoque et al. (2001), Chenhall and Langfield-Smith (1998), and Ittner et al. (1997).

6. However, as ANOVA assumes equality of variance between groups, the variance was checked earlier using the Levene test. The significance value of the Levene statistic was 0.159 (higher than 0.05), presenting homogeneity of variance.

ACKNOWLEDGMENT

The authors acknowledge the valuable comments made by two anonymous reviewers for the improvement of this article.

REFERENCES

Abernethy, M., & Lillis, A. M. (1995). The impact of manufacturing flexibility on management control system design. *Accounting, Organizations and Society*, *20*(4), 241–258.

Abernethy, M. A., & Guthrie, C. H. (1994). An empirical assessment of the 'fit' between strategy and management information system design. *Accounting and Finance*, *34*(2), 49–66.

Akhter, A. (2007). The practices of ABC costing – An empirical evidence of Bangladeshi companies. *Stamford Journal of Business Studies*, *2*(1), 86–98.

Atkinson, A. A., Balakrisnan, R., Booth, P., Cote, J. M., Groot, T., Malmi, T., Roberts, H., Uliana, E., & Wu, A. (1997). New directions in management accounting research. *Journal of Management Accounting Research*, *9*, 79–109.

Bangladesh Economic Review. (2007). Available at http://www.mof.gov.bd/en/index.php? option = com_content&view = article&id = 160&Itemid = 1. Retrieved on December 2, 2008, pp. 1–47.

Banker, R. D., Potter, G., & Srinivasan, D. (2000). An empirical investigation of an incentive plan that includes nonfinancial performance measures. *The Accounting Review*, *75*(1), 65–92.

Bartlett, M. S. (1954). A note on the multiplying factors for various chi square approximations. *Journal of the Royal Statistical Society Series B*, *16*, 296–298.

Begum, M., Hoque, & Shill, N. (2001). The prospect of JIT implementation in manufacturing facilities: Survey on large manufacturing business of Bangladesh. *Journal of Business Administration*, *25*(2), 33–45.

Bourne, M., Mills, J., Wilcox, M., Neely, A., & Platts, K. (2000). Designing, implementing and updating performance measurement systems. *International Journal of Operations & Production Management*, *20*(7), 754–771.

Bouwens, J., & Abernethy, M. A. (2000). The consequences of customization on management accounting systems design. *Accounting, Organizations and Society*, *25*(3), 221–259.

Bruggeman, W., & Slagmulder, R. (1995). The impact of technological change on management accounting. *Management Accounting Research, 6*(3), 241–252.

Chakravarthy, B. S., & White, R. E. (2002). Strategy process: Forming, implementing and changing strategies. In: A. Pettigrew, H. Thomas & R. Whittington (Eds), *Handbook of strategy and management*. London: Sage Publications.

Chenhall, R., & Morris, D. (1986). The impact of structure, environment and interdependence on perceived usefulness of management accounting systems. *The Accounting Review, 61*(1), 16–35.

Chenhall, R. H. (1997). Reliance on manufacturing performance measures, total quality management and organizational performance. *Management Accounting Research, 8*, 187–206.

Chenhall, R. H. (2003). Management control systems design within its organizational context: Findings from contingency-based research and directions for the future. *Accounting, Organizations and Society, 28*, 127–168.

Chenhall, R. H., & Langfield-Smith, K. (1998). Adoption and benefits of management accounting practices: An Australian study. *Management Accounting Research, 9*, 1–19.

Chong, V. K., & Chong, K. M. (1997). Strategic choices, environmental uncertainty and SBU performance: A note on the intervening role of management accounting systems. *Accounting and Business Research, 27*, 268–276.

Cooper, R. (1995). *When lean enterprise collide: Competing through confrontation*. Boston, MA: Harvard Business School Press.

Cronbach, L. J. (1951). Coefficient alpha and the internal structure of tests. *Psychometrika, 16*(September), 297–334.

Dearden, J. (1987). Measuring profit center managers. *Harvard Business Review, 65*(5), 84–88.

Defond, M. L., & Park, C. W. (1999). The effect of competition on CEO turnover. *Journal of Accounting and Economics, 27*, 35–56.

Dent, J. (1990). Strategy, organization and control: Some possibilities for accounting research. *Accounting, Organizations and Society, 15*(1/2), 3–25.

Dhaka Stock Exchange Official Directory of Listed Companies. (2008). Available at http://www.dsebd.org/company%20listing.php. Retrieved on October 4, 2008.

Dixon, J. R., Nanni, A. J., Jr., & Vollman, T. E. (1990). *The new performance challenge: Measuring manufacturing for world class competition*. Homewood, IL: Dow Jones-Irwin.

Donaldson, L. (2001). *The contingency theory of organizations* (pp. 1–38). California: Sage.

Duncan, R. (1972). Characteristics of organizational environments and perceived environmental uncertainty. *Administrative Science Quarterly, 17*(3), 313–327.

Dunk, A. S. (1992). Reliance on budgetary control, manufacturing process automation and production subunit performance: A research note. *Accounting, Organizations and Society, 17*(3–4), 195–203.

Emmanuel, C., & Otley, D. (1995). *Readings in accounting for management control*. London: Chapman and Hall.

Ezzamel, M. (1990). The impact of environmental uncertainty, managerial autonomy and size on budget characteristics. *Management Accounting Research, 1*(2), 181–197.

Fernandes, A. M. (2008). Firm-level productivity in Bangladesh manufacturing industries. *World Development, 36*(10), 1725–1744.

Gehl Sampath, P. (2007). *Intellectual property and innovation in least developed countries: Pharmaceuticals, agro-processing and textiles and RMG in Bangladesh*. Background Paper no. 9 for the least developed countries. Report 2007 on Knowledge, Technological Learning and Innovation for Development. UNCTAD, Geneva.

Gerdin, J., & Greve, J. (2004). Forms of contingency fit in management accounting research – A critical review. *Accounting, Organizations and Society, 29*(3–4), 303–326.

Ghoshal, S. (2003). Miles and Snow: Enduring insights for managers. *Academy of Management Executive, 17*(4), 109–114.

Gordon, L. A., & Naryanan, V. K. (1984). Management accounting systems, perceived environmental uncertainty and organizational structure: An empirical investigation. *Accounting, Organizations and Society, 19*(1), 330–348.

Gosselin, M. (1997). The effect of strategy and organizational structure on the adoption and implementation of activity-based costing. *Accounting, Organizations and Society, 22*(2), 105–122.

Gosselin, M. (2005). An empirical study of performance measurement in manufacturing firms. *International Journal of Productivity and Performance Management, 54*(5/6), 419–437.

Govindarajan, V. (1984). Appropriateness of accounting data in performance evaluation: An empirical examination of environmental uncertainty as an intervening variable. *Accounting, Organizations and Society*, 125–135.

Govindarajan, V., & Fisher, J. (1990). Strategy, control systems and resource sharing: Effects on business unit performance. *Academy of Management Journal, 33*(2), 259–285.

Govindarajan, V., & Gupta, A. K. (1985). Linking controls systems to business unit strategy: Impact on performance. *Accounting, Organizations and Society, 10*(1), 51–66.

Gupta, A. K., & Govindarajan, V. (1984). Business unit strategy, managerial characteristics, and business unit effectiveness at strategy implementation. *Academy of Management Journal, 27*(1), 25–41.

Halachmi, A. (2005). Performance measurement is only one way of managing performance. *International Journal of Productivity and Performance Management, 54*(7), 502–516.

Hambrick, D. C. (1983). Some tests of effectiveness and functional attributes of Miles and Snow's strategic types. *Academy of Management Journal, 26*, 5–26.

Hambrick, D. C. (2003). On the staying power of defenders, analyzers, and prospectors. *Academy of Management Executive, 17*(4), 115–118.

Hayes, D. (1977). The contingency theory of managerial accounting. *The Accounting Review, 52*(1), 22–39.

Hemmer, T. (1996). On the design and choice of modern management accounting measures. *Journal of Management Accounting Research, 8*, 87–116.

Hoque, Z. (2004). A contingency model of the association between strategy, environmental uncertainty and performance measurement: Impact on organizational performance. *International Business Review, 13*, 485–502.

Hoque, Z., & Hopper, T. (1997). Political and industrial relations turbulence, competition and budgeting in the nationalized jute mills of Bangladesh. *Accounting and Business Research, 27*(2), 125–143.

Hoque, Z., & James, W. (2000). Linking balanced scorecard measures to size and market factors: Impact on organizational performance. *Journal of Management Accounting Research, 12*, 1–17.

Hoque, Z., Mia, L., & Alam, M. (2001). Market competition, computer-aided manufacturing and use of multiple performance measures: An empirical study. *British Accounting Review, 33*, 23–45.

Horngren, C. T., Datar, S. M., Foster, G., Rajan, M., & Ittner, C. (2009). *Cost accounting: A Managerial Emphasis* (13th ed.). Upper Saddle River, New Jersey: Prentice Hall.

Hossain, H. (2008). Performance measurement practices in action: Financial vs non-financial: The case in Bangladesh. *Journal of Business Administration*, *12*(3), 15–27.

Industrial Policy of Bangladesh. (2005). Government of Bangladesh. Available at www.fbcci-bd. org/policy/Industrial_Policy_2005.htm. Retrieved on December 7, 2008, pp. 2–40.

Ishtiaque, A. N. A., Khan, Md. H. U. Z., Akhter, S., & Fatima, J. K. (2007). Perception analysis of balanced scorecard – An application over a multinational corporation of Bangladesh. *Dhaka University Journal of Business Studies*, *28*(2), 235–270.

Ismail, T. H. (2007). Performance evaluation measures in the private sector: Egyptian practice. *Managerial Auditing Journal*, *22*(5), 503–513.

Ittner, C. D., & Larcker, D. F. (1998a). Innovations in performance measurement: Trends and research implications. *Journal of Management Accounting Research*, *10*, 205–238.

Ittner, C. D., & Larcker, D. F. (1998b). Are non-financial measures leading indicators of financial performance? An analysis of customer satisfaction. *Journal of Accounting Research*, *36*, 1–35.

Ittner, C. D., & Larcker, D. F. (2001). Assessing empirical research in managerial accounting: A value-based management perspective. *Journal of Accounting and Economics*, *32*, 349–410.

Ittner, C. D., Larcker, D. F., & Rajan, M. V. (1997). The choice of performance measures in annual bonus contract. *The Accounting Review*, *2*(2), 231–256.

James, W. L., & Hatten, K. J. (1995). Research notes and communication: Further evidence on the validity of the self-typing paragraph approach: Miles and Snow strategic archetypes in banking. *Strategic Management Journal*, *16*(2), 161–168.

Jusoh, R., Ibrahim, D. N., & Zainuddin, Y. (2008). The performance consequence of multiple performance measures usage: Evidence from the Malaysian manufacturers. *International Journal of Productivity and Performance Management*, *57*(2), 119–136.

Jusoh, R., & Parnell, J. A. (2008). Competitive strategy and performance measurement in the Malaysian context. *Management Decision*, *46*(1), 5–31.

Kaiser, H. (1974). An index of factorial simplicity. *Psychometrika*, *39*, 31–36.

Kaplan, R., & Norton, D. (2001). Transforming the balanced scorecard from performance measurement to strategic management. *Accounting Horizons*, *15*(1), 87–104.

Kaplan, R. S. (1983). Measuring manufacturing performance: A new challenge for managerial accounting research. *The Accounting Review*, *58*(4), 686–705.

Kaplan, R. S., & Atkinson, A. (1998). *Advanced management accounting* (3rd ed.). New York: Prentice Hall.

Kaplan, R. S., & Norton, D. (1992). The balanced scorecard – Measures that drive performance. *Harvard Business Review*, *70*(1), 71–79.

Kaplan, R. S., & Norton, D. (1993). Putting the balanced scorecard to work. *Harvard Business Review*, *71*(5), 134–147.

Kaplan, R. S., & Norton, D. P. (1996a). *The balanced scorecard*. Harvard: Harvard Business School Press.

Kaplan, R. S., & Norton, D. P. (1996b). Using the balanced scorecard as a strategic management system. *Harvard Business Review*, *74*(1), 75–85.

Karathanos, D., & Karathanos, P. (2005). Applying the balanced scorecard to education. *Journal of Education for Business*, *80*(4), 222–230.

Keegan, D. O., Eiler, R., & Anania, J. V. (1989). An advanced cost management system for the factory of the future. *Management Accounting* (December), 31–37.

Khan, M. H. U. Z., & Halabi, A. K. (2009). Perceptions of firms learning and growth under knowledge management approach with linkage to balanced scorecard (BSC): Evidence from a multinational corporation of Bangladesh. *International Journal of Business and Management*, *4*(9), 257–282.

Khandwalla, P. N. (1972). The effect of different types of competition on the use of management controls. *Journal of Accounting Research*, *10*(2), 275–285.

Khundker, S., & Nasreen, K. (2002). Garment industry in Bangladesh. In: J. Gopal (Ed.), *Garment industry in South Asia: Rags or riches? Competitiveness, productivity and job quality in the post-MFA environment*. New Delhi: South Asia Multidisciplinary Advisory Team, ILO.

Langfield-Smith, K. (1997). Management control systems and strategy: A critical review. *Accounting, Organizations and Society*, *22*(2), 207–232.

Langfield-Smith, K., Thorne, H., & Hilton, R. W. (2009). *Management accounting: Information for creating and managing value* (5th ed.). Australia: McGraw-Hill.

Lambert, R. A. (1998). Customer satisfaction and future financial performance. Discussion of "Are nonfinancial measures leading indicators of financial performance? An analysis of customer satisfaction." *Journal of Accounting Research*, *36*(Supplement), 37–46.

Libby, T., & Waterhouse, J. H. (1996). Predicting change in management accounting systems. *Journal of Management Accounting Research*, *8*, 137–150.

Lynch, R. L., & Cross, K. F. (1991). *Measure up!*. Cambridge, MA: Blackwell Publishers.

Mahmud, W., Ahmed, S., & Mahajan, S. (2007). *Economic reforms, growth, and governance: The political economy aspects of Bangladesh's development surprise*. Working Paper Series no. 22. The World Bank, Washington, DC, USA, pp. 1–44.

Malmi, T. (2001). Balanced scorecards in Finnish companies: A research note. *Management Accounting Research*, *12*(2), 207–220.

Mazumder, B. C. (2007). Application of management accounting techniques in decision making in the manufacturing business firms in Bangladesh. *The Cost and Management*, *35*(1), 5–18.

McNair, C. J., & Mosconi, W. (1987). Measuring performance in an advanced manufacturing environment. *Management Accounting* (July), 28–31.

Merchant, K. (1981). The design of the corporate budgeting system: Influences on managerial behaviour and performance. *The Accounting Review*, *56*(4), 813–829.

Merchant, K. A. (1984). Influences on departmental budgeting: An empirical examination of a contingency model. *Accounting, Organizations and Society*, *9*(3/4), 291–310.

Mia, L., & Chenhall, R. H. (1994). The usefulness of management accounting systems, functional differentiation and managerial effectiveness. *Accounting, Organizations and Society*, *19*(1), 1–13.

Mia, L., & Clarke, B. (1999). Market competition, management accounting systems and business unit performance. *Management Accounting Research*, *10*, 137–158.

Miles, R. E., & Snow, C. (1994). *Fit, failure and the hall of fame*. New York: Free Press.

Miles, R. E., & Snow, C. C. (1978). *Organizational strategy, structure and process*. New York: McGraw-Hill.

Mlachila, M., & Yang, Y. (2004). *The end of textile quotas: A case study of the impact on Bangladesh*. IMF Working Paper no. 108. International Monetary Fund, Washington, USA, pp. 1–38.

Mossaraf, L., & Ahmed, F. (2008). Evaluating business performance with the presence of non-financial measures – An empirical investigation. *Prime University Journal of Business Administration*, *2*(2), 13–22.

Nanni, A. J., Jr., Dixon, J. R., & Vollmann, T. E. (1992). Integrated performance measurement: Management accounting to support the new manufacturing realities. *Journal of Management Accounting Research, 4*(Fall), 1–19.

Naranjo-Gil, D. (2004). The role of sophisticated accounting systems in strategy management. *International Journal of Digital Accounting Research, 4*(8), 125–144.

Nunnally, J. C. (1978). *Psychometric theory.* London: McGraw-Hill.

Otley, D. (1980). The contingency theory of management accounting: Achievement and prognosis. *Accounting, Organizations and Society, 5*(4), 413–428.

Otley, D. (1999). Performance management: A framework for management control systems research. *Management Accounting Research, 10,* 363–382.

Pallant, J. (2001). *SPSS survival manual* (1st ed.). Australia: Allen & Unwin.

Perera, S., Harrison, G., & Poole, M. (1997). Customer focused manufacturing strategy and the use of operations-based non-financial performance measures: A research note. *Accounting, Organizations and Society, 22*(6), 557–572.

Rahman, M., & Anwar, A. (2006). *Bangladesh apparels export to the US market: An examination of her competitiveness vis-à-vis China, CPD trade policy brief.* Paper no. 62 (September), pp. 1–59.

Schoenfeld, H. M. (1986). The present state of performance evaluation in multinational. In: H. P. Holzer & H. M. Schoenfeld (Eds), *Managerial accounting and analysis in multinational enterprises* (pp. 217–252). Berlin: Walter de Gruyter.

Sharkar, M. Z. H., Sobhan, Md. A., & Sultana, S. (2006). Management accounting development and practices in Bangladesh. *BRAC University Journal, 3*(2), 113–123.

Shields, M. D. (1995). An empirical analysis of firms' implementation experiences with activity-based costing. *Journal of Management Accounting Research, 7*(Fall), 148–166.

Shields, M. D. (1997). Research in management accounting by North Americans in the 1990s. *Journal of Management Accounting Research, 9,* 3–62.

Silk, S. (1998). Automating the balanced scorecard. *Management Accounting (USA), 79*(11), 38–44.

Simons, R. (1987). Accounting control systems and business strategy: An empirical study. *Accounting, Organizations and Society, 12,* 357–374.

Simons, R. (1990). The role of management control systems in creating competitive advantage: New perspectives. *Accounting, Organizations and Society, 15*(1/2), 127–143.

Simons, R. (1991). Strategic orientation and top management attention to control systems. *Strategic Management Journal, 12*(1), 49–62.

Simons, R. (1995). *Levers of control.* Boston, MA: Harvard Business School Press.

Simons, R. (2000). *Performance measurement & control systems for implementing strategy.* Prentice Hall, Upper Saddle River, NJ: Prentice Hall International.

Snow, C. C., & Hrebiniak, L. G. (1980). Distinctive competence and organizational performance. *Administrative Science Quarterly, 25*(June), 317–336.

Speckbacher, G., Bischof, J., & Pfeiffer, T. (2003). A descriptive analysis on the implementation of balanced scorecards in German-speaking countries. *Management Accounting Research, 14*(4), 361–387.

Thompson, J. (1967). *Organizations in action.* New York: McGraw-Hill.

Waterhouse, J., & Tiessen, P. (1978). A contingency framework for management accounting systems research. *Accounting, Organizations and Society, 3*(1), 65–76.

Woodward, J. (1965). *Industrial organization: Theory and practice.* London: Oxford University Press.

World Bank. (2005a). World development indicators database. Available at http://www.
    worldbank.org/data/dataquery.html. Accessed on October 12, 2005.
World Bank. (2005b). *End of MFA Quotas: Key Issues and Strategic options for Bangladesh
    Readymade Garments Industry*. Bangladesh Development Series – no. 2. The World
    Bank Office, Dhaka, Office of the World Bank, Washington, DC, USA, pp. 1–107.
Young, S. M., & Selto, F. H. (1991). New manufacturing practices and cost management:
    Review of the literature and directions for research. *Journal of Accounting Literature, 10*,
    265–298.
Zahra, S. A., & Pearce, J. A., II. (1990). Research evidence on the Miles and Snow typology.
    Journal of Management, 16, 751–768.

APPENDIX. STATISTICS OF RESPONDENT COMPANIES IN TERMS OF EMPLOYEES, ANNUAL SALES, AND ASSETS

Number of Employees

Firms	Number of employees			
	50–150 (%)	150–250 (%)	Over 250 (%)	Total
All sectors ($n = 50$)	4%	30.5%	65.5%	100%

Sales Turnover

Firms	Sales amount (in million Bd. Tk.)					
	Less than 100	100–199	200–299	300–399	400–499	Over 500
All sectors ($n = 50$)	5 %	10%	20%	45%	10%	10%

Total Assets

Firms	Total assets (in million Bd. Tk.)					
	Less than 100	100–199	200–299	300–399	400–499	Over 500
All sectors ($n = 50$)	5%	20%	20%	40%	10%	5%

Bd. Tk. = Bangladeshi taka (official currency).

THE ADOPTION OF ACCRUAL ACCOUNTING IN THE INDONESIAN PUBLIC SECTOR [☆]

Harun Harun and Peter Robinson

ABSTRACT

Purpose – *The purpose of this article is to examine the contextual variables that influence the pace of public sector reforms through the adoption of accrual accounting for the Indonesian public sector.*

Design/methodology/approach – *The study employs a historically informed study based on a modified version of the Luder's (1992) Contingency Model (LCM). The data are drawn from official documents issued by the Indonesian government about reporting system for the public sector in the country and interviews with the key figures involved in the public sector accounting reforms in Indonesia. The study also uses publicly available information addressing the recent progress in the implementation of the accrual accounting system in the Indonesian public sector.*

[☆]Early versions of the article were presented at the *Fourth Asia Pacific Interdisciplinary Research in Accounting Conference (APIRA Conference IV)* held in Singapore in 2004 and *1st Accounting Conference*, Faculty of Economics at The University of Indonesia in Jakarta, Indonesia, in 2007 (see Robinson & Harun, 2004; Harun, 2007a, 2007b). The authors thank the suggestions and comments from the referees and participants of both conferences.

Research in Accounting in Emerging Economies, Volume 10, 233–250
Copyright © 2010 by Emerald Group Publishing Limited
All rights of reproduction in any form reserved
ISSN: 1479-3563/doi:10.1108/S1479-3563(2010)0000010014

Key findings – *The adoption of accrual accounting in the Indonesian public sector was stimulated by the economic crisis, prodemocratic movements, and international pressures for the reform of the public sector. However, the public sector accounting reforms in the country are confronted with significant implementation barriers which include legal issues, the lack of political supports, and skilled human resources. These barriers in turn threaten the intended purposes to be achieved through the greater economic and public sector reforms in the newly democratic Indonesia.*

Research limitations/implications – *The arguments of the study should be understood in the context of the institutional setting of Indonesia as a developing country. Nonetheless, the findings of this study show an example of the complexity faced through the use of the private sector accounting practice in the public sector context.*

Originality/value – *The findings of the study support the notion that the nature of legal system, political support, and human resource capacity influence the extent to which an accounting system is adopted in the public sector.*

Keywords: Accrual accounting; local government; decentralization; implementation barriers.

1. INTRODUCTION

In many jurisdictions, public sector reforms have been accompanied by accounting reforms (Guthrie, 1998; Ryan, 1998; Carlin, 2005; Connolly & Hyndman, 2006; Christensen & Parker, 2010). The change from cash-based accounting or budgetary accounting to accrual accounting is often a significant element in reforms of the public sector, a process which Power and Laughlin (1992) suggest is a shift toward the accountingization of the public sector. The introduction of accrual accounting, perceived to be a superior accounting technology, is intended to facilitate greater transparency in public sector agency activities, strengthen the accountability of government, and improve the quality of decision making within government.

However, while public sector reforms delivered through the introduction of accrual accounting aim at improving the performance of the public sector operation, there is no guarantee that a government will be any more accountable for its achievements and that provision of goods and services will be any better. Hopwood (1983) notes that it is difficult to distinguish between the advance of accounting for ritualistic, legitimizing, and rationalizing reasons and its advance from the belief that it can change and improve organizational performance. In addition, recent literature in the public sector accounting also critically questions the benefits of the use of the private style accounting systems for the public sector (e.g., Carlin, 2005; Connolly & Hyndman, 2006; Christensen, 2007; Christiaens & Rommel, 2008; Nor-Aziah & Scapens, 2007).

Therefore, to provide evidence of the links between broader changes in the public sector and changes in accounting techniques, it is important to examine the political and economic context in which changes to financial reporting have taken place and to assess the impact of these changes on public sector management practices. The rest of this article is structured as follows: (1) the purpose and context of the study; (2) research questions, theoretical model, and methods used in the study; (3) the background of Indonesian public sector reform taken after the fall of President Suharto in 1998; (4) the introduction of accrual accounting in the Indonesian public sector; (5) an interpretational history of the introduction of accrual accounting in the Indonesian public sector drawn from Luder's (1992) Contingency Model (LCM); (6) conclusion, implication of the findings, and limitations of the study.

2. PURPOSE AND CONTEXT OF STUDY

The purpose of the study is to examine the pace of current public sector reform in Indonesia, which is adopting accrual accounting as part of the waves of political and economic reforms flowing from the fall of the Suharto regime in 1998. As most published accounting research on public sector accounting reforms has focussed on developed countries (see Neu, 2001; Sharma & Lawrence, 2008), this study is set to address the experience of an emerging economy in undertaking a public sector accounting reform as most research tends to be written from the perspective of, and in reverence for, first-world institutions and a wealthy subset of first-world population (Lawrence & Wynne, 2010, p. 1). Therefore, this study not only documents and provides an understanding of accounting regulation within Indonesia, but also investigates the contextual variables affecting the pace and extent of Indonesian public sector reform realized through the adoption of accrual accounting.

3. RESEARCH QUESTIONS, THEORETICAL MODEL, AND METHODS

In relation to the purpose of the study, three research questions are raised as the basis in collecting and analyzing the data of the study: (1) What were the stimuli of the public sector reforms in Indonesia? (2) Who were the main promoters of the adoption of the accrual accounting system in Indonesia? (3) What were the main problems with respect to the public sector accounting reforms in Indonesia?

The model that is used as the lens in this study is the LCM for governmental accounting innovation developed by Luder (1992). According to Luder (2001), the primary objectives pursued by the model were twofold. First, it was intended to serve as a framework for empirical investigations into governmental accounting reforms and to thereby facilitate the comparison of the findings reported by different research studies. Second, it was meant to constitute a complex hypothesis explaining the influence of context on a specific reform or innovation process, and to trigger further research directed at confirming, falsifying, and amending the hypothesis.

Luder (1992) also suggests that the model is fundamentally an economic model that posits an information market exists for the users and producers of governmental accounting information. The attitude and behavior of users and producers is shaped by their respective environments. If the conditions are ripe, as occasioned by some stimuli (such as financial scandals or a government financial crisis), the interaction between demand and supply could spark governmental accounting innovations. The model suggests that there are contextual and behavioral variables relevant to explaining the outcome of the governmental accounting innovation process. The contextual variables can be placed into several categories: (1) stimuli, (2) the social environment for government, (3) characteristics of the political administrative system, and (4) barriers to implementation (Monsen, Nazi, & Jyvaskyla, 1998).

With respect to the research questions of the study, the most relevant notions of the LMC model used in this study are focused on three aspects: stimuli, promoter, and implementation barriers of the accounting change.

3.1. Stimuli

The LCM suggests that situational factors in the form of financial problems, financial scandals, the sophistication of capital markets, the influence of external standard setting, and professional interests stimulate reforms.

These situations or events usually occur at the initial stage of the innovation process and create a need for improved financial information on the part of the users of accounting information. This need for more informative financial information exerts pressure on the producers of information to adopt accrual accounting. The LCM suggests that the economic crisis is one of the primary factors in stimulating public sector accounting reform.

3.2. Promoter of Change

According to Luder (1992), promoters of change in public sector accounting are people and organizations with a vested interest in wanting the change. Those promoters could include international donors, members of legislative, international accounting firms, accounting profession, and academics.

3.3. Implementation Barriers

Implementation barriers are the features of a political or bureaucratic environment that impede the adoption of a public sector reform such as accrual accounting (Luder, 1992). According to Luder (1992), a policy of decentralizing government, a civil law system (i.e., a non-Anglo-Saxon system), and a lack of qualified accountants are important barriers to the reform of public sector accounting.

The LCM has been widely used in comparative international governmental accounting research (CIGAR) studies of the factors affecting adoption of public sector accounting innovations (Monsen et al., 1998). In addition, this model also has been used for application to developed and developing nations (e.g., Godfrey, Devlin, & Merrouche, 1996; Christensen, 2002; Saleh, 2007). A further development of the LCM model was shown by Luder and Jones (2003) in exploring the mass move to adopt the accrual accounting system by local governments in nine Europe countries. In the study, they suggest that although the accrualization process of reporting systems at local level in Europe continues, the stage of implementation is diverse in different ways.

4. METHODS

As this study investigates the contextual variables that influence the pace of public sector reform in Indonesia through the adoption of accrual accounting, the validation of data through across verification was necessary and important. Therefore, in informing the study the data were drawn from three sources. First, this study explores official documents issued by the Indonesian government in relation to the government reporting systems in the country issued since the early 1990s (e.g., laws, government regulations, presidential decrees, ministerial decrees, Indonesian governmental accounting standards). Table 1 outlines key rules about the public sector reporting system in Indonesia.

Second, the data are based on interviews with six key individuals in their roles as the promoters, producers, and users of governmental accounting information. The interviews were conducted by the first author with representatives from the Ministry of Finance, the State Audit Board, Indonesian Institute of Accountants, as well as academics in Indonesia. These people were involved in the early efforts of the government in reforming the public sector accounting system in Indonesia. The interviewees are grouped into three categories on the basis of the revised contingency model (Christensen, 2002; see Table 2). Face-to-face interviews were conducted with four interviewees, while responses from two interviewees were obtained through electronic mail.

All interviewees agreed to the audio taping of their interview, and while notetaking did take place during the interviews, this was kept to a minimum. The interviews took place in Jakarta in 2004. In addition, to cope with recent progress of public sector accounting reforms in Indonesia, this study

Table 1. Key Regulations Related to the to the Public Sector Reporting System in Indonesia.

Year	Regulations	Content
1907	Belasting Accountantdienst in 1907	The establishment of state accounting bureau
1917	Tax accounting bureau	Auditing regulations
1925	State finance (*Indische Comtabiliteistswet*)	Budgeting and reporting system for central and local governments
2002	Financial Minister Decree 308 (2002)	The adoption of accrual accounting for central and local governments
2003	• Financial Minister Decree 337 (2003) • Law 17 on state finance	All government institutions at all levels are required to adopt accrual accounting
2005	Government Accounting Standards (GAS)	All government institutions at all levels are required to adopt accrual accounting as part of their annual accountability report

Table 2.   Interviewees.

Cohort	Interviewees (Organization)
User of information (UoI)	Interviewees 1 and 2 (State Audit Board)
Producers of information (PoI)	Interviewees 3 and 4 (Ministry of Finance)
Promoters of change (PoC)	Interviewees 5 and 6 (a partner of an accounting firm and a professor in accounting, respectively; both interviewees participated in the formulation of the Government Accounting Standards in 2005)

also draws attention to the recent data in documentation and literature such as the mass media and the audit reports issued by the State Audit Board since the early 2000s to 2008. As a historically informed field study, the analysis of data was conducted through two steps: (a) interpreting the data obtained from interviewees and archival data (in this procedure, responses recorded from interviewees and other resources were analyzed to determine which comments or suggestions were relevant to the issues addressed) and (b) analyzing the interpretation of evidence from previous step to conform to the LCM in public sector accounting reform in Indonesia.

5. THE ADOPTION OF ACCRUAL ACCOUNTING

The Indonesian government's efforts to improve the reporting system had existed since the 1980s during the Suharto era (Prawiro, 1987). However, these efforts failed to formally replace the cash-based system due to the lack of human resource and low political commitment from the government reflected in its failure to replace the old state finance law (i.e., *Indische Comtabiliteistswet* (ICW) issued in 1925 during colonial era) which only required the use of accrual-based reporting system (Nasution, 2009; Prodjoharjono, 1999).

A more systematic public sector accounting reform was only prompted recently as part of wider economic and political reforms in the country following the collapse of the Suharto's administration in 1998 (Manao, 2008).

The first draft of accrual-based Government Accounting Standards (GAS) was issued in 2000. The draft was called "Accounting Standards for the Central and Local Governments" (2002) issued by a committee established by the Ministry of Finance. After receiving comments and views from the State Audit Board, Indonesian Institute of Accountants, universities, and others, the Ministry of Finance through Financial Minister Decree 337 (2003) promulgated "Accounting Standards for the Central and Local Governments" (2003). Importantly, Law 17 (2003) that later required all government institutions to adopt accrual accounting added significant support to the provisions of Financial Minister Decree 337. In 2005, the government finally issued a set of GAS (2005) as the basis from the government to prepare the financial statement of the Indonesian government at central and local levels. The GAS formally replaces the old system which required the government to prepare budget realization reports only. The GAS requires all government institutions at central and local levels to implement the system in 2006.

The nature of the GAS substantially differs from the cash-based system previously used. It is stated that the objective of the GAS is to provide information that will be useful to a wide range of users in making and evaluating decisions about the allocation of resources. The GAS also states that these objectives are very important in developing public sector accountability, managerial performance, transparency, and intergenerational equity. According to the GAS, the central and local governments are required to present six components of financial statements: budget realization, balance sheet, financial performance statements, changes in equity, cash flows, and notes to the financial statements. The old reporting rule only required the government to produce budget realization reports (see Table 3).

5.1. Implementation Constraints

Although legal reforms have been undertaken to support the adoption, the study identifies that the government is still confronted with significant implementation barriers that undermine its effort in developing a more

Table 3. Comparison on the Indonesian Reporting System.

Accounting System	Features
Old system (pre-2005)	• Budget realization reports
New system (after 2005)	• Budget realization • Balance sheets • Financial performances • Changes in equities • Cash flows • Notes on financial statements

transparent and reliable public sector accounting system. These barriers include legal issues, lack of political will and support from the parliament, and the deficiencies in skilled human resources.

5.1.1. Legal Issues

With respect to the legal issues, two important issues need to be noted. First, although Law 17 (2003) supports the adoption of accrual accounting within the Indonesian public sector, the GAS (2005) have yet to be set by an independent body. It is apparent that the committee assigned the responsibility for the setting of accounting standards remains a government-backed organization. This signifies the government's inconsistency and the lack of coherence approach in bridging the wish of the laws issued and the government strategy in setting the new GAS.

> ... in a more democratic era, the government should not dominate how its own accountability and accounts should be set up .... (Interviewee 5)

Second, it is important to note that Law 17 (2003) that requires the adoption of accrual accounting at the national and local levels, runs counter to Law 22 and Law 25 about local autonomy issued in 1999. As these two laws provide a greater autonomy for local governments in determining their own programs, financial management and reporting system, thus all local governments in the country also have the right to select any accounting systems (i.e. an accounting regime) which suit their capacities. Such an interpretation of the effect of Law 22 weakens the power of Law 17 (2003) and the GAS (2005) in directing the accounting practices to be implemented by local government. This contradiction between the two laws potentially weakens the efforts of central government in its attempt to implement uniform accounting standards throughout the nation.

> We don't really understand why the government issues contradicting laws. I think the implementation of the new accounting system has made the accounting function in the government more complicated. (Interviewee 1)

5.1.2. Lack of Political Will

This factor will potentially undermine any attempt to improve the accountability of financial management in the public sector. As stated by Interviewee 1, this problem led to the failure of prior public sector accounting reforms undertaken during President Suharto's era. The interviewee also suggests that while Indonesia has entered a new economic, social, and political era, the government remains somewhat reluctant to embrace a greater level of responsibility for reforming public sector accounting. Moreover, Interviewee 2 claims that the government does not follow up the audit findings and recommendations of the State Board Auditor. Interviewee 2 stated:

> It is the task of auditor to state their findings and to give recommendations and it is the responsibility of the government to implement the recommendations. However, since President Habibie [1998–1999], including the current President Megawati [1999–2004], the government simply lacks the will for improving government accountability.

Interview 3 claims the resistance of the government to the implementation of a more informative accounting system is also fueled by the low commitment of government bureaucrats toward accountability. A very clear example of this problem was indicated in a report issued by the State Audit Board (*Kompas Daily*, 2008). This report suggests that the Constitution Court declined to review Law 28 (2007) on tax that prevents the State Audit Board to audit the tax revenue account in the Ministry of Finance. This resistance is against the 1945 Constitution (basic constitution of the country) which assigns the State Audit Board to audit every account belonging to the government. Commenting on the fact, Interviewee 3 claims that the main problem in the implementation of the accounting system in the government is the fact that most of high-level managers in all departments have low commitment to accountability. Interviewee 3 states:

> For one thing they do not know the importance of accountability but for another, that almost nobody has much interest in accountability since the money is not there any longer.

The State Audit Board (2008) also finds seven obstacles that potentially undermine the public sector accounting reform in Indonesia: (1) limited access given to auditors on tax revenues and payable tax and Court Revenue account; (2) the weakness of internal control systems and review mechanism within the government; (3) fragmented government bank accounts; (4) insufficient information system technology; (5) low compliance of the government officials to related regulations regarding the revenues and disbursements; (6) the lack of coordination within the government at the central and local levels; (7) rapid changes in regulations leading to different interpretations.

5.1.3. Lack of Response from Society and Parliament
It is important to acknowledge that previous reforms in the Indonesian public sector accounting were initiated by the central government (Prawiro, 1987). The Central Government Accounting System (1992), the Accounting

Standards for the Central and Local Governments (2003), and GAS were set up by a committee under the coordination of the State Accounting Agency at the Department of Finance. While Indonesian society seems to be concerned about reforms intended to improve the accountability of government, it is less bothered about the reform of public sector accounting practices. As Interviewee 4 states:

> Now we have a board in the Indonesian Accounting Institute that develops accounting standards for the public sector. However, Indonesia society is not concerned about participating by responding to the exposure draft promulgated by Indonesian Accountants Associations. The Parliament also lacks concern accounting issues.

Interviewee 3 notes:

> Somehow the parliament is also concerned with this issue; however they do not exactly know what it is. Accountability report is not really what they would like to see. They know the importance of accountability but they could not understand and could not comprehend the accounting process. Even if we use the term like accounting system or accounting standards, it is something outside their capability.

Moreover, Interviewee 5 suggests that those who were involved in formulation process of the GAS were only those who formulated the new accounting standards. The interviewee also indicates that the diffusion process of the previous drafts of the new accounting standards only involved the same people. The lack of participation from parliamentary members and other group people in the country is also supported by Interviewee 6.

5.1.4. Lack of Qualified Staff

The lack of skilled and experienced accounting staff within the government represents a serious problem affecting the adoption of accrual accounting throughout all levels of the Indonesian public sector. Interviewees 5 and 6 of the study point out that the lack of skilled staff within the accounting function of the government across the nation is the biggest problem faced in adopting the new reporting system. A senior auditor at the State Audit Board also suggests that the government now requires at least 21,700 accountants to support the implementation of the new accounting system at the central and local levels (Prodjoharjono, 2008). Other report also suggests the government requires at least 46,000 more skilled staff in accounting. The capital Jakarta alone still lacks about 5,000 accountants as it employs only 22 qualified accountants (*Detik News*, 2008). The lack of qualified accountants in the government is mainly caused by the disparity in remuneration rates for accountants in the public sector when compared with their private sector counterparts, inducing many accountants to seek better

paid jobs in the private sector. While training existing personnel is a solution
to the problem of insufficient public sector accountants, it takes time, and
the outcome is not always as effective as recruiting new skilled personnel
(Ministry of Finance, 2001).

6. INTERPRETING THE EVIDENCE

On the basis of evidence discussed above, this section examines the adoption
of accrual accounting in the context of broader public sector reforms within
Indonesia. We employ the LCM as the skeleton in examining the data. Our
approach is consistent with the aim of Luder (1992) model in seeking to
explain the attempts of the Indonesian government in moving from the
traditional government accounting to a more informative accrual-based
accounting system.

6.1. Stimuli

The LCM hypothesizes that the economic crisis is the main factor that led a
government to adopt accrual-based accounting for the public sector.
However, we find evidence that the initiative to reform Indonesian public
sector accounting has existed since Suharto's era in the early 1990s prior to
the economic crisis in 1997 and 1998. This is consistent with the policy
adopted by the Suharto administration in the late 1960s to implement a free
market economy policy by encouraging foreign investment in Indonesia.
For much of the Suharto administration, accounting reforms were not
intended to make the government more accountable but were the result of
international pressure. As stated by Rosser (1999):

> accounting reform in Indonesia was not the product of rational choices by wise
> technocrats or neo-colonial domination but rather of structural pressures generated by
> periodic economic crises. It is also argued that accounting policies in developing
> countries have, for the most part, been imposed by developed countries initially through
> colonialism, and then through the influence of transnational corporations, foreign aid
> donors, and professional accounting institutes. (p. 2)

However, current public sector accounting reforms in Indonesia cannot
be isolated from the broader reforms occurring within Indonesia's economy
and political system that followed the resignation of Suharto in 1988. While
the role of donor countries and international pressure are still influential in
directing public sector accounting reforms as part of broader reforms in

economic, banking, and financial sectors (Khambata, 2001), domestic forces are also exerting some influence as stated by Interviewees 5 and 6 of the study. These interviewees also view that democratization, the need for greater accountability, and the reduction of corrupt practices have been important stimuli pressuring government toward a more fulsome embrace of accrual accounting. Therefore, it was not only the economic crisis, as proposed by the LCM, but also the prodemocratic movement and pressure from the international donors that has further stimulated the Indonesian government's attempts to reform public sector accounting.

6.2. Promoters of Change

In accordance with the LCM, the potential promoters of public sector accounting reforms in the public sector are international donors, members of parliament, international accounting firms, accounting profession, and academics. We find evidence to support this view except for the minor roles of parliamentary members and international accounting firms. Since the early 1990s and in spite of the failure of the early reforms sought by the IMF and the World Bank (Interviewees 3 and 6), international donors continue to be active promoters of public sector accounting reform (Marwata & Alam, 2006). This reality can be understood as the world and IFM played crucial roles in the economic reforms following the collapse of the Suharto's administration in 1998 (Grenville, 2004).

Moreover, academics and representatives from accounting profession (i.e., Indonesian Institute of Accountants) have been influential as the promoters of public sector accounting reforms in the country. This can be seen from members of the Public Sector Accounting Standards Committee who set up the government. Most of them are academics and from accounting profession (PSAC, 2005). In addition, as noted by Interviewees 2 and 4, the Indonesian Institute of Accountants has actively provided comments and suggestions on drafts of public sector accounting standards issued earlier. However, there is little evidence to suggest that members of parliament (Interviewee 3) have been active promoters of public sector accounting reform in Indonesia (Interviewee 2). Interviewees 5 and 6 also support this notion as there is no member of the legislative body who has a good understanding on accounting issues. Despite the potential role of the Indonesian parliament in promoting the reform process, as many parliamentary members do not appreciate the importance of accrual accounting to improving the accountability of government, the actual support offered by the parliament has been minimal (Interviewee 3).

International accounting firms do not appear to be actively participating in the recent process of reforming Indonesia's public sector accounting or in ensuring compliance with those public sector accounting reforms in the form of the GAS as stated by Interviewees 3 and 6. The minimal influence of international accounting firms over public sector accounting reforms may be due in part to the nature of the Indonesian legal system. In Indonesia, the authority of the state determines any administrative and procedural system that is to be used within the public sector. Thus, the reform agenda for Indonesian public sector accounting is totally controlled by the government although the members of the public sector accounting committee represent a different group of people (Interviewees 2 and 4). Thus, this evidence indicates that international donors, accounting profession, and academics were the main promoters of accounting reforms for the Indonesian public sector.

6.3. Implementation Barriers

According to the LCM, the main barriers to the successful adoption of accrual accounting by the public sector include a policy of decentralizing government, a civil law system (i.e., a non-Anglo-Saxon system), and a lack of qualified accountants. Drawing from recent experience of the Indonesian government in using the new accounting system, the obstacles proposed by the LCM fit the contextual situation faced by the country.

First of all, currently the conflict between legal requirements and how those laws are implemented constitutes a serious barrier to the successful implementation of accrual accounting at all levels of government. As discussed above, Law 17 (2003) is in conflict with Law 22 (1999). Law 17 (2003) requires government agencies to adopt accrual accounting while Law 22 (1999), in delegating responsibility to local government for the management of its own development programs, suggests that local government is under no obligation to implement any particular form of accounting practice as part of its own administrative systems (e.g., accrual accounting).

Furthermore, while Law 17 (2003) assigns the responsibility for the setting of governmental accounting standards to an independent body, this has yet to occur. The GAS has been set up by a committee under the control of the government and not by an independent body as required by Law 17 (2003). This can be understood as the Indonesian legal system which upholds the Continental System provides little opportunity for nongovernment organizations to have a significant role in formulating government policies as proposed by the LCM. Nonetheless, a similar situation also occurs in European countries (Grossi & Pepe, 2009). Furthermore, the adoption of accrual accounting by central and local governments in Indonesia will be retarded by the lack of suitably qualified accountants. As discussed earlier, the majority of local government accountants can only call upon their experience of the cash-based accounting system, a system inherited from the Dutch colonial era. Thus, the lack of skilled and experienced accountants within local government represents a serious threat to the successful adoption of accrual accounting. In addition, the public sector accounting reform in the Indonesian public sector also encounters the lack of political will and support from public sector organizations, the parliament, and the society in general in the country. In this vein, although legal reforms have been undertaken which requires the adoption of a better reporting system, the lack of political will and commitment to the introduction of accrual accounting from senior government officials and parliamentary members and the low level of citizen participation also constitute significant barriers to the successful implementation of accrual accounting within the Indonesian public sector.

7. CONCLUSION, IMPLICATION, AND LIMITATION

Using LCM, we demonstrate how the economic crisis, the prodemocratic movement, and international pressures for the reform of the Indonesian public sector stimulated the reform process that culminated in the passage of legislation that requires all levels of government to adopt accrual accounting (see GAS) for the central and local governments. However, despite these legislative provisions and decree, significant barriers to the adoption of accrual accounting by the Indonesian public sector are identified. We believe that these barriers are of sufficient magnitude to retard the pace and extent of reform achieved through the adoption of accrual accounting.

The most significant barriers to the reform process include: (1) Law 22 (1999) which grants powers to local government to determine its own administrative requirements, (2) the lack of suitably qualified accounting staff within the Indonesian public sector, and (3) minimal parliamentary and citizen interest in the introduction of accrual accounting. As the policy to adopt the accrual accounting system was part of greater economic and political reforms as a means to strengthen the accountability, transparency and efficiency of the public sector in the country — these barriers potentially undermine the very conditions that stipulated the process of the reforms itself. In other words, the failure of the Indonesian public sector to fully embrace accrual accounting would undermine the purposes intended to be achieved through the economic and public sector reforms.

One implication of the findings of this study is that any adoption of the private sector–style accounting in the public sector context would not automatically bring intended outcomes. In this case, social, political, and institutional contexts of a country shape the extent to which an accounting reform takes place. As the legal system and the attitudes of powerful political actors to accounting reforms in developing economies potentially differ from developed countries, the intended outcomes of any public sector reforms for improving efficiency and performance in these countries may not be realized. This notion must be taken into account by the policy makers of public sector accounting reforms in the developing countries (Nor-Aziah & Scapens, 2007; Rahaman, 2009).

This study has several limitations. First, we examine efforts to adopt accrual accounting in the Indonesian public sector by analyzing what we believe to be the significant historical events surrounding the reform process. As Christensen (2002) suggests, the history that we analyze by way of a version of the LCM may be criticized as being "doctrinal" in approach. Second, the model that has been employed to inform our study of the adoption of accrual accounting in Indonesia is too coarse in its analysis. It could be argued that a more finely detailed differentiation of the "groups" of actors (e.g., promoters, producers, and users of accounting information) could have been used to sift through the events surrounding the adoption of accrual accounting by the Indonesian public sector. Thus, subsequent studies could examine the introduction of accrual accounting through the perceptions of public servants at the level of central and local governments.

REFERENCES

Carlin, T. M. (2005). Debating the impact of accrual accounting and reporting in the public sector. *Financial Accountability and Management*, *21*(3), 309–336.

Christensen, M. (2002). Accrual accounting in the public sector: The case of the New South Wales government. *Accounting History*, *7*(November), 93–124.

Christensen, M. (2007). What we might know (but aren't sure) about public sector accrual accounting. *Australian Accounting Review*, *17*(1), 51–65.

Christensen, M., & Parker, L. (2010). Using ideas to advance professions: Public sector accrual accounting. *Financial Accountability and Management*, *26*(3), 246–266.

Christiaens, J., & Rommel, J. (2008). Accrual accounting reforms: Only for businesslike (part of) government. *Financial Accountability and Management*, *24*(1), 309–336.

Connolly, C., & Hyndman, N. (2006). The actual implementation of accruals accounting: Caveats from a case within the UK public sector. *Accounting, Auditing and Accountability Journal, 19*(2), 272–290.

Detik News. (2008). The country needs 46 thousand accountants. *Detik*, November 17. Available at http://www.detikfinance.com/read/2008/11/17/111440/1038063/4/negara-butuh-46.000-tenaga-akuntan

Godfrey, A. D., Devlin, P. J., & Merrouche, C. (1996). Governmental accounting in Kenya, Tanzania and Uganda. In: J. L. Chan (Ed.), *Research in governmental and nonprofit accounting* (Vol. 9, pp. 193–208). Greenwich, CT: JAI Press.

Grenville, S. (2004). The IMF and Indonesian crisis. *Bulletin of Indonesian Economic Studies, 40*(1), 77–94.

Grossi, G., & Pepe, F. (2009). Consolidation in the public sector: A cross-country comparison. *Public Money and Management, 23*(4), 251–256.

Guthrie, J. (1998). Application of accrual accounting in Australian public sector: Rhetoric or reality? *Financial Accounting and Management, 14*(1), 549–573.

Harun. (2007a). Accrualization of the Indonesian public sector accounting: An analysis of rhetoric–reality gap. *Presented at 1st accounting conference*, Faculty of Economics of University of Indonesia, Depok, Indonesia.

Harun. (2007b). Obstacles to Indonesian public sector accounting reforms. *Bulletin of Indonesian Economics Studies, 43*(3), 365–375.

Hopwood, A. G. (1983). On trying to study accounting in the contexts in which it operates. *Accounting, Organization and Society*, 287–305.

Khambata, D. (2001). Bank restructuring in Indonesia. *Journal of International Banking Regulation, 3*(1), 79–87.

Kompas Daily. (2008). The State Audit Board greets Anti Corruption Commission to investigate the Supreme Court [translated]. *Kompas*, June 16. Available at http://www.kompas.com/read/xml/2008/06/12/16383438/bpk.sambut.baik.kpk.selidiki.ma

Lawrence, S., & Wynne, A. (2010). Accounting for government in the global South African. *The Australasian Accounting Business & Finance Journal, 3*(2), 1–25.

Luder, K., & Jones, R. (Eds). (2003). *Reforming governmental accounting and budgeting in Europe*. Frankfurt: Fachverlag Modern.

Luder, K. G. (1992). A contingency model of governmental accounting innovations in the political–administrative environment. *Research in Governmental and Nonprofit Accounting, 7*, 99–127.

Luder, K. G. (2001). Research in comparative governmental accounting over the last decade – achievements and problems. Paper presented at the 7th CIGAR conference, Valencia, Italy.

Manao, H. (2008). Government accounting developments: The Indonesian experience. In: *The American Accounting Association annual meeting*, Anaheim, CA.

Marwata, & Alam, M. (2006). The interaction amongst reform drivers in governmental accounting changes: The case of Indonesian local government. *Journal of Accounting and Organizational Change, 2*(2), 144–163.

Ministry of Finance. (2001). Accrual accounting and budgeting: Indonesian experience. Paper presented at OECD-ASEAN Senior Budget Official meeting, Singapore, November 19–20.

Monsen, N., Nazi, S., & Jyvaskyla. (1998). The contingency model of governmental accounting innovations: A discussion. *The European Accounting Review, 7*(2), 257–288.

Nasution, A. (2009). Kemajuan Peningkatan Transparansi dan Akuntabilitas KeuanganNegara Periode 2004–2009. Keynote speech at Department of Finance, Rakernas Akuntansi dan Pelaporan Keuangan Pemerintah. *National workshop on government accounting and financial reporting*, Jakarta.

Neu, D. (2001). Banal accounts: Subaltern voices. *Accounting Forum*, 25(4), 319–333.

Nor-Aziah, A. K., & Scapens, R. W. (2007). Corporation and accounting change: The role of accounting and accountants in a Malaysian public utility. *Management Accounting Research*, 18, 209–247.

Power, J., & Laughlin, R. (1992). Critical theory and accounting. In: N. Alverson & H. William (Eds), *Critical management studies* (pp. 112–135). London: Sage.

Prawiro, R. (1987). Reforming financial management in government: The Indonesian agenda. *International Journal of Government Auditing*, 14(1), 9–17.

Prodjoharjono, S. (1999). *Accrual accounting in Indonesian local government*. Unpublished PhD thesis, Birmingham University, Birmingham, UK.

Prodjoharjono, S. (2008). Kegalauan pemerintah daerah dalam menerapkan akuntansi pemerintahan [The confusion of local government in implementing the government accounting standards]. Available at http://pomphy.blogspot.com/2008/11/kegalauan-pemerintah-daerah-dalam.html. Retrieved on December 12, 2009.

PSAC [Public Sector Accounting Committee]. (2005). *Government Accounting Standards*. Ministry of Finance: Jakarta.

Rahaman, A. (2009). Independent financial auditing and the crusade against government sector financial mismanagement in Ghana. *Qualitative Research in Accounting & Management*, 6(4), 224–246.

Robinson, P., & Harun. (2004). The introduction of accrual accounting in the context of Indonesian public sector reforms. In: *APIRA conference IV 2004*, Singapore.

Rosser, A. (1999). *The political economy of accounting reform in developing countries: the case of Indonesia*. Working Paper no. 93, Asia Research Centre, Murdoch University. Available at http://wwwc.murdoch.edu.au/wp/wp93.pdf. Retrieved on 21 January 2008.

Ryan, C. (1998). The introduction of accrual reporting policy in the Australian public sector: An agenda setting explanation. *Accounting, Auditing and Accountability Journal*, 11(5), 518–539.

Saleh, Z. (2007). Malaysian governmental accounting: National context and user orientation. *International Review of Business Research Papers*, 3(2), 376–384.

Sharma, U., & Lawrence, S. (2008). Stability and change at FPTL. An institutional perspective. *Australian Accounting Review*, 18(1), 25–34.

State Audit Board. (2008). *The summary of audit findings for semester I 2008 on the financial statements of Palu municipal government for the budget year 2006*. Badan Pemeriksa Keuangan, Jakarta.

TOWARD IFRS: ECONOMIC CONSEQUENCES OF ACCOUNTING CONVERGENCE IN AN EMERGING ECONOMY

Vinícius Simmer de Lima, Gerlando Augusto Sampaio Franco de Lima, L. Nelson Guedes de Carvalho and Iran Siqueira Lima

ABSTRACT

Purpose – *The purpose of this article is to investigate whether underlying firm-level incentives influence firms' compliance with International Financial Reporting Standards (IFRS) convergence practices and whether this adoption impacts firms' cost of equity capital and market liquidity in Brazil, a setting with a poor institutional environment but high growth opportunities.*

Methodology/approach – *Using a sample of 54 companies from the São Paulo Stock Exchange, this article employs three measures of accounting convergence based on: (i) compliance to a 37-item index, called the International Accounting Standards Convergence Index (IASCI), (ii) increase in annual reports disclosure, and (iii) increase in accounting earnings quality. Furthermore, the article employs statistical analysis to*

Research in Accounting in Emerging Economies, Volume 10, 251–295
Copyright © 2010 by Emerald Group Publishing Limited
All rights of reproduction in any form reserved
ISSN: 1479-3563/doi:10.1108/S1479-3563(2010)0000010015

test the influence of firm-level incentives on IFRS compliance and its economic consequences for the capital market.

Findings – *The results indicate that firm-level incentives are important drivers of compliance with IFRS convergence practices. The results suggest that firms that (i) are larger, (ii) are more exposed to international markets, and (iii) have greater financing needs are more likely to adopt IFRS practices by implementing material changes in their accounting policies. The economic consequence analysis shows that cost of capital does not seem to be related to any of the convergence measures used. However, there is a statistically significant relationship between all the market liquidity variables and the IASCI, indicating that companies that best meet the convergence requirements have lower trading costs and greater liquidity, and their share price is less susceptible to the influence of individual investors.*

Research limitations and implications – *The scope of the study is limited to a relatively small sample of listed Brazilian companies, and they may not represent all listed companies. The sample restriction is due to information availability, since the study requires earnings estimates from the Thomson ONE Analytics database.*

Originality/value – *The study extends the work of Barth (2008) considering Ball's (2006) observation that superior accounting standards do not necessarily translate into higher quality reporting, since reporting quality may be largely shaped not only by accounting standards, but also by economic/political forces and firm-level economic incentives.*

Keywords: Accounting convergence; IFRS; cost of capital; liquidity; incentives.

1. INTRODUCTION

Two recent trends have emerged in the debate over the regulation of accounting practices and the content of financial reports around the world. First, international financial crises and corporate scandals have prompted reforms in regulations and heightened disclosure requirements in the capital market. The 1997 Asian crisis, the Enron meltdown in the United States, and the recent global credit crisis are just a few examples. Second, stock exchanges and setters of accounting standards in many countries have been adopting the

International Financial Reporting Standards (IFRS), with the declared objective of "converging" to a single set of international accounting practices.

Despite the importance of transparency as a recurring matter of regulation, the adoption of the IFRS by countries has brought two contrasting but not mutually exclusive viewpoints. One view, which favors the adoption of international standards, holds that the IFRS are better than local GAAPs (Barth, 2008). It is further argued that convergence to a single set of accounting standards makes the information disclosed by firms more comparable. According to these two arguments, IFRS adoption will improve the informational environment and help reduce the cost of capital (Barth, 2008). In contrast, according to Ball (2006), enhanced accounting standards do not necessarily translate into better quality of disclosure, because the quality of financial statements is influenced not only by accounting standards, but also by the political and economic forces present in each country.

We empirically assess these questions by using firm-level observations in an emerging market, Brazil. Our aim is to shed light on the impact of adopting practices to converge to international standards, in terms of the economic consequences for firms, considering the conditional incentives given by the institutional setting. To reinforce our considerations on the role of the institutional setting in this analysis, we also evaluate whether the adoption of convergence practices is in some way related to the specific underlying incentives of companies.

To investigate this question, we need a scenario with reduced institutional requirements for accounting statements, so as to present significant heterogeneity both in the quality of the numbers reported and the adoption of international practices. An ideal setting would be a country with (i) poor accounting and corporate governance standards, a code law legal system, a relatively underdeveloped capital market where firms use private sources of financing more than the public capital market, government-defined accounting rules, a close relationship between tax and corporate accounting rules, and weak investor protection and legal enforcement, together with (ii) significant opportunities for growth, resulting in a strong demand for capital by many firms (Lopes & Walker, 2008).

We believe that Brazil, considering the above characteristics and the objectives of our study, has outstanding experimental potential. Other reasons, related specifically to the process of IFRS adoption, also indicate Brazil is a good candidate for the present analysis.[1] First, Brazil is one of the few emerging economies that have adopted IFRS in its local accounting rules. For this purpose, over the past three years a huge legal effort has been made to include the adoption of these international standards as part of the transformation of the country's corporate accounting framework. In the second place, Brazil provides a unique database to measure the adoption of convergence practices. Brazilian legislation exempts companies from immediate observance of certain practices. This creates an interesting aspect for our study due to the mix between voluntary and mandatory adoption. This particular aspect, along with the limited ability of Brazilian institutions to enforce accounting rules, provides a setting with considerable hetero- geneity regarding the conformity of firms to international standards. Finally, empirical evidence indicates that the effects of adopting interna- tional standards tend to be stronger in countries where the difference between local GAAP and IFRS is larger (Daske, Hail, Leuz, & Verdi, 2008; Hail, Leuz, & Wysocki, 2009). This is certainly true of Brazil.

One may question the relevance of a study of a single country. However, disclosure incentives can differ significantly among countries because they are influenced by many hard-to-measure factors, including the institutional system, level of legal enforcement, capital market mechanisms, competition of products in the market, ownership structure, and corporate governance characteristics. Indeed, recent empirical research has shown the important influence of the system of incentives on firms' disclosure practices (e.g., Ball, Kothari, & Robin, 2000; Fan & Wong, 2002; Leuz, Nanda, & Wysocki, 2003; Haw, Hu, Hwang, & Wu, 2004; Burgstahler, Hail, & Leuz, 2006). In this respect, Holthausen (2003, p. 282) proposed that within-country studies are necessary to control for institutional variables so as to maintain specific characteristics of the disclosure regime constant. As he additionally noted, "Perhaps international comparisons are not the most powerful tests of the hypothesis that that institutional structures beyond accounting standards affects the characteristics of financial reporting, because there are so many things that are difficult to adequately control in cross-country work."

International rules, just as any other set of accounting standards, give managers a good deal of discretion in their accounting choices. Furthermore, the measurement process itself is largely based on private information. The way firms use this discretion should depend on their underlying incentives as well as the mentioned institutional characteristics. This concept is also at the heart of the literature on accounting choices and earnings management.

Therefore, one of the main reasons for this investigation is that few international studies have examined the different cross-sectional effects of the process of accounting convergence in a single country, and the reasons for these differences. The majority of studies have investigated the relationship among firms at the international level (Daske et al., 2008; Daske, Hail, Leuz, & Verdi, 2009; Leuz, Triantis, & Wang, 2008; Hail et al.,

2009). Therefore, we believe a more detailed within-country study can complement the results of the cross-country investigations.

We use a sample of 54 companies with shares listed for trading on the São Paulo Stock Exchange (Bovespa) and belonging to the portfolio of its tracking index, the Ibovespa, between September and December 2009. We individually analyze these firms' annual reports for 2008, the year when application of the new corporate rules became mandatory. We construct three measures to characterize information disclosure in light of the new accounting standards, following the study by Daske et al. (2009). The proxies are based on our own International Accounting Standards Convergence Index (IASCI), the change in the length (volume of information) of the firms' complete financial statements, and the change in the quality of accounting earnings (Section 3.4.3 describes these proxies in detail). Our analysis of the economic consequences is restricted to identifying cross-sectional differences in the cost of capital and market liquidity of the companies studied.

For the dependent variable, cost of equity capital, we use the average implied internal rate of return, calculated recursively, by applying four valuation models: those of Claus and Thomas (2001), Gebhardt, Lee, and Swaminathan (2001), Easton (Modified PEG) (2004), and Ohlson and Juettner-Nauroth (2005). In these models the estimated cost of equity capital primarily depends on analysts' forecasts. For the market liquidity variable we use three proxies: the bid–ask spread, the impact on price, and the share turnover. We discuss these choices and validation of the variables in Sections 3.4 and 4.

This study contributes directly to a recent branch of the literature on the effects of IFRS adoption on firms' economic variables (Ball, 2006; Barth, 2008; Daske et al., 2008; Leuz et al., 2008; Hail et al., 2009; Leuz & Wysocki, 2008). First, this study adds to these works by investigating the effects on the cost of capital and market liquidity for companies in a country with weak governance and legal enforcement. Second, because Brazil is adopting the international standards as its own local accounting rules, this study stands out from others by examining convergence instead of IFRS adoption. Third, we use a considerable amount of information gathered individually from the firms' annual reports, allowing us to identify, in a descriptive approach, some characteristics of the Brazilian accounting convergence process. Lastly, this study allows inferring whether the Brazilian market, characterized by a weak institutional structure and corporate governance, manages to differentiate firms according to their strategies of adopting the new accounting practices.

To clarify the contributions of this study, we highlight some important points. First, Armstrong, Barth, Jagolinzer & Rield (2010) and Daske et al.

(2008) documented a small effect of IFRS adoption for companies located in countries characterized as having weak institutions. Our study examines firms in a country with weak legal enforcement and finds considerable variability in firms' levels of convergence to international standards. In terms of market liquidity, the results also indicate that – despite the evidence of Armstrong et al. (2010) and Daske et al. (2008) – Brazilian firms also benefit from the adoption of convergence practices, because those with higher levels of observance have higher Turnovers, lower Bid–Ask Spreads, and lower Price Impacts. This suggests that obligatory IFRS convergence also can provide benefits to companies in countries with weak enforcement, since they can have economic incentives to meet higher standards.

Our study also has regulatory implications. The results suggest that regulatory attempts to apply international rules to a wide set of companies should consider the characteristics of the institutional setting as well as private incentives of firms. Our results show that firm-level incentives significantly influence the propensity to conform to international accounting standards. In this respect, these results present a counterpoint to the idea that the mere adoption of international practices necessarily implies improved information quality.

This article is organized into six sections including this section. In the second section we develop the hypotheses and review the relevant literature; in the third section we delineate the research design and describe the sample; in the fourth section we define and validate the proxies used; in the fifth section we analyze the results; and in the sixth section we summarize our conclusions and indicate possible topics for future research. The construction of the IASCI is presented in Appendix A. Appendix B present assumptions and model-specific overviews of implied cost of capital accounting models. Appendix C shows the details of earnings quality changes estimation (Kang and Sivaramakrishnan accrual-based model).

2. UNDERLYING CONCEPTS AND REVIEW OF THE LITERATURE

2.1. Market Characteristics and Convergence to International Standards in Brazil

There are two main reasons to focus on Brazil in this study. First, we believe Brazil has the typical characteristics of an emerging economy, combining accounting reports with low informational quality with the existence of significant growth opportunities (Chong & Lopez-de-Silanes, 2007). In a study covering the period before the convergence phase, Lopes and Walker (2008) described the Brazilian market as having low legal enforcement, government-defined accounting rules, high state participation in the economy, prevalence of private instead of capital market financing, a relatively underdeveloped capital market, incentives to manipulate earnings because of close association of taxation and accounting rules, a volatile financial market, and weak governance standards. Brazil is a typical developing country with a code law system where the financial statements, before the requirement for convergence, were prepared more to meet tax and regulatory needs than to inform investors. The country also certainly presents excellent growth prospects for firms, with well-behaved inflation (since macroeconomic reform in 1994), better control of public spending, a relatively stable floating exchange rate, and good openness to external capital.

Second, the process of converging to international standards in Brazil has involved not only the adoption of IFRS for consolidated financial statements, but also covers a set of significant regulatory changes that apply international rules locally. There are many examples of these changes: the creation of the Accounting Pronouncements Committee (*Comitê de Pronunciamentos Contábeis* (CPC)), established by CFC[2] Resolution 1,055/05, the enactment of Federal Law 11,638/07, the Letter to the Market of January 14, 2008, from the Brazilian Securities Commission (*Comissão de Valores Imobiliários* (CVM)), the issuance of Provisional Measure[3] 449/08, subsequently transformed into Federal Law 11,941/09, and the translation of the IAS by the CPC and their approval by the CVM. Other evidences of the relevance of this process are the numerous seminars and conferences held by academic institutions and auditing firms to discuss the effects of Law 11,638/07 and the adoption of IFRS in Brazil (Cardoso, 2008).

2.2. Development of the Hypotheses

Although adoption of the recent convergence practices is mandatory for all companies with shares listed on the São Paulo Stock Exchange, we do not expect all firms to have identical compliance. Differences in this respect can arise from the ability of firms to bear the costs involved in adapting their financial demonstrations (Barth, Landsman, Lang, & Williams, 2010). Such differences tend to be more important in emerging economies because more firms do not have the resources necessary for immediate convergence. Additionally, there is an undersupply of accountants with the required knowledge of IFRS in these countries, requiring high costs for training courses.

Besides costs, differences in compliance with convergence practices can arise from specific firm-level incentives. Evidence indicates that the incentives to meet disclosure practices more than formal rules affect the quality of the numbers reported (e.g., Ball, Robin, & Wu, 2003; Leuz, 2003; Ball & Shivakumar, 2005; Burgstahler et al., 2006). In this respect, firms with strong incentives should be more likely to adopt the new provisions for convergence to international standards than those that do not have the same incentives. Based on the accounting and economic theory of the past two decades, we postulate that (i) larger firms, (ii) firms more exposed to the international market, (iii) firms with greater external financing needs, and (iv) firms with greater growth opportunities will show more propensity to issue financial statements with better information quality (Daske et al., 2009). We also consider the error in analysts' earnings projections. This variable aims to capture whether the level of observance of international practices is associated with difficulty in projecting the firm's earnings. Consequently, our first hypothesis is:

H_1. Companies subject to greater specific incentives are more compliant with accounting convergence practices.

To the extent that IFRS improve the quantity and quality of specific information about firms, they should contribute to greater transparency and facilitate estimation of future cash flows. Greater transparency and facility of estimating cash flows hence can raise share liquidity (positive effect) and lower the cost of capital (negative effect). Easley and O'Hara (2004) observed that asymmetric information puts less-informed investors at a disadvantage and can limit demand and discourage share turnover. The bid–ask spread and low liquidity impose transaction costs on investors, which need to be compensated in equilibrium. Thus, a stock's rate of return per period increases by a magnitude consistent with the transaction cost (Amihud & Mendelson, 1989). Besides this, adverse selection can distort investors' choices and result in inefficient and hence more costly capital allocations, for which investors need to be compensated, leading to higher capital costs (Garleanu & Pedersen, 2004).

In contrast, when more information is available about a firm, well-informed investors have less of an advantage, resulting in a lower bid–ask spread, increased share demand, and reduced cost of capital (Diamond & Verrecchia, 1991). Additionally, an increased demand for a firm's shares can reduce the price impact – the ability of investors to have a strong effect on the asset's quotation (Amihud, 2002).

Previous studies have shown that the adoption of international accounting standards affects firms' cost of capital and market liquidity.[4] Unlike in developed markets, Brazil has relatively few information intermediaries such as analysts to gather and disseminate specific information on firms. Indeed, few Brazilian firms have analysts' coverage from I/B/E/S. This situation means that the information from financial reports is more important because there are few alternative sources of information. In line with these arguments, we assess the impact of convergence on the informational situation through the following hypotheses:

H₂. The level of compliance with convergence practices affects firms' cost of capital in an environment characterized by weak governance, low enforcement, and high growth opportunities.

H₃. The level of compliance with convergence practices affects firms' market liquidity (Share Turnover, Bid-Ask Spread and Price Impact) in an environment characterized by weak governance, low enforcement, and high growth opportunities.

2.3. Related Empirical Studies

The accounting literature contains strong evidence that greater information disclosure is negatively associated with the cost of capital (Botosan & Plumlee, 2002; Hail, 2003; Francis, LaFond, Olsson, & Schipper, 2004; Francis, Nanda, & Olsson, 2008) and reduces the information asymmetry component of the bid–ask spread, resulting in greater liquidity (e.g., Welker, 1995; Ng, 2008).

Since international standards generally require a higher level of disclosure than local ones, the literature contains a series of arguments in favor of convergence to an international model. According to Hail et al. (2009), the adoption of international standards should improve the quality of financial statements for external investors, benefiting the information environment. This improvement should benefit firms by reducing the adverse selection costs and risk of estimates, helping to reduce the cost of capital (e.g., Leuz & Verrecchia, 2000; Lambert, Leuz, & Verrecchia, 2007). Armstrong et al. (2010) and Covrig, DeFond, and Hung (2007) indicated that disclosure according to IFRS reduces the costs related to comparison of companies between different countries and markets, leading to an increase in cross-border investments. Moreover, Bushman and Smith (2001) suggested that this can limit the range of managers' discretion by increasing the capacity of external investors to monitor management practices.

A series of empirical studies provide evidence of the above arguments. Leuz and Verrecchia (2000) found that German companies that adopted IFRS had lower bid–ask spreads and higher turnovers than those that only followed local GAAP. Ashbaugh and Pincus (2001) found a negative association between the differences between IAS and local GAAP and the precision of analysts' forecasts. After the adoption of IFRS, the authors found an improvement in analysts' estimates, suggesting an improved information environment. Barth, Landsman, and Lang (2008) directly examined the accounting properties of firms using local GAAP and those using IAS. Based on observations from 21 countries, they found that firms following IFRS show less earnings management, greater conditional accounting conservatism, and higher relevance of accounting numbers. Utilizing the expected returns of the Fama–French three-factor model, they also documented a decrease in the cost of capital on the date near the first publication of accounts according to IFRS.

Despite the above evidence, however, questions have been raised about whether a shift from local GAAP to IFRS necessarily will improve the quality of financial reports and whether accounts prepared according to IFRS are really more precise, to achieve the objective of greater transparency (Ball, 2006). In this sense, the questions raised focus on (i) whether the positive effects expected from convergence exist independent of the institutional conditions of each country (Daske et al., 2008) and (ii) whether the adoption is voluntary or mandatory. There are many reasons for these concerns. First, the characteristics of accounting reports are in large part molded by firms' disclosure incentives (e.g., Leuz et al., 2003; Ball et al., 2003). In this sense, it is possible that the process of converging to a single set of standards will have no effect on firms, since IFRS give managers substantial discretion, and in this case the institutional arrangements of countries (e.g., Ball et al., 2003) and specific incentives of firms (Ball & Shivakumar, 2005; Burgstahler et al., 2006) tend to play an important role. Considering these incentives, it is far from obvious that IFRS adoption will naturally mean better quality financial reports, irrespective of a particular country's enforcement regime.

Second, the enforcement regime plays an important role in the effects of IFRS adoption. Ball et al. (2003) found that the financial statements of firms in Hong Kong, Malaysia, Singapore, and Thailand, all of which are countries generally following the UK common law tradition, were no better than those of firms in code law countries. Daske et al. (2008), examining the effects of mandatory introduction of IFRS in 26 countries, documented: (i) an increase in market liquidity of 3%–6%; (ii) a reduction in the cost of capital; and (iii) an increase in share values, but only in countries with high legal enforcement. In a second study, Daske et al. (2008) differentiated firms into two categories – called "label" and "serious" adopters – and found that firms that appear to have a "serious" commitment to transparency by adopting international standards have a lower cost of capital in relation to those that do so only superficially ("label" adopters). Other recent studies have made relevant contributions to the theme. Christensen, Lee, and Walker (2009) analyzed whether the reconciliations between IFRS and UK GAAP near the date of adopting the former rules provided additional information to the market. Capkun, Cazavan, Jeanjean, and Weiss (2008) found that the reconciliation of earnings for companies in the European Union in the transition period had informational value. Horton, Serafeim, and Serafeim (2010) and Wang, Young, and Zhuang (2008) found that certain properties of analysts' forecasts, such as precision of the estimates, number of analysts, and dispersion of projections, improved after the obligatory adoption of IFRS. Finally, some studies conducted by auditing firms have concluded that despite the substantial convergence, financial statements prepared according to IFRS still have a strong national flavor (KPMG, 2006).

Third, accounting rules should reflect society's interests, formulated by regulators considering the costs and benefits that are particular to each country. Viewed in this form, it is not clear that IFRS are better than a country's own GAAP. Barth et al. (2008) observed that limiting managers' discretion to choose accounting alternatives can eliminate firms' ability to disclose accounting measures that best reflect their economic position and performance. Also, IFRS, which are based on principles, may actually give more discretion to managers than local GAAP. This increase in the leeway for discretion, without the necessary constraint of enforcement, can lead to abuse and undermine the quality of disclosures (Bova & Pereira, 2010).

Finally, preparing financial statements in IFRS can involve substantially higher costs, especially initially, than those required for reporting according to local GAAP (Barth et al., 2010). These costs can weigh particularly heavily on companies with limited resources. Once again the implication is that the better quality of the rules may not be carried over to better disclosure.

In summary, IFRS can improve the quality of financial statements to the extent that they are better than local GAAP and require greater transparency. Additionally, the use of a uniform set of accounting standards among countries enhances comparability, which can also improve the information content of disclosures. Nevertheless, the link between IFRS and the quality of financial statements is subject to certain caveats, in the sense that disclosure also depends on incentives and enforcement. To address these questions, this article examines the economic consequences of convergence to international standards in an emerging economy, with typical characteristics of weak enforcement and ample growth opportunities.

3. RESEARCH DESIGN AND SAMPLE

3.1. Determinants of the Level of Compliance with Convergence Practices

Our first analysis compares the levels of compliance with convergence practices against firms' underlying incentives (H_1). We theorize that firms that (i) are larger, (ii) are more exposed to the international market, (iii) have greater needs for external financing, and (iv) have greater growth opportunities are more willing to provide accounting reports to external investors that are more informative (Daske et al., 2009). We also include the error of analysts' earnings projections with the aim of capturing whether the level of observance of these practices is associated with the difficulty of projecting future earnings. We do not control for the quality of auditing, since nearly all the firms in our sample are audited by one of the Big Four. The empirical model estimated is:

$$IASCI_i = \alpha + \beta_1 MV_i + \beta_2 ADR_i + \beta_3 LEV_i + \beta_4 MTB_i + \beta_5 AERR_i + \varepsilon_i$$

$$(1)$$

where IASCI is the score on our convergence index of firm i; MV a proxy for size, measured by market value, of company i; ADR a proxy for international market exposure, represented by a dummy variable equal to 1 if the firm has American Depositary Receipts (level I, II, or III) and 0 otherwise; LEV a proxy for the need for financing, measured by the indebtedness of firm i (i.e., ratio of total liabilities to total assets); MTB a proxy for growth opportunities, represented by the market-to-book ratio of firm i; and AERR the analysts' forecasting error (i.e., the absolute value of the percentage difference between the consensus earnings projection and the observed earnings, scaled by total assets) of firm i.

If the cost of implementing the changes is an economic barrier for firms, we expect greater compliance with convergence practices to be associated with larger firms. Besides this, given the generally low quality of the accounting numbers and governance regime in Brazil, some firms (probably those with better growth perspectives and opportunities) should have stronger incentives to seek external financing for new projects. These firms will thus have a greater need to be more transparent voluntarily, by adopting more rigorous accounting practices. In particular, we expect that these companies will be more committed to adopting international standards as a way to improve the quality of their financial reporting. Therefore, we expect the signs of the correlation coefficients of MV, ADR, LEV, and MTB with the IASCI to be positive.

The analysis of the degree of compliance with convergence practices has two specific objectives. First, it allows making inferences about the underlying incentives that influence firms' commitment to the convergence process (in response to H_1). Second, it provides an important result about the validity or degree of theoretical consistency of our index, since the literature contains recurring interrelations between IFRS adoption and the variables studied (size, international market exposure, financing need, growth opportunities, and analysts' forecasting errors) (e.g., Daske et al., 2008).

3.2. Economic Consequences of Convergence to International Standards

In this section we focus on the main objective of this study, which is to investigate the effect of adopting international standards on the cost of equity capital and share liquidity of Brazilian firms, considering the conditional incentives of the institutional environment (H_2 and H_3). To do this, we need variables that measure the cost of capital and liquidity along with classifications that capture differences in the disclosure strategies followed. These latter variables serve to identify the degree to which companies make material changes in their disclosure policies or how strongly they are committed to transparency. Besides this, some control variables are necessary to enable isolating the effects of interest, ceteris paribus. These aspects are combined in the following general model:

$$\text{EconCon}_i = \alpha_0 + \beta_1 \text{DiscPol}_i + \sum_{j=1}^{n} \beta_j \text{ContVar}_{ji} + \varepsilon_i \qquad (2)$$

where EconCon refers to the economic consequence in question (Cost of Capital or market liquidity – Bid–Ask Spread, Price Impact, and share

Turnover), DiscPol is any of the three proxies utilized to measure the disclosure policies of firm i (i.e., IASCI, variation of pages in financial statements, or quality of earnings), and ContVar represents the value resulting from the control variables selected for firm i. To estimate the equation we used cross-sectional data.

Note that this approach does not allow identifying the marginal effect of adopting accounting convergence practices. On the contrary, the point of this study is to show that the estimated coefficient of a variable indicating convergence cannot simply be attributed to the adoption of new practices alone, because it probably also reflects differences in factors that determine how strongly companies are committed to transparency.

3.3. Sample

Our sample consists of companies present in the Bovespa Index (Ibovespa) according to its portfolio from September to December 2009. Additionally, we restricted the sample to companies with analysts' earnings forecasts available in *Thomson ONE Analytics*. Analysts' estimates are fundamental for application of models that calculate the implied cost of capital suggested in the literature. Therefore, when faced with a tradeoff between number of observations and precision of the estimates, we gave higher priority to the second aspect. In this respect, we restricted our analysis only to companies that at least had analysts' earnings per share estimates for two years ahead and an estimate of earnings per share for the period $t + 3$ (x_{t+3}) or a long-term growth estimate (ltg). This procedure substantially reduced the final sample, which was composed of 54 firms for which all the required information was available.

International studies, usually examining developed economies, contain a large amount of information on market analysts' forecasts. Unlike these studies, which generally use large numbers of observations (firms between countries and followed over time) – such as Cuijipers and Buijink (2005), Barth et al. (2008), and Daske et al. (2009) – this study relies on a high volume of descriptions of companies themselves, gathered manually.

Despite the limitation of our sample, there is an important counterpoint. Bushman, Piotroski, & Smith (2004) observed that information intermediaries, namely market analysts, have an impact on firms' informational environment. In this respect, in a recent study Armstrong et al. (2010) documented that the reaction to IFRS adoption is more positive in countries with a weak informational environment. Therefore, while the small number of observations tends to limit our analysis, the relative lack of analysts' coverage in Brazil increases the role of financial reports in providing specific information on companies.

3.4. Variables

3.4.1. Cost of Equity Capital

Following Hail and Leuz (2006) and Daske et al. (2009), we compute the cost of capital using four models suggested by the literature – Claus and Thomas (2001), Gebhardt et al. (2001), Easton (2004), and Ohlson and Juettner-Nauroth (2005). The basic idea of all these models is to substitute the price and analysts' estimates in the valuation equation and to get back the cost of capital as the internal rate of return that equates the current share price and the sequence of expected future residual earnings or abnormal earnings. The models differ from each other with respect to the use of analysts' forecast data, premises about short- and long-term growth, the forecasting horizon, and how the inflation rate is incorporated in the steady-state terminal value (Hail & Leuz, 2006).

The share price and analysts' forecasts are measured in month $+10$ (October 2009) after the end of the fiscal year (calendar year). We chose this lag to permit the financial data, especially earnings and shareholders' equity, to be publicly available and reflected in the prices at the moment of computing the cost of capital (Daske et al., 2009). However, this implies that the earnings projection one year ahead is for a fiscal year that only ends two months later (December 2009). To consider this appreciation in price and keep the estimate in annual terms, we discount the cost of capital from the price in month $+10$ (P_t) by means of the expression $[1 + r]^{-10/12}$. This adjustment returns an annualized estimate of the cost of capital while at the same time reflecting the set of information available in month $+10$ after the fiscal year-end.

Since many of the valuation equations do not have a closed-form solution, we use an iterative numerical calculation method (linear iteration method) to determine the internal rate of return. This return represents the cost of capital calculated implicitly. The numerical approximation identifies the annual discount rate that equals the price on the right-hand side of the expression. We adopted a difference of 0.001 between the imputed price and the observed value to stop the iteration. In this method, the cost of capital estimates is necessarily positive, resulting in nonconvergent numerical values if there is any mathematical problem in the calculations (e.g., division by zero or negative cost of capital).

3.4.2. Market Liquidity

We use three proxies for market liquidity. First we analyze the percentage Bid–Ask Spread, which is usually used as a proxy for information asymmetry (Welker, 1995; Leuz & Verrecchia, 2000). We calculate the difference between the closing bid and ask prices for each day and divide it by the midpoint. To obtain a semiannual estimate, we calculate the median of the daily measures. Second, we use a measure of illiquidity suggested by Amihud (2002), the Price Impact. The idea behind this proxy is to capture the ability of an investor to trade a stock without affecting its price. Following Amihud (2002), we measure the price impact by the semiannual median of the absolute value of the difference in daily stock price divided by the trading volume (in R). Finally, we use the stock turnover, computed by the average of all shares outstanding. The semiannual measure is obtained by the median of the monthly values. The following are the formulas of each proxy:

$$\text{Bid} - \text{Ask Spread}_i = \text{median}\left(\frac{\text{Bid Price}_{it} - \text{Ask Price}_{it}}{P_{it,\text{mean}}}\right)$$

$$\text{Price Impact}_i = \text{median}\left[\frac{|\text{Maximum Price}_{it} - \text{Minimum Price}_{it}|}{\text{Volume}_{it}}\right]$$

$$\text{Share Turnover}_i = \text{median}\left(\frac{\text{Volume}_{it}}{\text{Market Value}_{it}}\right)$$

where i represents the firm and t the trading days between May and October 2009; Volume the average daily stock price times the number of shares traded that day; and Market value the stock price times the number of shares outstanding.

We obtained all the data necessary to calculate the variables from *Datastream* in daily frequency, for the period from May to October 2009, resulting in 126 observations (trading days) for each input of each variable of each firm. We chose May to start the series because by law all listed companies must publish their financial statements by April every year. The existence of some interval can be interpreted as the time necessary for investors to interpret the information to adjust their decisions.

3.4.3. Compliance with Convergence Practices

We use three measures to characterize the observance of the new practices, based on the study of Daske et al. (2009). We believe the application of these measures also is a big contribution to national empirical research. We intend to associate characteristics such as objectivity and direct and indirect measurements of convergence. The first and most important of these is our IASCI, constructed based on the criteria employed for giving the Transparency Trophy of the ANEFAC–FIPECAFI–SERASA Award and the Checklist for Preparation of Financial Statements published by Deloitte. The ANEFAC–FIPECAFI–SERASA Award was created in 1997 to recognize the best accounting statements published in the country. The aim is to encourage corporate transparency, by supplying clear and trustworthy information. The Deloitte checklist was developed to help companies prepare their financial statements, including the notes and the annual management report, according to the requirements of Law 6404/76 (Corporations Law), as well as the rules established by the Brazilian Securities Commission (CVM) and the CFC and the pronouncements of the Brazilian Institute of Independent Auditors (IBRACON).

From these we isolated the content related to accounting convergence in Brazil. The result is 37 binary classifications applied to firms' complete annual reports/financial statements, named the IASCI. We sought to observe not only compliance or noncompliance with corporate legislation on convergence, but also firms' choices in relation to the items the legislation made optional.

The IASCI contemplates the following aspects: initial adoption, impairment, cash flow statement, intangible assets, adjustment to present value, functional currency, exchange rate variation, compensation of directors and officers, related parties, leasing, classification of investments, financial instruments, accounting for bad debt provisions, deferred assets, economic depreciation, transitional tax regime, revaluation, and auditors' opinion (see Appendix A for details on each aspect). Not all items making up the index apply to all firms. In these cases, the item is excluded from the checklist for that firm. Each firm's score is obtained by adding the response to each item and dividing this by the number of items applicable to that company.

The second measure is based on the idea that the demand for more information, as well as the commitment to comply with the new practices, should increase the volume of information a firm discloses in its annual report. We believe this variable is an important measure in Brazil, since we expect it will have greater significance the longer the lag between local GAAP and IFRS. We analyzed the length of the complete annual financial statements (including the management report, auditors' opinion, accounting statements, and notes) of the firms by the percentage change in the number of pages around the transition date. We used the reports in Portuguese (some firms also publish them in English) as published in the *Official Federal Gazette*, because the standardized formatting allows comparison of length. The percentage variation is computed as the difference between the number of pages in the 2008 report (published in 2009) and the average number of pages in the preceding two years (2007 and 2006), divided by the average for the past two years. Although this measure potentially contains serious deviations, we believe it permits approximating firms' convergence by a strictly objective criterion.

The third and last proxy is based on the changes in the quality of earnings around the date of introducing the new accounting provisions. In this case we want to create an indirect measure of the quality of accounting practices. If one of the characteristics of the convergence process is the premise that IFRS are better than local GAAP (in the sense of better reflecting the firm's financial situation), we expect that accounting earnings will have better informational quality. Unlike many other countries, in Brazil the introduction of convergence practices considerably altered the measurement of earnings. Some examples are: (i) recognition of financial instruments at fair value (previously they were carried at cost, except by financial institutions), (ii) introduction of the figure of impairment, and (iii) introduction of economic depreciation (previously the rates allowable for tax purposes were preponderant). Therefore, we believe it is important to use a proxy for changes in earnings quality in Brazil. According to Leuz et al. (2003), this variable can be measured by the difference in discretionary accruals from one year to the next. This proxy is commonly applied in empirical investigations of earnings management. We use the model of Kang and Sivaramakrishnan (1995), which according to Lopo (2008) presents the best results for the Brazilian case among the earnings management models based on accruals.[5] However, for our purposes here, we assume this measure only provides a way to measure the quality of earnings (Healy & Whalen, 1999; Dechow & Skinner, 2000), so we make no inferences about firms' behavior in managing their earnings. Based on the literature and the purposes of the changes in accounting rules in Brazil, we assume that firms with lower discretionary accruals have better earnings "quality." Hence, this variable measures the magnitude of the decrease (or increase) in accruals.

Measurement of information quality is usually indicated in the literature as one of the main constraints of research into accounting disclosure. The measures are generally qualitative and narrative by nature, making objective empirical measurement difficult. It is also argued that these measures capture the existence of particular disclosure instead of measuring the effective quality, and ignore activities that can complement or substitute annual reports. Furthermore, theoretical studies provide little guidance on how the quantity of information and frequency of disclosure are relevant for various stakeholders.

To minimize these problems, we extend the analysis of the IASCI, with the intent of empirically validating it. To do this we evaluate the association of the IASCI with the underlying economic incentives of firms. This analysis of the determinants of the degree of complying with convergence practices has two specific aims in our study. First, it permits inferences about the underlying incentives that influence firms' commitment to the convergence process (in response to H_1). Second, it gives us an indication of the degree of theoretical consistency of this measure, since the literature contains important observations about the interrelationships between compliance with IFRS and variables such as size, international market exposure, financing needs, growth opportunities, and analysts' forecasting errors (e.g., Daske et al., 2008).

3.5. Control Variables

Following Hail and Leuz (2006), Daske et al. (2009), and Lopes and Alencar (2008), we use the following control variables for general orientation in the regressions: ADR, indebtedness, size, beta, MTB ratio, and analysts' forecasting errors. We also use other variables, such as the number of analysts (Botosan, 1997), turnover (in the market liquidity regressions, when it is not the dependent variable) (Chordia, Roll, & Subrahmanyam, 2000), trading variables (financial volume, number of trades or shares traded), and earnings/price (E/P). All of these have been shown to be important controls in analyses to validate the cost of capital and market liquidity (see Section 4). Each equation can contain different controls, or not contain all of them, in function of their elimination by econometric criteria. We believe these control variables mitigate the concerns raised by Ruland, Shohn, and Zhou (2007) about this type of study, and also consider the specific characteristics of the Brazilian setting associated with the cost of capital.

ADR controls for excessive differences that arise, because firms with securities traded in the American market are subject to the stricter reporting rules of the Securities and Exchange Commission (SEC). LEV measures the firms' indebtedness, which is likely related to the cost of capital. This variable is measured by the ratio between total liabilities and equity. Size is measured by total assets and is included because we expect larger firms to present less risk than smaller ones. Beta controls for the market component of the cost of capital. MTB is a proxy for risk and growth opportunities. AERR controls for analysts' forecasting errors. We compute this variable to at least partly reduce a sample problem that can arise in calculating the cost of capital. The reason is that it is possible for the convergence process to impair analysts' ability to project earnings, at least in the convergence period. Another justification, more subtle, is that any bias introduced by analysts' projections can mechanically affect the implied estimate of the cost of capital if the market is contaminated by this bias. Finally, NANALYSTS controls for the effect of the number of analysts covering a particular firm on the ratios studied. Table 1 presents the descriptive statistics of the variables.

4. VALIDATION OF THE COST OF CAPITAL AND MARKET LIQUIDITY

To verify the reliability of our proxies, we performed individual analyses of the cost of capital and market liquidity. In terms of cost of equity capital, there can be a problem in the implied metric used if there is some systematic bias (intentional or not) in analysts' forecasts. Besides this, there is a debate over the validity of implied cost of capital estimates (Botosan & Plumlee, 2002; Guay, Kothari, & Shu, 2005). To overcome these questions, we gathered other measures associated with firms' risk to verify the trust-worthiness of the estimates (Beta, Size, MTB, and Earnings/Price).

To study the empirical validity of the r_{MEAN}, we mainly relied on Penman (1996) and Fama and French (1992, 1993). Those authors established that the cost of capital should be positively correlated with E/P and Beta and negatively correlated with Size and MTB. Penman (1996) argued that the E/P index can be used to estimate the cost of capital, but only in the rare situations when the expected future earnings are a function of current earnings adjusted by a rate that equals the cost of capital. The three-factor model of Fama and French (1992, 1993) motivated our use of the other measures (Size, Beta, and MTB).

In terms of market liquidity, we expect that the Bid–Ask Spread, because it contains transaction cost components, will be negatively correlated with Share Turnover and the other trading variables, because a greater volume or

Table 1. Descriptive Statistics of the Dependent, Control, and Validation Variables.

Variable	N	Mean	SD	P1	P25	Median	P75	P99
Panel A: Dependent variables								
Mean Cost of Capital– r_{MEAN}	50	13.5%	3.1%	4.0%	11.5%	14.2%	15.5%	20.9%
Cost of Capital – r_{CT}	50	12.5%	3.5%	4.0%	10.5%	12.7%	14.3%	24.2%
Cost of Capital – r_{GLES}	47	11.2%	6.0%	1.2%	7.0%	11.0%	16.6%	28.0%
Cost of Capital – r_{OJ}	43	15.6%	3.6%	8.3%	13.6%	15.5%	17.8%	25.1%
Cost of Capital – r_{PEG}	40	16.5%	5.7%	6.9%	12.4%	15.9%	20.3%	30.8%
Bid–Ask Spread	51	0.00314	0.00266	0.00035	0.00176	0.00266	0.00384	0.01856
Price Impact	51	0.00563	0.02672	0.00004	0.00054	0.00141	0.00213	0.19184
Share Turnover	51	0.10745	0.08758	0.00059	0.04696	0.08791	0.13133	0.37145
Panel B: Independent/Validation variables								
Total Assets	51	70.122	154.571	1.559	6.578	14.645	31.497	638.727
Leverage	51	76.6%	11.3%	51.4%	68.3%	75.2%	82.5%	102.9%
Market-to-Book	51	2.598136	4.703782	-12.97785	0.8524317	1.331586	2.667565	22.46323
Market Value	52	18.661	33.973	0.707	3.713	6.776	14.815	195.079
Number of Analysts	53	7.85	3.78	1	5	9	11	14
Estimation Error	51	0.336	1.906365	0.0000208	0.0027079	0.0099969	0.0648361	13.64187
Beta	51	0.889	0.209	0.512	0.738	0.893	1.002	1.315
Earnings/Price	50	0.033	0.143	-0.420	0.021	0.060	0.114	0.241
Trading Volume	51	60543.4	111285.9	1648.5	16853.5	23002.0	47554.5	581651.0

Table 1. (*Continued*)

Variable	N	Mean	SD	P1	P25	Median	P75	P99
Number of Trades	51	3360.2	3440.4	230.5	1479.0	2272.5	3917.5	17074.5
Number of Securities Traded	51	2593.9	3874.3	47.5	530.5	1287.0	2713.0	17745.0
Liquidity	51	1.208	1.686	0.053	0.450	0.656	1.185	8.556

The sample consists of 54 Bovespa Index (Bovespa) listed companies from September to December 2009, limited by availability of earnings estimates of market analysts. This financial information was collected from *Economática*, projections data were obtained from *Thomson ONE Analytics*, and daily market information from *Datastream*. The table reports the descriptive statistics of the dependent (Panel A), independent, and validation variables (Panel B). We used four dependent variables in our analysis: (1) Cost of Capital is the average implied cost of capital − r_{MEAN} − estimated through actual stock price and consensus projected earnings by market analysts. The models used are described in greater detail in Appendix A. (2) Bid–Ask Spread is computed as the six-month median of the difference between daily bid and ask price, divided by the midpoint (measured at the end of each trading day). (3) Price Impact is measured by median daily price impact over the year, following Amihud (2002) in computing price impact as the daily absolute price change per dollar of trading volume. (4) Share Turnover is computed by monthly share volume divided by average total shares outstanding (Bushee & Leuz, 2005). The independent and validation variables consist of the following measures: Total Assets are denominated in R\$ billion. Leverage is computed by total liabilities divided by total assets. Market-to-Book (MTB) is obtained by market value divided by book value. Market Value is the stock price times the total number of shares. Number of Analysts is obtained from *Thomson ONE Analytics*. Estimation Error is equal to the absolute percentage change from average projected earnings per share to actual price (scaled by total assets). Beta is calculated using prices from the last 60 months, adjusted for dividends, obtained directly from *Economática*. Earnings/Price (E/P) is the earnings per share divided by stock price. Trading volume, Number of Trades and Number of Securities Traded are yearly averages of the respective daily variables expressed in thousands. Liquidity is provided by the Liquidity Ratio (ILB) of *Economática*, which considers the number of days on which the stock was traded, number of shares outstanding, and trading volume.

number of trades should be associated with a smaller spread. However, we expect the Bid–Ask Spread to be positively correlated with the Price Impact, reflecting the greater ability of investors to influence the prices of stocks with higher transaction costs (which also implies an information asymmetry component). Analogous interpretations apply to both Price Impact and Share Turnover.

4.1. Validation: Cost of Capital

Table 1 presents, among other variables, the descriptive statistics of the implied cost of capital estimates of the four models used (Claus & Thomas, 2001; Gebhardt et al., 2001; Easton (Modified PEG), 2004; Ohlson & Juettner-Nauroth, 2005). For all four estimates both the mean and median are between 10% and 20%. The standard error varies from a low of 3.5% (r_{CT}) to a high of 6.0% (r_{GLES}), with relatively stable measures. We use the mean of the four models (r_{MEAN}) to estimate the regression models (mean and standard deviation equal, respectively, to 13.5% and 3.1%). The Pearson correlation coefficients of r_{MEAN} are equal to 41%, 61%, 72%, and 66% (significant at 1%), respectively, with the four models: r_{CT}, r_{GLES}, r_{OJ}, and r_{PEG}. Hail and Leuz (2006), utilizing the same models in a sample of companies from 40 countries over 10 years, found correlation values for the average cost of capital between 75% and 96%. This indicates that the differences in the theoretical premises of the four models (details in Appendix A) show greater empirical divergence when only using Brazilian firms. The result, however, is satisfactory, since the study by Hail and Leuz (2006) used 35,118 firm-years. Table 2 presents the results of the univariate and multivariate correlation analyses of r_{MEAN}. As predicted in the literature, the cost of capital estimate is positively correlated with E/P and negatively with MTB. The sign of the correlation with Beta is positive, as expected, but the coefficient is not significant at the usual levels. The regression analysis presents relations as predicted in the literature for all the variables, and once again MTB and E/P are statistically significant. Lastly, we include the error in analysts' earnings forecasts in function of the implied cost of capital based on the projections. The coefficient is positive and significant at 1%, as expected, indicating a higher risk premium for firms whose parameters are harder to estimate.

Table 2. Correlation Analysis of Cost of Capital (r_{MEAN}).

	MTB	E/P	BETA
Panel A: Univariate analysis			
Pearson coefficient	$-27.5\%^{**}$	$43.0\%^{**}$	13.5%
P-value	0.027	0.001	0.177
No. of observations	50	50	49

	Intercept	MTB	E/P	BETA	MV	AERROR
Panel B: Multivariate analysis						
Coefficient	0.1242^{*}	-0.002^{**}	0.13246^{*}	0.0134	-0.0001	0.0003^{*}
T-statistic	9.31	-2.12	3.29	0.99	-1.01	4.29
P-value	0.000	0.040	0.002	0.327	0.320	0.000
Adj. R^2	39.6%					
Prob. $> F$	0.0000					
No. of observations	49					

The table shows the correlation analysis of Mean Cost of Equity – r_{MEAN} – with variables indicated in the literature. Panel A presents the results of the Pearson coefficient analysis (univariate), while Panel B presents the results of multiple regression analysis (multivariate). The variables consist of the following measures: Market-to-Book (MTB) is obtained by market value divided by book value. Earnings/Price (E/P) is the earnings per share divided by stock price. BETA is calculated using prices from the last 60 months, adjusted for dividends, obtained directly from *Economática*. Market Value (MV) is the stock price times total number of shares. Estimation Error (AERROR) is equal to the absolute percentage change from average projected earnings per share to actual price (scaled by total assets). *, **, Denote values significantly different from zero at the 1%, 5%, and 10% level, respectively, using a two-tailed test.

4.2. Validation: Market Liquidity

Table 3 presents the individual Pearson correlations of the proxies, adding the trading variables: trading volume, number of shares, number of trades, and a liquidity measure, computed by *Economática*.[6] The expected behavior of the variables, or whether they really represent what we intend to study, closely depends on this analysis.

Of the 21 Pearson correlations in Table 3, all have the expected sign, according to the interpretations above. Of them, 20 are significant at the usual levels, 17 of them at 1%. Besides this, all the correlations of the three proxies have high economic meaning, with percentages that range from a significant minimum of 25.4% to a maximum of 87.1%. This preliminary evidence adds a degree of validity to the variables necessary to interpret the results and relations studied.

Table 3.   Correlation Analysis of Bid–Ask Spread, Price Impact, and
Share Turnover.

Variable	Bid–Ask	Price Impact	Share Turnover	Volume	N_{Shares}	N_{Trades}
Price Impact	87.1%*					
	(0.000)					
Share Turnover	−58.6%*	−48.6%*				
	(0.000)	(0.000)				
Volume	−77.8%*	−82.7%*	25.4%***			
	(0.000)	(0.000)	(0.072)			
N_{Shares}	−73.2%*	−64.1%*	32.5%**	84.6%*		
	(0.000)	(0.000)	(0.020)	(0.000)		
N_{Trades}	−77.1%*	−75.6%*	32.3%**	94.3%*	96.3%*	
	(0.000)	(0.000)	(0.021)	(0.000)	(0.000)	
Liquidity	−74.4%*	−73.3%*	20.4%	81.6%*	68.5%*	75.5%*
	(0.000)	(0.000)	(0.151)	(0.000)	(0.000)	(0.000)

Bid–Ask Spread is computed as the six-month median of the difference between the daily bid price and the ask price, divided by the midpoint (measured at the end of each trading day). Price Impact is measured by the median daily price impact over the year, following Amihud (2002) in computing price impact as the daily absolute price change per R$ of trading volume. Share Turnover is computed by the monthly share volume divided by average total shares outstanding (Bushee & Leuz, 2005). Trading Volume, Number of Trades, and Number of Securities Traded are yearly averages of the respective daily variables expressed in thousands. Liquidity is provided by the Liquidity Ratio (ILB) of *Economática*, which considers the number of days on which the stock was traded, number of shares outstanding, and trading volume. All variables are average of daily observations from May 2009 to October 2009. The beginning of the semester series in month +5 reflects an average interval of one month after official publication of comprehensive financial statements. The intentional choice allows variables to reflect the financial information published previously. *, **, *** denote values significantly different from zero at the 1%, 5%, and 10% level, respectively, using a two-tailed test.

5. EMPIRICAL RESULTS

5.1. Determinants of the Level of Compliance with Convergence Practices

In this section we present the result of the relation between the level of compliance with convergence practices and the economic incentives of firms (H_1). In line with Ball (2006), our hypothesis is that the underlying conditional incentives exercise an influence on firms' commitment to convergence.

Appendix A shows the average of each aspect included in the IASCI for the 54 firms in the sample. The analysis of this information is by itself of great interest, since it shows the average behavior of companies with respect to adopting and disclosing practices during the accounting convergence phase in Brazil. As can be seen, there is great dispersion in compliance with the items, ranging from 6.8% (disclosure of the criteria followed to determine the economic depreciation rates) to 100% (publication of the cash flow statement for the 2007 fiscal year).

We next analyze the IASCI variable. Table 4 presents the correlation and regression analyses (respectively, Panels A and B) of the IASCI (dependent) with the other variables described (independent). It can be seen, in Panel A, that with the exception of the MTB ratio (measure of growth opportunity),

Table 4. Correlation Analysis of the International Accounting Standards Convergence Index (IASCI).

	ADR	SIZE	MV	LEV	MTB	AERROR
Panel A: Univariate analysis						
Pearson coefficient	24.5%**	31.5%**	22.1%***	13.8%	−20.1%***	−26.6%**
P-value	0.043	0.013	0.062	0.169	0.080	0.031
No. of observations	50	50	50	50	50	50

	Intercept	ADR	MV	LEV	MTB	AERROR
Panel B: Multivariate analysis						
Coefficient	0.1939	0.0551***	0.0213**	0.1675***	−0.0053***	−0.0008*
T-statistics	1.20	1.78	2.42	1.69	−1.74	−9.25
P-value	0.235	0.082	0.020	0.098	0.089	0.000
Adj. R^2	26.0%					
Prob.>F	0.000					
No. of observations	50					

The table shows the correlation analysis of the International Accounting Standards Convergence Index (IASCI) with variables indicated by the literature. Panel A presents the results of the Pearson coefficient analysis (univariate analysis), while Panel B presents the results of multiple regression analysis (multivariate). The IASCI is a self-constructed index, composed of 37 binary questions, based on specific disclosure related to new international accounting oriented practices (Laws 11,638/07, 11,941/09 and published pronouncements from the Accounting Pronouncements Committee – CPC). Other variables consist of the following measures: ADR consists of a binary variable indicating whether or not the company issues American Depositary Receipts (in all modalities). Total Assets (TA) are denominated in R$ billion. Market Value (MV) is the stock price times the total number of shares. Leverage (LEV) is computed by total liabilities divided by total assets. Market-to-Book (MTB) is obtained by market value divided by book value. Estimation Error (AERROR) is equal to the absolute percentage change from average projected earnings per share to actual price (scaled by total assets). *, **, *** denote values significantly different from zero at the 1%, 5%, and 10% level, respectively, using a two-tailed test.

the signs of the Pearson[7] coefficients of all the variables are as expected. Of these, only Leverage is not significant at 10%. In the regression analysis, only MTB is contrary to the expectation, and all the other variables are significant at the indicated level. This result agrees with findings in the literature that firms' economic incentives have important effects on their disclosure behavior. The results suggest that firms that (i) are larger, (ii) are more exposed to the international market, and (iii) have greater financing needs are more likely to adopt the new rules, shown by material changes in their accounting practices, in relation to firms that do not have the same incentives.

5.2. Economic Consequences of Convergence to International Standards

We now examine the effects of adopting accounting convergence practices in Brazil on the cost of capital and market liquidity, the latter represented by the variables Bid–Ask Spread, Price Impact, and Share Turnover (H_2 and H_3). If the market and the three variables constructed to analyze convergence are able to differentiate firms regarding their behavior in the transition to the international standards, we expect to find a negative relation with the Cost of Capital, Bid–Ask Spread, and Price Impact, and a positive one with Share Turnover.

Table 5 presents the analysis by sector (Panel A) and the descriptive statistics (Panel B) of the convergence variables. The firms in our sample make up 87.5% of the Ibovespa. The average IASCI, expressed as a percentage, was 68.6%, the variation in the number of pages in the complete financial statements was 24.0%, and the variation in the quality of earnings between 2007 and 2008, measured through the concept of discretionary accruals (Kang & Sivaramakrishnan model, 1995), was 0.093. The descriptive statistics, shown in Panel B, have high standard deviations for the variables ΔPages and ΔDiscrAccruals, demonstrating the natural instability of these measures.

Next we present the cross-section regression analysis by OLS of Eq. (2), estimated with robust standard errors. Table 6 presents the results of multiple regressions. The main variable of interest is that indicating convergence of accounting practices.

Panel A reports the cost of capital results. Two of the three convergence variables have the expected sign (IASCI and ΔPages), but neither of them is significant at the usual levels (1%, 5%, or 10%). This means that even though these variables point in the expected direction, it is not possible to

Table 5. Analysis per Sector and Descriptive Statistics of Accounting Convergence Variables (Independents).

ID	Sector	N	IBOV Part (%)	IASCI (%)	ΔPages (%)	ΔDiscrAccruals
Panel A: Convergence per sector variables						
1	Food	4	4.07	0.6152	0.1258	0.6407
2	Retailing	5	3.75	0.6678	0.3815	0.1241
3	Construction	3	2.81	0.6457	0.5682	−0.1937
4	Energy	9	5.55	0.6941	0.0158	0.1202
5	Banking and finance	5	17.10	0.6835	0.4303	−
6	Mining	2	14.39	0.6708	0.2302	−0.1992
7	Others	5	5.32	0.6932	0.1828	−0.2230
8	Pulp and paper	3	0.43	0.5556	0.0139	0.1603
9	Oil and gas	2	15.60	0.6280	0.0903	0.0168
10	Chemicals	2	0.93	0.8626	0.3719	0.5251
11	Steel and metallurgy	4	11.02	0.7154	0.1810	0.1150
12	Telecommunications	5	3.09	0.6748	0.1104	−0.0018
13	Transportation	4	3.37	0.7082	0.2146	−0.1899
14	Vehicles	1	0.54	0.7838	0.4393	0.3075
	Total/mean	54	87.96	0.6856	0.2397	0.0925

Variable	N	Mean	SD	P1	P25	Median	P75	P99
Panel B: Descriptive statistics of accounting convergence variables								
IASCI	50	0.687	0.101	0.472	0.639	0.694	0.778	0.892
ΔPages %	49	22.0%	26.7%	−29.2%	7.1%	16.7%	34.3%	92.7%
ΔDiscrAccruals	35	0.0462343	0.430124	−0.962567	−0.097437	0.0197765	0.1602583	1.478114

The sample consists of Bovespa Index (Bovespa) listed companies from September to December 2009, limited by availability of information on analysts' projections. This results in a total of 54 companies from 14 sectors of the economy, according to the *Economática* sector classification. The information for the composition of the IASCI and ΔPages variables were collected from comprehensive financial statements for 2008, published at the Brazilian Securities Commission website (www.cvm.org.br) in 2009. We used only officially published documents, which include the management report, auditors' report, financial statements, and notes. (1) IASCI – Brazilian Convergence Index to International Accounting Practices is a self-constructed index composed of 37 binary questions ("1" if yes and "0" if no – see Appendix B), based on specific disclosure related to new international accounting oriented practices (Laws 11,638/07, 11,941/08 and published pronouncements from the Accounting Pronouncements Committee – CPC). (2) ΔPages is computed as the percentage change in number of pages of comprehensive financial statements for 2008 compared to the average of the two previous years (2007 and 2006). (3) ΔDiscrAccruals is measured by the change in discretionary accruals computed for 2008 and 2007 through the model of Kang and Sivaramakrishnan (1995) – see Appendix C.

Table 6. Regression Analysis of Cost of Capital, Bid–Ask Spread, Price Impact, and Share Turnover.

	Expected Sign	International Accounting Convergence Related Variables		
		IASCI	ΔPages	ΔDiscrAccruals
Panel A: Cost of capital as dependent variable				
Accounting Convergence Variable	−	**−2.423**	**−0.853**	**0.362**
T-statistics		**(−0.57)**	**(−0.65)**	**(0.30)**
Intercept	¢	6.521***	4.514	2.511
		(1.84)	(1.02)	(0.51)
Control variables				
Market Value	−	−0.011	−0.021***	−0.009
		(−1.29)	(−1.95)	(−0.9)
Leverage	+	7.061**	5.461***	12.700***
		(2.18)	(1.76)	(2.18)
Market-to-Book	−	−0.236*	−0.245*	−0.232***
		(−2.96)	(−3.54)	(−3.58)
Estimation Error	+	0.040*	0.034*	–
		(4.75)	(4.21)	–
Beta	+	–	–	1.317
		–	–	(0.71)
E/P	+	16.058*	15.011*	15.248***
		(3.92)	(3.59)	(−3.30)
Trading Variable	−	–	0.539	–
		–	(1.37)	–
R^2 (%)		45.1	46.4	45.9
No. of observations		50	46	35
F-test		0.000	0.000	0.000
Panel B: Bid–Ask Spread as dependent variable				
Accounting Convergence Variable	−	**−3.526***	**−0.110**	**−0.314**
T-statistics		**(−1.68)**	**(−0.68)**	**(−1.09)**
Intercept	¢	2.241	−3.923***	13.063*
		(0.65)	(−4.08)	(6.76)
Control variables				
Market Value	−	−0.018***	−0.170*	−0.266***
		(−1.85)	(−2.74)	(−1.72)
American Depositary Receipts	−	1.009***	0.054	0.368
		(1.69)	(0.60)	(1.06)
Share Turnover	−	−1.748**	−0.368*	−7.954*
		(−2.55)	(−12.42)	(−3.38)
Trading Variable	−	−0.120	−2.163*	−0.900*
		(−0.34)	(−3.36)	(−4.39)

Table 6. (*Continued*)

	Expected Sign	International Accounting Convergence Related Variables		
		IASCI	ΔPages	ΔDiscrAccruals
Number of Analysts	−	−0.102***	−0.026***	−0.088**
		(−1.77)	(−2.01)	(−2.46)
Beta	+	–	–	2.021*
		–	–	(2.95)
R^2 (%)		66.2	80.5	78.1
No. of observations		50	47	35
F-Test		0.000	0.000	0.000
Panel C: Price Impact as dependent variable				
Accounting Convergence Variable	−	**−2.280****	**−0.504****	**−0.063**
T-statistics		**(−2.30)**	**(−2.67)**	**(−0.69)**
Intercept	¢	−2.083	5.992*	4.387*
		(−1.09)	(10.09)	(4.18)
Control variables				
Market Value	−	−0.018*	−0.900*	−0.814*
		(−3.31)	(−15.61)	(−10.18)
American Depositary Receipts	−	0.457**	0.171	0.204
		(2.03)	(1.62)	(1.47)
Turnover	−	−0.474***	−0.861*	−0.811*
		(−1.96)	(−11.98)	(−8.81)
Trade Variables	−	−0.516**	−0.062	−0.004**
		(−2.46)	(−1.14)	(−2.20)
Number of Analysts	−	−0.043***	−0.030**	−0.044*
		(−1.92)	(−2.55)	(−3.58)
R^2 (%)		81.3	95.3	94.7
No. of Observations		50	47	35
F-Test		0.000	0.000	0.000
Panel D: Share Turnover as dependent variable				
Accounting Convergence Variable	+	**1.355****	**0.351**	**−0.107**
T-statistics		**(2.02)**	**(1.07)**	**(−0.79)**
Intercept	¢	6.757*	−8.575*	0.595
		(5.44)	(−6.97)	(0.91)
Control variables				
Market Value	+	−0.689*	−0.013*	−0.706*
		(−7.77)	(−2.88)	(−9.82)
American Depositary Receipt	+	–	0.568**	0.276**
		–	(2.20)	(2.67)
Trade Variables	+	0.021*	0.795*	0.794*
		(7.53)	(4.53)	(10.19)

Table 6. (*Continued*)

	Expected Sign	International Accounting Convergence Related Variables		
		IASCI	ΔPages	ΔDiscrAccruals
Number of Analysts	+	0.012	−0.048	−0.028***
		(0.63)	(−1.57)	(−1.80)
Estimation Error	−	−0.353*	−0.370*	−
		(−34.73)	(−29.26)	−
R^2 (%)		80.5	66.0	86.3
No. of observations		50	46	35
F-test		0.000	0.000	0.000

The sample consists of Bovespa Index (Bovespa) listed companies from September to December of 2009, limited by availability of analysts' earnings estimates. This results in a total of 54 companies from 14 economic sectors, according to the *Economática* sector classification. The financial information was collected from *Economática*, projections data from *Thomson ONE Analytics*, and daily market information from *Datastream*. Panels A, B, C, and D present the analysis results for each different dependent variable. They are (1) Cost of Capital is the average of implied cost of capital – r_{MEAN} – estimated through actual stock price and consensus projected earnings by market analysts using Claus and Thomas – r_{CT} (2001), Gebhardt et al. – r_{GLES} (2001), Ohlson and Juettner-Nauroth – r_{OJ} (2005), and Easton – r_{PEG} (2004) models. The models are described in greater detail in Appendix A. (2) Bid–Ask Spread is computed as the six-month median of the difference between the daily bid price and ask price, divided by the midpoint (measured at the end of each trading day). (3) Price Impact is measured by median daily price impact over the year, following Amihud (2002) in computing price impact as the daily absolute price change per R$ of trading volume. (4) Share Turnover is computed by monthly trading volume divided by average total shares outstanding (Bushee & Leuz, 2005). The independent variables consist of the following measures: Leverage is computed by total liabilities divided by total assets. Market-to-Book (MTB) is obtained by market value divided by book value. Market Value is the stock price times the total number of shares. Number of Analysts is obtained from *Thomson ONE Analytics*. Estimation Error is equal to the absolute percentage change from average projected earnings per share to actual price (scaled by total assets). Beta is calculated using prices from the last 60 months, adjusted for dividends, obtained directly from *Economática*. Earnings/Price (E/P) is the earnings per share divided by stock price. Trading Variable consists of one of the following variables: Trading Volume, Number of Trades, and Number of Securities Traded, which are yearly averages of the respective daily variables expressed in thousands. ADR consists of a binary variable indicating whether or not the company issues American Depositary Receipts (in all modalities). No. of observations may vary, and does not represent the total sample, due to the absence of observations of some regression variables. For exhibition reasons, the coefficients in Panel A (Panel B) are multiplied by 100 (1000). *, **, *** denote values significantly different from zero at the 1%, 5%, and 10% level, respectively, using a two-tailed test. Values in bold represent the main important variables in each regression model.

affirm with acceptable security that they are significantly different than zero. The control variables in all the regressions have the expected sign and are statistically significant in the majority of cases (the exception being Trading), confirming the findings in the literature on their relevance in explaining the cost of capital, and thus their status as important control instruments. The basic idea is, for example, that since more leveraged companies have higher capital costs, it is important to consider firms' debt level before making inferences about the association between their disclosure of accounting convergence provisions and cost of capital. In summary, then, the Brazilian market apparently does not differentiate firms in terms of associating lower costs of capital with firms that are more committed to accounting convergence.

Panel B shows the results for the Bid–Ask Spread. The coefficients of the convergence variables are negative for all three constructions (IASCI, ΔPages, and ΔDiscrAccruals), according to the predicted direction. However, the results are mixed: the only statistically significant variable is IASCI, the main variable in the analysis, or at least the one least subject to containing serious deviations. IASCI is also statistically more stable than ΔPages and ΔDiscrAccruals, as shown by analysis of the mean and standard deviation in Panel B of Table 5. For the IASCI variable, the impact of convergence on Bid–Ask Spread has even greater economic significance. The control variables inserted in all three regressions have the predicted sign and in nearly all cases are significant (the exception being ADR), confirming the findings in the literature on their relevance in explaining the bid–ask spread, and thus their importance as control instruments.

Panel C reports the results for the Price Impact variable. Once again the convergence variables are negative for all three constructions (IASCI, ΔPages, and ΔDiscrAccruals), as expected. In this case, IASCI and ΔPages are statistically significant. This result hence suggests there is an association between firms that are more committed to convergence and those whose investors have lower ability to trade in these firms' stocks without influencing the price. For the IASCI variable, the relation between convergence and Price Impact shows even greater economic significance. The control variables in all three regressions again have the expected sign and are statistically significant in the majority of cases (except for ADR), confirming the findings in the literature on their relevance in explaining the price impact, and thus their importance as control instruments.

Panel D gives the results of the analysis of Share Turnover. This variable measures the financial volume traded divided by the total number of shares outstanding. It is commonly used as a proxy for market liquidity. Therefore, in this case, unlike in the previous ones, the convergence variables should be positively related to Share Turnover. Two of the three convergence variables (IASCI and ΔPages) have the expected sign, but only IASCI is statistically significant at the usual levels. The control variables, except for Market Value and Number of Analysts for some cases, have the expected signs in accordance with the literature and are significant.

In summary, the results of analyzing the market liquidity variables (Panels B–D) indicate statistically significant relations with IASCI for the three measures: Bid–Ask Spread, Price Impact, and Share Turnover. This result thus provides evidence, though not under all study conditions, that the level of compliance with accounting convergence is associated (i) negatively with transaction cost – asymmetric information (Bid–Ask Spread), (ii) negatively with investor capacity to influence the stock price (Price Impact), and (iii) positively with liquidity (Share Turnover).

In general, the ΔPages and ΔDiscrAccruals variables are excessively unstable, making it impossible to obtain conclusive results from their parameters. As shown in Table 5, the degree of dispersion of these variables possibly prevents them from being good measurement instruments, at least in the context of this study. The ΔPages metric could well be misleading in some cases, such as when an unusual corporate event requires increasing the amount of information reported without any relation to convergence, undermining this metric's validity as a proxy. The ΔDiscrAccruals is subject to the criticisms expressed in the earnings management literature on the use of accruals models. Nevertheless, it is possible the problem lies in the measurement instrument (Kang and Sivaramakrishnan model) rather than the validity of the "earnings quality" metric itself.

6. CONCLUSIONS

Despite our focus on regulation, this article should not be taken as an argument in favor of the need for greater regulation or regulatory reform. Indeed, we stress the important influence of the market on firms' disclosure choices, as well as the interaction of these forces with regulatory acts.

We investigated two questions related to the level of adoption of convergence practices. First, do firms' underlying incentives influence the level of their commitment to convergence in a setting of weak legal enforcement? Second, is the level of adopting convergence practices associated with economic improvements of firms (reduced cost of capital and increased market liquidity) provided by the informational environment in an economy with weak enforcement?

Two contrasting views motivated this investigation. The first holds that because the IFRS require a higher discloser level in relation to local GAAP, the informational environment of firms will benefit from better financial reports and greater transparency (Barth, 2008). The contrasting view is that more rigorous accounting rules do not necessarily improve financial disclosure (Ball, 2006). The main argument supporting this view is that the quality of accounting reports is molded not only by accounting rules, but also by the country's political and economic forces and legal framework, along with firms' underlying conditional incentives. We evaluated these questions in the setting of an emerging economy, characterized by weak institutions and enforcement and high growth opportunities.

Initially, the analysis of the variables indicates considerable heterogeneity in convergence to international accounting standards, as expected in the weak institutional setting investigated here. With respect to the underlying incentives for compliance with convergence practices, our results suggest that (i) larger firms, (ii) firms more exposed to the international market, and (iii) firms that have greater financing needs are more likely to adopt the new provisions, by making material changes in their accounting policies, in relation to firms that do not have the same incentives.

Examining the effects of convergence, we found evidence for the argument that the IFRS can improve the informational environment of firms. Nevertheless, our results indicate that these improvements are limited, since only our market liquidity variables were statistically significant. For the cost of capital, although we obtained negatively correlated coefficients, these were not statistically significant after controlling for known determinants of this measure. For market liquidity, tested via the variables Bid–Ask Spread, Price Impact, and Share Turnover, the evidence points to an association with the adoption of accounting convergence measured by the IASCI, with the respective expected signs. This result suggests that the level of compliance with convergence practices is (i) negatively associated with the transaction cost (Bid–Ask Spread), (ii) negatively related to the ability of investors to influence the stock price (Price Impact), and (iii) positively related to market liquidity (Share Turnover). These results corroborate other findings in the literature that the market manages to differentiate (albeit not perfectly) firms' disclosure strategies.

The results here agree with the evidence found by Daske et al. (2008) regarding market liquidity, with the exception that they only found significant relations for countries with high enforcement. In this respect, our results add to the literature by providing similar results in an emerging market with weak enforcement. We believe that the main limitation of cross-country studies, as argued by Holthausen (2003), is that they cannot adequately control for institutional variables so as to keep constant specific characteristics of disclosure regimes. Therefore, we have shown that convergence to international accounting standards can improve the informational environment of firms in emerging markets with weak enforcement and high growth opportunities, considering that these firms have economic incentives to comply with enhanced accounting practices.

NOTES

1. In the next section we present characteristic aspects of the process of IFRS adoption in Brazil.
2. CFC stands for the Federal Accounting Board (*Conselho Federal de Contabilidade*).
3. A provisional measure (*medida provisória*) is a presidential decree that takes effect immediately with status of ordinary law but is then subject to congressional approval and/or amendment.
4. See Section 2.3
5. See Appendix C. For the estimation we applied the model using instrumental variables.
6. The Market Liquidity Index (*Índice de Liquidez em Bolsa* (ILB)) of *Economática* considers the number of days a stock was traded, the number of trades of the stock under analysis and of all others, and the monetary trading volume.
7. We used Pearson's coefficient after confirmation of the hypothesis of normality of the *IOPC* variable by the Kolmogorov–Smirnov and Shapiro–Wilk tests.

ACKNOWLEDGMENTS

We are grateful for the helpful comments and suggestions of Josué Braga, Marcelo Álvaro, Marcelo Bicalho, Raquel Zanon, and the participants at the *Contemporary Topics in Accounting Seminar* at the University of São Paulo – Ênio Bonafé, Fabio Araújo, Cássio Callegaro, Luciano Gilio, and Roberta Alencar. We express particular thanks to Rogério Abrahão for the important help in gathering the data to construct the variables. Vinícius Simmer de Lima acknowledges financial support from the São Paulo State Research Support Foundation (FAPESP). Any errors are entirely the authors' responsibility.

REFERENCES

Amihud, Y. (2002). Illiquidity and stock returns: Cross-section and time-series effects. *Journal of Financial Markets*, *5*, 31–56.

Amihud, Y., & Mendelson, H. (1989). The effects of beta, bid–ask spread, residual risk and size on stock returns. *Journal of Finance*, *44*, 479–486.

Armstrong, C. S., Barth, M. E., Jagolinzer, A. D., & Rield, E. J. (2010). Market reaction to the adoption of IFRS in Europe. *The Accounting Review*, *85*(1), 31–61.

Ashbaugh, H., & Pincus, M. (2001). Domestic accounting standards, international accounting standards, and the predictability of earnings. *Journal of Accounting Research*, *39*, 417–434.

Ball, R. (2006). International Financial Reporting Standards (IFRS): Pros and cons for investors. *Accounting and Business Research: International Accounting Policy Forum*, 5–27.

Ball, R., Kothari, S. P., & Robin, A. (2000). The effect of international institutional factors on properties of accounting earnings. *Journal of Accounting and Economics*, *29*, 1–51.

Ball, R., Robin, A., & Wu, J. S. (2003). Incentives versus standards: Properties of accounting income in four East Asian countries and implications for acceptance of IAS. *Journal of Accounting & Economics*, *36*, 235–270.

Ball, R., & Shivakumar, L. (2005). Earnings quality in U.K. private firms. *Journal of Accounting and Economics*, *39*, 83–128.

Barth, M. (2008). Global financial reporting: Implications for U.S. academics. *The Accounting Review*, *83*, 1159–1180.

Barth, M., Landsman, W., & Lang, M. (2008). International accounting standards and accounting quality. *Journal of Accounting Research*, *46*, 467–498.

Barth, M., Landsman, W., Lang, M., & Williams, C. (2010). Are international accounting standards-based and U.S. GAAP-based accounting amounts comparable? Available at http://papers.ssrn.com/sol3/papers.cfm?abstract_id = 1585404

Botosan, C. (1997). Disclosure level and the cost of equity capital. *The Accounting Review*, *72*, 323–349.

Botosan, C., & Plumlee, M. (2002). A re-examination of disclosure level and the expected cost of equity capital. *Journal of Accounting Research*, *40*, 21–40.

Bova, F., & Pereira, R. (2010). The determinants and consequences of heterogeneous IFRS compliance levels following mandatory IFRS adoption: Evidence from a developing country. SSRN. Available at http://ssrn.com/abstract = 1542240

Burgstahler, D., Hail, L., & Leuz, C. (2006). The importance of reporting incentives: Earnings management in European private and public firms. *The Accounting Review*, *81*, 983–1016.

Bushee, B., & Leuz, C. (2005). Economic consequences of SEC disclosure regulation: Evidence from the OTC bulletin board. *Journal of Accounting and Economics*, *39*, 233–264.

Bushman, R. M., Piotroski, J., & Smith, A. J. (2004). What determines corporate transparency. *Journal of Accounting Research*, *42*, 207–252.

Bushman, R., & Smith, A. (2001). Financial accounting information and corporate governance. *Journal of Accounting and Economics*, *32*, 237–333.

Cardoso, R. L. (2008). Accounting regulation and regulation of accounting: Theories and the Brazilian case of convergence to IFRS. SSRN. Available at: http://ssrn.com/abstract = 1288068

Capkun, V., Cazavan, A., Jeanjean, T., & Weiss, L. (2008). *Earnings management and value relevance during the mandatory transition from local GAAPs to IFRS in Europe.* Working Paper. HEC Paris. Available at SSRN http://ssrn.com/abstract = 1125716

Chong, A., & Lopez-de-Silanes, F. (2007). *Investor protection and corporate governance – Firm evidence across Latin America.* Inter-American Development Bank and Stanford University.

Chordia, T., Roll, R., & Subrahmanyam, A. (2000). Co-movements in bid–ask spreads and market depth. *Financial Analysts Journal, 56,* 23–27.

Christensen, H., Lee, E., & Walker, M. (2009). Do IFRS reconciliations convey new information? The debt contraction effect. *Journal of Accountinng Research, 47,* 1167–1199.

Claus, J., & Thomas, J. (2001). Equity premia as low as three percent? Evidence from analysts' earnings forecasts for domestic and international stock markets. *Journal of Finance, 56,* 1629–1666.

Covrig, V., DeFond, M., & Hung, M. (2007). Home bias, foreign mutual fund holdings, and the voluntary adoption of international accounting standards. *Journal of Accounting Research, 45,* 41–70.

Cuijpers, R., & Buijink, W. (2005). Voluntary adoption of non-local GAAP in the European union: A study of determinants and consequences. *European Accounting Review, 14,* 487–524.

Daske, H., Hail, L., Leuz, C., & Verdi, R. (2008). Mandatory IFRS reporting around the world: Early evidence on the economic consequences. *Journal of Accounting Research, 46,* 1085–1142.

Daske, H., Hail, L., Leuz, C., & Verdi, R. (2009). *Adopting a label: Heterogeneity in the economic consequences of IFRS adoptions.* Working Paper. University of Pennsylvania and University Of Chicago. Available at http://ssrn.com/

Dechow, P., & Skinner, D. (2000). Earnings management: Reconciling the views of accounting academics, practitioners, and regulators. *Accounting Horizons, 14*(June), 235–250.

Diamond, D., & Verrecchia, R. (1991). Disclosure, liquidity, and the cost of capital. *Journal of Finance, 46,* 1325–1359.

Easley, D., & O'Hara, M. (2004). Information and the cost of capital. *Journal of Finance, 59,* 1553–1583.

Easton, P. (2004). PE ratios, PEG ratios, and estimating the implied expected rate of return on equity capital. *The Accounting Review, 79,* 79–95.

Fama, E. F., & French, K. R. (1992). The cross section of expected stock returns. *Journal of Finance, 47,* 427–465.

Fama, E. F., & French, K. R. (1993). Common risk factors in the returns on stocks and bonds. *Journal of Financial Economics, 33,* 3–56.

Fan, J., & Wong, T. (2002). Corporate ownership structure and the informativeness of accounting earnings in East Asia. *Journal of Accounting and Economics, 33,* 401–425.

Francis, J., LaFond, R., Olsson, P., & Schipper, K. (2004). Costs of equity and earnings attributes. *The Accounting Review, 79,* 967–1010.

Francis, J., Nanda, D., & Olsson, P. (2008). Voluntary disclosure, earnings quality, and costs of capital, *Journal of Accounting Research, 46,* 53–99.

Garleanu, N., & Pedersen, L. (2004). Adverse selection and the required return. *Review of Financial Studies, 17,* 643–665.

Gebhardt, W. R., Lee, C., & Swaminathan, B. (2001). Toward an implied cost of capital. *Journal of Accounting Research, 39,* 135–176.

Guay, W. R., Kothari, S. P., & Shu, S. (2005). *Properties of implied cost of capital using analysts' forecasts.* MIT Sloan Working Paper no. 4422-03. Available at SSRN http://ssrn.com/ abstract = 26560 or doi:10.2139/ssrn.426560

Hail, L. (2003). The impact of voluntary corporate disclosures on the ex ante cost of capital for Swiss firms. *European Accounting Review, 11*, 741–743.

Hail, L., & Leuz, C. (2006). International differences in the cost of equity capital: Do legal institutions and securities regulation matter? *Journal of Accounting Research, 44*, 485–531.

Hail, L., & Leuz, C. (2009). Cost of capital effects and changes in growth expectations around U.S. cross-listings. *Journal of Financial Economics, 93*, 428–454.

Hail, L., Leuz, C., & Wysocki, P. (2009). *Global accounting convergence and the potential adoption of IFRS by the United States: An analysis of economic and policy factors.* Working Paper. February 25, Available at SSRN http://ssrn.com/abstract = 1357331

Haw, I., Hu, B., Hwang, L., & Wu, W. (2004). Ultimate ownership, income management and legal and extra-legal institutions. *Journal of Accounting Research, 42*, 423–462.

Healy, P., & Whalen, J. (1999). A review of the earnings management literature and its implications for standards setting. *Accounting Horizons, 13*, 365–383.

Holthausen, R. (2003). Testing the relative power of accounting standards versus incentives and other institutional features to influence the outcome of financial reporting in an international setting. *Journal of Accounting and Economics, 36*, 271–283.

Horton, J., Serafeim, G., & Serafeim, I. (2010). *Does mandatory IFRS adoption improve the information environment?* HBS Working Paper Number: 11-029. London School of Economics. Available at http://hbswk.hbs.edu/item/6515.html

Kang, S. H., & Sivaramakrishnan, K. (1995). Issues in testing earnings management: An instrumental variable approach. *Journal of Accounting Research, Rochester, 32*(2), 353–367.

KPMG. (2006). *The application of IFRS: Choices in practice.* Technical Handbook. KPMG IFRG Limited. Available at http://www.kpmg.sk/dbfetch/52616e646f6d4956aff42b fa91e4e4fc9c34347444eadb4e938871a42eceae07/application_of_ifrs_choices_in_practice_ 2006.pdf

Lambert, R., Leuz, C., & Verrecchia, R. (2007). Accounting information, disclosure, and the cost of capital. *Journal of Accounting Research, 45*, 385–420.

Leuz, C. (2003). IAS versus U.S.-GAAP: Information asymmetry-based evidence from Germany's new market. *Journal of Accounting Research, 41*, 445–472.

Leuz, C., Nanda, D., & Wysocki, P. (2003). Earnings management and investor protection: An international comparison. *Journal of Financial Economics, 69*, 505–527.

Leuz, C., Triantis, A., & Wang, T. (2008). Why do firms go dark? Causes and economic consequences of voluntary SEC deregistrations. *Journal of Accounting and Economics, 45*, 181–208.

Leuz, C., & Verrecchia, R. (2000). The economic consequences of increased disclosure. *Journal of Accounting Research, 38*, 91–124.

Leuz, C., & Wysocki, P. (2008). *Economic consequences of financial reporting and disclosure regulation: A review and suggestions for future research.* University of Chicago Working Paper. Available at SSRN http://ssrn.com/abstract = 1105398

Lopes, A. B, & Alencar, R. C. (2008). *Disclosure and cost of equity capital in emerging markets: The Brazilian case.* Working Paper. Available at SSRN http://ssrn.com/abstract = 1099900

Lopes, A. B., & Walker, M. (2008). *Firm-level incentives and the informativeness of accounting reports: An experiment in Brazil.* Working Paper. Available at http://ssrn.com/ abstract = 1095781

Lopo, A. M. (2008). Detectando earnings management no Brasil: Estimando os Accruals Discricionários. *Revista Contabilidade e Finanças, 19*(46), 7–17.

Ng, J. (2008). *The effect of information quality on liquidity risk*. PhD Thesis, University of Pennsylvania, PA, USA.

Ohlson, J., & Juettner-Nauroth, B. E. (2005). Expected EPS and EPS growth as determinants of value. *Review of Accounting Studies, 10*, 349–365.

Penman, S. (1996). The articulation of price–earnings ratios and market-to-book ratios and the evaluation of growth. *Journal of Accounting Research, 34*, 235–259.

Ruland, W., Shohn, J., & Zhou, P. (2007). Effective controls for research in international accounting. *Journal of Accounting and Public Policy, 26*, 96–116.

Wang, X., Young, D., & Zhuang, Z. (2008). *The effects of mandatory adoption of International Financial Reporting Standards on information environments*. Working Paper. Chinese University of Hong Kong. Available at http://aaahq.org/AM2008/abstract.cfm?submissionID = 1623

Welker, M. (1995). Disclosure policy, information asymmetry, and liquidity in equity markets. *Contemporary Accounting Research, 11*, 801–827.

APPENDIX A. INTERNATIONAL ACCOUNTING STANDARDS CONVERGENCE INDEX (IASCI)

		Percentage
Initial adoption		
1	Did the company give the base for preparation and presentation of financial statements?	96.0
2	Did the company demonstrate earnings and equity effects of initial adoption of the rules of Laws 11,638/07 and 11,941/09?	88.0
3	Were retroactive adjustments made to previous statements related to Laws 11,638/07 and 11,941/09?	42.9
4	Was the cash flow statement for 2007 presented?	100.0
5	Was the statement of value added for 2007 presented?	85.7
6	Did the company disclose the leading practices in the adoption of new standards?	98.0
Impairment		
7	Did the company specify an explanatory note or indicate the application of an impairment test?	82.0
8	Did the company disclose the criteria for impairment testing?	26.0
Cash flow statement		
9	Did the company disclose the components of cash and cash equivalents?	84.0
10	Did the company disclose the policy adopted in determining the composition of cash and cash equivalents?	70.0
11	Did the company announce the investing and financing transactions not involving cash use?	26.0
12	Did the company disclose the total interest and dividends paid and received, separately?	30.0
Intangible assets		
13	Did the company specify a separate explanatory note on intangible assets?	94.0
14	Did the company present both book value and useful life of intangible assets individually?	72.0
15	Did the company segregate intangible assets from those with indefinite and definite useful life?	16.7
16	Did the company disclose total spending on research and development as expenses in the period?	52.3

Adjustment to present value

17   Did the company indicate the application of adjustment to present value in the main accounts of noncurrent assets and liabilities?   82.0

18   Did the company report assumptions used to calculate the adjustment to present value?   54.0

Functional currency

19   Did the company indicate its functional currency and presentation currency?   46.0

Exchange rate variation

20   Did the company report net exchange rate variation, classified in a specific equity account?   47.8

Compensation of directors and officers

21   Did the company disclose the compensation of directors and officers in total and separated into categories?   68.0

Related parties

22   Did the company disclose the nature of its relationship with related parties?   88.0

Leasing

23   Did the company disclose whether or not there were changes in the accounting of previous leasing agreements?   80.0

Classification of investments

24   Did the company determine whether there were changes in the classification of investments measured by the equity method?   30.6

Financial instruments

25   Did the company present a specific note on financial instruments (including derivatives)?   100.0

26   Did the company demonstrate the criteria and assumptions adopted for the classification of financial instruments?   80.0

27   Did the company disclose the policy on the use of derivative financial instruments?   95.7

28   Did the company present the sensitivity analysis for financial instruments?   91.5

29   Did the company disclose the fair value of derivatives contracts?   97.7

30   Did the company publish the criteria for measuring the fair value of contracted derivatives?   91.1

Accounting for bad debt provisions

31   Were the criteria for accounting for bad debt provisions disclosed?   74.0

APPENDIX A. (Continued)

	Percentage
Deferred assets	
32 Did the company disclose the option adopted in relation to items classified as deferred assets?	83.3
Economic depreciation	
33 Did the company indicate the application of economic depreciation rates?	28.6
34 Did the company publish the criteria and assumptions adopted in determining the depreciation rates?	6.8
Transitional tax regime	
35 Did the company disclose the adoption of the transitional tax regime?	70.0
Revaluation of assets	
36 Did the company disclose the treatment of the "revaluation of assets" balance accounts?	87.0
Auditors' opinion	
37 Did the auditors' attest to compliance with recent rules?	96.0

The IASCI is a self-constructed index, composed of 37 binary questions, based on specific disclosure related to new international accounting-oriented practices in Brazil (Laws 11,638/07 and 11,941/09, and published pronouncements from the Accounting Pronouncements Committee – PC). Besides questions 3–5 and 32, all questions mention mandatory elements introduced by the regulatory framework cited above. Notes on specific questions: (5) Besides the international accounting standards, the referred laws in Brazil require the presentation of the statement of value added for 2008 onward. For comparison, companies were supposed to present the statement of value added also at least for 2007, which was exempted from the cited laws. (24) Changes in the criteria for recognizing an investment by the equity method require companies to disclose whether there will be changes in individual classifications. (31) Before the introduction of the referred laws, the accounting for bad debt provision was primarily oriented by tax regulations, which specified the required depreciation rate for tax purposes. With the separation and independence of corporate and tax rules, companies are oriented to determine such provisions based on individual economic reasons (except for financial institutions, which are regulated by the Central Bank of Brazil). (32) Before 2008, the balance sheet included a "deferred asset account" which was eliminated with the introduction of the intangible asset account. (35) The referred laws introduced a transitory regime for tax adjustments from recognizing as expenses the amounts classified in this account. (36) The referred laws prohibited the revaluation of assets in Brazil.

APPENDIX B. IMPLIED COST OF CAPITAL MODELS – OVERVIEW AND MODEL-SPECIFIC ASSUMPTIONS

Claus and Thomas (2001) (CT) – r_{CT}

$$P_t = bv_t + \sum_{\tau=1}^{T} \frac{\hat{x}_{t+\tau} - r_{CT}bv_{t+\tau-1}}{(1+r_{CT})^{\tau}} + \frac{(\hat{x}_{t+\tau} - r_{CT}bv_{t+\tau-1})(1+g)}{(r_{CT} - g)(1+r_{CT})^{T}}$$

Gebhardt et al. (2001) (GLES) – r_{GLES}

$$P_t = bv_t + \sum_{\tau=1}^{T} \frac{\hat{x}_{t+\tau} - r_{GLES}bv_{t+\tau-1}}{(1+r_{GLES})^{\tau}} + \frac{\hat{x}_{t+\tau} - r_{GLES}bv_{t+T}}{r_{GLES}(1+r_{GLES})^{T}}$$

Ohlson and Juettner-Nauroth (2005) (OJ) – r_{OJ}

$$P_t = \frac{\hat{x}_{t+1}}{r_{OJ}} \frac{\left(g_{cp} + r_{OJ}\hat{d}_{t+\tau}/\hat{x}_{t+1} - g_{lp}\right)}{r_{OJ} - g_{lp}}$$

Easton (Modified PEG) (2004) (PEG) – r_{PEG}

$$P_t = \frac{\hat{x}_{t+2} + r_{PEG}\hat{d}_{t+1} - \hat{x}_{t+1}}{r_{PEG}^2}$$

APPENDIX B. (*Continued*)

Variable	Symbol	Description	Database
Market price	P_t	Market price of a firm's stock in 2009	*Economática*
Book value	bv_t	Book value per share at the beginning of the fiscal year (end of 2008)	*Economática*
Expected future earnings per share	$x_{t+\tau}$	Expected future earnings per share by market analysts, or estimated from expression $x_{t+\tau} = x_{t+\tau-1}(1+ltg)$ when earnings are missing for any period greater than $t+2$	*Thomson ONE*
Expected future book value per share	$bv_{t+\tau}$	Expected future book value per share at date $t+\tau$, where $bv_{t+\tau} = bv_{t+\tau-1} + x_{t+\tau} - div_{t+\tau}$	*Economática/Thomson ONE*
Expected future net dividends per share	$div_{t+\tau}$	Expected future net dividends per share, derived from the dividend payout ratio times the earnings per share forecast	*Economática/Thomson ONE*
Expected perpetual future growth rate	G	One-year-ahead projected IGP-M (2010)	*Datastream*
Expected short-term future growth rate	g_{cp}	Average between the forecasted percentage change in earnings from year $t+1$ to $t+2$ and from year $t+4$ to $t+5$ provided by financial analysts	*Thomson ONE*
Expected long-term future growth rate	g_{lp}	One-year-ahead projected IGP-M (2010)	*Datastream*
Long-term growth rate	ltg	Obtained from financial analysts' estimations or, if missing, estimated from percentage change in earnings from year $t+2$ to $t+3$	*Thomson ONE/Estimated*

Source: Adapted from Hail and Leuz (2009).

APPENDIX C. DETAILS OF EARNINGS QUALITY CHANGE ESTIMATION – KS MODEL

Kang and Sivaramakrishnan model (1995)

$$TACC_{it} = \phi_0 + \phi_1\left[\delta_1\frac{NI_{it}}{TA_{it-1}}\right] + \phi_2\left[\delta_2\frac{OEXP_{it}}{TA_{it-1}}\right] + \phi_3\left[\delta_1\frac{PA_{it}}{TA_{it-1}}\right] + \varepsilon_{it}$$

$$\delta_1 = \frac{REC_{it-1}}{NI_{it-1}}$$

$$\delta_2 = \frac{\Delta WC - REC_{it-1}}{OEXP_{it-1}}$$

$$\delta_3 = \frac{DEPRE_{it-1}}{PA_{it-1}}$$

Here $TACC_{it}$ is the total accrual ($= NWC -$ depreciation and amortization); TA_{it} the total assets; NI_{it} the net income (excluding taxes); $OEXP_{it}$ the operating expenses before depreciation and amortization; NWC the net working capital excluding cash, short-term financing, and taxes; PA_{it} the fixed assets, deferred assets, and intangible assets; REC_{it} the receivables; and $DEPRE_{it}$ the depreciation expenses.

The table presents details of the KS model's construction, used for calculating the proxy quality of accounting earnings. We estimated changes in discretionary accruals by the variation in regression residuals for 2008 and 2007. Positive changes represent a proxy for improvement in earnings quality. The KS model operates directly on a single balance sheet account for a given accounting year, avoiding the problem of comparing current values in different periods. The technique of instrumental variables is used to reduce the correlation problem between residuals and independent variables. The instruments are δ_1, δ_2, and δ_3. We used *Economática* to obtain the necessary accounting parameters to estimate the model. The variables were obtained directly from the *Economática* database, except for costs and expenses before depreciation and amortization, which were estimated by the difference between net sales and operating profit.